"This extremely timely and much-needed study of the media's role in covering COVID-19 provides an excellent global and comparative perspective of how different societies' media are responding to the unprecedented risk brought on by the pandemic. Covering all inhabited continents, it provides fascinating and in-depth accounts of the media's role in the pandemic. This book should be mandatory reading."

University Professor Folker Hanusch, *Ph.D., Professor of Journalism, Department of Communication, University of Vienna; Editor-in-Chief,* Journalism Studies; *Vice-Chair, Worlds of Journalism Study*

"Pollock and Vakoch have assembled a formidable collection that demonstrates the richness of communication theories and analysis for understanding multiple aspects of the COVID-19 pandemic. The book features stellar contributions from around the world that examine the communicative, technological, political and cultural complexities of the pandemic, as well as different government responses and performance."

Dr. Silvio Waisbord, *Director and Professor, School of Media and Public Affairs, George Washington University; Past Editor-in-Chief,* Journal of Communication, *2015–2018*

"In the midst of a global crisis, *COVID-19 in International Media: Global Pandemic Perspectives* presents a rich and timely panoply of the way governments, citizens, and the media around the world have framed the Corona pandemic. An exemplary effort of internationally collaborative scholarship, this book is a must-read for scholars in health communication and journalism as well as in political and strategic communication."

Dr. Thomas Hanitzsch, *Chair and Professor of Communication, Department of Media and Communication, LMU Munich; Chair, Worlds of Journalism Study; Editor of* Worlds of Journalism: Journalistic Cultures around the Globe *and The Handbook of Journalism Studies*

"A pandemic is a global event, handled and experienced in many different ways in different contexts and creating important global information flows, debates and competitions. Scholarship on communication in pandemics rarely reflects this global character. But here is an exception—a highly diverse collection that explores COVID communication in a wide range of national and transnational contexts across the world, deeply informed by first-hand knowledge of those contexts."

Daniel C. Hallin, *Distinguished Professor, Department of Communication, University of California, San Diego*

"The COVID-19 pandemic has precipitated unprecedented challenges to society to reduce the spread of viral infection, death, and suffering around the globe. However, some countries did a better job than others in avoiding the (pandemic misinformation) 'infodemic' by using media strategically to mobilize public acceptance of prevention guidelines. This important book examines which media communication strategies worked effectively to help minimize danger from the pandemic, and which mediated communication practices made the pandemic even worse in different parts of the world. There are important lessons to be learned about effective communication and strategic use of media to address important public health threats that this book powerfully illustrates."

Gary L. Kreps, *Ph.D., FAAHB, University Distinguished*
Professor, Department of Communication; Director,
Center for Health and Risk Communication,
George Mason University

"The COVID-19 pandemic underscores the critical importance of media of all kinds in the precarious efforts to forge a shared understanding of the health threats we all face. With accounts from every continent, this volume carefully and effectively explores the social and political contexts in which media respond to once-in-a-century challenge."

Tim P. Vos, *Professor and Director of the School of Journalism,*
Michigan State University; Co-author of Gatekeeping Theory,
and President, Association for Education in Journalism
and Mass Communication, 2020–2021

"COVID-19 in International Media offers an important and timely account of the roles and responsibilities of news and social media in the face of a pandemic of massive proportions. Authors from around the world contribute to a discussion that will for years to come set an agenda for researchers and policymakers alike."

Theodore L. Glasser, *Professor Emeritus, Department of*
Communication, Stanford University; Past President,
Association for Education in Journalism and
Mass Communication

"This book delves into some of the continued injurious consumption practices— ecologically insensitive social behavior, wet markets, and environmental destruction—that will continue when the medical hype of COVID-19 is long past, and when the next pandemic will inevitably again punish societies for their inability to adapt to the natural world. The solutions are known, but is anyone listening? The authors of this book explain what needs to be done."

Keyan G. Tomaselli, *Distinguished Professor, University of Johannesburg;*
Johns Hopkins Health and Education South Africa Lifetime Achiever's Award;
Co-editor, Development and Public Health Communication

COVID-19 in International Media

COVID-19 in International Media: Global Pandemic Responses is one of the first books uniting an international team of scholars to investigate how media address critical social, political, and health issues connected to the 2020–2021 COVID-19 outbreak.

The book evaluates unique civic challenges, responsibilities, and opportunities for media worldwide, exploring pandemic social norms that media promote or discourage, and how media serve as instruments of social control and resistance, or of cooperation and representation. These chapters raise significant questions about the roles mainstream or citizen journalists or netizens play or ought to play, enlightening audiences successfully about scientific information on COVID-19 in a pandemic that magnifies social inequality and unequal access to healthcare, challenging popular beliefs about health and disease prevention and the role of government while the entire world pays close attention.

This book will be of interest to students and faculty of communication studies and journalism, and departments of public health, sociology, and social marketing.

John C. Pollock is Professor of Health and Human Rights Communication at the Departments of Communication Studies and Public Health, The College of New Jersey.

Douglas A. Vakoch is Professor Emeritus at the Department of Clinical Psychology, California Institute of Integral Studies.

Routledge Research in Journalism

For more information about this series, please visit:
www.routledge.com/Routledge-Research-in-Journalism/book-series/RRJ

COVID-19 in International Media

Global Pandemic Perspectives

**Edited by John C. Pollock and
Douglas A. Vakoch**

 Routledge
Taylor & Francis Group

LONDON AND NEW YORK

First published 2022
by Routledge
2 Park Square, Milton Park, Abingdon, Oxon OX14 4RN

and by Routledge
605 Third Avenue, New York, NY 10158

Routledge is an imprint of the Taylor & Francis Group, an informa business

British Library Cataloguing-in-Publication Data
A catalogue record for this book is available from the British Library

Library of Congress Cataloging-in-Publication Data
A catalog record for this book has been requested

ISBN: 978-1-032-02066-2 (hbk)
ISBN: 978-1-032-02067-9 (pbk)
ISBN: 978-1-003-18170-5 (ebk)

Typeset in Times New Roman
by Apex CoVantage, LLC

To Peggy, who brightens every day
and
To Julie, who transforms my life

Contents

Figures

Foreword

Perceptions of pandemics: communicating about COVID-19 in international ecosystems

Culture and the conceptualization of care

Perspectives on "healthy" and "ill" are not universal; rather, such distinctions represent the perspectives of the individuals communicating about those concepts. These factors can affect how groups share healthcare information in different national contexts. They can also affect how organizations convey health-related content across countries. Such variations include the information collected when evaluating someone's medical status. They also encompass the rubrics used to assess a person's health and the prescribed method for treating a condition.

Such differences can occur across a range of healthcare processes and affect how cultures and nations communicate about issues of public health. These communication variations, moreover, often involve different perspectives on *ecosystems of care*—or the locations where healthcare activities occur and where individuals use health-related information (St.Amant 2020). In these ecosystems, certain elements influence how individuals conceptualize the credibility and viability of healthcare information. These factors affect how audiences use texts, visuals, and other communication artifacts to engage in care-related activities in a setting.

Ecosystem dynamics and international healthcare communication

Variations in ecosystems of care often involve information on certain aspects of healthcare. These areas include cultural perspectives on health and medicine as well as the realities of where caregiving occurs. These aspects also influence how individuals communicate about healthcare when creating and using information in a setting. Addressing such factors requires an understanding of how seven core elements affect perceptions, behaviors, and communication practices across ecosystems of care.

Ecosystem element 1: approaches to assessment

The criteria cultures used to assess an individual's health can vary from nation to nation, and such differences can affect how audiences respond to health-related communiques. According to the US-based American Heart Association, for example, the condition of high blood pressure starts at the systolic/diastolic reading of 130/80 (Berg 2017). In many EU nations, however, it is a systolic/ diastolic reading of 140/90 that indicates high blood pressure (Neale 2018). This difference means individual considered healthy in one nation could be classified as having a particular medical condition in another. As certain organizations consider hypertension a COVID-19 risk factor, this difference can affect how individuals approach care-related information—such as who is at risk of coronavirus infection—in different nations (Mayo Clinic Staff 2020; Center for Disease Control 2020).

Ecosystem element 2: information to evaluate

The data individuals use to assess health-related issues can also vary across national and cultural lines. The notion of reviewing a patient's qui—or life force—to assess health is a common part of traditional medical practices in China but considered spurious by many US-based healthcare professionals (Zhu and St.Amant 2007; Nature 2017). As a result, patients could be diagnosed as having a medical condition in one nation but be considered healthy in another depending on the information healthcare professionals use to assess wellness. Per the COVID-19 pandemic, the biomedical data used to determine deaths caused by COVID-19 has varied across countries. This variation has made it difficult to compare COVID-19 mortality rates internationally and coordinate communication for effective public health responses (Morris and Reuben 2020).

Ecosystem element 3: treatment for conditions

What processes constitute valid treatment for a condition can also vary across nations and cultures. In certain cultures, healthcare professionals might consider acupuncture or herbal remedies effective treatments for a medical condition— approaches that healthcare providers in other nations might consider "noncredible" (Zhu and St.Amant 2007; Nature 2017). Such variations mean patients who receive similar diagnoses might be prescribed different treatments for a condition. During the COVID-19 crisis, for example, Spain has continued to use hydroxychloroquine (HCQ) to treat infections. Other European nations, such as France and Italy, however, have limited the use of HCQ as a COVID-19 treatment due to safety concerns (WINON Web Team 2020; Smith 2020; Reuters 2020). Such variations mean information on treatment for a COVID-19 infection in Spain might be considered problematic and not be used by peers in France or Italy.

Ecosystem element 4: providers of care

Who provides care and where to seek care can also vary across nations and cultures. For many US-based patients, care generally involves visiting a hospital or clinic and meeting with a physician or a nurse who diagnoses a condition and prescribes a course of treatment. In France, by contrast, many individuals first visit their local pharmacies. This is because pharmacists in France are approved to diagnose certain (generally more minor) conditions, prescribe related care, and even dispense medications for treatment (P-O Life n.d.). As a result, instructions on how to engage in healthcare activities in one nation might not align with and be usable by individuals in another—a factor that could affect international communication around COVID-19. In Peru, for example, the families of COVID-19 patients have become increasingly responsible for providing the oxygen needed to treat sick relatives versus expecting healthcare facilities will provide such resources (Armario 2020). Such factors mean information on using oxygen to treat COVID-19 in Peru might require realignment to focus on receiving treatment from family members and at home versus from healthcare providers and in a hospital.

Ecosystem element 5: context of care

The physical locations where healthcare activities occur can affect approaches to providing care in different nations (St.Amant 2017). Climatic conditions, for example, can affect the spread of infectious diseases and lead to different courses of treatment across nations. Accordingly, as warm, humid temperatures might slow the spread of COVID-19, instructions for containing outbreaks and coordinating treatment might vary from nation to nation based on climatic factors (Chaufen 2020). Similarly, infrastructure variations can affect the care available in a region. Nations with effective road and train systems, for example, can ensure that patients receive medications on a relatively regular schedule—something perhaps not possible in regions with less reliable infrastructure. Such factors have played a central role in the resources available to treat COVID-19 in different parts of the globe. One result has been the need to communicate alternative approaches to providing treatment in different areas (Armario 2020).

Ecosystem element 6: notions of acceptability

Further confounding this situation are cultural norms of acceptability when communicating about health and wellness (St.Amant 2017). Cultures can have markedly different perspectives on what constitute a sensitive healthcare topic. Such differences can affect how the individuals in a nation communicate about sensitive healthcare issues—if they discuss them at all. The core concept involves acceptability and how it is acceptable to discuss, or if it is acceptable to discuss, certain healthcare topics, conditions, or procedures. Some critics, for example, have claimed national differences involving when to communicate an outbreak occurred affected the global spread of COVID-19 (Davidson 2020; Ma 2020; Gander 2020). Moreover, if COVID-19 mutates into a sexually transmissible disease, sharing related health information could vary internationally based on differing attitudes toward sexual activities. (Such was the case with AIDS detection and prevention campaigns in different nations (Thomas et al. 2015; Uwah 2013).)

Ecosystem element 7: technologies of access

Finally, nations and cultures can differ in terms of how individuals use technologies to convey health-related content (Bonfadelli 2017; Ahmed 2018; Ghebreyesus and Ng 2020). Such variations can affect how individuals respond to medical information shared via a particular medium. Differing international approaches to circulating COVID-19 information online, for example, prompted the Director-General of the World Health Organization to suggest international measures to coordinate the sharing of health information during the pandemic (Ali and Kurasawa 2020; Ghebreyesus and Ng 2020). Doing so was considered central to avoiding an "infodemic" similar to those that caused confusion during earlier crises involving media use and international public health (Ali and Kurasawa 2020).

Each of these seven elements affects the sharing of healthcare information across cultures. As a result, nations can vary in terms of how individuals perceive and respond to illnesses during pandemics such as the COVID-19 crisis. The challenge involves addressing the global spread of infection through quick, coordinated, and consistent information sharing across nations. However, if opinions vary in terms of what a condition entails or how to treat it, then communication disconnects can occur, and diseases can continue to spread across borders. The solution involves understanding the expectations affecting how nations and cultures share information associated with ecosystems of care.

Experience and international health communication

Our expectations of what healthcare processes involve and what medical conditions entail are not inherent to humans. Rather, the nation and culture in which we have lived shape our understanding of such factors. Essentially, the more we encounter a process performed a certain way in a setting, the more we associate those experiences with the expected way for communicating about healthcare (St.Amant 2017, 2020). This situation means individuals cannot assume the approaches used to communicate care in their own national and cultural contexts will easily export to other nations and cultures. Rather, as experiences in ecosystems of care vary from nation to nation, so too do the expectations individuals associate with communicating about such ecosystems (St.Amant 2017, 2020). Addressing these ecosystem expectations is thus central to sharing information in ways audiences in other nations consider credible and worth using. The better we understand the experiences that shape ecosystem expectations in other nations, the more effectively we can create commutation materials—from informational texts to instructional visuals—audiences in other countries can and will use to address healthcare concerns.

With global pandemics, such as COVID-19, the better one understands the seven factors affecting ecosystem expectations, the more readily one can provide information individuals in other nations can use to address a public health concern. The goal is to address the ecosystems of care dynamics of a nation to provide individuals with needed information in a format they consider credible and is usable. If addressed effectively, the speed with which information is acted upon across nations increases, and the ability to effectively contain healthcare threats grows. Achieving such success, however, means individuals need to identify the factors affecting communication expectations in different nations during a pandemic.

The need for new knowledge

By studying international communication approaches during the COVID-19 crisis, individuals can better understand ecosystem of care expectations in other cultures. Such understanding can help identify factors that affect information sharing during global pandemics. The entries in this volume represent an important step in achieving this objective, for they provide a comparative review of ecosystem of care dynamics across different nations during a global healthcare crisis.

While these chapters focus on one particular disease, how societies responded to and shared information during the COVID-19 pandemic will likely affect future attempts to address disease outbreaks in different nations. As such, each entry in this volume provides insights on the ecosystem of care dynamics affecting health communication in a nation. Each entry also encompasses different ecosystem of care aspects and provides important insights on how societies might respond to such dynamics in the future. By reviewing these chapters, readers can gain a more comprehensive picture of forces shaping ecosystems of care in certain nations. They can then use these insights to develop strategies for sharing healthcare information across and within nations in the future. In applying ideas described in this volume, readers can enhance the exchange and use of information during a global crisis in public health.

Conclusion

The Spanish-American historian George Santayana is credited for the adage "Those who cannot remember the past are condemned to repeat it." In global pandemics, such advice must be taken to heart. While awareness of a global health crisis can fade quickly once infections wane, similar threats will appear again. The better we understand the factors affecting communication practices during the global COVID-19 crisis, the more effectively we can plan for similar challenges in the future. The key involves understanding audience experiences and related expectations involving ecosystems of care.

By studying communication patterns in different nations during the COVID-19 pandemic, we can identify the experiences affecting information sharing during a global pandemic in the twenty-first century. The knowledge we collect on such experiences provides essential insights on how humans might approach similar situations in the future. The understanding we gain from such experiences can help us plan responses to and coordinate international efforts around future crises in public health.

Kirk St.Amant

References

Ahmed, Rukhsana. 2018. "Challenges of Migration and Culture in a Public Health Communication Context." *Journal of Public Health Research* 7, no. 2: 93–94.

Ali, S. Harris, and Fuyuki Kurasawa. 2020. "#COVID19: Social Media both a Blessing and a Curse During Coronavirus Pandemic." *The Conversation*, March 22, 2020. Accessed April 25, 2020. https://theconversation.com/covid19-social-media-both-a-blessing-and-a-curse-during-coronavirus-pandemic-133596.

Armario, Christine. 2020. "Peru is Running Out of Oxygen for COVID-19 Patients." *The Washington Post*, June 5, 2020. Accessed June 5, 2020. www.washingtonpost.com/world/the_americas/peru-is-running-out-of-oxygen-for-covid-19-patients/2020/06/05/f5abff3c-a743-11ea-898e-b21b9a83f792_story.html.

Berg, Sara. 2017. "New BP Guideline: 5 Things Physicians Should Know." *American Medical Association (AMA)*, November 13, 2017. Accessed April 10, 2020. www.ama-assn.org/delivering-care/hypertension/new-bp-guideline-5-things-physicians-should-know.

Bonfadelli, Heinz. 2017. "Media Effects: Across and Between Cultures." In *The International Encyclopedia of Media Effects*, edited by Patrick Rössler, Cynthia A. Hoffner, and Liesbet van Zoonen, 1–16. Hoboken, NJ: John Wiley and Sons, Inc.

Center for Disease Control. 2020. "Groups at Higher Risk for Severe Illness." Last Reviewed May 14, 2020. Accessed May 20, 2020. www.cdc.gov/coronavirus/2019-ncov/need-extra-precautions/groups-at-higher-risk.html.

Chaufen, Alejandro. 2020. "How Latin America Is Faring with COVID-19." *Forbes*, April 25, 2020. Accessed June 1, 2020. www.forbes.com/sites/alejandrochafuen/2020/04/25/how-latin-america-is-faring-with-covid-19/#2ab052e75d2f.

Davidson, Helen. 2020. "First Covid-19 Case Happened in November, China Government Records Show—Report." *The Guardian*, March 13, 2020. Accessed April 15, 2020. www.theguardian.com/world/2020/mar/13/first-covid-19-case-happened-in-november-china-government-records-show-report.

Gander, Kashmira. 2020. "Some Scientists Think COVID-19 May Have Been Spreading Far Earlier than Previously Thought." *Newsweek*, May 6, 2020. Accessed May 30, 2020. www.newsweek.com/covid-19-spreading-earlier-thought-scientists-1502077.

Ghebreyesus, Tedros Adhanom, and Alex Ng. 2020. "Coronavirus: How the WHO Is Leading the Social Media Fight Against Misinformation." *South China Morning Post*, February 13, 2020. Accessed April 25, 2020. www.scmp.com/comment/opinion/article/3050080/coronavirus-how-who-leading-social-media-fight-against.

Ma, Josephine. 2020. "Coronavirus: China's First Confirmed Covid-19 Case Traced Back to November 17." *Asiaone*, March 12, 2020. Accessed April 30, 2020. www.asiaone.com/china/coronavirus-chinas-first-confirmed-covid-19-case-traced-back-november-17.

Mayo Clinic Staff. 2020. "COVID-19: Who's at higher risk?" Last Updated May 29, 2020. Accessed June 5, 2020. www.mayoclinic.org/diseases-conditions/coronavirus/in-depth/coronavirus-who-is-at-risk/art-20483301.

Morris, Chris, and Anthony Reuben. 2020. "Coronavirus: Why are International Comparisons Difficult?" *BBC*, May 18, 2020. Accessed June 1, 2020. www.bbc.com/news/52311014.

Nature. 2017. "Traditional Chinese Medicine Needs Proper Scrutiny." November 29, 2017. Accessed April 10, 2020. www.nature.com/articles/d41586-017-07650-6.

Neale, Todd. 2018. "New European Hypertension Guidelines Not in Harmony with US Guidance." *tctMD*, June 11, 2018. Accessed April 10, 2020. www.tctmd.com/news/new-european-hypertension-guidelines-not-harmony-us-guidance.

P-O Life. n. d. "French 'Pharmacies'—More Than Just a Chemist." Last Updated April 3, 2018. Accessed May 15, 2020. http://anglophone-direct.com/chemists-in-france/.

Reuters. 2020. "France, Italy, Belgium to Stop Use of Hydroxychloroquine for Coronavirus Over Safety Fears." *New York Post*, May 27, 2020. Accessed April 20, 2020. https://nypost.com/2020/05/27/france-italy-belgium-act-to-stop-use-of-hydroxychloroquine/.

Smith, Lydia. 2020. "Spain Launches Large-scale Study of Hydroxychloroquine and Antiretrovirals to Prevent COVID-19 in Health Workers." *Newsweek*, April 10, 2020. Accessed April 30, 2020. www.newsweek.com/spain-study-hydroxychloroquine-antiretrovirals-covid-19-health-workers-1497277.

St.Amant, Kirk. 2017. "The Cultural Context of Care in International Communication Design: A Heuristic for Addressing Usability in International Health and Medical Communication." *Communication Design Quarterly* 5, no. 2: 62–70.

———. 2020. "Culture and Causal Chains of Care: A Perspective on the Chronology of Health and Medical Communication in Cross-Cultural Contests." *Journal of Technical Writing and Communication* 50, no. 2: 123–40.

Thomas, Tami L., Hossein N. Yarandi, Safiya George Dalmida, Andrew Frados, and Kathleen Klienert. 2015. "Cross-Cultural Differences and Sexual Risk Behavior of Emerging Adults." *Journal of Transcultural Nursing* 26, no. 1: 64–72.

Uwah, Chijioke. 2013. "The Role of Culture in Effective HIV/AIDS Communication by Theatre in South Africa." *Journal of Social Aspects of HIV/AIDS* 10, no. 3–4: 140–49.

WION Web Team. 2020. "Spain Will Not Stop Use of HCQ to Treat COVID-19 Patients, Unlike Other European Nations." *WION*, May 28, 2020. Accessed June 1, 2020. www.wionews.com/world/spain-will-not-stop-use-of-hcq-to-treat-covid-19-patients-unlike-other-european-nations-301593.

Zhu, Pinfan, and Kirk St.Amant. 2007. "Taking Traditional Chinese Medicine International and Online: An Examination of the Cultural Rhetorical Factors Affecting American Perceptions of Chinese-Created Web Sites." *Technical Communication* 54, no. 2: 171–86.

COVID-19 in global media: questions and challenges for health communication

Media responsibility: critical questions

The coronavirus pandemic represents an unusual opportunity and responsibility for media worldwide. The global focus on a particular health issue is a special challenge for health education and communication. Since news media (print, TV, radio, internet/digital) and social media are more accessible to the public than longform communication platforms such as magazines, journals or books, professional journalists, citizen journalists, and netizens (all "communicators") have an unusual opportunity to enlighten readers, viewers, and listeners about accurate information on COVID-19 at a time when the entire world is paying close attention. That opportunity is joined to a health communication responsibility for news communicators as well: to balance competing interests between, for example, scientists and policymakers, in order to do what media do best in relatively open societies and political systems: present citizens with as many intelligent choices as possible to facilitate informed civic action and decision-making.

Some of the compelling health communication questions addressed by scholars in "COVID-19 in International Media" include the following:

1   How well do media appear to understand their critical "investigative" role, warning not only of health risks and dangers, but also balancing reporting on the risks of government regulation (China by Li and Meinhof, Serbia by Cendic) with coverage of the benefits of cooperation among governments, mainstream media, and social media to represent the interests of a wide range of citizens (communication in the UK and India by Lahiri et al., New Zealand by Martin-Anatias, Vietnam by Dinh and Nguyen, Nigeria by Lasisi and Oyedele, and the United States by Pollock et al.).

2   How robustly do media illuminate disparities in health access among different cultural, racial, ethnic, and income groups, as well as corresponding differences in risk for contracting COVID-19? Some media may foreground disparities in order to manifest compassion, others to "other" those who are "different" (examples include chapters on China by Gao; Taiwan by Huang; Africa by Santos; and Russia and its diaspora by Smoliarova, Sharkova, and Gromova).

3   How effectively do media report on the dangers of COVID-19 communication, including the threat of dangerous disinformation, urging caution about abuse of legitimate public health concerns to defraud others through phishing and online scams (Kikerpill and Siibak), issuing alerts about cybercriminals involved in bogus donation campaigns for aid and relief, products purporting to identify or cure the virus, or insurance and commercial fraud.

4   What kinds of "role models" do media select as heroic actors or villains, "belonging" or "non-belonging" in the pandemic? What proportion are scientists, what proportion policymakers or lawmakers? In identity or "solidarity" discourses, what proportion of "heroes" belong to a particular nationality, government, or political party, and what proportion belong to those not included in a particular nationality, government, or political party? (China by Gao, Spain by del Campo Tejedor, Indonesia by Pitaloka and Martin-Anatias, Cyprus by Nunziata, multiple countries by Auschner et al.)

5   What social norms of behavior and expectations do media promote or discourage, risking unstoppable and contagious "infodemics" (Lin), deciding how much to foreground or background different effective examples of "agency" or "efficacy," including coping behaviors or concepts such as "social distancing," quarantine," "lockdowns," or "opening up"? (Examples include Africa by Santos; "infodemics" in West Africa by Obi and Endong; "riskscapes" in Turkey by Tabur; Cyprus by Nunziata, and "risk society" in the United States by Miller and Davis Bivens.)

Undergirding all of these questions is a foundational question about "reflexivity": how aware are communicators of the special responsibilities they bear in reporting on a world crisis costing more fatalities than at any time since World War II? How much evidence is apparent in mainstream or citizen media reports on the pandemic that reporters understand the special moment in history that they occupy now? Do they comprehend the social, political, and ethical issues they face in a period of almost unprecedented risk?

COVID-19 in International Media represents an unprecedented global effort by scholars to investigate how media use a health communication lens to address critical social, political, and health issues. Scholars also raise significant questions about the roles mainstream or citizen journalists play or ought to play when faced with a pandemic that magnifies social inequality and unequal access to healthcare, and that challenges popular beliefs about health and disease prevention, the role of government, and the capacity of science to address health issues in countries throughout the world.

John C. Pollock

Notes on editors

John C. Pollock (Ph.D., Stanford, M.I.P.A., Maxwell School-Syracuse, B.A., Swarthmore) is Professor, Departments of Communication Studies and Public Health, The College of New Jersey. His teaching and research interests focus on health communication and community structure theory, a subset of media sociology, exploring the impact of society on media. Serving on the editorial boards of *Journal of Health Communication, Communication Theory, and Mass Communication and Society,* he has published articles in *Journalism and Mass Communication Quarterly, Journal of Health Communication, Journal of Human Rights, The New York Times, The Nation, and Industry Week.* His authored or edited books include *Tilted Mirrors: Media Alignment with Political and Social Change—A Community Structure Approach* (2007); *Media and Social Inequality: Innovations in Community Structure Research* (2013); *Journalism and Human Rights: How Demographics Drive Media Coverage* (2015); and (with Mort Winston) *Making Human Rights News: Balancing Participation and Professionalism* (2017). He has received grants from the Social Science Research Council, National Cancer Institute, United Nations Foundation, and Senior Fulbright Scholar program (Argentina, 2010).

Douglas A. Vakoch, Ph.D., is President of METI, a research organization dedicated to Messaging Extraterrestrial Intelligence and sustaining civilization on multigenerational timescales. As Director of Green Psychotherapy, PC, he helps alleviate environmental distress through ecotherapy. He is a frequent commentator on television programs that explore astrobiology—the hunt for life in the cosmos. His expertise includes space exploration, the societal impact of science, and environmental threats to humanity's long-term survival. Dr. Vakoch has published over 20 books covering the search for life beyond the Earth, the psychology of space exploration, COVID-19, environmental health, and ecofeminism. He has been featured in such publications as *The New York Times, The Economist, Nature,* and *Science,* and he has been interviewed on radio and television shows on the BBC, NPR, ABC, the Science Channel, the Discovery Channel, and many others, with recent appearances on PBS's *NOVA Wonders* and the Netflix documentary series *Alien Worlds.* Dr. Vakoch is Editor-in-Chief of the book series *Space and Society,* as well as general editor of *Ecocritical Theory and Practice.*

Notes on contributors

Maryam Alsulaimi is Head of the Department of Public Relations in the Directorate of Civil Aviation, Kuwait. Her Ph.D. research focuses on public relations practitioners' use of social media in Kuwait organizations. Her research critically compares the use of social media strategies adopted by the public relations practitioners in Kuwait organizations in both government and nongovernment sectors. Maryam's research interests are gender and feminist studies, social media and technologies, public relations, cultural studies, and health and nutrition.

Eika Auschner graduated in Latin American Sciences from the University of Cologne, Germany, and holds a Ph.D. from the University of Jena, Germany, in the area of Intercultural Business Communication. Her research is focused on international and intercultural topics, especially on intercultural communication and intercultural competence development in Higher Education. After living and working in Medellin, Colombia, for some years, she currently works at the Technical University Braunschweig, Germany.

Debanjan Banerjee has completed his postgraduation (M.D.) in psychiatry from National Institute of Mental Health and Neurosciences (NIMHANS), Bangalore. Subsequently, he has worked as Senior Resident in General Psychiatry for two years before starting his postdoctoral (D.M.) in geriatric (old-age) psychiatry from the same institute. His research interests include social psychiatry, stigma, old-age psychiatry, psychotherapy, and qualitative methods.

Nicola Davis Bivens is an Associate Professor of Criminology at Johnson C. Smith University, where she also serves as the Program Coordinator. She is a Research Fellow at the Homeland Security and Workforce Development Institute at North Carolina Central University. Recent examples of her scholarship are found in *Journal of Applied Security Research, Journal of Justice Studies, Paradigm Shift: An Interdisciplinary Journal on the African American Experience*, and *Journal of Criminal Justice and Law Review*.

Kristina Ćendić holds a Ph.D. in Communications and currently works as Expert Associate for the Law Faculty, University of Zenica, Bosnia and Herzegovina and as Senior Researcher for SHARE Foundation in Serbia. Kristina worked for USAID's Strengthening Independent Media Project in Bosnia and Herzegovina, on the component of media law and policy led by Annenberg School for Communication, University of Philadelphia. She specializes in freedom of expression online issues.

Anish V. Cherian is Associate Professor of Psychiatric Social Work at the Department of Psychiatric Social Work, National Institute of Mental Health and Neuro Sciences. His research interests are in Public Mental Health, Stigma, Suicide Prevention, and Community Mental Health. Their current project is "Development of evidence based lay health worker delivered psycho-social intervention module for women with common mental disorders in rural India."

Miranda Crowley is a Communication Studies major with a Women, Gender, and Sexuality Studies minor at The College of New Jersey. She was a panelist at the 2018 New Jersey Communication Association Conference, presenting on the sociopolitical consequences of news convergence. Crowley has also coauthored several community structure theory studies on both US multi-city and cross-national levels, some published, others accepted at academic conferences, including the Kentucky and DC biannual conferences on health communication.

Lisa DeTora is Associate Professor and Director of STEM Writing at Hofstra University in Hempstead, NY, where she also serves as guest faculty at the Donald and Barbara Zucker School of Medicine at Hofstra/Northwell. Before joining Hofstra, Lisa worked in medical and scientific affairs roles associated with vaccines and pharmaceutical research and development. Her research interests include medical rhetoric, embodiment, medical humanities, and graphic narrative. An active member of professional societies for biomedical publication professionals, she also publishes on regulatory documentation practice.

Alberto del Campo Tejedor gained three degrees in Law, Language Studies, and Social Anthropology (Ph.D. in 2003). He is currently Associate Professor at the Universidad Pablo de Olavide (Seville, Spain). He has written 20 books and around 100 articles, on subjects such as interethnic relations, stereotypes, stigma, religion, literature, and comicalness. His work has been recognized with seven national and international awards, including the Marqués de Lozoya, the Ángel Carril, and the Manuel Alvar Prizes.

Hang Thi Thuy Dinh is currently working as both Senior Lecturer at the Academy of Journalism and Communication (AJC) and Director of the Center for Further Training of the Vietnamese Journalists, Vietnam Journalist Association (VJA). Hang Dinh has an extensive hands-on experience from professional training, including international capacity building projects as she worked with many international media development projects.

Floribert Patrick C. Endong is of the Department of Theatre, Film and Carnival Studies, University of Calabar (Nigeria). His areas of interest include visual anthropology, media laws, international communication, digital cultures, cinema, religious communication, and gender studies. He is a prolific author, having published more than 100 peer-reviewed journal articles and book chapters in the aforementioned areas of interest. He recently edited *Deconstructing Images of the Global South through Media Representations and Communication*.

Zhipeng Gao holds a Ph.D. (2018) degree in psychology from York University and is currently conducting postdoctoral research at Simon Fraser University, Canada. He studies Chinese immigrants' identity and belonging, intergroup relations, and mental health amid the COVID-19 pandemic and international political tensions. In addition, he has been publishing on a range of psychological topics in Chinese socialism and in China-West interactions. He is currently guest editing a special issue for *Integrative Psychological and Behavioral Science*.

Suchir Govindarajan is a senior English major and Honors student with minors in Public Health and Russian Studies at the College of New Jersey. Govindarajan currently serves as Executive President for Student Government, representing the student stakeholder perspective to College administration and in campus governance. He has coauthored several community structure theory studies published in academic journals and accepted for conferences, including the N.J. Communication Association and DC Health Communication Conference (2021).

Tamara Gromova is Lecturer at the Department of International Journalism, St. Petersburg State University. Her research interests include innovation policy and media, gender studies, and media in the Nordic countries. She has participated in the research projects "Transformation of migrants' media repertoires as an adaptation strategy" and "Media consumption among Russian-speaking immigrants." She authored a section on journalism and gender in an international training manual on intercultural understanding, human rights, and ethics in journalism.

Julia Heitsch is an International Business undergraduate student at the University of Applied Sciences Muenster. Her academic interests in innovation, sustainability, and international negotiation have allowed her to work at the business incubator at the Universidad Pontificia Bolivariana in Medellín, Colombia. She currently works on the internationalization of engineering courses at the Münster University of Applied Sciences. Heitsch also serves as a volunteer at TechLabs, a student-run non-profit organization aiming a world without digital illiterate.

Ling-Yi Huang holds a Ph.D. degree in Communication and Journalism from National Chengchi University in Taipei, Taiwan. She has worked as a lecturer at the Literature and Media Studies Department at Nanfang College of Sun Yat-Sen University, Guangzhou, China, between 2015 and 2107 and as a postdoctoral researcher and a lecturer at the Media and Journalism Department in Linnaeus University, Sweden, between 2017 and 2020.

Kristjan Kikerpill (MA in Information Technology Law) is a doctoral student at the Institute of Social Studies (University of Tartu, Estonia). His main areas of research are online deception, the mechanics of social engineering attacks, the social impact of deepfakes, and crime prevention in online environments. Recent publications include a socio-legal analysis of phishing e-mails, a critical analysis of cybercrime case law, and a criminological perspective on the role of individuals in cybercrime prevention.

Michael J. Klein, Ph.D., is Professor of Writing, Rhetoric and Technical Communication at James Madison University. He directs the Cohen Center for the Humanities and coordinates the interdisciplinary minor in medical humanities. He teaches courses in technical communication, scientific and medical communication, and writing in the health sciences. His recent scholarship focuses on medical narratives and intercultural communication, graphic embodiment memoirs in interdisciplinary writing, and technical communication pedagogy.

Indrani Lahiri is Senior Lecturer, Leicester Media School, Faculty of Computing, Engineering and Media, De Montfort University, Leicester. She is an interdisciplinary researcher working on digital media and society. She is the Fellow of the Royal Society of Arts, Senior Fellow of HEA, and an Academic Consultant in public relations. Her research focuses on digital media, mental health, society, and politics.

Mutiu Iyanda Lasisi is a research and communications professional with a special bias for data and computational management consulting. He is Chief Visionary Officer of Infoprations Limited, a data-driven management consulting company in Nigeria. His research interests include data and computational journalism, development communication, media studies, and strategic management.

Abigail Lewis is a senior Public Health student at The College of New Jersey with a secondary major in Women, Gender, and Sexuality Studies and a minor in Arabic. As an honors student, she concentrates on population health and public policy evaluation in her studies. She has coauthored several community structure theory studies (US multi-city and cross-national levels) that have been accepted for publication in academic literature and for the DC Health Communication Conference (2021).

Yawen Li is currently a Ph.D. student in English Literature at the National University of Singapore jointly with King's College London. Her research interests include trauma and memory studies, postcolonial and diaspora studies, as well as different forms of representation.

Carolyn A. Lin is Professor of Communication at the University of Connecticut. Her research interests focus on digital, environmental, science, risk, political, marketing, and intercultural communication. She has developed/codeveloped a commercialized bioinformatics system, two interactive serious games, and two mobile apps. A recipient of a University Distinguished Research Faculty award, she is also the founder of the *Communication Technology Division* at the Association for Education in Journalism & Mass Communication.

Alexis Marta is a senior Public and Mass Communication major with a minor in Public Health on a Pre-Health track at The College of New Jersey. Marta has coauthored several community structure theory studies published in academic journals and accepted for conferences, including the N.J. Communication Association and D.C. Health Communication conferences. In fall 2021, she will be attending Johns Hopkins University to earn her MPH.

Nelly Martin-Anatias is Research Fellow at the School of Social Sciences and Public Policy Auckland University of Technology, New Zealand. Her research interests include but are not limited to language, identity, gender, language ideology, code-switching, textual and interpretive analysis, and autoethnography. Her recent publications are accessible on the journals of *World Englishes*, *South East Asia Research, Humanity and Society, the Journal of Homosexuality, Language@internet*, and *Text&Talk*.

Zully Paola Martinez Torres is an International Business undergraduate student at Universidad Pontificia Bolivariana and an active member of her faculty's International Business research group. She currently works as a student assistant of the UPB's Office of International Relations, and she serves as a volunteer in non-profit organizations: in AIESEC, assisting the development of global youth leadership and cultural understanding; and in TechLabs where she helps to equip youth with technological domain expertise.

K. S. Meena is Additional Professor and Head of the Department of Mental Health Education, National Institute of Mental Health and Neuro Sciences [NIMHANS], Karnataka, India. Her main areas of interest include suicide prevention, stigma, media and mental health, community mental health, and developing various methodologies (brief documentaries, print and video for imparting mental health education). She also heads the Media Cell at NIMHANS, Bangalore, which is instrumental in connecting to various media houses for accurate reporting of mental health to bring down the stigma and discrimination.

Marius Meinhof works as a research associate in the Faculty of Sociology at Bielefeld University in Germany. His research interests revolve around postcolonialism, governmentality, and notions of modernity in China. He has authored the award-winning monography *Shopping in China* (2018) in the German language and coedited the special issue *Postcolonialism and China* (2017) in English. Since 2020, he has started research on mass media discourses on COVID-19 in China, the United States, and Germany.

DeMond Shondell Miller is Professor of Sociology and Professor of Crisis & Emergency Management at Rowan University. His primary area of specialization is environmental sociology (disaster studies), community development, and emergency management. Several of his scholarly articles are in the

International Journal of Sociology and Social Policy, Space and Culture, Sociological Spectrum, Journal of Applied Security Research: Prevention and Response in Asset Protection, Terrorism and Violence.

Hien Thi Minh Nguyen is Dean of Public Relations and Advertising, Academy of Communication and Journalism (AJC). With more than 17 years working at AJC, she is the author, coauthor of a number of academic journal articles, books, head of many research projects and trainers of many courses in communication management and media studies as well as public relations and advertising.

Daniele Nunziata, D.Phil., is Lecturer in English Literature at the University of Oxford. He is the author of *Colonial and Postcolonial Cyprus: Transportal Literatures of Empire, Nationalism, and Sectarianism* (Palgrave Macmillan, 2020). His other research into postcolonial literature has been published in *PMLA*, the *Journal of Postcolonial Writing*, and the Studies in World Literature book series. He contributes to *Writers Make Worlds* and *Great Writers Inspire* and has discussed his writing on BBC Radio.

Paul Obi is a journalist/researcher interested in political communication, and how the media interact with elections, politics, and democracy. He has presented a paper on protest at the University of Westminster, London; his book chapters on US/UK media coverage of African elections and Donald Trump's Insult Politics have appeared in *Deconstructing Images of the Global South through Media Representations and Communication*. In 2020, his paper 'Insider Peddling. . .' on hate speech won UNESCO second best paper. He is a 2017 Fellow, ICFJ/UN Fellowship on Migration/Climate. He was educated at Cardiff University, UK, and University of Abuja, Nigeria.

Obasanjo Joseph Oyedele is Lecturer in the Mass Communication Department of the Federal University, Oye-Ekiti Ekiti State, Nigeria. He got his Ph.D. degree on climate change communication in 2017 from the University of Ibadan and his research interests are in climate change, environmental, health, and risk communication.

Dyah Pitaloka was a Fulbright scholar who completed her PhD in 2014. She is currently Senior Lecturer in Communications and Media Studies at the School of Arts and Social Sciences, Monash University Malaysia. Dyah has been working on issues related to communications, marginalization and health, and ICT and social change, within the contexts of Southeast Asia (Indonesia, Singapore, and Vietnam) and Australia.

John C. Pollock (PhD, Stanford), Professor, departments of Communication Studies and Public Health, The College of New Jersey, authored or edited *Tilted Mirrors: Media Alignment with Political and Social Change – A Community Structure Approach* (2007), *Media and Social Inequality: Innovations in Community Structure Research* (2013), and *Journalism and Human Rights: How Demographics Drive Media Coverage* (2015). A Senior Fulbright Scholar

(Argentina, 2010), Pollock advances community structure theory, exploring the impact of society on media.

Radhika Purandare, a senior at The College of New Jersey (TCNJ), pursues majors in Public Health and Communication Studies and a minor in Law, Politics, and Philosophy. She serves as president of the TCNJ Public Health Communication Club and has coauthored several papers on community structure theory (US multi-city and cross-national levels) and health-related stigma communication. These papers have been accepted to academic journals (published articles) and conferences, including the D.C. Health Communication Conference (2021).

Phillip Santos is Senior Lecturer at the Namibia University of Science and Technology where he teaches Media and Globalization, Critical Discourse Analysis, Journalism for Development, and Advocacy Journalism. He holds a Ph.D. degree in Journalism and Media Studies from Rhodes University, South Africa. His research interests are in the areas of mediated rhetoric and argumentation, political communication, the sociology of digital media, and the mediation of social memory, identity, development, inequality, and social justice.

Ekaterina Sharkova, Ph.D., Associate Professor, Department of PR in Business, St. Petersburg State University. Her research interests include environmental communication, public health communication, and strategic communication. She chaired the *Environmental Communication* section on the annual international conference "Strategic Communication in Business and Politics," St. Petersburg State University. She has participated in the research projects "Transformation of migrants' media repertoires as an adaptation strategy" and "Professional practices and ethics of PR specialists in today's Russia."

Andra Siibak (Ph.D. in media and communication) is Full Professor of Media Studies at the Institute of Social Studies (University of Tartu, Estonia). Her main areas of research are related to internet and social media use, privacy, online audiences, and datafication.

Anna Smoliarova, Ph.D., is Associate Professor in the Department of International Journalism, St. Petersburg State University, Russia. Her research interests include global public, media and migration, and mass-self communication. She was the head of the following research projects: "Transformation of migrants' media repertoires as an adaptation strategy" (2020–2021) and "Media consumption among Russian-speaking immigrants" (2018–2019) funded by Russian Presidential Grant for Young Ph.D. Scientists; and "Transformation of foreign Russian-language journalism in national media systems" (2014–2015).

James N. Sparano, Communication Studies major, The College of New Jersey, coauthored a poster presented at the 2020 biannual Kentucky Conference on Health Communication: *Nationwide Media Coverage of Gun Safety: Community Structure Theory and Community Vulnerability*. Sparano has coauthored several community structure theory studies (US multi-city and cross-national levels), one on US COVID-19 coverage, published in Spanish journal *Tripodos*, others accepted to the New Jersey Communication Association (2020) and DC Health Communication (2021) academic conferences.

Kirk St.Amant is the Eunice C. Williamson Chair in Technical Communication at Louisiana Tech University and serves as Director of the University's Center for Health and Medical Communication (CHMC). Kirk is also an Adjunct Professor of Health and Medical Communication with the University of Limerick in Ireland, and he researches how cognition affects communication, usability, and design in international health and medical contexts.

Şemsettin Tabur is a full-time faculty member in the Department of Translation Studies at Ankara Yildirim Beyazit University, Turkey. He gained his Ph.D. at Bayreuth University, Germany, where he worked as a lecturer and assistant professor of American Studies until recently. His monograph titled *Contested Spaces in Contemporary North American Novels: Reading for Space* was published in 2017. Tabur's research interests include literary and cultural studies, decoloniality, spatial studies, risk studies, and Anglophone Muslim fiction.

Introduction

Coronavirus disease 2019 (COVID-19) and international media—issues, challenges, and opportunities

Lisa DeTora, Michael J. Klein, and John C. Pollock

Providing a rich overview of COVID in the media, the volume's four main sections explore relationships among media, culture, government agencies, and technology. *COVID-19 in International Media: Global Pandemic Responses* is one of the first books uniting a diverse international team of scholars to investigate how media address critical social, political, and health issues connected to the 2020–2021 COVID-19 outbreak. The book evaluates unique civic challenges, responsibilities, and opportunities for media worldwide, exploring pandemic social norms that media promote or discourage, and how media serve as instruments of social control and resistance (Frankfort School), or of cooperation and representation (media sociology and community structure theories). Hailing from continents across the globe, the authors provide deep insights into media representations of COVID, from individual nations or specific social media platforms to transnational and even global contexts.

Introduction

In early 2020, the world became gripped by a global pandemic of coronavirus disease 2019 (COVID-19) caused by the circulation of a novel coronavirus strain called SARS-CoV-2. The pandemic significance of COVID-19 derives equally from its novelty—no humans have yet developed immunity against the virus—and from its characteristics such as virulence, how quickly it can be transmitted, and the proportion of people it kills (Andersen et al. 2020). This constellation of characteristics differentiates COVID-19 from the three influenza pandemics that occurred after 1918 as well as the AIDS pandemic during the twentieth century: for the first time in over 100 years, a new pathogen has an ability to spread rapidly through the population causing significant illness and mortality, but without a known and easily made vaccine or treatment.

The earliest cases of COVID-19 were identified in Wuhan, Hubei Province, in China, and have been associated with potential animal vectors, including bats and pangolins (Andersen et al. 2020; Wu et al. 2020; Zhou et al. 2020). All of this sounds rather scientific; however, of interest, a group of researchers, whose work has also been represented by the mass media, have conducted analyses strongly suggesting that SARS-CoV-2 was not the product of intentional engineering in a laboratory (Andersen et al. 2020). One might well wonder where the idea of intentional creation of a disease-causing organism originated. Why did the authors seek to test and publish a refutation of this hypothesis?

Narratives that depict the purposeful development and release of a dangerous virus or bacterium to devastate the world population should be familiar to viewers of science fiction and thriller movies and television programs. These productions, which proliferated during the late twentieth and early twenty-first centuries with information about Ebola, SARS, and fears of a possible H5N1 influenza pandemic, generally feature the machinations of malign or captive scientists working for personal or corporate gain. For example, *Mission: Impossible 2* (Woo 2000) sees agent Ethan Hunt (Tom Cruise) traveling the globe to stop the release of a deadly pathogen unwillingly engineered by a Russian scientist captive to corrupt multinational corporation. Fortunately, through numerous car chases, erotic encounters, helicopter rides, horse races, and an in-the-nick-of-time intervention, Hunt saves the world. This melodramatic construct is one type of dominant cultural storyline that interferes with the dissemination of accurate scientific, medical, and policy information around the world. This collection examines communications about COVID-19 and their place in global public health and policy discourses even as COVID-19 communications struggle for space against popular expectations.

Estimating SARS-CoV-2 viral characteristics, managing public opinion, and influencing public health can be complicated by the flow of information— scientific, cultural, and emotional—through various media outlets. Inaccurate information may affect the behavior of individuals who have not yet become infected. This uncertainty complicates not only communication about policymaking, healthcare delivery, and day-to-day experiences, but also the substance of these communications. Further, new scientific and medical information must be understood in the light of not only current developments but also a history of past information. Thus, the current coronavirus SARS-CoV-2 pandemic is being compared with prior pandemics like the 1918 Spanish influenza, H1N1 Swine flu, and the polio epidemics of the twentieth century. The significance of these choices might tell an informed reader about story-building and the power of melodramatic narratives in the media.

One might well wonder why the current pandemic is not being discussed more consistently in the light of scientific information about coronaviruses. While such information has been collected and published at an unprecedented rate since the SARS and MERS outbreaks in 2002–2003 and 2012, coronavirus has been a feature of biomedical research since the 1960s. Viral outbreaks are not new but the ongoing representation of the ensuing pandemic in media across the globe via proliferating media channels is quite novel. The most recent example of widespread fear may have been anticipation of an H5N1 pandemic of 2004–2007, given the lethality of infection in humans, but the current situation is also unprecedented, especially insofar as world governments have had to institute fairly restrictive measures to protect public health.

This chapter reviews information about pandemics, coronaviruses, and SARS-CoV-2 information in particular. The review and subsequent analysis will situate that information relative to other pandemics, specifically in terms of media response. The focus is upon how COVID-19 and SARS-CoV-2 scientific information is presented and analyzed. How media influence scientific publishing will be explored. We will consider scientific publication as a stand-in for influence on scientific research questions.

Pandemics

The World Health Organization (WHO) specifically defines the term "pandemic" as "the worldwide spread of a new disease" (np) and on March 11, 2020, COVID-19 was designated as a pandemic disease (World Health Organization (WHO) 2020). Pandemics vary in duration over time and the number of fatalities they cause. Although several different viruses and bacteria have caused illnesses that spread worldwide, influenza virus has been the most frequent cause of pandemics because it mutates quickly and can be transmitted easily from person to person but causes relatively few deaths among the infected, which means that survivors are able to continue to spread the virus to others.

Pandemics occur because people and animals carry pathogens from place to place. And ease and frequency of global travel was at a peak just before the COVID-19 pandemic. According to the World Bank, registered global air carriers conducted 35.7 million departures in 2017 compared with only 9.2 million in 1975 (The World Bank 2019). Mass gatherings of people from across the world might also play a role accelerating pandemics. In 2019, for example, the Kingdom of Saudi Arabia hosted 7.5 million visitors for Hajj and Umrah, as compared with over 2.5 million ten years earlier (Kingdom of Saudi Arabia Ministry of Hajj and Umrah 2020). Realizing the potential hazard, the Saudi government has long set strict vaccination requirements for pilgrims. Sporting events like the FIFA World Cup have provided opportunities to assess disease transmission in a more controlled environment. During the 2014 FIFA World in Brazil, there was concern that dengue cases might foster disease outbreaks, but interventions were successful because experts took various disease and environmental factors into account (Aguiar et al. 2015). Unfortunately, COVID-19 was not prevented and contained as successfully.

Coronavirus background

Coronaviruses have been a well-known threat to both humans and animals since their discovery in the 1960s. The name coronavirus comes from the Latin *corona*, meaning crown or halo because the virus particle in electron micrographs appears to have a solar corona on its surface. This corona is formed because "spike" proteins stick out from the sides of the virus: these proteins are the target of many vaccines. Coronaviruses typically cause respiratory, gastrointestinal, and central nervous system diseases like SARS and the common cold.

The first widespread public interest in coronaviruses was caused by the original SARS-CoV outbreak in 2002—commonly known as SARS—which infected approximately 8000 people in Asia, North America, South America, and Europe before it was eventually contained (Li 2016). About 10% of identified SARS patients died. In 2013, a coronavirus outbreak killed almost all young pigs and eliminated 10% of the US pig population (Li 2016). The most recent human outbreak of coronavirus disease was Middle East respiratory syndrome coronavirus (commonly referred to as "MERS") in 2012, which had a fatality rate of approximately 36% of identified patient (Li 2016). The COVID-19 pandemic, which had caused hundreds of thousands of confirmed cases and thousands of deaths by early April 2020, was caused by a virus that is now thought likely to have originated in bats. The virus was first discovered in December 2019 when pneumonia of unknown origin was observed in people who visited a local fresh seafood market in Wuhan, Hubei province in central China (Zhou et al. 2020; Wu et al. 2020). Although different strains of SARS-CoV-2 have been identified, they are very similar genetically (Zhou et al. 2020).

COVID-19 disease has several characteristics that make it particularly dangerous to human health, despite the current belief that it kills fewer than 5% of infected patients. First, no human had immunity to SARS-CoV-2 before it transferred to humans. Second, the majority of COVID-19 cases are mild, which makes them difficult to detect as compared with other common illnesses like colds or the flu (CDC COVID-19 Response Team 2020). Also, the virus has a long incubation period during which the infected person has no disease symptoms. Finally, older individuals are more likely to suffer serious illnesses or death. This means that the virus can be transmitted asymptomatically among people at low risk of serious illness until the virus encounters a vulnerable person. In contrast to previous coronavirus diseases with much more severe symptoms, where affected individuals could be rapidly separated from the general population, those with COVID-19 might never realize they are sick. This allows SARS-CoV-2 to contact the most vulnerable category of individuals with relative ease. This unusual disease profile has been the root of the increasing number of severe COVID-19 illnesses and deaths with resultant overloading of health resources across the globe. Efforts to develop vaccines and therapies might be aided by the knowledge that SARS-CoV-2 can be neutralized by sera from several COVID-19 patients. Furthermore, it has been confirmed that SARS-CoV-2 uses the ACE2 protein as the cell entry receptor, which is identical to the cell entry receptor of SARS-CoV, highlighting the possibility that current vaccine and drug development efforts may be useful against several coronaviruses (Zhou et al. 2020).

One tension in communication about COVID-19 is the very real difference in understanding and expectations between scientific and other audiences. A key characteristic of scientific writing is that the content should convey scientific information and also instruct a reader how to replicate the described experiments. Other audiences, like healthcare providers or patients, have different needs that professional medical writers might also need to understand and meet. The content of the clinical manuscript must be presented in a neutral manner and attempts to sway readers with emotional or melodramatic presentations are sharply frowned upon. This tone contrasts with how media outlets currently discuss SARS-CoV-19 infection and COVID-19 disease. And the contrast between media presentations of information about COVID-19 and scientific presentations is important because reader expectations are very different among people seeking medical or health-care information and those seeking to make social or political commentary.

Melodrama as a mode of thinking

In popular culture, pandemics are not necessarily understood terms of their epide-miologic characteristics but rather tend to capture the imagination because of their potential to ravage human bodies and devastate life as we know it on earth. Daniel Dinello (2005) locates an increased impact of "horrific images of mutilated bod-ies and corrupted flesh" (246) occurring after the end of the Cold War in his book *Technophobia: Science Fiction Visions of Posthuman Technology*. Dinello notes that anxieties about nuclear war in Hollywood science fiction films, which was a common trope during the Cold War, were gradually displaced by other fears, of which viruses became the most potent by the early 2000s. In narratives like *Hot Zone, Outbreak*, and *28 Days Later*, uncontrollable and deadly diseases or viral infections undermine not only individual health but the very fabric of global soci-ety. Dinello's observations draw on both specific film representations and their historical situation relative to global public health and international policy; in other words, he sees film representations as operating in conversation with cur-rent events, creating mutual influences. For Dinello, the rise of public and popular discourses that identify viruses as the most potent potential threat to humanity is significant in part because dystopian visions of viral futures attenuate the fabric of humanity itself. That is, dystopian futures create situations in which people are no longer free to be fully human. Technological posthumanity deadens emotions, limiting access to the most basic characteristics of humanity, such as love or trust, replacing these feelings with machinery, media, or other trappings of modern and futuristic lifestyles.

Hollywood narratives about plagues and pandemics participate in melodramatic traditions that date back to the foundations of popular culture itself. Melodramatic forms originated in stage productions outside officially sanctioned entertainments like ballet, opera, or drama and came to include certain stock characters engaged in a life or death struggle between clearly defined forces of good and evil. In his book *The Melodramatic Imagination*, Peter Brooks (1995) described what he called "the mode of excess" in nineteenth-century popular forms. He identi-fied this mode in French and British stage melodramas, in which stock characters enacted various scenarios whose ultimate resolutions were predefined by the inher-ent nature of the characters themselves. In this model of popular culture, heroes were always rewarded and villains always punished, not because of the specific actions they undertook but because of the essential identification of heroic or vil-lainous identity. An added feature of these productions was the open expression of emotions normally kept hidden from public view, a tendency that he identified in many popular forms, even more highbrow productions like the novels of Balzac, Henry James, and the Great Tradition. Film critic Linda Williams (1998) went a step further, building on Brooks' theory to state that all popular culture in the United States, an important source for global popular culture, is dominated by melodramatic expectations. Williams's essay "Melodrama Revised" outlines several key elements of twentieth-century melodramatic productions. These include moral elements—what Brooks referred to as a "moral occult"—as well as thematic and stylistic ones. Critically, heroes are also identified with innocence and victimization, and they engage in Manichaean conflicts between good and evil forces. The plot of these productions toggles between interventions that occur too late or in the very nick of time.

While Hollywood sensibilities inform current understandings, it is also important to note that these productions participate in a much longer tradition of literary production. For example, diaries and other sources about plagues extend back at least to the Black Death in Europe. For the purposes of understanding current productions, the relationship of melodramatic modes to older models of narrative, like the Hero's Journey, is of interest. As described by Joseph Campbell, the Hero's Journey is transformative, taking an ordinary individual and following their path from everyday life through magical realms and the underworld and back to gain renown and responsibility. Whereas the Hero's Journey differentiates realistic experiences from the magical realm, as Williams notes, melodramatic forms collapse these distinctions, which means that realism serves only to reinforce predefined outcomes.

The implications of melodramatic thinking in and around COVID-19 communication include the idea that membership in a certain group *de facto* confers immunity, which Trevor Noah asked about in a recent interview with Anthony Fauci (Noah and Fauci 2020). This idea mirrors the melodramatic tendency to assign specific outcomes based on a character's identity rather than their behavior. Fauci contrasted the idea that certain age groups are immune with the idea that probabilities of bad outcomes are lower in some groups, substituting a heuristic for rational decision-making with a melodramatic model. Similarly, Governor Andrew Cuomo castigated the "arrogance" of New Yorkers (Cuomo 2020) who failed to maintain appropriate social distancing because of the misplaced notion that because going outside was permitted, that no changes needed to be made in their usual behavior while outside. Like Fauci, Cuomo called on citizens to think about what they were doing and to weigh and consider risks and benefits rather than seeking automatic results. These requested behaviors are at odds with a lifetime of immersion in melodramatic modes of representation.

Media, control, and resistance

Recent trends in world leadership and national identity have been attributed, at least in part, to the rise of social media as a force for propaganda and information sharing that, while potentially not intended as propaganda per se, still acts to sway public opinion. Unlike melodramatic modalities, which serve merely to reinforce specific moral and ideological beliefs, propaganda is intended as a persuasive medium, aimed to induce specific actions. This is one reason why the rise of mass media, like radio, prompted intellectuals to develop theories about the role of such materials in the quest to, as Horkheimer (1972 [1992]) put it, "create a world which satisfies the needs and powers" of the people who inhabit it (246). Horkheimer, widely recognized as a member of the Frankfurt School, worked in a theoretical and intellectual tradition that sought to empower people, to break free of various forms of coercion and slavery to become fully realized human beings. Of course, as Dinello observed, certain types of melodramatic productions undercut these goals. And as Douglas Kellner (2007) observes, members of the Frankfurt School saw in forms like radio and television exemplars of a "culture industry" (1) that produced mass culture under the aegis of other powerful actors.

Kellner describes origins and approaches to a critical study of mass culture, as suggested initially by Horkheimer, Theodor Adorno, and other members of the Frankfurt school, including Jürgen Habermas, that would help identify and counteract the propagandistic elements of all forms of popular media. For these thinkers, who, as Kellner notes, "experienced at first hand" (1) not only the rise of popular media, but also its efficacy in inculcating populist impulses that led to the rise of Nazism, the culture industry was an important tool for reinforcing social inequity and economically driven power dynamics. Kellner highlights the ongoing importance of this work:

Indeed, the systematic thrust of the Frankfurt School approach that studies television and other institutions of media culture in terms of their political economy, text, and audience reception of cultural artifacts continues to be of use. Overcoming the divide between a text-based approach to culture and an empiricist social-science-based communication theory, the Frankfurt School sees media culture as a complex multidimensional phenomenon that must be taken seriously and that requires multiple disciplines to capture its importance and complexity (6).

For example, recent works on health communication have drawn on Habermas's notion of communicative action. Kellner himself integrates various other approaches to popular media with the foundational work of the Frankfurt School, creating a site for multicultural, multidisciplinary inquiry that accounts for differences in race, gender, social class, and relative involvement with lifestyle choices that depend on what Eisenhower called "the military industrial complex."

Various other theorists have offered models for examining the effects of media and propaganda delivered by various media outlets, as, again, Kellner notes. For example, a tension exists between freedom of thought and what Edward S. Herman and Noam Chomsky called "manufacturing consent" which is the appearance of independent choice constructed in many media productions. In *Manufacturing Consent, The Political Economy of the Mass Media*, Herman and Chomsky (2002) describe what they term "systematic propaganda" that is used to create the appearance of free choice and democratic process that have already been undermined by media control designed to provide predetermined outcomes. They describe how powerful entities use various forms of popular media "to inculcate individuals with the values, beliefs and codes of behavior that will integrate them into the institutional structures of the larger society." The result of these actions is the creation of what operates practically as an economic and social oligarchy that steers media messages behind the scenes and for its own purposes. In this context, and in the contexts that Kellner and various members of the Frankfurt School described, melodramatic constructs, by reinforcing what Brooks referred to as a "moral occult," create and reinscribe powerful cultural ideologies that undercut rather than encourage critical thinking.

This idea is related to what Slavoj Žižek called "the desert of the real" following 9/11: the idea that fabricated reality supplants actual knowledge and lived experience. Harry Collins gets at similar ideas about the erosion of expertise in his work, when he suggests that all readers believe that they are scientific experts on the basis of superficial familiarity with headlines and social media content. The chapters in this volume examine how meaning is made, disseminated, and circulated in various global contexts, keeping in mind the idea that popular reception is often constrained by forces outside the realities of healthcare delivery and research.

Media, cooperation, and representation

Although media may be understood in terms of propaganda, they also function as instruments of cooperation and representation rooted in sociological sensibilities that highlight interaction, value alignment, and awareness of inequality. As Waisbord (2014) notes, the "sociological sensibility . . . links the analysis of media . . . to questions about stratification, order, collective identity, sociability, institutions, domination/control, and human agency" (15). In short, media sociology considers connections between media and a wide range of human behaviors. A modern media sociology viewpoint envisions examining not simply the impact of "media" on society, but also the impact of "society" on media (Pollock 2007, 2013a, 2013b, 2015).

Several chapters in the current volume reveal that social media played critical interactive roles connecting publics and authorities during the COVID-19 pandemic. Beyond the speeches of government leaders, group chat participants in China (Li and Meinhof), citizen journalists in Serbia (Cendic), social media users in Vietnam (Dinh and Nguyen), bloggers in the Russian diaspora in Italy and China (Smoliarova, Gromova, and Sharkova), social media inhabitants in the UK and India (Lahiri et al.) as well as New Zealand (Martin-Anatias), netizens in Taiwan (Huang), and a wide range of cybercriminals (Kikerpill and Siibak) have abundantly demonstrated that the COVID-19 pandemic opens a cornucopia of opportunities for citizen media interaction with political leaders and institutions. In many countries, authorities and governments are compelled to witness the vibrant participation of citizen media activists.

Media also demonstrate cooperation and representation through attempts at message universalization. This perspective represents the effort by message creators to take into account the attitudes and values of intended audiences to craft persuasive messages that successfully engender attitudinal and behavioral change. A classic study by Herbert Gans (1980) found that most US journalists have in mind a few "enduring values" when they write for their audiences, including ethnocentrism or a value of their own nation above all others; altruistic democracy; responsible capitalism; small-town pastoralism, or the rural and anti-industrial values of Jefferson; environmentalism in which nature and smallness are desirable; individualism; and moderatism that discourages excess or extremism. Consistently, some chapters in the current volume suggest that various media universalize their messages by appeals to and alignment with values perceived as shared. These include Chinese nationalism (Gao; Li and Meinhoff) and the use of soccer as a source of national pride in Spain (del Campo).

Further examples of universalization involve national and political leaders. In New Zealand, Prime Minister Ardern's regular Facebook appearances in sweatshirts or pajamas after putting her baby to bed normalized both her and her appeals for coronavirus caution and social distancing as something ordinary citizens can do. Similar efforts at universalized messaging occurred after a UK government public health information campaign was launched employing several social media platforms, and ultimately a WhatsApp information service was developed that allowed the public to post responses or questions to social media feeds. In India, Prime Minister Modi called upon print and online media and enlisted the support of Bollywood actors to reduce social stigma associated with COVID-19 and promote basic health hygiene. Consistently, a substantial literature affirms that the use of "entertainment-education," whether through television or radio serial dramas or through more traditional song, dance, acting, and music, effectively encourages healthy behavior and reduces risk, in particular in developing countries (Singhal and Rogers 1999; Singhal et al. 2004; Tomaselli and Chasi 2011).

Media also demonstrate cooperation and representation through messages that illuminate inequality. Waisbord (2014) sees sociological approaches to media as necessary to foreground "questions about . . . history, power, inequality, control, institutions, autonomy, and human agency" (17). Since few scholars have attempted to fashion building blocks to construct a systematic, cross-national research framework for health communication or health issues (Pollock and Storey 2012), contributions to this endeavor are welcome. For example, one chapter documents that "asymmetries" and inequalities in resource and information access between the Global North and the Global South foment inequalities in health information access (Santos). Similarly, social media and infodemics reveal a plethora of issues connected to inequality in media access and therefore in health information access as well (Lin), including digital divides, knowledge gaps, and variations in social support. Illuminating unequal communication access, community structure theory (Pollock 2007), a subdivision of media sociology, "a form of quantitative content analysis that focuses on the ways in which key characteristics of communities, such as cities, are related to the content coverage of newspapers in those communities" (23), is useful. Community structure theory focuses on demographic characteristics of communities as "bottom-up" shapers of news instead of "top-down" national news leaders as "intermedia agenda-setters" (McCombs 2004) and drivers of public perception. Consequently, as Funk and

McCombs (2017) observe, community structure theory is a "central pillar of modern communication research" (845).

One of community structure's major umbrella predictions (Pollock 2007) is that media often report on critical issues in accord with the interests of a community's most vulnerable residents, for example, those below the poverty level, the unemployed, or Hispanics. Reporting on critical health issues, this "vulnerability" hypothesis has been supported by results of several US cross-city and cross-national studies, in coverage of universal healthcare (Kiernicki, Pollock, and Lavery 2013), immigration reform (Pollock et al. 2014), and genetically modified organisms (Pollock et al. 2017). In cross-national coverage, specific measures of national "health vulnerability," such as percent without improved water access or infant mortality rate or "macro" vulnerability conditions, such as agricultural dependence or political instability, are linked to "government" responsibility coverage for a wide range of health issues (Pollock 2020). In the current volume, a US multi-city study of coverage of state/local government responses to the coronavirus pandemic revealed that newspapers reported negative coverage in a way that "represented" the interests of relatively vulnerable populations (Pollock et al.). Overall, community structure theory's "bottom up" perspective reveals how the vulnerable are empowered by their demographic alignment with variations in health reporting/communication. By demonstrating the capacity of media to manifest inclusive, interactive behavior; message universalization; and the interests of underserved populations, several chapters in this collection foreground media's role as an instrument of cooperation and representation.

Organization of the current volume

The current volume is organized into four main sections that consider the relationships between media, culture, government agency, and technology. The authors of the individual chapters that comprise this work, most of whom hold advanced or terminal degrees in their fields, derive from varied educational and professional backgrounds to provide a rich overview of COVID in the media. It is worthy of note that the authors hail from all continents across the globe and therefore represent all areas affected by the COVID-19 pandemic. Overall, the chapters that contribute to this volume illustrate and enact a series of different approaches to examining the media that parallel, evoke, and either builds on the trajectory of the Frankfurt School in the twentieth century or adheres to the more recent tenets of media sociology. The authors provide deep insights into media representations of COVID on various scales, from the individual nation or specific social media platform to transnational and even global contexts.

Cultural differences in communication and identity

The five chapters in Section I examine cultural differences in communication and identity that impact how COVID-19 is represented and understood in various contexts spanning multiple continents and using varied methodologies. The authors consider cultural differences insofar as they might correspond to national or ethnic identities as well as the distinctions often drawn between persons with varied economic and social status. Several essays present the representation of COVID-19 by government leaders, while others interpret social media platforms or the news media more broadly. In addition, the researchers who contributed to Section I eloquently call for an understanding of communication and culture as persons cross national and cultural boundaries.

The New World Information and Communication Order forms the basis for Phillip Santos's discussion of the role of neoliberal policies in sustaining massive inequalities between the Global North and Global South. In his essay "Coronavirus response asymmetries in the Global North and Global South: new challenges and recommendations," Santos argues that by attending to global and local inequalities as proposed by dependency theorists and developing countries during earlier debates about communication, more effective local responses to global crises such as viral pandemics can be realized. For instance, calls for self-isolation and social distancing ignore the informality and ephemerality of daily earnings in African countries as well as the lack of fund for governments to compensate businesses and workers for lost earnings. Although this incapacity may arise from local failures and incompetence, neoliberal policies are also to blame.

In "Between declarations of war and praying for help: analyzing heads of state's speeches from an intercultural point of view," Eika Auschner et al. take a quantitative content analysis approach to speeches about COVID by various heads of state in order to highlight how cultural differences play out in this politically influential context. Auschner notes that public health measures toward COVID-19 differ around the globe and also that communication regarding the implementation of these measures varies. Some heads of state have declared war while others appeal to reason or encourage religious devotion and still others issue threats. Reasons for this range of approaches are manifold. Thus, Auschner considers theories of intercultural communication and management by figures like Hall, Hofstede, and Meyer, which highlight differences in trust-building, leadership, and sense of belonging. Taking these theories and further research findings into account, the proposed chapter aims at analyzing the speeches of the heads of state from different countries and continents, applying qualitative content analysis.

Echoing Auschner, Zhipeng Gao uses Stuart Hall's theories of ideology and media to unpack rhetorical approaches to COVID in Chinese government communications that impacted both persons living in China and immigrants from China residing in other nations. Of particular interest are the political imaginaries generated by such media portrayals, irresponsible Western governments as contrasted with a capable, trustworthy Chinese government, and the overindulged Western citizenry as contrasted with the collectivist, altruistic Chinese people. Gao argues that various common media strategies, such as fake news and othering, adeptly tap into cultural differences and goes on to reflect on the role of media in the cultural politics of diasporic (un)belonging in the process of de-globalization catalyzed by the COVID-19 pandemic, providing an anchoring point for this section that bridges the initial and later chapters.

In "Framing the pandemic as a conflict between China and Taiwan: analysis of COVID-19 discourse on Taiwanese social media," Ling-Yi Huang examines several cases and key questions in terms of the Taiwanese strategy and policy approaches to prevent and control infectious diseases. Huang also examines the interaction of social media and government policy and their grounding in either populist or rational thinking. Three central questions inform this research study. A semantic analysis was employed to analyze the content of public debates against the timeline of public health policy events. The chapter aims to reveal the connections between online debates and Taiwanese public health policy regarding COVID-19 and furthermore to contribute to the discussions of the role of social media in policymaking during the epidemic outbreak more generally.

Mutiu Iyanda Lasisi and Obasanjo Joseph Oyedele employ quantitative content analysis, computational analysis, and big data analytics of news stories between December 2019 and March 2020 to determine the causal relationship between internet information seeking of global data on local coronavirus and media reports containment and mitigation messages. In their chapter, "Comparing coronavirus online searching and media reporting: alignment or disconnect? A big data analysis of media reportage and public information seeking in Nigeria," the authors employ the health belief model, information seeking, and agenda setting, theories to predict the flow and identify patterns in audience information seeking about, and media reportage of the coronavirus. Studies have identified news values, topicality, and urgency of news items as major factors determining news reportage, which may align with information-seeking behavior of media audiences. However, during an outbreak of a pandemic disease, efforts at understanding the symptoms, causes, preventive mechanisms, and treatment options must also be considered.

Responses to regulation: media as instruments of social control or resistance

Section II comprises four chapters that consider the use of various social media strategies and genres to counter or address government policies and communications. The authors, who work and live in various national contexts, employ various methods, including descriptive analysis, interviews, measurements of post shares, and qualitative coding to characterize the nature, content, and impact of social media relative to official communication and policies. A critical argument within this group of chapters is Li and Meinhof's work that characterizes the media situation of COVID-19 in China as almost tantamount to an internal war between authorities and ethical journalists, intellectuals, and netizens. This idea of the netizen recurs in an essay that detail media approaches in Serbia. The authors provide rich insights into the effects and distinctions in settings where social media is free and open relative to those in which speaking truthfully carries heavy consequences.

In "Imagining pandemic as a failure: writing, memory and forgetting under COVID-19 in China," Li and Meinhof reconsider and recontextualize insights proposed by Jing Tsu in *Failure, Nationalism, and Literature* in 2005 to argue that the media situation of COVID-19 in China is almost tantamount to an internal war between authorities and ethical journalists, intellectuals, and netizens. The rise of counter-official accounts of the COVID-19 crisis, together with the irrepressible record of its everyday experience, suggests the emergence of a split between two strands of public writing in contemporary China. The advancement of new media and online platforms in China exposes ugly sociopolitical realities while disseminating reflexive commentary, yet also makes it possible for such observations to be censored and erased. Many, for example, have construed the COVID-19 outbreak as a national failure, attributable to officials' conspiratorial self-silencing at the Central Hospital of Wuhan.

Kristina Ćendić, similarly, discusses the role of policing of social media in Serbia where limitations to free speech result in people being detained and arrested for allegedly causing panic in social networks. In her essay "Arrest of the public interest or fight for public health in Serbia: contrasting roles of professional and citizen journalists," Ćendić observes that the deeply polarized media landscape in Serbia followed its usual pattern with pro-government media approving actions against citizens, while pro-opposition media outlets emphasize the role of citizen journalists and the need to balance the state of emergency and public interest. This chapter analyzes media discourse about the arrests regarding coronavirus-related posts by ordinary citizens and explores the boundaries between measures to protect both public health and freedom of expression.

A different method informs the next entry, which considers how and why the Indonesian government spent weeks claiming to have zero cases of COVID-19. Pitaloka and Martin-Anatias use interpretive and discourse analysis to unpack the Indonesian government's discourse in handling and approaching the pandemic in their chapter, "'We don't want to cause public panic': pandemic communication of the Indonesian government in responding to COVID-19." The authors suggest that the Javanese tendency to avoid conflict appears strongly in the communication strategy of Indonesian president Joko Widodo, who initially denied the presence of COVID-19 in the nation before admitting the number of cases weeks later. Collecting data from the daily newspapers and other media, the authors analyze how President Jokowi and his government approached COVID-19 in speeches and directives using interpretive and discourse analysis.

The final chapter in this section examines and interprets communications about COVID in a specific national context on the border of Europe and the Middle East. Daniele Nunziata shows how Cyprus continues to play out existing problems in "Pathological borders: how the coronavirus pandemic strengthened depictions of the Cyprus partition in the media and government." The chapter analyzes government press releases and responses by mainstream media and resistance organizations to understand connections between the pandemic and the island's imperial history of conflict, sectarianism, and division through postcolonial theory.

Responses to regulation: media as instruments of cooperation and representation

Section III's seven essays consider how media works cooperatively to communicate with populations, demonstrating how the public sphere can operate separately from government control. Chapters in this section provide an "alternative" media sociology perspective, which expects media to be imbedded in "contexts" and to play a role in "representing" the interests of communities that surround locations where media are produced. Of specific interest in this grouping of chapters is work by Smoliarova and colleagues, who consider how bloggers working in foreign languages represent the pandemic in COVID hotspots. This situation contrasts with that in countries like New Zealand, whose social media and government media overlap to create better communication that reaches all cultural groups.

The idea of media literacy informs the UK-India interchange of ideas about COVID discussed by Lahiri et al in their chapter, "Digital media and COVID-19 in the UK and India: challenges and constructive contributions." The authors note that government officials in the UK and India have asked social platforms to start awareness campaigns, prevent misinformation, and promote authenticity on the outbreak by initiating advisories. Lahiri and colleagues explore this phenomenon from the sociocultural perspective and examine how people from both countries have used digital technology in adopting appropriate health measures. The chapter further explores how the digital public sphere influenced public response to the outbreak in both countries, which retain important cultural ties by their membership in the British Commonwealth. The authors deliver an outlook on the integration of social media as an essential tool for preparedness, response, and recovery that can be translated and applied in future health-related crisis situations.

Nelly Martin-Anatias uses discourse and interpretive analysis to show that the New Zealand government's social media use demonstrated quality leadership and functioned as an effective means of communication that reduced the perceived gap between the state and its citizens. Her chapter, "New Zealand's success in tackling COVID-19: how Ardern's government effectively used social media and consistent messaging during the global pandemic," bridges a personal and intellectual perspective as both an Indonesian citizen and a permanent resident of New Zealand.

Working in another cultural context of the Eastern Hemisphere, Dinh and Nguyen in "Coronavirus pandemic: a historical handshake between the mainstream media and social media in response to COVID-19 in Vietnam" employ agenda-setting theory, content analysis, and in-depth interviews to clarify how stories of COVID-19 are reflected on mainstream media and social media in Vietnam, and how the cooperative relationship between mainstream media and social networks is shown in the content and way of reporting COVID-19. "Bloggers against panic: Russian-speaking Instagram bloggers in China and Italy reporting about COVID-19" reports on effective modes of countering Russian national media by social media participants who have immigrated to other nations. The authors Smoliarova, Sharkova, and Gromova measured the share of posts focused on COVID-19 and coded their content into four categories: informative versus emotional tone; actors that are blamed or criticized; information sources; and calls for action that have been used in previous research. The findings suggest that Instagram bloggers clearly intend to provide balanced information about COVID-19 and show a willingness to combat fake news and to criticize Russian national media for spreading panic.

Alberto del Campo Tejedor's "Re-imagined communities in the fight against the invisible enemy: soccer and the national question in Spain," considers how the coronavirus crisis burst onto the stage in Spain in the midst of a sociopolitical crisis between the central government and the pro-independence government of Catalonia. On social media as well as other news media, the merits of localisms, regionalisms, and nationalisms began to be discussed in relation to the health crisis. The coronavirus crisis has revealed and cultivated a political arena for read-justing identity discourses in a struggle not only between government institutions, but also between associations, football clubs, political parties, and civil society, who from their confinement at home are putting the possibilities of social networks to imaginative uses.

In "US nationwide COVID-19 newspaper coverage of state and local government responses: community structure theory and community "vulnerability," John C. Pollock and colleagues explore COVID coverage in cities in the United States through the use of media frames: the act of creating a coherent story by organizing the facts in a favorable or unfavorable light. Utilizing quantitative content analysis called community structure theory, the authors explore how community demographics shape the associated local news coverage (Pollock et al. 2020). The chapter confirms that increased levels of "vulnerability" in a city, in particular proportions of those categorized as "Mainline Protestant" (a belief system category in decline since the 1960s), are associated with less favorable coverage of state/local government responses to the COVID-19 pandemic.

The section ends with an important concept, infodemics, in the context of the COVID pandemic. Carolyn Lin's chapter, "Exploring the COVID-19 social media *infodemic*: health communication challenges and opportunities," explores the theoretical and empirical aspects of this infodemic phenomenon. Specifically, she reviews the source and methods associated with the transmission of COVD-19 news and information as well as public sharing and discussion of such news and information. The chapter also relies on media psychology and health psychology theories as the basis for presenting a scientifically sound discussion of relevant empirical evidence. These theoretical perspectives include information source credibility, social norms, opinion spiral, health belief model, soical support, social capital theory, and protection motivation theory.

Risk, space, and cyberattacks

The four chapters in Section IV consider risk, space, and cyberattacks. The authors and essays in this section foreground these questions as of heightened significance for promoting more sustained support for theoretical scholarship. Critical to this section is the idea of presenting, understanding, and demystifying extreme uncertainty, ambiguity, xenophobia, and western bias discussed by DeMond Shondell Miller and Nicola Davis Bivens. Chapters in this section also provide critical frameworks for understanding the media representation of COVID and other disease phenomena through concepts like relational riskscapes, as theorized by Şemsettin Tabur. Specific problems like phishing scams, viruses, and Trojan horses are also contextualized and critiqued, with researchers not only presenting current information but making future predictions about patterns of ongoing wrongdoing in cyberspace. The scholars and researchers who contributed to this section therefore set up a means of understanding how media sets itself up to create risks as well as anticipating the long-term consequences of current practices.

Paul Obi and Floribert Patrick C. Endong's "Manufacturing fear: infodemics and scaremongering on coronavirus and Ebola epidemics on social media platforms in West Africa" compares the proliferation of misinformation associated with the 2014–2016 Ebola outbreak with the current COVID crisis. The authors contend that information on both epidemics has been characterized by fake cures propagated by traditional and new forms of media. The information, labeled by the World Health Organization as infodemics, has been a challenge to the dissemination of genuine health information and leads to calls for the tightening of media control.

In "Space matters in narrating the catastrophe: relational riskscapes of COVID-19, dominant discourses, and the example of Turkey," Şemsettin Tabur seeks to examine the diverse ways the COVID-19 pandemic has been represented in a number of real, imagined, and lived spaces, including media, political discourse, and everyday locales in Turkey. The author uses Ulrich Beck's definition of risk as anticipating catastrophe, focusing on the uncertain, complex, global, anthropocentric, culturally situated, anticipatory, and catastrophic features of the concept, to highlight the social construction. The concept of riskscape is then proposed as an interpretive tool to explore the complex relations between risk and space, and address the socially produced, relational, and multilayered spaces in coronavirus discourse.

DeMond Shondell Miller and Nicola Davis Bivens take up Beck's idea of a risk society to demystify extreme uncertainty, ambiguity, xenophobia, and western bias in the content of messages promoted in US media with regard to risk for both Ebola and COVID-19. Their chapter, "Risk society in the age of pandemics: disaster reporting in the media—Ebola and COVID-19," contributes to the extant literature by examining how these messages relate to risk perception to support individual risk assessment and decision-making when faced with ambiguity during public health crises.

Kristjan Kikerpill and Andra Siibak take a distinct approach to discussing COVID in the media. By exploring news stories related to COVID-19 phishing and online scams that appeared in international news media from January to April 2020. Qualitative and quantitative content analysis was employed to explore how the social context of COVID-19 pandemic was used in scams, the types of scams, and influencing techniques used to deceive victims. The authors find that the COVID-19 pandemic is a perfect storm for phishing scams because it encourages general panic.

References

Aguiar, Maíra, Giovanni Evelim Coelho, Filipe Rocha, Luis Mateus, José Eduardo Pessanha, and Nico Stollenwerk. 2015. "Dengue Transmission During the 2014 FIFA World Cup in Brazil." *Lancet Infect Dis* 15, no. 7: 765–66. DOI: 10.1016/S1473-3099(15)00073-0.

Andersen, Kristian G., Andrew Rambaut, W. Ian Lipkin, Edward C. Holmes, and Robert F. Garry. 2020. "The Proximal Origin of SARS-CoV-2." *Nat Med* 26, no. 4: 450–52. DOI: 10.1038/s41591-020-0820-9.

Brooks, Peter. 1995. *The Melodramatic Imagination: Balzac, Henry James, Melodrama and the Mode of Excess*. New Haven, CT: Yale University Press.

CDC COVID-19 Response Team. 2020. "Severe Outcomes Among Patients with Coronavirus Disease 2019 (COVID-19)—United States, February 12-March 16, 2020." *MMWR Morbidity Mortality Weekly Report* 69, no. 12: 343–46. DOI: 10.15585/mmwr.mm6912e2.

Cuomo, Andrew. 2020. "Cuomo: 'Arrogant,' 'Self-Destructive,' 'Disrespectful' People Not Taking Quarantine Seriously Are 'Making A Mistake.'" *Real Clear Politics*. Accessed April 19, 2020. www.realclearpolitics.com/video/2020/03/22/cuomo_arrogant_self-destructive_disrespectful_people_not_taking_quarantine_seriously_are_making_a_mistake.html.

Dinello, Daniel. 2005. *Technophobia! Science Fiction Visions of Posthuman Technology*. Austin, TX: University of Texas Press.

Funk, Marcus J., and Maxwell McCombs. 2017. "Strangers on a Theoretical Train: Intermedia Agenda Setting, Community Structure, and Local News Coverage." *Journalism Studies* 18, no. 7: 845–65.

Gans, Herbert J. 1980. *Deciding What's News: A Study of CBS Evening News, NBC Nightly News, Newsweek, and Time*. New York: Constable.

Herman, Edward S., and Noam Chomsky. 2002. *Manufacturing Consent: The Political Economy of the Mass Media*. New York: Pantheon.

Horkheimer, Max. 1972 [1992]. *Critical Theory: Selected Essays, translated by Matthew J. O'Connell, et al.* New York: Seabury Press; reprinted Continuum.

Kellner, Doug. 2007. "Critical Perspectives on Television from the Frankfurt School to Postmodernism." In *A Companion to Television*, edited by Janet Wasko, 29–47. Hoboken, NJ: Blackwell Publishing. DOI: 10.1002/9780470997130.ch3.

Kiernicki, Kristen, John C. Pollock, and Patrick Lavery. 2013. "Nationwide Newspaper Coverage of Universal Health Care: A Community Structure Approach." In *Media and Social Inequality: Innovations in Community Structure Research*, edited by John C. Pollock, 116–34. New York: Routledge.

Kingdom of Saudi Arabia Ministry of Hajj and Umrah. 2020. "Open Data Platform—Statistical Number of Pilgrims for the Last Five Years." Accessed April 18, 2020. www.haj.gov.sa/en/InternalPageCategories/Details/50.

Li, Fang. 2016. "Structure, Function, and Evolution of Coronavirus Spike Proteins." *Annual Review of Virology* 3, no. 1: 237–61. DOI: 10.1146/annurev-virology-110615-042301.

McCombs, Maxwell. 2004. *Setting the Agenda: The Mass Media and Public Opinion.* Malden: Blackwell Publishing.

Noah, Trevor, and Anthony Fauci. 2020. "Dr. Fauci Answers Trevor's Questions About Coronavirus." *The Daily Social Distancing Show.* Accessed April 19, 2020. www.you tube.com/watch?v=8A3jiM2FNR8.

Pollock, John C. 2007. *Tilted Mirrors: Media Alignment with Political and Social Change: A Community Structure Approach.* Cresskill, NJ: Hampton Press.

———, ed. 2013a. *Media and Social Inequality: Innovations in Community Structure Research.* New York: Routledge.

———. 2013b. "Community Structure Research." In *Oxford Bibliographies Online*, edited by Patricia Moy. New York: Oxford University Press.

———, ed. 2015. *Journalism and Human Rights: How Demographics Drive Media Coverage.* New York: Routledge.

———. 2020. "How Media Empower the Vulnerable: Using Community Structure Theory to Analyze Relationships between Demographics and Health Reporting." *International Journal of Nursing Sciences.* https://doi.org/10.1016/j.ijnss.2020.05.007.

Pollock, John C., Suchir Govindarajan, Alexis Marta, James N. Sparano, Miranda Crowley, Radhika Purandare, and Abigail Lewis. 2020. "US Nationwide Coronavirus Newspaper Coverage of Federal/National Government Responses: Community Structure Theory and a 'Violated Buffer.'" *Trípodos* 47, no. 1: 27–47.

Pollock, John C., Stefanie Gratale, Kevin Teta, Kyle Bauer, and Elise Hoekstra. 2014. "Nationwide Newspaper Coverage of Immigration Reform: A Community Structure Approach." *Atlantic Journal of Communication* 22, nos. 3/4: 259–74.

Pollock, John C., Krysti Peitz, Elizabeth Watson, Cara Esposito, Phil Nichilo, James Etheridge, Melissa Morgan, and Taylor Hart-McGonigle. 2017. "Comparing Cross-national Coverage of Genetically Modified Organisms: A Community Structure Approach." *Journalism & Mass Communication Quarterly* 94, no. 2: 571–96.

Pollock, John C., and Douglas Storey. 2012. "Comparing Health Communication." In *Handbook of Comparative Communication Research*, edited by Frank Esser and Thomas Hanitzsch, 161–84. New York: Routledge.

Singhal, Arvind, Michael Cody, Everett Rogers, and Miguel Sabido. 2004. *Entertainment-Education and Social Change: History, Research, and Practice.* New York: Routledge.

Singhal, Arvind, and Everett Rogers, eds. 1999. *Entertainment-Education: A Communication for Social Change.* New York: Routledge.

Tomaselli, Keyan, and Colin Chasi, eds. 2011. *Development and Public Communication.* Bloemfontein, South Africa: Pearson.

Waisbord, Silvio R., ed. 2014. *Media Sociology: A Reappraisal.* Cambridge, UK: Polity Press.

Williams, Linda. 1998. "Melodrama Revisited." In *Refiguring American Film Genres: Theory and History*, edited by Nick Browne, 42–88. Berkeley, CA: University of California Press.

Woo, John. 2000. *Mission: Impossible 2.* Hollywood, CA: Paramount Pictures. Original edition, May 24, 2000.

The World Bank. 2019. "Air Transport, Registered Carrier Departures Worldwide." Accessed April 18, 2020. https://data.worldbank.org/indicator/IS.AIR.DPRT.

World Health Organization (WHO). 2020. "WHO Director-General's Opening Remarks at the Media Briefing on COVID-19–11 March 2020." Accessed April 17, 2020. www. who.int/dg/speeches/detail/who-director-general-s-opening-remarks-at-the-media-briefing-on-covid-19–11-march-2020.

Wu, Fan, Su Zhao, Bin Yu, Yan-Mei Chen, Wen Wang, Zhi-Gang Song, Yi Hu et al. 2020. "A New Coronavirus Associated with Human Respiratory Disease in China." *Nature* 579, no. 7798: 265–69. DOI: 10.1038/s41586-020-2008-3.

Zhou, Peng., Xing-Lou Yang, Xian-Guang Wang, Ben Hu, Lei Zhang, Wei Zhang, Hao-Rui Si et al. 2020. "A Pneumonia Outbreak Associated with a New Coronavirus of Probable Bat Origin." *Nature* 579, no. 7798: 270–73. DOI: 10.1038/s41586-020-2012-7.

Part I

Cultural differences in communication and identity

1 Coronavirus response asymmetries in the Global North and Global South

New challenges and recommendations

Phillip Santos

Introduction

The explosive, devastating, and expansive impact of the new coronavirus induced COVID-19 pandemic on the complete horizon of modern human existence is by now a matter of common knowledge. Subsequent to its outbreak, most governments introduced extraordinary measures aimed at arresting, containing, and eliminating the deadly new coronavirus. Key among these were, on the one hand, those measures that severely restricted human mobility, intimacy, right to assembly, and economic activity among other things. On the other hand, and more significantly, are the different ways in which governments from across the divide between the Global North and Global South stepped in to mitigate the impact of the pandemic on their populations. These extraordinary developments reveal three old but still exigent issues about the unique vulnerabilities and position of the Global South, in particular Africa, relative to highly developed countries in the Global North.

First, that the way the global economy is currently organized exposes both the underclasses or marginalized social groups in the Global North and, more significantly, the economically disenfranchised masses of the Global South, to the extreme effects of global crises—health or otherwise. Second, that global media in highly developed societies still dominate the flows of information across the world with consequential implications on the ideas and information shaping responses to crises in the Global South. Third, that news media and opinion leaders in the Global North continue to portray Africa in ethnocentric, patronizing, and condescending colonist discursive frames. COVID-19 has also shown that vulnerability to viral pandemics is universal although their effects are suffered and experienced disparately by people across the world depending on their sociocultural practices and values as well as their economic circumstances. Moreover, it is now also axiomatic that as long as there is human mobility across national borders, regions, and continents, everyone is as safe as the weakest members of society across the world. Therefore, the baseline argument in this chapter is that without addressing the pervasive asymmetries in the distribution and circulation of economic as well as cultural resources across the globe, the human species remains wholly vulnerable to the mortal effects of viral pandemics as well as other catastrophic crises now and in the future.

Consequently thus, it seems logical and prudent if not ineluctable that countries in the Global North synergistically foster cooperation and solidarity in capacitating both the economic stamina and communications infrastructure of the Global South, in particular Africa, which is the weakest part of this region. If not out of a sense of moral obligation, this could be done at least for the former's own self-preservation. Either way, the human species will be left better positioned and prepared to collectively confront, contain, eliminate, and preclude potentially catastrophic global or localized crises in the future. This chapter draws on the dependency paradigm and the New World Information and Communication Order (NWICO) debates to bring attention to the unfinished business toward the achievement of an egalitarian, inclusive, and just global community, which is imperative to building national and regional capacities as well as mutual cooperation between countries of the Global North and the Global South, in response to any future epidemics, pandemics, and other crises.

The dependency paradigm and NWICO debates

The COVID-19 pandemic has shown the fundamental importance of quality, reliable, and credible information, and economic capacity to respond to arising challenges before, during, and after a viral pandemic or crisis situation. Accurate, relevant, and useful information is a key vector in the formulation of effective and contextually informed strategies to arrest, contain, and eliminate the virus behind any pandemic. In the same vein, superoptimal economic resources are equally important in capacitating any preparatory work before the onset of a pandemic, protecting and supporting commercial activity during and after the pandemic, and in providing socioeconomic and psychological support to ordinary citizens during and after the pandemic. However, African countries and the rest of the Global South are severely disadvantaged in respect of each of these critical aspects. But the situation could have been better if the issues raised by dependency theorists and the Non-Aligned Movement (NAM) during the NWICO debates from the 1960s onward had been taken seriously and addressed.

The dependency paradigm in development praxis emerged as a critical response to the modernization claim that countries in the Global South were underdeveloped primarily because of "the lack of necessary ingredients for development, whether they are cultural, psychological-sociological, economic, or institutional" (Chew and Lauderdale 2010, 1). It blamed the internal dynamics of developing countries for their lack of development (see Smith 1996; O'Byrne and Hensby 2011). But the theory could not account for "gaps in growth between countries, the lack of autocentric self-sustaining development, the particularized economic specialization of some countries, and the persistent impoverishment of most parts of the globe" (Chew and Lauderdale 2010, 2). It is these gaps that the dependency paradigm sought to explain and address through self-valorizing redemptive formulations. For instance, dependency scholars challenged the modernization paradigm's focus on internal conditions as barriers to development and instead directed attention toward the operation of global structural factors and vectors as causes of underdevelopment (see Frank 1966; Dos Santos 1970; Furtado 1971; Cardoso 1972). As Frank argues, "contemporary underdevelopment is in large part the historical product of past and continuing economic and other relations between the satellite underdeveloped and the now developed metropolitan countries" (2010, 8).

In addition, dependency scholars noted that the global economic system within which the Global South was integrated from the time of the Slave Trade and colonialism privileged the former colonial powers as the center, and marginalized former colonies as the periphery of the global economy (see Wallerstein 1979; Frank 1966; dos Santos 1970). The dependency paradigm provided a narrative of development from the perspective of the Global South arguing that underdevelopment "cannot be blamed on the Third World, but that responsibility must be placed historically on the Western and colonial powers" (Chew and Lauderdale 2010, 3; see also dos Santos 1970; Frank 1966). Also, as O'Byrne and Hensby (2011, 60) point out, from the dependency perspective, the problem of the Global South is not "one of *under-development*, but one of *capitalist* underdevelopment." From this perspective, globalization is seen as a fundamental factor in creating and sustaining the Global South's dependent relationship with the Global North (see O'Byrne and Hensby 2011). Sub-Saharan Africa's relationship with the International Monetary Fund in particular has been noted for subjecting local economies to international capital with "disastrous social consequences" on the former (see O'Byrne and Hensby 2011, 67). To redress these dynamics, Frank's work proposes the consideration of historical and structural factors in their totality (see Chew and Lauderdale 2010). As a solution, some have proposed, among other things, de-globalization, which replaces

> the dominant, polarizing model of the "new world order" with a democratic "one world community" committed to international law, human rights, environmental justice, and grassroots sustainable development: a globalization from below.
>
> (O'Byrne and Hensby 2011, 75)

If this envisaged order were to be realized, two problematic areas would at least begin to be addressed. First, rather than furthering an asymmetrical regionalist world order, it would foster cooperation and solidarity at the planetary level, with the human species and its surrounding environment as the unit of socioeconomic organization. Second, it would provide for the non-exploitative and inclusive sustainable development of all countries, in particular the marginalized Global South. This would provide a foundation for both fraternal cooperation and solidarity in times of crisis as well as independent capacity to preclude (where possible), respond to, and counteract the negative impact of perilous global crises.

While the dependency paradigm focused on the economic relationship between the Global North and the Global South, an equally important global conversation on imbalances in the flows and circulation of information and cultural resources across the world ensued in the 1970s. The debates on the New World Information and Communication Order (NWICO) held under the rubric of the United Nations Educational, Scientific and Cultural Organization (UNESCO) were spearheaded by members of the NAM who sought a redress to "structural inequities, such as unequal media flow, foreign-owned infrastructure, and prohibitively priced rates" within the global communications architecture (Pickard 2007, 122). The NWICO debates of the 1970s and 1980s focused on "the worldwide imbalance of media facilities and flows as well as on the lack of accuracy and fairness in international news reporting, particularly concerning developing countries, by Western media" (Nordenstreng 2010, 1). These concerns were informed by fundamental considerations of the media's role in perpetuating the colonial condition and perceptions in and about post-independence Africa as well as the rest of the Global South. As Nordenstreng points out, NAM's declaration in Algiers 1973 noted, "the activities of imperialism are not confined solely to the political and economic fields, but also cover the cultural and social fields" (2010, 4). This led them to demand "concerted action in the fields of mass communication" (Nordenstreng 1984, 9).

The NWICO debates culminated in the production of the MacBride Report that promoted a move "towards a new, more just and more efficient world information and communication order" (Nordenstreng 2010, 11). Some of the elements expected of a just communication order include establishing balance and equality in information circulation, guarding against corporate malfeasance arising from monopolistic tendencies, allowing for a plurality of sources, cultural expressions, the media, press freedom, cooperation between the North and South in building communication infrastructure in the Global South, and expanding egalitarian participatory frameworks across all levels of social interaction (Nordenstreng 2010; see also Pickard 2007). Regrettably, dysfunctions and foibles in respect of these issues remain the order of the day in contemporary society (see Pickard 2020; Murdock 2017). Arguably thus, the dominance by massive transnational corporate media of the global discursive space during COVID-19 narrowed the lens through which intervening mitigatory measures could be imagined and implemented across the world.

Asymmetrical responses to COVID-19

First, it is imperative to show how the asymmetries already referred to manifest themselves in the context of COVID-19 as the basis for thinking redemptive interventions going into the future. The differentials in the capacity to respond to the economic shocks induced by the pandemic invite us to reflect on the economic dynamics outlined by dependency theorists. To begin with, during the COVID-19 pandemic, it was evident that the economic muscle and privileges of the Global North allowed developed countries to make available massive amounts of funding to cushion their working and non-working people, business entities (big and small), to acquire or manufacture the necessary personal protection material, to expand intensive care and testing capacity, to build new industrial type hospitals, and to develop the necessary contact tracing technologies as well as work on and develop vaccines aimed at effectively thwarting the pandemic's proliferation. Examples include the United States' more than US$2.2 trillion economic stimulus package (Noy 2020), and the European Union's US$750 billion pandemic recovery package (Ewing and Eddy 2020). As of May 20, Japan's stimulus packages represented 21.1% of its gross domestic product (GDP), the United States 13%, Sweden 12%, Germany 10.7%, and France 9.3% among others (see McCarthy 2020). These packages ensured these countries met their citizens' basic needs, economic activity can spring back to life after stringent lockdown conditions, and that critical services such as public health systems are rebuilt (Noy 2020).

The picture in Africa is starkly different as most countries "have either not yet announced any assistance or their packages are less than 1% of GDP" (Noy 2020). This excludes South Africa, the only African member of the G-20, which announced a package worth 10% of its GDP (Perez 2020). Most governments in Africa demonstrated tremendous incapacity to compensate businesses and workers for lost earnings under conditions of total lockdown, to say nothing of support for extremely marginalized members of society. Although this incapacity may have largely arisen because of corrupt governance, local failures, and inept leadership, the role of neoliberal policies in sustaining massive inequalities between the Global North and Global South cannot be underestimated (see Stiglitz 2017; Chigudu 2020). The majority of countries in the Global South lack both the economic wherewithal to protect those in the lower rungs of society from the vagaries of deprivation amplified by conditions of severe restrictions and the infrastructural incapacity to handle severe cases of COVID-19. In fact, a significant chunk of their interventions has come through debt relief packages, donations, and other support mechanisms extended from outside.

In addition to Africa's subdued ability to handle the economic impact of COVID-19, the continent is expected to take a huge economic shock due to "(i) lower trade and investment from China in the immediate term; (ii) a demand slump associated with the lockdowns in the European Union and OECD countries; and (iii) a continental supply shock affecting domestic and intra-African trade" (OECD 2020). Following its evaluation of COVID-19's likely economic impact on African countries, the OECD (2020) recommends that

> beyond the immediate response, recovery strategies should include a strong structural component to reduce dependence on external financial flows and global markets, and develop more value-adding, knowledge-intensive, and industrialized economies, underpinned by a more competitive and efficient services sector.

This observation is consistent with the central concerns of most dependency theorists and arguably recognizes the perils that come with both economic and humanitarian dependency on both developed countries in the Global North and multilateral institutions. Moments of severe crises seem to drive most countries toward an inward-looking posture as they prioritize their own citizens before considering other afflicted but undercapacitated regions. Furthermore, as economic activities across the world suffer crisis-induced knocks, demand for multilateral financial support also increases, which can potentially undermine the capacity or scale of such support for the most vulnerable countries. Although, by an inexplicable stroke of fortune, most countries in Africa escaped the devastating impact of the new coronavirus that was dealt European countries such as Italy, Spain, Britain as well as the United States, Brazil, and China, at least as the case was at the time of writing, the economic challenges posed by the viral pandemic portend a grim future for most countries on the continent and the greater Global South.

Second, it is also imperative to examine the implications of disparities in the flows of information between countries in the Global North and those in the Global South as these have huge implications on the latter's capacity to handle or preclude the potentially catastrophic impact of an equally (if not worse) devastating pandemic in the future. Africa's wholesale adoption of measures used by countries in the Global North in response to COVID-19 arguably reflects the asymmetries in global information flows. In the early stages of the pandemic, African governments imposed the same restrictive measures as those used in the Global North without much, if any, consideration for contextual circumstances. Although the reasons for this trend are difficult to discern, in toto, they could be partially explained in terms of the dominant narratives circulating in the public domain especially through global media such as CNN and the BBC, which are followed by a significant part of the African population, not least by policy or decision-makers. The disjuncture between the contexts of developed and developing countries in terms of the applicability of proposed measures triggered the publication of a number of critical articles across a range of alternative and mainstream media, which brought attention to this dynamic.

Two distinct leitmotifs run through these articles. On the one hand, some of the articles focus on the uniquely grotesque impact of the pandemic on vulnerable populations in the Global South and Africa in particular. For instance, *The Conversation Africa* noted that "the current crisis is really worsening enormous existing inequalities, in addition to creating new ones" in South Africa (Valodia and Francis 2020). Basing its observations on a study by the Southern Africa Labour and Research Unit, *The Conversation Africa* goes on to note that "the poorest 10% of households will most likely lose 45% of their income through the shutdown" in South Africa (Valodia and Francis 2020; DataFirst 2020). During lockdown measures, the poor will always bear the worst of the crisis because, unlike their rich counterparts, they do not have any savings to fall back on, which makes some form of universal income imperative, a feature largely absent from much of Africa. This picture is reproduced across the continent, in forms more severe than is the case in South Africa.

On the other hand, they criticize the wholesale adoption of radically restrictive measures used by countries in the Global North. Although such interventions may partly address the problem, they may also at once amplify already existing challenges. For instance, calls for self-isolation and social distancing ignore the informality and ephemerality of daily earnings in African countries. The adoption of measures used in the West by countries in the Global South was also criticized by media contributors such as Sur and Mitra (2020), Broadbent and Smart (2020), and Roy (2020) and Noko (2020) among others. In the case of India, for instance, Roy (2020) notes that Prime Minister Narendra Modi "borrowed the playbook from France and Italy" which quickly exposed India's "brutal, structural, social and economic inequality." She notes that rather than enforcing physical distancing, the lockdown "resulted in the opposite—physical compression on an unthinkable scale" (Roy 2020). The many people whom she spoke to expressed their fear of the virus, but as she further avers "it was less real, less present in their lives than looming unemployment, starvation and the violence of the police" (Roy 2020).

In an opinion article written for *Al Jazeera*, Noko (2020) cites overlapping sociocultural groups, the existence of crowded "slums and informal settlements," informal economies and poor health systems as factors that make containment measures suited for developed countries unpalatable for the African context. Broadbent and Smart (2020) note that such measures as physical distancing and quarantining may lead to "malnutrition and starvation for millions of people, and for these horrors, children and especially infants are the most at risk." For them, it is paradoxical that "the net effect of measures that seek to enforce social distancing may thus be to prevent people from working, without actually achieving the distancing that would slow the spread of the virus" (Broadbent and Smart 2020).

These examples show that the availability of accurate, truthful, relevant, and timely information is imperative not only in informing people and policymakers about the virus, but also about the necessary and contextually appropriate mitigatory measures. Furthermore, some of the articles directed their criticism at the egregious colonist representation of Africa by Western opinion leaders and news media. Criticisms have been directed at the representation of Africa as an inevitable epicenter of a COVID-19 catastrophe, "the final frontier of coronavirus," as if to suggest disasters and crises are endemic to the continent (Pailey 2020). The World Health Organization even predicted that the pandemic would kill at least 300,000 people in Africa (BBC 2020).

Contemporary resonances

The foregoing exposition shows that both the issues raised by dependency theorists about the asymmetrical organization of the global economy and those raised during the NWICO debates about the imbalances in the flows of global information are as relevant today as they were back then. In fact, they bear existential implications for people in the Global South if COVID-19 spreads to Africa, to the extent that it did in Europe and the United States or in the event of an equally pernicious pandemic in the future. Based on a cursory analysis of global experiences of COVID-19, it is arguable that countries with a combination of healthy economies and widely inclusive high-quality public health systems faired very well considering the grave circumstances they found themselves confronted by. Therefore, by attending to global and local socioeconomic inequalities as proposed by dependency theorists as well as the asymmetrical flows of information and cultural resources between the Global North and Global South, an issue forcefully raised by developing countries during the NWICO debates, the capacity to effectively respond to global crises such as viral pandemics in the developing world can be realized.

While the preoccupation during NWICO debates were the political and cultural implications of such imbalances on, especially, the Global South, today the same questions must be raised within the context of viral pandemics and other catastrophic crises. The imbalances in information flows that still exist have meant prescriptions for situations in more advanced societies about ways to deal with the coronavirus among other things, are taken up by news media in the Global South without consideration for local dynamics, at least in the initial stages before reflexive criticism mainly in alternative media resonate with discourses circulating in mainstream media.

Conclusion

The coronavirus pandemic has made the need for mutual recognition, cooperation, and solidarity among all of the world's people not only axiomatic but also imperative. Going forward thus, as Mbembe argues, "the path is clear" and demands that "on the basis of a critique of the past, we must create a future that is inseparable from the notions of justice, dignity, and the *in-common*" (2017, 177). Nonetheless, to fully realize this outcome requires a radical realignment of economic and social relations between countries of the Global North and those of the Global South. In the face of a non-discriminatory and deadly virus, it is apparent that every human life is as indispensable as it is vulnerable to such a vicious threat. The way forward thus should be one characterized by mutual recognition between the affluent and impoverished populations of the world, as well as a new attitude toward each other. Powerful countries must recognize the humanity of those long seen as the 'Other' in the Global South and that humanity shares the same fate "for, in the end, there is only one world" which is "composed of a totality of a thousand parts. Of everyone. Of all worlds" (Mbembe 2017, 180). Roy (2020) rightly argues that, as with other pandemics before it, COVID-19 may potentially force "humans to break with the past and imagine their world anew." She notes that COVID-19 offers a "portal, a gateway between one world and the next" (Roy 2020). Such a world, for her, must be devoid of "our prejudice and hatred, our avarice, our data banks and dead ideas, our dead rivers and smoky skies" (Roy 2020).

In this regard, the Global North must now relate with Africa and the rest of the Global South as equal partners sharing the same fate and working in solidarity with each other as they pursue equal and inclusive human coexistence. For as Lopes (2020) notes, since "health conditions everywhere protect more anywhere" it follows that "a new partnership is important for Africa and Europe alike." This must be read to imply relations between the Global South and the Global North. Such a partnership must not be one characterized by Africa's dependence on the charity of developed countries, but one of cooperation, solidarity, equality, and mutual recognition. This means the economic development of Africa and the Global South is no longer a peripheral matter for the Global North, but one that is as consequential for the former as it is for the latter.

References

BBC. 2020. "Coronavirus: Africa could be Next Epicenter, WHO Warns." Accessed June 6. www.bbc.com/news/world-africa-52323375.

Broadbent, Alex, and T. H. Smart Benjamin. 2020. "Why a One-Size-Fits-All Approach to COVID-19 could have Lethal Consequences." Accessed June 5. https://theconver sation.com/why-a-one-size-fits-all-approach-to-covid-19-could-have-lethal-conse quences-134252.

Cardoso, Fernando H. 1972. "Dependent Capitalist Development in Latin America." *New Left Review* 74 (July–August).

Chew, Sing C., and Pat Lauderdale. 2010. "On National Development: The Development of Underdevelopment." In *Theory and Methodology of World Development: The Writings of Andre Gunder Frank*, edited by C. Chew Sing and Lauderdale Pat, 1–5. New York. Palgrave Macmillan.

Chigudu, Simukai. 2020. *The Political Life of an Epidemic: Cholera, Crisis and Citizenship in Zimbabwe*. Cambridge: Cambridge University Press.

DataFirst. 2020. "South Africa—National Income Dynamics Study 2017, Wave 5." Accessed June 6. www.datafirst.uct.ac.za/dataportal/index.php/catalog/712.

Dos Santos, Theotonio. 1970. "The Structure of Dependence." *The American Economic Review* 60, no. 2: 231–36.

Ewing, Jack, and Melissa Eddy. 2020. " 'Europe Finally Got the Message': Leaders Act Together on Stimulus." Accessed June 6. www.nytimes.com/2020/06/04/business/europe-coronavirus-economic-support.html.

Frank, Andre Gunder. 1966. "The Development of Underdevelopment." *Monthly Review* 18, no. 4. https://doi.org/10.14452/MR-018-04-1966-08_3.

———. 2010/1966. "The Development of Underdevelopment." In *Theory and Methodology of World Development: The Writings of Andre Gunder Frank*, edited by C. Chew Sing and Lauderdale Pat, 6–17. New York. Palgrave Macmillan.

Furtado, Celso. 1971. *Development and Underdevelopment*. Berkeley: University of California Press.

Lopes, Carlos. 2020. "Europe and African Relations Post COVID-19: Time to Add Size, Scale and Speed." Accessed June 5. https://theconversation.com/europe-and-african-relations-post-covid-19-time-to-add-size-scale-and-speed-135017.

Mbembe, Achille. 2017. *Critique of Black Reason*. Translated by Laurent Dubois. Johannesburg: Wits University Press.

McCarthy, Niall. 2020. "Global Coronavirus Stimulus Packages Compared." Accessed June 5. www.statista.com/chart/21672/financial-responses-to-the-covid-19-pandemic-as-a-share-of-gdp/.

Murdock, Graham. 2017. "Mediatisation and the Transformation of Capitalism: The Elephant in the Room." *Javnost—The Public* 24, no. 2: 119–35.

Noko, Karsten. 2020. "In Africa, Social Distancing Is a Privilege Few Can Afford." Accessed June 5. www.aljazeera.com/indepth/opinion/africa-social-distancing-privilege-afford-20 0318151958670.html.

Nordenstreng, Kaarle. 1984. *The Mass Media Declaration of UNESCO*. Norwood: Ablex Publishing Corporation.

————. 2010. "MacBride Report as Culmination of NWICO." Keynote at International Colloquium 'Communication et changement social en Afrique' Université Stendhal, Grenoble 3, January 27–29, 2010.

Noy, Ilan. 2020. "Coronavirus Support Packages Will Reshape the Future Economy, and That Presents an Opportunity." Accessed June 5. https://theconversation.com/corona virus-support-packages-will-reshape-the-future-economy-and-that-presents-an-oppor tunity-135296.

O'Byrne, Darren J., and Alexander Hensby. 2011. *Theorizing Global Studies*. New York: Palgrave Macmillan.

OECD. 2020. "COVID-19 in Africa: Regional Socio-Economic Implications and Policy Priorities." Accessed June 5. https://read.oecd-ilibrary.org/view/?ref=132_132745-u5pt1rdb5x&title=COVID-19-in-Africa-Regional-socio-economic-implications-and-policy-priorities.

Pailey, Robtel Neajai. 2020. "Africa Does Not Need Saving During This Pandemic." Accessed June 5. www.aljazeera.com/indepth/opinion/africa-saving-pandemic-00408 180254152.html.

Perez, Francisco. 2020. "Financing Africa's COVID-19 Response." Accessed June 5. https://africasacountry.com/2020/05/financing-africas-covid-19-response.

Pickard, Victor. 2007. "Neoliberal Visions and Revisions in Global Communications Policy from NWICO to WSIS." *Journal of Communication Inquiry* 31, no. 2: 118–39.

————. 2020. *Democracy without Journalism? Confronting the Misinformation Society.* New York: Oxford University Press.

Roy, Arundhati. 2020. "The Pandemic Is a Portal." Accessed June 1. www.ft.com/content/10d8f5e8-74eb-11ea-95fe-fcd274e920ca.

Smith, B. C. 1996. *Understanding Third World Politics: Theories of Political Change and Development*. London: Palgrave Macmillan.

Stiglitz, Joseph. 2017. *Globalisation and Its Discontents Revisited: Anti-Globalisation in the Era of Trump*. New York: W. W. Norton.

Sur, Priyali, and Esha Mitra. 2020. "Social Distancing Is a Privilege of the Middle Class. For India's Slum Dwellers, It Will Be Impossible." Accessed June 5. https://edition.cnn.com/2020/03/30/india/india-coronavirus-social-distancing-intl-hnk/index.html.

Valodia, Imraan, and Francis David. 2020. "South Africa Needs to Mitigate the Worst of Its Inequalities in Tackling Coronavirus." Accessed June 6. https://theconversation.com/south-africa-needs-to-mitigate-the-worst-of-its-inequalities-in-tackling-corona virus-135564.

Wallerstein, Immanuel. 1979. *The Capitalist World-Economy*. Cambridge: Cambridge University Press.

2 Between declarations of war and praying for help

Analyzing heads of states' speeches from a cross-cultural point of view

Eika Auschner, Julia Heitsch, and Zully Paola Martinez Torres

Introduction

The spread of COVID-19 is a phenomenon that presents a huge challenge for governments around the globe. With a still-rising number of confirmed cases in more than 200 countries, areas, and territories, almost all governments have been forced to respond to the virus and implement measures to protect their societies. Not only do these measures differ around the globe, but also the communication regarding the implementation of these measures varies. Some Heads of State have declared a war against the virus; others appeal to reason or encourage prayers. Some have even threatened people who do not follow the rules. Reasons for this range of approaches are manifold, but cultural differences may represent one. This research analyzes 11 speeches given by Heads of State around the globe regarding the implemented measures to contain the spread of the virus. Criteria for the analysis were derived from models used in Intercultural Management that identify differences between cultures. The purpose of this analysis is to identify differences in communication among Heads of State and their populations that can be linked to these models. Results show that the speeches differ regarding the dimensions used in the respective models, but they do not always correspond with the expectations generated by the country analyses in these models. However, more research is needed to confirm our findings, including research on speeches in more countries, speeches by the same Heads of State at different points of time, and on the people's reactions to the implemented measures.

Theoretical background

Before focusing on cultural differences and ways to visualize them, it is important to define the term "culture." Woltin and Jonas (2009) define culture as the "vital world of a group of individuals characterized by shared patterns of interpretation in the context of shared knowledge" (Woltin and Jonas 2009, 469). For Geert Hofstede, culture is "the collective programming of the mind that connects the members of a group and distinguishes them from other groups of people" (Hofstede,

Hofstede, and Minkov 2010, 6). Culture, therefore, not only unites a group of people but also differentiates them from other people and groups at the same time.

Research that compares (management) practices in different cultures is referred to as "cross-cultural (management) research" (Perlitz 2004). Research findings in this area suggest that the way we communicate, work, and solve problems differs around the globe. Various researchers have tried to describe these differences and to categorize them. Hall (1977) formed the terms "high" and "low context" communication as well as "monochronic" and "polychronic" cultures. High context cultures refer to those cultures that apply a rather indirect form of communication, where messages are sent and received between the lines, relying also on non-verbal communication, whereas low context cultures use a more direct, clear, and straightforward way of communicating. The terms "monochronic" and "polychronic" refer to the use and management of time, with "monochronic" describing a linear and structured time management, and "polychronic" a more flexible way of organizing time, allowing doing several tasks at the same time.

Taking this research into account, several models have been developed that facilitate cross-cultural comparisons, with Hofstede, Hofstede, and Minkov's model (2010) and Erin Meyer's Culture Map (2014) probably the most popular ones. Both models describe different dimensions of culture, define two extremes, and place a country's characteristics on a continuum, allowing relative cross-cultural comparison between countries. These models were developed to facilitate the comparison between (national) cultures regarding different managerial functions and aspects of work (e.g., time management, leadership, communication, feedback, and trust). At the same time, the models allow analyzing and reflecting on one's own culture, seeing it in global comparison, thus facilitating a change of perspective. Although criticized a lot (e.g., McSweeney 2002; Ailon 2008), these models have been used to support organizations in their international activities, for example, in the negotiation, marketing, and management of global projects.

The model compares six dimensions:

1   *Power distance:* To which extent do people accept and expect that power is distributed unequally?
2   *Individualism:* How interdependent are members of a certain society?
3   *Masculinity:* Are people rather motivated by being the best or doing what they like?
4   *Uncertainty avoidance:* Are people trying to avoid unknown and ambiguous situations?
5   *Long-term orientation:* Does a society maintain links with the past or are changes made easily and in a pragmatic way?
6   *Indulgence:* To which extent do people try to control their desire and impulses?

Erin Meyer's Culture Map (2014) analyzes eight different scales related to management functions:

1   *Communicating:* Do you use high or low context communication?
2   *Evaluating:* How direct or indirect are you when giving negative feedback?

3   *Leading:* Is your leading style rather hierarchical or egalitarian?
4   *Deciding:* Are decisions taken top-down or in consensus?
5   *Trusting:* How do you build trust—based on tasks or relationships?
6   *Disagreeing:* Are you confrontational when expressing disagreement or do you avoid confrontations?
7   *Scheduling:* Do you organize your time linearly or more flexibly?
8   *Persuading:* Are people convinced based on facts and theories or rather based on the application and benefits?

Although these models rely on the idea of national cultures determining how people behave and have therefore been criticized (e.g., Ray 2017), the Culture Map has been used widely to identify and understand cultural differences in managerial behavior and business communication (e.g., Caldwell and Prizant 2017; Jean 2019).

Cultural differences in communication have been analyzed from several perspectives, especially from linguistic (e.g., Malyuga and Tomalin 2017) and rhetorical (e.g., Kammhuber 2008) viewpoints. Authors have concluded that parameters of communication are flexible and depend, among other variables, on the cultural context of communication partners.

As Hofstede's and Meyer's models have been developed in a business context and are mainly applied to analyze cultural differences in organizations, the purpose of this research is to identify differences in communication among Heads of State and their population in times of a crisis with the use of these models. The guiding research question is: how can differences in official communication of Heads of State toward their population be identified using Hofstede's and Meyer's model? The purpose of this analysis is to find out whether the cultural differences described by the models can also be found in political speeches.

Crisis communication around the globe: an empirical study

A qualitative study was undertaken to analyze differences in the form of communication in times of COVID-19. In total, 11 speeches by Heads of State in different countries were analyzed, in which they informed their populations about the measures taken to prevent the virus from spreading. For the analysis, qualitative content analysis (Mayring 2010) was used. The aforementioned models developed by Hofstede and Meyer served as a theoretical framework to build categories.

The following speeches were analyzed for this chapter (Tables 2.1 and 2.2).

These countries were selected because of their official language (Spanish, English, or German), location (with the purpose to cover many different regions), and accessibility of the speeches. We focused on speeches about measures that governments have implemented to protect their populations in the early stages of COVID-19 in their countries. The speeches were analyzed based on the following criteria derived from the aforementioned models. The guiding questions have been developed on the basis of the explanations of the respective dimensions.

Table 2.1 Overview of analyzed speeches

Country	Speech given by:	Links	Date	Language
1 Canada	Justin Trudeau	https://pm.gc.ca/en/news/speeches/2020/03/11/prime-ministers-remarks-canadas-response-covid-19	03/11/20	English
2 Peru	Martin Vízcarra	https://cdn.www.gob.pe/uploads/document/file/566444/Mensaje_a_la_Nación_15-03-20.pdf	03/15/20	Spanish
3 Malaysia	Tan Sri Muhyiddin Yassin	https://www.pmo.gov.my/2020/03/perutusan-khas-yab-perdana-menteri-mengenai-covid-19-16-mac-2020/	03/16/20	English
4 Germany	Angela Merkel	https://www.bundesregierung.de/resource/blob/975954/1732744/1d4e0fda2fec2a700a381d7e7fa7effd/37-1-bkin-ansprache-corona-data.pdf?download=1	03/18/20	German
5 Argentina	José Fernandez	https://www.casarosada.gob.ar/informacion/discursos/46803-palabras-del-presidente-de-la-nacion-alberto-fernandez-acerca-de-la-pandemia-del-coronavirus-covid-19-desde-olivos	03/20/20	Spanish
6 New Zealand	Jacinda Ardern	https://www.tvnz.co.nz/one-news/new-zealand/full-speech-prime-minister-jacinda-arderns-address-nation	03/23/20	English
7 India	Narendra Modi	https://www.narendramodi.in/text-of-prime-minister-narendra-modi-s-address-to-the-nation-on-vital-aspects-relating-to-the-menace-of-covid-19–548941	03/24/20	English
8 South Africa	Cyril Ramaphosa	https:// www.presidency.gov.za/speeches/statement-president-cyril-ramaphosa-escalation-measures-combat-covid-19-epidemic%2C-union	03/24/20	English
9 Colombia	Ivan Duque	https://id.presidencia.gov.co/Paginas/prensa/2020/Palabras-Presidente-Ivan-Duque-especial-television-Solidaridad-Cooperacion-Disciplina-Contagiemonos-solidaridad-200324.aspx	03/24/20	Spanish
10 Great Britain	Boris Johnson	https://www.gov.uk/government/speeches/pm-address-to-the-nation-on-coronavirus-23-march-2020	03/24/20	English
11 Dominican Republic	Danilo Medina	https://www.primeradama.gob.do/index.php/noticias/item/2009-discurso-del-presidente-danilo-medina-con-nuevas-medidas-por-la-pandemia-del-coronavirus	03/25/20	Spanish

Table 2.2 Overview of analyzed criteria and guiding questions

No.	Criteria	Guiding questions
1	High/low context communication	Is the message clear and direct or between the lines? Does the text talk clearly about consequences? Does it mention clear forms of expected behavior?
2	Individualism or collectivism?	Does the text include many terms that refer to personal relationships (friends, family, . . .)? If so, how often?
3	Hierarchical or egalitarian?	Is the speaker positioning him/herself at the same level as the audience? Are there any signs of hierarchy in the text ("Me as your president . . .")? Or does the speaker avoid mentioning her/his power?
4	Task- or relationship-based?	Does the speech appeal to reason or emotion? Does it mention personal relationships, for example, family and friends, or uses it more often terms like "task," "responsibility," "logic"?
5	Confrontational or avoiding confrontation?	Does the text name consequences if people don't stick to the rules? For the individuals but also for society? Are the consequences painted scarily?
6	Persuasion via facts/numbers from the past or by expected results?	How is the audience convinced to stick to the rules? Based on numbers/data/facts from the past? Or by picturing the post-COVID-world?
7	Consensus or top-down decision?	Does the text mention who decided on the measures? Who was included in the process?
8	Linear time or flexible time?	Does the text state explicit timelines, for example, the duration of the measures taken? Does it state procedures for the future if plans change?
9	Short-term or long-term approach?	Is there any time mentioned in the text? Does it refer to the (distant) future? Or focus more on the present and immediate future?
10	Uncertainty avoidance?	Does the text give clear instructions regarding the rules? Or does it leave room for personal interpretation? Can people decide by themselves what they want to do in the situation?
11	Self-control?	Are there any hints in the text that the population of the respective country is self-controlled and can stick to rules? Or are they expected to break the rules for their benefit?

Source: © Eika Auschner, Julia Heitsch, and Zully Paola Martinez 2021; own elaboration based on Hofstede, Hofstede, and Minkov 2010; Meyer 2014.

Categories were built on the aforementioned questions and tested with two exemplary speeches. After the first test, the speeches were analyzed by two undergraduate students with the necessary language skills and knowledge of cross-cultural theories and models, and simultaneously by the main researcher to guarantee coherence in the coding process. No differences in coding among the researchers were found.

Results

1 High or low context communication

    Most Heads of State (Germany, Great Britain, Canada, Argentina, Peru, the Dominican Republic, South Africa, India, and New Zealand) used low context communication: the message is clear and leaves little room for interpretation ("And if you are outside, keep your distance from others. That means 2 meters at all times. This is the single most important thing we can do right now to stop further community transmission."—New Zealand). In Malaysia and Colombia, the message was communicated more indirectly ("And I want to reiterate those three messages that are very important so that we remember them at all times. Let's stay home, stop the virus from spreading, and save lives."—Colombia)

2 Individualism or collectivism?

    The speeches that were given in Great Britain, New Zealand, South Africa, Canada, and India followed a rather individualistic approach, not referring to relationships ("New medical modeling considered by the Cabinet today suggests that without the measures I have just announced up to tens of thousands of New Zealanders could die from COVID-19."—New Zealand). The Heads of State of Malaysia, Colombia, the Dominican Republic, Argentina, and Peru, in contrast, mentioned relationships often or stated the necessity of getting through this situation collectively ("I believe that this pandemic is the greatest challenge to individualism, here no one can think in the first person anymore, we act personally to protect others."—Colombia). In Germany, the Head of State used elements of both, individualism and collectivism ("Without exception, it all depends on each individual and therefore on all of us.").

3 Hierarchical or egalitarian.

    The majority of the Heads of State did not mention their positions or differentiate between them and the audience regarding a hierarchical level. The leaders of Germany and Great Britain referred to their position once ("No Prime Minister wants to enact measures like this."—Great Britain). The president of Colombia, in general, used "we" and thus included himself ("We are a few hours away from starting what will be our national quarantine, a very important moment for our country, where our behavior, our attitude, our discipline, our solidarity, our commitment can save lives."), and the leader of India referred to the population several times as "friends" ("Friends, All of you are listening to and watching news items regarding Corona Global Pandemic situation around the world."). Hierarchies in form of a distance between the speaker and the audience can most clearly be seen in the speeches given by the Heads of State of Peru ("I assumed the office of President of the Republic because of a responsibility to Peru. And in each of the problems that we face, we have always made the best decision, thinking of the welfare of all") and the Dominican Republic ("So I say to you once again: Do not take it lightly.").

4 Task- or relationship-based

Most speeches (Great Britain, New Zealand, India, South Africa, Canada, Argentina, and Peru) appeal more to reason than to relations and/or emotions ("You should not be meeting family members who do not live in your home."—Great Britain). In Colombia, the president mentioned social relations ("Protect grandparents, grandfathers, and grandmothers, that we know we will give them our affection, but that we have to do it with the proper distance to protect their days."), and in Germany, the Dominican Republic, and Malaysia, indicators for both ways could be found ("Indeed, it is our collective responsibility to do so, as a citizen who cares for the well-being of our families, our communities, and our nation."—Malaysia).

5 Confrontational or avoiding confrontation.

Regarding the consequences, some differences can be found among the speeches. While the Heads of State of South Africa, Canada, Colombia, and Peru did not explicitly talk about the consequences of misbehavior ("If we do not take these steps, the promotion will be constant and permanent. Therefore, I believe that this is a circumstance that requires urgent and extreme decisions, however difficult they may be, but absolutely necessary"—Peru), the leaders of Germany and New Zealand mentioned the death of others as a possible consequence ("Failure to play your part in the coming days will put the lives of others at risk. There will be no tolerance for that and we will not hesitate in using enforcement powers if needed."—New Zealand). In India, Great Britain, the Dominican Republic, and Argentina, negative consequences were mentioned ("If you don't follow the rules, the police will have the powers to enforce them, including through fines and dispersing gatherings."—Great Britain). Only in Malaysia, the Head of State focused on positive consequences ("I believe that with these measures undertaken by the government, we will be able to stop the spread of this virus expeditiously.").

6 Persuasion via facts/numbers from the past or by expected results.

Almost all leaders justified their decisions by referring to the experiences of countries that had been affected by the virus, or by relying on data and the opinions of experts and scientists ("On the epidemic—and everything I tell you about it comes from the ongoing consultations of the Federal Government with the experts from the Robert Koch Institute and other scientists and virologists."—Germany). The only Head of State who did not refer explicitly to data, sources, or experiences is the Prime Minister of Great Britain ("Without a huge national effort to halt the growth of this virus, there will come a moment when no health service in the world could possibly cope; because there won't be enough ventilators, enough intensive care beds, enough doctors and nurses.").

7 Consensus or top-down decision.

Most leaders (New Zealand, Malaysia, Colombia, the Dominican Republic, Argentina, and Peru) stated that the respective Government or even the Head of State decided on the measures ("This is the most drastic decision that a government and a president have taken, and we are doing it to protect the life and health of all Colombians."—Colombia). In the speeches given in Great Britain and South Africa, nobody was explicitly mentioned ("Our analysis of the progress of the epidemic informs us that we need to urgently and dramatically escalate our response."—South Africa), whereas the leader of India referred to experts ("In light of health sector experts and experiences of other countries, the nation is taking a very important decision today."). In Germany and Canada, the Heads of State explained that the governments made the decisions and that they consulted with experts. They also included regional entities ("We are working very closely with our municipal, provincial, and territorial counterparts to mitigate the risks to the population."—Canada).

8   Linear time or flexible time.

While some leaders (Great Britain, Canada, and the Dominican Republic) did not explicitly mention a period for the measures, the leaders of New Zealand and Argentina proposed a clear plan ("After 48 hours, the time required to ensure essential services are in place, we will move to Level 4."—New Zealand), and Germany's leader explained the procedure of the implementation of new measures in detail ("This is a dynamic situation and we will remain capable of learning so that we can rethink and react with other instruments at any time. We'll explain that, too."). In India, South Africa, Malaysia, Colombia, and Peru, leaders focused on the duration of the current measures only, without talking about the next steps ("Considering the circumstances at present, this lockdown will last 21 days."—India).

9   Short-term or long-term approach

Given the urgency of the measures, all speeches focused on the present and the immediate future.

10   Uncertainty avoidance

The leaders of India, Great Britain, Germany, New Zealand, South Africa, the Dominican Republic, and Peru gave very clear and direct instructions that left little room for interpretation ("That is why people will only be allowed to leave their home for the following very limited purposes."—Great Britain). In Malaysia, Colombia, and Argentina, instructions were given more vaguely ("The current scenario requires drastic measures to be taken to resolve the situation as soon as possible."—Malaysia). The speech given in Canada did not contain any information regarding expected behavior and could therefore not be analyzed under this perspective.

11   Self-control.

The speeches did not contain enough information that could be related to this dimension to come to a conclusion. In general, the Heads of State asked people to behave accordingly to what had been established. The only exception is the Head of State of Argentina who apparently expected his population to break the rules ("Somehow, we wondered if we Argentines would be able to stay in our homes and I really want to say—to all of you—that I am very happy with how we are behaving as a society. . . . That is why I would say that—after 10 days—we have to be very happy as Argentineans, because we were able to stay in our homes and fulfill the commitment.")

Discussion

As the analysis has shown, cultural differences explained through the dimensions of Hofstede's and Meyer's model can (partially) also serve to visualize differences in the communication between Heads of State and the population. We could find differences in almost all dimensions, with long-term and short-term orientation being the exception, because all analyzed speeches focused on the present and immediate future. A second exception is the self-control dimension proposed by Hofstede; we didn't find enough evidence to compare the speeches under this angle.

For the remaining criteria, differences in the speeches could be identified. Interestingly, the analysis of the speeches did not always lead to the expected results, as they did not always correspond with the descriptions for the countries that can be found in the cross-cultural models. Based on our analysis and taking findings from cross-cultural management research into account, the speeches can be classified as culturally expected (in line with findings from previous research and descriptions in the models), culturally ambiguous (containing elements that correspond to earlier research as well as elements that do not), and culturally unexpected (the speeches do not employ a form of communication as expected based on earlier research).

Culturally expected

Countries that correspond to results from previous research are Malaysia, where elements of a collectivistic culture were reflected in the speech, as well as Great Britain, Canada, South Africa, and New Zealand. In these speeches, more direct forms of communication were applied. This form of communication is in line with the description of these countries in the models. Additionally, the speeches appeal to reason and logic rather than to emotions.

Culturally ambiguous

Latin American cultures are in the models categorized as rather high context and collectivistic cultures, using a more indirect form of communication. The speeches given in the Latin American countries considered in this research showed some elements of collectivistic cultures, such as using the term "we" rather than "I" and "you," but, for example, did not mention relationships as much as expected. The exception is Colombia, whose president mentioned family members and their protection to motivate people to stick to the rules.

Culturally unexpected

India is considered a rather high-context and collectivistic country, but the speech used a low-context communication style, without referring to personal relationships a lot. Germany, a country that scores rather high on individualism and applies low-context communication, would supposedly be suited for a very clear speech with direct instructions, but its leader used elements that are expected in collectivistic countries. Therefore, these countries did not apply the communication style that was expected.

Research limitations

The deviations of the presented results from previous research can be explained with a different context, as the models applied for this analysis have been developed in Business and Management and not for (political) communication. They are usually used to explain differences in Business behavior, not in speeches given by Heads of State. For Hofstede's model, it is also worth mentioning that the model was developed decades ago and does not necessarily reflect today´s practices. It is also important to keep in mind that the database for this research is very limited, as only one speech per country was considered. Public speaking is very personal, and of course, the personalities and experiences of the Heads of State also need to be taken into consideration.

Also, the role of the researchers who analyzed the speeches might have an impact on the results. This impact was reduced by applying scientific methods for qualitative research, but it cannot be neglected. Further research is needed, taking more countries, Heads of State, and situations into account to confirm or reject these results. It would also be interesting to connect these results with cross-cultural research on rhetoric and linguistics. Additionally, research could focus on the citizens´ response to the measures from a cross-cultural point of view. Finally, it is important to keep in mind that the current situation is a global challenge that we can only overcome together, despite our differences.

References

Print works

Ailon, Galit. 2008. "Mirror, Mirror on the Wall: Culture's Consequences in a Value Test of its Own Design." *Academy of Management Review* 33 (4): 885–904.

Hall, Edward T. 1977. *Beyond Culture*. New York: Anchor.

Hofstede, Geert, Gert Jan Hofstede, and Michael Minkov. 2010. *Cultures and Organizations: Software of the Mind*, 3rd ed. New York: McGraw Hill Professional.

Jean, Jessica. 2019. "Negotiating with Managers from France." In *The Palgrave Handbook of Cross-Cultural Business Negotiation*, edited by Mohammad Ayub Khan and Noam Ebner, 189–218. Cham: Palgrave Macmillan.

Kammhuber, Stefan. 2008. "Psychologie interkultureller Rhetorik als Grundlage des interkulturellen Dialogs." In *Psychologie des interkulturellen Dialogs*, edited by Alexander Thomas, 51–67. Göttingen: Vandenhoeck & Ruprecht.

Malyuga, Elena, and Barry Tomalin. 2017. "Communicative Strategies and Tactics of Speech Manipulation in Intercultural Business Discourse." *Training, Language and Culture* 1, no. 1: 28–45.

Mayring, Philipp. 2010. *Qualitative Inhaltsanalyse: Grundlagen und Techniken*, 11th ed. Weinheim: Beltz.

McSweeney, Brendan. 2002. "Hofstede's Model of National Cultural Differences and their Consequences: A Triumph of Faith—a Failure of Analysis." *Human Relations* 55, no. 1: 89–118.

Meyer, Erin. 2014. *The Culture Map: Breaking through the Invisible Boundaries of Global Business*, 1st ed. New York: Public Affairs.

Perlitz, M. 2004. *Internationales Management*, 5th ed. Stuttgart: Ullstein.

Ray, Tim. 2017. "Why Invisible Boundaries Matter: Imagined Institutions and Power." *Prometheus—Critical Studies in Innovation* 35, 4: 305–23.

Woltin Karl-Andrew, and Jonas Kai. 2009. "Interkulturelle Kompetenz – Begriffe, Methoden und Trainingseffekte." *Diskriminierung und Toleranz*, edited by Andreas Beelmann and Kai Jonas. Wiesbaden: VS Verlag für Sozialwissenschaften. https://doi.org/10.1007/978-3-531-91621-7_23

Online works

Caldwell, Christie, and Prizant, Ethan. 2017. "Influence and Global Leadership: China, India, and the Multinational Corporation." *Global and Culturally Diverse Leaders and Leadership. New Dimensions and Challenges for Business, Education and Society*, edited by Jean Lau Chin, Joseph E. Trimble and Joseph E. Garcia. 85–103. Bingley: Emerald Publishing Limited. https://doi.org/10.1108/S2058-880120170000003005.

3 Unsettled belongings in deglobalization

Chinese immigrants' struggle for political identity by using transnational media in the COVID-19 pandemic

Zhipeng Gao

Prologue: the puzzle of an uninvited donation

On April 11, 2020, *College Daily* (2020b), a New York-based online publication in Chinese that enjoys much popularity among Chinese students living in North America, made a public announcement that it would like to donate a ventilator to Jiayang Fan, a staff writer at *The New Yorker*. According to *College Daily*, it was responding to Fan's tweeted call for a ventilator needed by her mother, whose situation remained unclear in this announcement. But *College Daily*'s frequent references to the novel coronavirus created an impression that the virus was the reason for her illness.

The announcement appeared to demonstrate a collegial spirit—given that *College Daily* and Fan both are in the media industry, as well as perhaps a degree of compatriotism—as Fan is an ethnic Chinese who immigrated to the United States with her mother when she was 7. I was intrigued and went to Fan's twitter feed for more details. After scrolling down for several seconds, I found a shocking revelation: Fan's mother was not infected with the coronavirus, nor did her predicament truly lie in the lack of a ventilator. The truth is that she had been suffering amyotrophic lateral sclerosis (ALS), a severe illness that had paralyzed her and left her hospitalized in palliative care. In addition to life support from a ventilator, Fan's mother had been assisted by a full-time healthcare aide, who had learned how to read her facial expressions and eye blinks in order to attend to her needs. Thus, when the hospital detected positive COVID-19 cases in the facility and expelled this caregiver to prevent further infections, Fan's mother faced a devastating situation: her caregiver could not be replaced by just any other nurse. That was why the anguished Fan reached out for help. Among her many tweets, she briefly pondered the possibility of bringing her mother under homecare, in which case she would purchase a ventilator. Even this option was complicated by the unwillingness of the hospital to immediately discharge her mother. Fortunately, the hospital eventually did allow the caregiver to return, ending this heart-wrenching plight.

It should be noted that Fan shared the news of the caregiver's return promptly on April 10, one day before *College Daily* made the donation announcement. Readers who wish to entertain the possibility that *College Daily* had failed to keep itself updated would be dismayed by its publication soon thereafter of a lengthy article explaining the reasoning behind the donation. In this article, *College Daily* (2020a) bared its teeth and revealed a grudge against Fan and her employer, *The New Yorker*. Its grudge was based on Fan's support for Hong Kong's democratic protest in 2019, her slightly unfavorable commentary on China's role in the trade war, and *The New Yorker*'s investigative report that considered *College Daily* to be representative of Chinese post-truth media (H. Zhang 2019). After scrutinizing all the deeds of Fan and *The New Yorker*, *College Daily* claimed that its ventilator donation stemmed from a Chinese virtue: repay injury with kindness [*yi de bao yuan*]. *College Daily*'s narrative and the nationalist repercussion it generated in many Chinese media eventually reached the ears of Fan's mother, who, fully lucid in her mind, communicated to Fan, even with her limited means, that she should maintain grace, because "true blue will never stain" [*qing zhe zi qing*].

Transnational media, international tensions, and diasporic belonging

As striking as it might be, *College Daily*'s passive-aggressive engagement with Fan is not an isolated incident in Chinese-based media. Days before the hospital blunder, Fan had just received from her aunt a news message claiming that the United States was murdering its citizens. Another Chinese-subtitled video featuring that Trump Tower in New York was currently burning brought the healthcare aide to tears and panic because her son works near this building. Placing *College Daily* within the entire infoscape of anti-Western Chinese media, we may begin to recognize that *College Daily* was performing a task much grander than feuding with Fan and her employer. It was participating in the frontline of China's wrestle with Western countries, one that had intensified over the past several years. China's global expansion plan, as exemplified by the Belt and Road Initiative—a multitrillion-dollar project that involves infrastructure development and investment in more than 70 countries across Asia, Europe, and Africa, has since led to strong pushback from Western countries, which are concerned with China's rising economic power as well as its political ideology that spreads along the way.

Indeed, *College Daily* deftly wove the story of Fan's mishap into a larger catastrophic scene to the disadvantage of the United States. Based on the discovery of COVID-19 cases in the hospital, *College Daily* suspected whether the United States has professional standards at all to deal with the epidemic. By creating the false impression that Fan's mother lost her medical support because her hospital was called on to relieve the COVID-19 emergency, *College Daily* hinted at the country's lack of medical resources. Further, its fake claim that the hospital forcibly unplugged Fan's mother's ventilator painted the United States as being cruel. While denouncing the US "arrogant and willful stigmatization of other people and other countries," *College Daily* proudly stated that every day, hundreds and thousands of ventilators were ceaselessly shipped from China to the United States to provide aid. The image of China helping the United States, according to *College Daily*, demonstrated how to build a "community of shared future for mankind," Chinese President Xi Jinping's buzzword for advancing his global expansion.

College Daily belongs in the category of Chinese transnational media (CTM). Transnational media are defined as those which address audiences beyond and across national borders (Brüggemann and Schulz-Forberg 2009). Due to globalization and immigration, transnational media has played an increasingly prominent role in how people stay in touch with international news. The rise of transnational media brings with it both hope and challenge. Taking the European Union for example, transnational media promises to bring various countries together toward pan-Europeanism (Brüggemann and Schulz-Forberg 2009). Meanwhile, there has also been a fear that transnational media has the potential to Americanize European cultures (Schou 1992).

While these European-based studies are concerned with the impact of globalization, this study investigates CTM's potential to catalyze a reverse process, namely, deglobalization. In the Chinese context, transnational media serve as circuits of information that tie overseas Chinese with China through their shared linguistic-cultural background, socioeconomic connections, as well as topics of common interest (Sun and Sinclair 2015a; Yin 2015). Thus, even though CTM are typically hosted by Chinese diasporas and target audience living there, they sometimes share China's recent raising nationalism (Schneider 2018; Hyun and Kim 2015; Nyíri 2001; Zhao 2013). The portion of CTM that this chapter concentrates on, which should not be taken as representative of the entire field, are defined by their anti-Western sentiment. While many new Chinese immigrants already experience unsettled belongings between the home country and the host countries (Rushdie 2012; Y. Zhang 2017; Liu, Maher, and Sheer 2019), anti-Western CTM creates more conflict than mutual understanding across cultures and ethnicities (Sawyer and Chen 2012). This chapter is particularly interested in how anti-Western CTM is capable of constructing new Chinese immigrants' sense of belonging at a time of crisis.

Over the past several years, CTM has received concentrated scholarly attention against the backdrops of China's rise in world prominence as well as the international migration of Chinese (Sun and Sinclair 2015b; Thussu, Burgh, and Shi 2017). Now, the COVID-19 pandemic has created new social and existential conditions in which CTM need be reexamined. No longer consisting of chitchat topics to entertain at the dinner table, CTM headlines are now filled with nerve-racking updates of new diagnoses and death tolls, as well as information about public health measures that may have an impact on the safety of Chinese immigrants. Under the acute and pervasive threat from the coronavirus, whether the host societies can promise security has come to influence new Chinese immigrants' sense of belonging (Gao 2021b). CTM have nimbly tapped into the practical and existential needs of new Chinese immigrants during this crisis, and used these needs as a springboard to comment on key topics of dispute in China's tension with the

Western world, including the administrative capacity of different governments, human rights, and the implications of liberal democracy for public health.

Methods and data

The study is based on two sets of data collected in the first half of 2020. The first dataset is comprised of CTM in the forms of digital news reports, online forums, and social media used in the five core Anglosphere countries (Australia, Canada, New Zealand, the United Kingdom, and the United States) as well as continental Europe. Coming from a wide range of sources, the news coverages and postings total approximately 400 pieces. Although it is impossible to exhaust materials on the internet, the database has reached saturation, namely, that any new data were likely to repeat the same patterns previously identified. New media were the chosen focus because they better embody transnationalism and are favored by new Chinese immigrants who arrived in Canada over the past three decades (Laguerre 2010; Alonso and Oiarzabal 2010; Ip and Yin 2015). My discourse analysis and narrative analysis concern the question of how CTM's portrayals of the two contrasting approaches to COVID-19 intervene in international competition on the one hand, and construct new Chinese immigrants' sense of identity on the other (Bischoping and Gazso 2016; Fairclough and Wodak 1997; Van Dijk 2001). The second dataset comes from fieldwork on new Chinese immigrants' media usage conducted in Vancouver and Toronto, Canada, comprising 23 study participants and approximately 350 observational notes made on international Chinese immigrant communities to which the author maintains connections online. It is found that various common media strategies, such as othering and disinformation, adeptly tap into cultural differences regarding, for example, one's sense of privacy, conformity to the government, and the habit of wearing face masks. In other words, this chapter highlights the assimilating power of political discourse, instead of ascribing all cultural characteristics to political causes.

Asymmetrical media portrayal of two public health approaches

During the COVID-19 pandemic, millions of overseas Chinese living in the core Anglosphere and continental Europe find themselves torn between two contrasting approaches to public health: one in China and one in their host societies. When the coronavirus first struck China, after weeks of denial, the Chinese government launched a drastic campaign. Modeled after Wuhan, the entire country entered various degrees of lockdown that restricted people's mobility: private vehicles were banned from the streets; checkpoints were set up outside of residential buildings to ensure that people stayed home except for essential needs; mass surveillance was applied to monitor the movements of individuals. While Western media were shocked by what they termed "draconian" measures, CTM played down the numerous resulting tragedies, while highlighting the Chinese government's determination to stamp out the coronavirus.

Having learned much about the effectiveness of China's forceful approach, some new Chinese immigrants see their host countries' governments as being lamentably sluggish and irresolute (Gao, 2021a). Such perception is not unwarranted; Western countries were well aware of China's lockdown as of late January but failed to prepare themselves for the looming pandemic (Johnson 2020). Nevertheless, many CTM played a troubling role in that they displayed little willingness to explore Western countries' general strategy of "flattening the curve." In many CTM reports, the rationale behind such a strategy, namely, that the highly contagious coronavirus could not be fully eradicated in today's globalized and mobile world, was simply missing. It was not until early April, when China began to witness recurrences of COVID-19 in small outbreaks, when "flattening the curve" received more recognition in CTM.

Particularly in early March, CTM's suspicion of the Western strategy was bolstered by the contrast that, while China had largely put its own epidemic under control, new epicenters were emerging in Europe and North America, resulting in panic among new Chinese immigrants living there. Drawing on this contrast, the Chinese government promoted a discourse that its approach should serve as the very role model to be emulated by the Western world, apparently omitting the highly successful responses made by a few other societies such as Taiwan. This view even won approval from the World Health Organization. When Bruce Aylward, Senior Advisor to the Director-General of WHO, was asked by a Hong Kong journalist to assess Taiwan's public health response, Aylward awkwardly evaded the question. Nevertheless, many CTM adopted the discourse of the Chinese role model, scolding Western countries for their failure to "copy China's homework."

The idea of "copying China's homework" is highly problematic. By replicating this discourse, anti-Western CTM not only flippantly ignored the tremendous suffering brought on by COVID-19, but also failed to recognize various historical, cultural, and political factors that feed into each society's public health strategy. Regarding the Chinese approach, anti-Western CTM largely omitted the Chinese Communist Party's long history of using mass mobilization to eliminate public health threats (Gross 2016), as well as the fact that the Party today has a gigantic membership of 90 million to exercise its unhampered power. Regarding the Western approaches, CTM tended to ignore or downplay the concerns of Western societies with human rights issues and the possibility that the governments might take advantage of this "state of exception" to expand their powers (Agamben 2005). Without adequate background information, readers were left with the impression that Western governments were simply irresponsible in not adopting the radical, and seemingly effective, measures undertaken by the Chinese government.

Mr. New York's controversial disinformation campaign

If the aforementioned problems—inadequate contextualization, partial representation, and ideological distortion—might have originated from lack of professional competence, there was a second, more disconcerting category of problems that can be attributed to calculated disinformation. In the latter case, some CTM concocted fake news to demonize Western responses to the pandemic. *Mr. New York*, an online magazine that purports to have more than a million overseas Chinese subscribers, recently sparked major controversies for its disinformation. Its false charges included that the US Centers for Disease Control and Prevention (CDC) had been hiding the real number of diagnosed cases, reporting only a tiny fraction; that the CDC stopped publicizing the number of diagnoses and deaths; and that the sale of guns and ammunition in the United States increased by three times due to the epidemic (Mr. New York 2020a, 2020b). To support these fabricated stories, *Mr. New York* showcased incomplete images cropped from the CDC website and made reference to dodgy sources. One source it drew from was "Dr. Paul Cottrell," an American who, without possessing substantial biological or medical expertise, had been spreading the conspiracy theory that the coronavirus was bioengineered. As of April 2020, his LinkedIn profile described him as being a "future medical student": namely, a candidate for a master's degree in biology at Harvard University as of 2017, and a "pre-medical student" at Fordham University between 2017 and 2019. As Cottrell himself confessed, his claim about the CDC hiding data, which he did not verify, came from a random Facebook user's text message.

Mr. New York did have more formal sources. One argument it—as well as *College Daily*—passionately defended is that the coronavirus originated in the United States, rather than in China. With this claim, *Mr. New York* not only exonerated China but further asserted that China deserves gratitude from the whole world for its sacrifices made in containing the coronavirus. In this regard, *Mr. New York* quoted from *People's Daily*, the Chinese government's official mouthpiece, as well as from tweets made by several Chinese diplomats. The fact that these diplomats announced their charges using Twitter is noteworthy, given that Twitter is banned in China, making ordinary Chinese citizens who use it potentially subject to legal punishment.

The more the controversial, the more the hits. Some of *Mr. New York*'s articles received over 100,000 views per piece, spreading the disinformation far and wide. Protests by many Chinese immigrants, including many CTM writers, led to the intervention from WeChat, China's most popular social media app that serves as the platform where *Mr. New York* publishes its articles. As a result, one of the articles had its title replaced by a warning message "Title contains exaggerated and misleading content." This is certainly a very lenient treatment by WeChat, given that any articles critical of the Chinese government are typically deleted within a matter of hours.

Distrusting Western governments: the cruelty of herd immunity

Some Chinese immigrants display paradoxical, ambivalent attitudes toward the Chinese regime. On the one hand, as mentioned earlier, they prefer the Chinese government's forceful approach to COVID-19 for its efficiency. On the other hand, they do not necessarily trust the Chinese government's commitment to its people. Such attitudes are reflected in the views of one study participant of mine, George (pseudonym), who, after harshly criticizing the Chinese government, gave up his successful law firm in China two years ago and became a political refugee in Vancouver. Since the outbreak of COVID-19, he accused the Chinese government of, among many other things, allowing its military laboratories to produce the coronavirus. This conspiracy theory enjoyed much popularity among Chinese political dissidents but had little scientific support. After weeks, when the coronavirus spread to Canada, George transferred his lack of trust in the Chinese government to the Canadian one, suspecting the latter of deliberately hiding the number of diagnoses and refusing to deliver enough tests. These claims replicate exactly his criticisms of the Chinese government.

In my conversations with George, I realized that the strategy of "flattening the curve" never impressed him. His understanding of the Western strategy to COVID-19 was instead encapsulated in "herd immunity," a controversial concept made popular by British Prime Minister Boris Johnson and his associates. While many Western scholars criticize herd immunity from a scientific perspective, George's criticism came from a very different angle. According to him, the British government planned to "deliberately let the plague run loose, in order to eliminate hundreds of thousands of individuals who are old, weak or unhealthy," and the Canadian government followed suit.

George's understanding of herd immunity, which took the place of "flattening the curve" as the definition of the Western public health approach, was not his brainchild. He was rehashing the dominant message inside China that spilled over to many CTM. Such a portrayal wholly neglects the British and Canadian governments' calls to protect the elderly—a request that has been enacted to a certain degree—and presents these governments as cold-bloodedly letting their senior citizens die. This demonizing discourse intertextually underlies *College Daily*'s false claim that the US hospital forcibly stopped Fan's mother's access to a ventilator. Indeed, in another article, by highlighting tragedies that occurred in various nursing homes in the West, *College Daily* (2020c) suggested that Western countries had failed to live up to their advocacy of human rights. This criticism might appear to resonate with many Westerners' concerns, but its ultimate focus was on the China-West rivalry. Ignoring calamities caused by stringent lockdowns in China, *College Daily* positions China as the foremost champion of human rights that takes good care of its citizens.

Distrusting Western liberal citizenship

While holding Western governments at fault for implementing an inhumane "herd immunity" policy, George was equally skeptical of whether the liberal-minded local citizens could actually adhere to the quarantine standards. By March 19, it was reported that Canada had carried out more than 55,000 COVID-19 tests. George was suspicious of this number. One reason behind his doubt is that individuals who suspected themselves of having caught the coronavirus would need to voluntarily visit a hospital in order to be tested. China, in contrast, enforced stricter measures, including taking individuals' temperature at checkpoints outside of residential buildings, grocery stores, and public transport stations, and by sending personnel to enter households. Keeping this mass control in mind as the standard practice, George wondered: "how did the Canadian government manage to find so many people who would voluntarily go to hospitals to be tested?"

George was also highly suspicious of the Canadian notion of voluntary self-isolation, which was later mandated by law but not strictly enforced. In his view, this lax state also stood in stark contrast with China's rigorously monitored isolation at medical centers. George's disbelief in citizens' voluntarism appears to instantiate Bilodeau's (2014) argument that although immigrants from authoritarian societies have strong democratic desires, some of them might still display certain inprints of their socialization under authoritarian rule. Another study participant of mine, who had been passionately critical of the Chinese government because of its previous oppressions on her families, now told me that she wished the Canadian government would emulate China by implementing enforced isolation. After the author explained that the Canadian government does not have as massive an administrative-police system to put such strictures into effect, she responded that GPS trackers would solve the problem. Even as political dissidents, she and George both, under the influence of anti-Western CTM, endorse the Chinese government's approach to COVID-19 in a time of crisis.

Indeed, motivated by a distrust of liberal citizenship, some CTM took Chinese authoritarianism as the gold standard in attempts to intervene in the host society's public health campaign. When criticizing the Canadian health authority's initial recommendation that healthy individuals need not wear masks, one CTM article found support from *The National Post*, and, to buttress its authority, claimed that this *de facto* commercial press was similar to China's *People's Daily*, the official newspaper of the Chinese Communist Party (Mao 2020). Another CTM article, critical of certain Canadians' lack of conformity with the government's order to stay home, posed a particularly grim rhetorical question in its title: "Really Need the Government to Send Tanks?" (Nancy 2020). The mention of tanks makes no sense in the Canadian context, but to Chinese ears, it is an immediate reminder of the Tiananmen Square Massacre in 1989, in which tanks were famously employed in the killing of thousands of protesters. The COVID-19 crisis has likely bred the kind of authoritarian thinking that dismisses human rights. After months, as Western countries gradually escalated their policies and legal measures against COVID-19, a CTM article claimed that "as the entire world enters the Wuhan (lockdown) mode, Westerners finally realized that human lives are more important than human rights" (Bobby 2020).

Conclusion

This chapter focuses on a group of anti-Western Chinese transnational media (CTM), which, instead of facilitating cross-cultural understanding, cause some new Chinese immigrants to be alienated from their host societies. This analysis is positioned in the COVID-19 pandemic, which has created a state of crisis where one's safety depends on the efficacy of public health measures. Thus, to an unprecedented level, new Chinese immigrants' sense of belonging became linked to their host societies' public health responses and the political values underlying them (Gao 2021b).

With its Chinese linguistic-cultural background, CTM plays an important role in representing the Chinese and Western public health approaches to overseas Chinese. Anti-Western CTM tends to demonize the Western approach by means of decontextualization, partial representation, ideological distortion, and disinformation. In so doing, this chapter argues that anti-Western CTM intervene in China's ongoing conflict with the Western world by commenting on key issues of international contention, including different governments' administrative capacity, human rights conditions, and the implications of liberal democracy for public health.

As demonstrated in the discussion of *College Daily*, *Mr. New York*, and some Chinese immigrants' use of CTM, the contrastive imaginaries created by anti-Western CTM function to construct new Chinese immigrants' sense of political identification. This is achieved through political appropriation of cultural characteristics. That is, various common media strategies, such as othering and disinformation, adeptly tap into cultural differences regarding, for example, one's sense of privacy, conformity to the government, and the habit of mask-wearing. In peaceful times, cultural difference has been often celebrated to be the basis of diversity in a globalized, cosmopolitan world. However, at a time of crisis, cultural difference can be easily usurped to shape immigrants' identity to generate intergroup conflicts (Cottle 2006). By capitalizing on the unsettled belongings of new Chinese immigrants amid the COVID-19 crisis, anti-Western CTM is catalyzing a significant part of the trend of deglobalization.

Funding: This research project is funded by the Social Sciences and Humanities Research Council of Canada, 756–2019–0092.

References

Agamben, Giorgio. 2005. *State of Exception*. Translated by Kevin Attell. Chicago, IL: University of Chicago Press.

Alonso, Andoni, and Pedro Oiarzabal. 2010. *Diasporas in the New Media Age: Identity, Politics, and Community*. Reno: University of Nevada Press.

Bilodeau, Antoine. 2014. "Is Democracy the Only Game in Town? Tension Between Immigrants' Democratic Desires and Authoritarian Imprints." *Democratization* 21, no. 2: 359–81.

Bischoping, Katherine, and Amber Gazso. 2016. *Analyzing Talk in the Social Sciences: Narrative, Conversation and Discourse Strategies*. London, UK: Sage.

Bobby. 2020. "As the entire world enters the Wuhan mode, Westerners finally realized that human lives are more important than human rights." *Jiazhong Shenghuo Quan*, April 15, 2020. https://mp.weixin.qq.com/s/a0ClvS5h43mDZ9xCWUOlsA.

Brüggemann, Michael, and Hagen Schulz-Forberg. 2009. "Becoming Pan-European? Transnational Media and the European Public Sphere." *International Communication Gazette* 71, no. 8: 693–712.

College Daily. 2020a. "235 Days after Being Smeared by The New Yorker, College Daily Donated a Ventilator to Its Journalist." *College Daily*, April 11, 2020. https://mp.weixin. qq.com/s/JNj4K8xKqc0__WmqndjZ8g.

———. 2020b. "The New Yorker Journalist Jiayang Fan: College Daily Would like to Donate a Ventilator to You." *Zhihu*, April 11, 2020. https://zhuanlan.zhihu.com/p/128975683.

———. 2020c. "Is Human Civilization Something That Forces Lonely Seniors to Forsake Resuscitation and Consent to Die?" *College Daily*, April 14, 2020. https://mp.weixin. qq.com/s/HtFz9O2C6Ziz0l5dIIko9w.

Cottle, Simon. 2006. *Mediatized Conflict: Developments in Media and Conflict Studies*. Maidenhead: Open University Press.

Fairclough, Norman, and Ruth Wodak. 1997. "Critical Discourse Analysis." In *Discourse as Social Interaction*, edited by Teun A. Van Dijk, vol. 2, 258–84. London: Sage.

Gao, Zhipeng. 2021a. "Political identities of Chinese international students: Patterns and change in transnational space." *International Journal of Psychology*, online first.

Gao, Zhipeng. 2021b. "Unsettled Belongings: Chinese Immigrants' Mental Health Vulnerability as a Symptom of International Politics in the Covid-19 Pandemic." *Journal of Humanistic Psychology* 61, no. 2: 198–218.

Gross, Miriam. 2016. *Farewell to the God of Plague Chairman Mao's Campaign to Deworm China*. Oakland, CA: University of California Press.

Hyun, Ki Deuk, and Jinhee Kim. 2015. "The Role of New Media in Sustaining the Status Quo: Online Political Expression, Nationalism, and System Support in China." *Information, Communication & Society* 18, no. 7: 766–81.

Ip, Manying, and Hang Yin. 2015. "Cyber China and Evolving Transnational Identities: The Case of New Zealand." In *Media and Communication in the Chinese Diaspora*, edited by Wanning Sun and John Sinclair, 165–83. New York: Routledge.

Johnson, Ian. 2020. "China Bought the West Time. The West Squandered It." *New York Times*, March 13, 2020. www.nytimes.com/2020/03/13/opinion/china-response-china. html.

Laguerre, Michel S. 2010. "Digital Diaspora: Definition and Models." In *Diasporas in the New Media Age: Identity, Politics, and Community*, edited by Andoni Alonso and Pedro Oiarzabal, 49–64. Reno, NV: University of Nevada Press.

Liu, Shuang, Jessica Maher, and Vivian C. Sheer. 2019. "Through the Eyes of Older Chinese Immigrants: Identity, Belonging and Home in a Foreign Land." *China Media Research* 15, no. 2: 39–49.

Mao, Xiaoyang. 2020. "National Post Blasts Canada's Health Officer and WHO: History Is Not Going to Look at Your Kindly!" *Vancouver Headlines*, April 2, 2020. https:// mp.weixin.qq.com/s/hJyeYnOUY3ziOH_4JcVArw.

Mr. New York. 2020a. "The U.S. Admits That Covid-19 to Explode; Whistleblower Reveals That CDC Deliberately Hides That More than 1000 Cases Diagnosed Across the Country." *Mr. New York*, February 22, 2020. https://mp.weixin.qq.com/s /0eKTC1RJvMYkja_QGycUSg.

———. 2020b. "Frenzied CDC of the U.S. Announced to Stop Publicizing the Number of Diagnoses and Deaths!" *Mr. New York*, March 4, 2020. https://mp.weixin. qq.com/s/2V7mOm6UbEhqDs2Ux6LcsQ.

Nancy. 2020. "Suiciding! Confirmed Diagnoses Exceed 12000, Canadians Still Gathering and Having Fun Nonstop! Soccer Competition, Partying in Park, Sunset Watching on Beach, Enjoying All You Can! Really Need the Government to Send Tanks?" *This Is Vancouver*, April 2, 2020. https://mp.weixin.qq.com/s/5Edy2vY8bgB7Q D7sNohOxQ.

Nyíri, Pál. 2001. "Expatriating Is Patriotic? The Discourse on 'New Migrants' in the People's Republic of China and Identity Construction among Recent Migrants from the PRC." *Journal of Ethnic and Migration Studies* 27, no. 4: 635–53.

Rushdie, Salman. 2012. *Joseph Anton: A Memoir*. New York: Random House.

Sawyer, Rebecca, and Guo-Ming Chen. 2012. "The Impact of Social Media on Intercultural Adaptation." *Intercultural Communication Studies* 21, no. 2: 151–69.

Schneider, Florian. 2018. *China's Digital Nationalism*. New York: Oxford University Press.

Schou, Soren. 1992. "Postwar Americanisation and the Revitalisation of European Culture." In *Media Cultures: Reappraising Transnational Media*, edited by Michael Skovmand and Kim Christian Schrøder, 142–58. London, UK: Routledge.

Sun, Wanning, and John Sinclair. 2015a. "Introduction: Rethinking Chinese Diasporic Media." In *Media and Communication in the Chinese Diaspora*, edited by Wanning Sun and John Sinclair, 1–14. New York: Routledge.

———, eds. 2015b. *Media and Communication in the Chinese Diaspora: Rethinking Transnationalism*. New York: Routledge.

Thussu, Daya Kishan, Hugo de Burgh, and Anbin Shi. 2017. *China's Media Go Global*. New York: Routledge.

Van Dijk, T. A. 2001. "Critical Discourse Analysis." In *The Handbook of Discourse Analysis*, edited by Deborah Schiffrin, Deborah Tannen, and Heidi E. Hamilton, 352–71. Oxford, UK: Blackwell Publishers.

Yin, Hang. 2015. "Chinese-Language Cyberspace, Homeland Media and Ethnic Media: A Contested Space for Being Chinese." *New Media & Society* 17, no. 4: 556–72.

Zhang, Han. 2019. "The 'Post-Truth' Publication Where Chinese Students in America Get Their News." *The New Yorker*, August 19, 2019. www.newyorker.com/culture/culture-desk/the-post-truth-publication-where-chinese-students-in-america-get-their-news.

Zhang, Yaying. 2017. "Conflict and Negotiation: Transnational Ties and Competing Identities of Chinese Immigrants in Kamloops, British Columbia." In *Canadian Perspectives on Immigration in Small Cities*, edited by Glenda Tibe Bonifacio and Julie L. Drolet, 99–118. New York: Springer.

Zhao, Suisheng. 2013. "Foreign Policy Implications of Chinese Nationalism Revisited: The Strident Turn." *Journal of Contemporary China* 22, no. 82: 535–53.

4 Framing the pandemic as a conflict between China and Taiwan

Analysis of COVID-19 discourse on Taiwanese social media

Ling-Yi Huang

Introduction

Taiwan, with strong language, economic, and cultural links to China, and situated in close proximity to it, has managed to date to keep its deaths to single digits. Despite the fact that Taiwan is effectively barred from both the United Nations and the World Health Organization (WHO), it has proven to be most effective in protecting its nearly 24 million citizens from the COVID-19.

Taiwan recorded only 441 cases and 7 reported deaths as of May 21, 2020. Many reasons may help Taiwan beat COVID-19. One of the secrets of Taiwan's success lies in the painful memories of the 2002 outbreak of the Severe Acute Respiratory Syndrome, known as SARS. Besides, the immediate response by the government and the public as soon as reports of a virus originating in Wuhan, China, has contributed to the success. This study attempts to provide another explanation in that the framing of the pandemic as a conflict between China and Taiwan on the Taiwanese social media has contributed to the success. This study is interested in the question: can Taiwanese social media play a role in public policymaking in Taiwan? Due to the limitations of the research timeline, the research question is narrowed down: how was COVID-19 framed on Taiwanese social media? To answer these questions, online debates and the news reports posted by the netizens on Taiwanese social media were collected. Hopefully, this study can contribute to the discussions of framing effects of social media in the process of public health policy agenda building.

Framing and public health policy

A frame is often defined as a "central organizing idea or storyline that provides meaning to an unfolding strip of events" (Gamson and Modigliani 1987, 143). Framing—portraying an issue from one perspective to the necessary exclusion of alternative perspectives—can have a significant influence on public attitudes toward important policy issues (Chong and Druckman 2007).

Semetko and Valkenburg (2000, 95–96) pointed out the common frames in the news include:

(1) *Conflict:* Conflicts between individual people, groups, institutions, etc.
(2) *Economic consequences:* It looks at the economic consequences of a situation in the news and how it may affect people, groups, institutions, etc. economically.
(3) *Human interest:* It adds emotion or a human side to an issue, event, etc.
(4) *Morality:* It applies religious or moral beliefs to a situation.
(5) *Responsibility:* It makes someone responsible for a situation.

Framing techniques introduced by Fairhurst and Sarr (1996, 125) include: (1) Metaphor: to frame a conceptual idea through comparison to something else. (2) Stories (myths, legends): to frame a topic via narrative in a vivid and memorable way. (3) Tradition (rituals, ceremonies): Cultural mores that imbue significance in the mundane, closely tied to artifacts. (4) Slogan, jargon, catchphrase: to frame an object with a catchy phrase to make it more memorable and relatable. (5) Artifact: Objects with intrinsic symbolic value—a visual/cultural phenomenon that holds more meaning than the object itself. (6) Contrast: to describe an object in terms of what it is not. (7) Spin: to present a concept in such a ways as to convey a value judgement (positive or negative) that might not be immediately apparent; to create an inherent bias by definition.

Public health policy is determined by a process of consultation, negotiation, and research, which leads to a plan of action that sets out a vision of identified public health goals (Martin 2008, 30). During this process, framing of the health issue is critical in forming public opinions and changing collective actions. Regarding COVID-19, why do some government react quickly and accept it as a state of emergency while others react slowly and refuse to accept it as a real risk? One of the reasons could be related to how the COVID-19 is framed through the government, the media, and the public. According to Nathanson (1999, 446), three key dimensions of how public health risks are framed that influence public policy were identified: (1) whether the health risk is portrayed as "acquired deliberately or involuntarily; (2) whether it is portrayed as "universal (putting us all at risk) or as particular (only putting them at risk); and (3) whether it is portrayed as "arising from within the individual or from the environment." Based on Nathanson (1999), Lawrence (2004) concluded that the more an issue is framed in terms of involuntary risk, universal risk, environmental risk, and knowingly created risk, the more likely the opinion environment is to be conducive to public policy solutions that burden powerful groups. This study argues that COVID-19 was framed as an involuntary risk, universal risk, environmental risk, and knowingly created risk due to the special political background between Taiwan and China.

Conflict framing

Conflict is a type of media framing that is employed in the production of news. Framing a situation as a conflict highlights incompatibilities, disagreements, or oppositional tensions between individuals, groups, and institutions (Putnam and Shoemaker 2007, 167). Conflict frames are also found to cause an increase in support for certain policies (Vliegenthart et al. 2008). In conflict situations, framing refers to the way that participants define the situation—that is, what they attend to or ignore in an ongoing stream of events, what counts as important, and what actions should they take (Putnam and Shoemaker 2007, 168). Schuck, Vliegenthart, and deVreese (2016, 182) used content analysis of the media and defined that a conflict frame was considered to be present in a news story when it mentioned (1) two or more sides of a problem or issue, (2) any conflict or disagreement, (3) a personal attack between two or more actors, or (4) an actor's reproaching or blaming another. Bartholomé, Lecheler, and de Vreese (2018, 1689) pointed out two types of conflict framing: (1) intervention level by the journalists and (2) substantive and non-substantive conflict frames. This study focuses on substantive and non-substantive frames since the journalists are not the focal point of this study. Substantive conflict frames focus mainly on political ideas, policy issues, ideological issues and values, while non-substantive conflict frames address mainly the political process, politics as a game, or personal attacks.

Who framed the health issue: Netizens in Taiwan?

Not only news media but also individuals can frame a story and attempt to influence others. In the traditional media age, audiences are considered passive receivers. The news media "frame" the issue and when communicative frames affect individual cognitive frames, a "framing effect" has occurred. However, in the digital age, users can be active players. They can actively participate in the framing process and furthermore they can try to influence the media to set the agenda and to change the public policy. Ahmed, Cho, and Jaidka (2019) distinguished the frames from the news coverage and the citizens' tweets. They pointed out that the comparison of news coverage and citizens' tweets will shed light on whether political discourse on social media is merely a reflection of media discourse or is a source of alternative perspectives. This study further argues that both the articles on the social media and the netizens' discussions online co-frame the issue COVID-19. However, due to the affordance of anonymity on the internet, it is difficult to recognize the real identities of the users. Framings from the users online may not be a pure "people's voice." Online users can be connected to all kinds of interest groups who attempt to have influence on the public opinions.

Fear has been used as a political tool in Taiwan for the past elections. During the past elections, it is a repeated debate argument that the Democratic Progressive Party (DPP) exploits the "fear of unification with China," and the Kuomintang (KMT) exploits the "fear of isolation and war of independence". During the recent years, the young generation's identification with Taiwan as a nation has increased. The DPP has greater support than KMT. Besides, the young generation has higher digital media literacy than the older generation. They use the social media to express their political attitudes and perspectives. Young people who fear unification with China and support the ideologies of Taiwan as a country are often referred to as "Netizens." Besides, the DPP has strong support from young generations. These netizens have created a strong pressure on the DPP ruling government. In other words, the public opinions from the internet has big influence on the political agenda and policymaking.

Social media, agenda setting, and public policy

In the digital age, social media have played a role in agenda setting. For journalists, social media have become news beats for picking up stories, contacting and getting access to sources informally or formally (Broersma and Graham 2013). Social media are potentially yet another channel for sources to influence journalism, as they allow sources to control staging and content, and thereby a means to influence the agenda-building and agenda-setting processes of the news media. However, the sourcing of content from social media and the transfer of news items from one platform to another may vary across different media systems and political systems. In Taiwan, social media play an important role in influencing the journalists' daily practices. However, Twitter is not commonly used by the public. The journalists in Taiwan often cite the content from the social media PTT Bulletin Board System (PTT). Denham (2010) proposed three different models of agenda building. (1) *Outside initiative model:* it accounts for the process through which issues arise in non-governmental groups and are then expanded sufficiently to reach, first, the public agenda and, finally, the formal agenda. (2) *The mobilization model:* it accounts for the ways decision-makers attempt to implement a policy by expanding an issue from the formal to the public agenda. (3) *The inside initiative model:* it describes issues that arise within the governmental sphere and whose supporters do not try to expand them to the mass public. Different political and cultural system may afford the different chances for the agenda-building models.

For example, the Taiwan government has reacted to the public agenda quickly and made the public agenda a formal agenda. In Taiwan, the outside initiative model has been adopted during the coronavirus outbreak. To react to the public agenda quickly may be a good thing at the first glance, however, it could also lead to the danger that the country is ruled by populists. Besides, politicians may utilize social media as a fake "public opinion" to achieve their political purposes. It looks like an outside initiative model in the beginning. However, it could be a disguised one.

Research methods

I collected the events on Taiwanese news media and argued the important role of Taiwanese social media in the COVID-19 policymaking. Examples of the conflict frames and the relationship between debates on social media and the government policy were described as follows: *Case 1:* On January 28, Singer Fan Weiqi advocated on her Facebook account that face masks should be donated to rescue the people in Wuhan. She was attacked by a large number of netizens. The Taiwan premier has pointed out that to rescue ourselves was the only way to save others. The government also introduced a face mask rationing plan later. *Case 2:* WHO has renamed the Wuhan pneumonia to 2019-nCoV. However, some online voices insist that it should be called Wuhan pneumonia. The government also suggested to continue to call it Wuhan pneumonia. *Case 3:* A debate has started whether to allow Chinese children with Taiwanese residency to come back to Taiwan during the coronavirus outbreak. The general opinion was that as long as they do not have a Taiwanese passport, they cannot enter Taiwan. The government policy has undergone a major turn. Originally these children were allowed to come to Taiwan but later the policy has changed.

In case 1, the slogan used by the Taiwan premier "to rescue ourselves was the only way to save others "was employed as a framing technique to respond to the debate whether to offer humanitarian aid to China. In case 2, the metaphor that COVID-19 is called Wuhan pneumonia suggested by Taiwan government was employed to imply that the virus originated from Wuhan, China. It was also employed as a framing technique to increase the negative emotions toward China. In case 3, a story that describes the special situation of a child of a Chinese spouse was employed as a framing technique to the public debate whether to accept the Chinese with Taiwanese residency but without the Taiwan passport to enter Taiwan for the purpose of humanitarian aid. In all of the cases, Taiwan was depicted to suffer an involuntary, universal, environmental, and knowingly created risk from China. Since many Taiwanese work in China, they could bring back the virus. Taiwanese suffer a universal high risk. In these three cases, the conflict frames between Taiwan and China were adopted to deepen the sense of COVID-19 as a knowingly created risk from China. It should be noted that the examples are based on my personal observations.

Two types of framing analysis were suggested: deductive and the inductive frame analysis (Semetko and Valkenburg 2000). Deductive frame analysis predefines frames and then looks for them in the news to see which stories fit into the definitions. Inductive frame analysis requires that a story is analyzed first. This study looks at the predefined frame "the conflicts between China and Taiwan" and sees whether the netizens' discourses online fit into the conflict frames. Data was collected through the PTT COVID-19 forum (PTT is the largest online forum in Taiwan). The PTT COVID-19 discussion forum was set up on January 26 in 2020. To limit the irrational discussions, only four types of posts were accepted. These are "news," "live," "summary," and "organized data." Besides, each post is required to provide "the full title," "the media outlets which published the article," "time of publication," "the name of the writer," and "the original text link." Netizens can leave their messages under each post. Due to the limitations of the API, the most recent 20 pages were collected from May 9 to May 22. Python 3.7 was employed to collect the data. Regarding the data analysis, semantic analysis and framing analysis were used to explore the conflict frames between Taiwan and China.

Using sentiment analysis to explore the frames from the netizens

The problem of the framing analysis in the digital age lies in that the big data from the user content can overwhelm the researcher and make it difficult to conduct the study. This study attempts to use sentiment analysis to present the words occurrence and frequency related to the issue. Sentiment analysis can be considered a subfield of information extraction, the research area within information, and computer science that aims to condense, summarize, and draw inferences from collections of textual documents (Puschmann and Powell 2018, 2). Issues arise when sentiment dictionaries developed for one genre are seldom applied to another and context-dependent word meanings no longer fit with the original context. A solution widely employed to overcome precision issues is to inductively develop sentiment dictionaries that are tailor-made to particular genres, rather than universally applied. Therefore, this study also developed the user dictionary. The user dictionary can reflect the user content in the context.

Research findings

1 Semantic analysis

Top 20 mentioned words by the netizens after stopwords being deleted were Taiwan (1329 times), China (1207 times), surgical masks (1058 times), journalists (727 times), appreciations (627 times), nations (508 times), health minister (467 times), confirmed cases (466 times), Japan (465 times), epidemic prevention (448 times), new COVID-19 cases (423 times), Chen Shih-Chung (395 times), USA (394 times), open (381times), we (380 times), many (363 times), quarantine (348 times), government (346 times), virus (296 times), and Wuhan (280 times) (Figure 4.1).

The top three keywords were Taiwan, China, and surgical masks. Overall, they expressed their appreciation to the government and health minister Chen Shih-Chung online. They also talked about the pandemic situations in "Japan" and "the United States." Not surprisingly, the most mentioned words related to COVID-19 were Taiwan and China. In order to understand how the netizens framed the conflict frames between China and Taiwan, several words were added to the user dictionary to explore the "conflict frames" of the issue. A selection of the words was made based on the netizens' comments. After that, the researcher proposed these words that were related to China and the conflict frames. (1) *Chinese communist party:* it was mentioned 127 times. Netizens use this word to represent China and the communist party. (2) *Conceal:* it was mentioned 43 times. Netizens use this word to describe that China conceals the real numbers of the confirmed cases. (3) *CHO* (which means China and WHO): it was mentioned 64 times. Netizens use this word to point out the close relationship between China and WHO. (4) *Zero new cases:* it was mentioned 56 times. Netizens use this to refer to the pandemic situation in Taiwan. It is a daily report announced by the Taiwanese

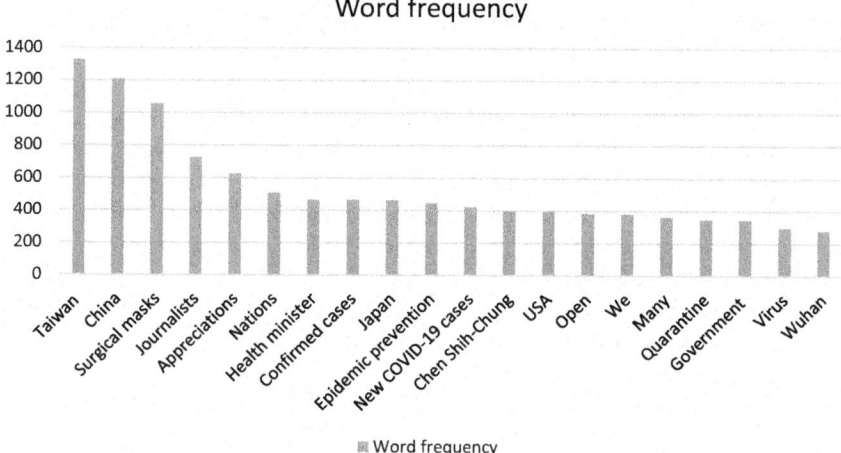

Figure 4.1 Semantic analysis of top 20 mentioned words by the netizens on the PTT COVID-19 Forum

Source: © Ling-Yi Huang, 2021

government. To have "zero new cases" gives pride to Taiwanese and strengthens the identity of Taiwanese. (5) *Conspiracy:* it was mentioned 12 times. Netizens use this word to describe that the COVID-19 is a Chinese conspiracy. (6) *WHO Director-General Tedros:* he was mentioned 22 times. Netizens mentioned him to describe the unfair treatment of Taiwan by the WHO.

2 Framing analysis of COVID-19 related to China from the news articles

Semantic analysis can help us understand the netizens' focal points, but the results alone can't disclose the whole picture of the conflict frames. Therefore, 35 news articles related to China posted by netizens from May 9 to May 22 were analyzed to understand the framing. The top three most frequently used frames were conflict frames and responsibility frames, non-substantive frames, and economic frames. The conflict frames were often used together with the responsibility frames.

Some articles adopted both the conflict frames and non-substantive frames or economic frames. (1) *Conflict frames and responsibility frames:* 20 out of 35 news articles adopted the conflict frames and responsibility frames together in blaming China for the outbreak of the pandemic and the spread of the fake information. These news article titles include: "China conceals the real numbers of infected people," "China objected to Taiwan joining the WHO," "The underlying relationship between China and the WHO," "China should have helped investigating and reporting the pandemic situation in the beginning of the outbreak," "China delays the report of the pandemic," "Fake news from China," "Fake surgical masks from China," Doubtful accuracy of tests from China, "Doubtful vaccine test results," "China steals vaccine research from the US," and "US professor said the pandemic originated in Wuhan." (2) Non-substantive framing: total four news articles "China objected to Taiwan joining the WHO," "The underlying relationship between China and the WHO," and "China steals vaccine research from US" were related to this frame. It implied that "politics is a game." (3) *Economic framing:* totally two articles have focused on the economic frames. One article mentioned the "Monetary profit in China due to exporting medical goods" and the other one added the conflict frame: "UK does not want to rely on medical goods from China." (4) *Human interest framing:* only one news article "It is difficult for Chinese citizens to return to China" adopted this frame.

Besides, COVID-19 was framed as a knowingly created risk, involuntary risk, universal risk, and environmental risk. (1) *Knowingly created risk:* 19 news articles have framed COVID-19 as a knowingly created risk. For example: "China conceals the real numbers of infected people," "China should have helped investigating and reporting the pandemic situation in the beginning of the outbreak," "China delays the report of the pandemic," and so on. (2) *Involuntary risk, universal risk, and environmental risk:* 11 articles were related to new confirmed cases in China. These articles depicted COVID-19 as an involuntary risk, universal risk, and environmental risk.

Conclusions and suggestions

Both the netizen discussions and the article titles of COVID-19 related to China were analyzed. Regarding the discussions of the netizens, the results have demonstrated that China has been the second most discussed issue between May 9 and May 22. China (mentioned 1207 times), Japan (465 times), and the United States (394 times) were the top three countries the netizens discussed. Furthermore, to understand the words in "conflict frames," a bag of words related to the context were selected to add to the user dictionary in Python. The results showed that "Chinese communist party" (mentioned 127 times), "CHO" (64 times), "Zero new cases" (56 times), "Conceal" (43 times), "WHO Director-General Tedros" (22 times), "Conspiracy" (12 times) were discussed by the netizens. The semantic analysis can help us understand the netizens' focal points, however, the results alone can't disclosure the whole picture of the conflict frames. Therefore, 35 news articles related to China posted by the netizens from May 9 to May 22 were analyzed to understand the framing. The top three most frequently used frames were conflict frame and responsibility frames, non-substantive frames, and economic frames. The conflict frames were often used together with the responsibility frames. Some articles adopted both the conflict frames and non-substantive frames or economic frames. Nineteen news articles have framed COVID-19 as a knowingly created risk. Eleven articles depicted COVID-19 as an involuntary risk, universal risk, and environmental risk.

Based on Schuck, Vliegenthart, and de Vreese's (2016) study, conflict frames can refer to the news articles using blaming strategies. In this study, 20 of the news articles posted by the netizens have adopted conflict and responsibility frames together since the articles have implied that China should be blamed for the pandemic outbreak. Besides, the result could be in line with Nathanson's (1999) and Lawrence's (2004) conclusions in that the more an issue is framed in terms of involuntary risk, universal risk, environmental risk, and knowingly created risk, the more likely the opinion environment is to be conducive to public policy solutions that burden powerful groups. Fifty-four percent of the news articles posted by the netizens framed COVID-19 as a knowingly created risk related to China. Thirty-one percent of the news articles framed COVID-19 as an involuntary risk, universal risk, and environmental risk.

By framing COVID-19 as a knowingly created risk, involuntary risk, universal risk, and environmental risk, PTT, the most influential Taiwanese social media, have formed the opinion environment that pressured the politicians to react toward the pandemic. It could be a good example of the outside initiative model of agenda-building. It accounts for the process through which COVID-19 issues arise among netizens and are then expanded sufficiently to reach, first, the public's attention and, finally, the formal agenda. However, due to the limitations of the research timeline, more evidence is needed to justify the outside initiative model of agenda building. For example, has the government attempted to influence the public opinions on social media? Are the netizens employed by the government? Could it in fact be a mobilization model? In order to study the role of social media in the process of different models of public health policy agenda-building, future studies are suggested to (1) collect data over a longer period to understand the changes of the frames, (2) compare frames between traditional media and social media, (3) collect data of changes of the government policy, and (4) interview opinion leaders on social media and policy decision-makers. Hopefully, this study can contribute as a starting point to discuss the framing effects of social media in the process of public health policy agenda-building.

References

Ahmed, S., J. Cho, and K. Jaidka. 2019. "Framing Social Conflicts in News Coverage and Social Media: A Multicountry Comparative Study." *International Communication Gazette* 81, no. 4: 346–71. DOI: 10.1177/1748048518775000.

Bartholomé, G., S. Lecheler, and C. H. de Vreese. 2018. "Towards A Typology of Conflict Frames." *Journalism Studies* 19, no. 12: 1689–711. DOI: 10.1080/1461670X.2017.1299033.

Broersma, M., and T. Graham. 2013. "Twitter as a News Source." *Journalism Practice* 7, no. 4: 446–64. DOI: 10.1080/17512786.2013.802481.

Chong, D., and J. N. Druckman. 2007. "Framing Theory." *Annual Review of Political Science* 10: 103–26.

Denham, B. E. 2010. "Toward Conceptual Consistency in Studies of Agenda-Building Processes: A Scholarly Review." *Review of Communication* 10, no. 4: 306–23. DOI: 10.1080/15358593.2010.502593.

Fairhurst, G., and R. Sarr. 1996. *The Art of Framing*. San Francisco, CA: Jossey-Bass.

Gamson, W. A., and A. Modigliani. 1987. "The Changing Culture of Affirmative Action." In *Research in Political Sociology*, edited by R. G. Braungart and M. M. Braungart, 137–77. Greenwich, CT: JAI Press.

Lawrence, R. 2004. "Framing Obesity: The Evolution of News Discourse on a Public Health Issue." *The Harvard International Journal of Press Politics* 9: 56–75.

Martin, R. 2008. "Law and Public Health Policy." In *International Encyclopedia of Public Health*, edited by Harald K. Heggenhougen and Stella R. Quah, vol. 4, 30–38. San Diego, CA: Academic. DOI: 10.1016/B978-012373960-5.00236-7.

Nathanson, C. A. 1999. "Social Movements as Catalysts for Policy Change: The Case of Smoking and Guns." *Journal of Health Politics and Law* 24, no. 3: 421–88.

Puschmann, C., and A. Powell. 2018. "Turning Words into Consumer Preferences: How Sentiment Analysis is Framed in Research and the News Media." *Social Media + Society* 4, no. 3: 1–12. DOI: 10.1177/2056305118797724.

Putnam, Linda L., and M. Shoemaker. 2007. "Changes in Conflict Framing in the News Coverage of an Environmental Conflict." *Journal of Dispute Resolution* 1: 167–75.

Schuck, A. R. T., R. Vliegenthart, and C. H. de Vreese. 2016. "Who's Afraid of Conflict? The Mobilizing Effect of Conflict Framing in Campaign News." *British Journal of Political Science* 46: 177–94. DOI: 10.1017/S0007123413000525.

Semetko, H. A., and P. M. Valkenburg. 2000. "Framing European Politics: A Content Analysis of Press and Television News." *Journal of Communication* 50, no. 2: 93–109. DOI: 10.1111/j.1460-2466.2000.tb02843.x. ISSN 0021-9916.

Vliegenthart, R., A. R. T. Schuck, H. G. Boomgaarden, and C. H. de Vreese. 2008. "News Coverage and Support for European Integration, 1990–2006." *International Journal of Public Opinion Research* 20, no. 4: 415–39. DOI: 10.1093/ijpor/edn044.

5 Comparing coronavirus online searching and media reporting

Alignment or disconnect? A big data analysis of media reportage and public information seeking in Nigeria

Mutiu Iyanda Lasisi and Obasanjo Joseph Oyedele

Introduction

Every pandemic disease is a public health issue with global attention needed in the areas of prevention, control, and/or containment. Apart from known morbidity and mortality losses, it comes with significant social, political, and economic costs. Usually, handwashing and social distancing are initial and proven control mechanisms generally recommended by public health experts where vaccines and drugs are unavailable. Salvation and help also come in form of mass media campaigns as agents of information, education, mobilization, and behavior modification capable of reducing the pandemic. The world turns to the media because of its capacity to reach millions of people with information, clear misinformation, encourage the right attitudes, and ensure that audiences take up recommended strategies for preventing and controlling the disease. As it stands, surveillance and quality tracking of contacts of index cases are done using the digital media (Collinson, Khan, and Heffeman 2015).

News values (especially currency, impact, immediacy, gravity, topicality, and urgency), apart from other factors influencing news gathering, production, and coverage, determine what is reported by news media. These values and factors are expected to arouse and sustain audiences' interests, aligning with their information-seeking behavior. There is also the aspect of framing and agenda setting to the discourse of media coverage with underlying motives different from news values and audiences' interests. This alignment is also greatly expressed during an outbreak of a pandemic disease, when there is a significant relationship between availability and access to critical health information and ability to prevent, control, or manage the spread of that diseases. Since media audiences could predictably be interested in understanding the symptoms, causes, preventive mechanisms, and treatment options available, the same agenda could underline media coverage.

During the Zika virus onslaught, mass media informatics enhanced disease surveillance systems; the digital media could be influential to requisite awareness, knowledge, understanding, attitude, and practices among the populace when an infectious disease breaks. To raise epidemic forecasting and produce quality preventive mechanisms aimed at reducing the spread of diseases, media coverage is also sacrosanct. Where media agencies do their works, transmission of infectious diseases is controlled as information is released to increase people's capacity to practice self-protection by adhering to standard measures for disease prevention (Kim, Fast, and Markuzon 2019; Falade 2019; Sell et al. 2018; Pavelka 2014; Majid and Rahmat 2013).

In December 2019, the coronavirus (COVID-19) outbreak was reported in Wuhan, China; by March 2020, it became a global pandemic infection attracting predominant media attention after reported thousands of infection and death worldwide. At the end of March 2020, there were more than 800,000 reported cases globally and Nigeria had 151 cases of COVID 19 with most cases in Lagos and Abuja. As expected, traditional and digital media spaces in the country rose to the challenge of breaking local and international news on the virus even before the first case of an Italian man who tested positive for coronavirus was reported. Such a situation comes with heightened tension, fear, and misinformation, as offline and online media agents rise to the responsibility and opportunity to satisfy the information-seeking behavior of media audiences.

Statement of the problem

There are studies on media coverage of disease outbreak. Collinson, Khan, and Heffeman (2015) investigated the effects of media reports of diseases spread and important public health measurements. For Petersen et al. (2017), an examination of customers' online, wed-based interaction with a national travel agency during the outbreak of Zika virus and internet searches for information within the period showed an agreement between the two, but not true for media information on the Rio Olympics.

A computerized textual analysis of contents of four newspapers—*O Estado, O Globo, Times of London*, and *New York Times*—on Zika virus in 2017, comparing their texts with Google Trends, was conducted by Falade (2019), who reported that audiences' attention to Zika virus was very high when attention was on Rio Olympics. However, the two foreign newspapers (*New York Times* and the *Times of London*) raised a greater anxiety than the local newspapers as the world was preparing for the Rio Olympics in Brazil. Randle et al. (2018) also examined the impact of the same outbreak of Zika virus on health-seeking and information-seeking behaviors of residents of Ontario. Data were collected from "trends in web searches, calls to a provincial telemedicine advice line, test submissions to the provincial laboratory and Zika-related media coverage" to determine information-seeking and health-seeking behaviors of Ontarians relating to the Zika virus outbreak. Findings showed that as soon as the WHO declared Zika as a pandemic, media coverage peaked within one week, with a corresponding increase in web searches within the period. This also affected telemedicine calls on information about Zika virus and increased requests testing and specimen submission.

In Nigeria, where there was a delayed onslaught of the coronavirus and only two reported cases within the specified period, it is important to determine the relationship between online information-seeking behavior of audiences overnight and what the mass media report as news on the coronavirus the following day. In this study, we employ the health belief model and agenda-setting theories to predict the flow and identify patterns in audience information seeking about, and media reportage of the coronavirus. Through quantitative content analysis, computational analysis, and big data analytics of news stories between February and April 2020, we determine the causal relationship between the audiences' information seeking through the internet in a day on coronavirus and media reports (containment and mitigation messages) in the following day, considering the confirmed cases, deaths, and recoveries globally.

Health belief model and agenda setting

How do people build knowledge, gain understanding, and be motivated to adopt a lifestyle? The health belief model is an important framework in health behavior research as it explains the process of change and maintenance of positive health behaviors after exposure to information. That is why interventions on changing people's health-related behaviors are premised on the model. For people to engage in health behaviors, proper information on risks or severity involved in adoption must be available. They need to be equipped with requisite information and understanding of the benefits associated with behavior change, barriers against the recommended actions, and their efficacy to take up such recommendations (Schiavo 2007; Champion and Skinner 2008). In the health belief model, whenever there is an epidemic or a pandemic disease, information provision is a constant variable as stakeholders seek to raise awareness, build knowledge and positive attitudes needed for prevention and control, and engender the right actions or practices. For these to happen, potential change agents endowed with intellect usually process information supplied and then evaluate their perceived susceptibility to the disease mentioned. If they believe that they are susceptible, the next cue is to look for information on severity of the infection. Once these two levels are positive, perceived threat is ignited. Constant information supply would need the change agents to consider the benefits and barriers that can accrue if they adopt the recommended change. The tilt leads them to actions to be taken and they also consider their capacity and ability to take such actions (Champion and Skinner 2008).

On agenda-setting theory, the question is: how does news media and their contents make some impact on people? From a discourse an almost all-powerful media determining what people think and do to the limited effects paradigm, agenda setting is a theory of interest when news consumption and people's reactions and beliefs are discussed. If the media are no longer powerful as to determine what news-consumers or media audiences do, they have some subtle influence on what people pay attention to and build as knowledge from exposure to the media. Media may be able to raise some issues to the fore for public discussion and attention, and such issues become the leading topics in the society. The mass media through their contents suggest what the audiences should think about; by doing this, there is a movement of media agenda through reportage to issue agenda. When audiences discuss these topical issues, they become public agenda through interpersonal and online comments among news consumers and later policy agenda if the society sustains its agitation for change (McCombs and Shaw 1972).

The two frameworks are symbolic to this study because there is a possibility that the information-seeking behavior of news consumers on coronavirus could trigger a media agenda the following day, while the discussion of what the media presented during the day can raise further discussion among the people, which may later become or raise another twists for media engagement the next day. This cycle is usually present during media coverage of pandemic diseases.

Methods

Quantitative approach and positivism philosophy of understanding problems were employed for the determination of possible causal relationship between public information seeking about the virus and media reportage about the virus the following day. Both the approach and philosophy led to the adoption of quantitative content analysis driven by computational analysis and emerging big data, from the information seeking behavior of the public and the media reportage of the issues and needs around the virus between February 27 and April 30, 2020.

Measures and data

The researchers specifically investigated a possible causal relationship between the audiences' information seeking through the internet in a day on coronavirus and media reports (containment and mitigation messages) the following day, considering the confirmed cases, deaths, and recoveries globally. Within this study, containment messages are the news about how governments at the state and federal levels in Nigeria provided measures and efforts toward controlling the spread of the virus. Containment messages also represent specific symptoms information and updates about the efforts of governments at reducing the number of cases. However, mitigation messages signify measures and efforts of the concerned stakeholders aimed at reducing the virus' severe impact on socioeconomic activities of the people and businesses.

Two sources were explored for data generation; the first was Google Trends, which normalizes public search terms on the Search Engines, especially Google. Google Trends is a tool that allows researchers and other professionals to understand relative score of specific terms or words between 0 and 100 scores (Randle et al. 2018). Using this tool, the researchers used "Coronavirus" as keyword and selected "Nigeria" to understand public interest in the virus within the study period. For adequate data collection, date of each day was set following the instructions associated with the use of the tool, while "All Category" was selected for the retrieval of the relative score per day. It should be noted that the scores for the trending of "coronavirus" were not used as the main data for the analysis. They only helped the authors in getting "related search terms" (related queries). The related search terms were the focus since the goal was to understand public information-seeking behavior related to the coronavirus.

Specifically, "coronavirus" was used as Search Term Index, while the first five search related terms (coronavirus Nigeria, coronavirus in Nigeria, coronavirus in Lagos, coronavirus in Kano, coronavirus Symptoms, Is coronavirus in Nigeria, Symptoms of coronavirus, coronavirus Update, coronavirus Cure) were considered as topical issues or needs the public wanted to understand each day. The expectation was that news-reports of Nigerian newspapers and some broadcast media that have websites for news dissemination would follow the dominant issues and need (the search related terms) of the people. The terms were also used as categories for determining the containment and mitigation messages.

Google News was the second data source. It is a news aggregation tool from the Google. Like the Google Search Engine that enables people to search for specific information, Google News also helps in reading news from newspapers across the world. The researchers used the tool to track and mine headlines of coronavirus related news. The headlines were extracted into a Microsoft Word document, coded in Microsoft Excel Sheet and transferred into the Statistical Package for the Social Sciences for analysis. The headlines and content of the news constituted the unit of analysis considered for the coding vis-à-vis the content categories (containment and mitigation messages). In the contents, the reflection of containment and mitigation messages was determined using the process tracing approach. It is an approach that helps researchers to detect meaning not easily discernible from news headlines.

Analysis and results

This section entails the analysis and results in line with the researchers' causal relationship investigation of public information seeking in a day and media reportage of the issues and needs that occupied minds during the day, on the following day. In Figure 5.1, the mean score of public information seeking in terms of understanding the disease through general information about the country and specific locations such as Lagos and Kano. The mean score also encompasses data that establish public understanding of the disease through searching of information regarding symptoms, existence, cure, and updates on the disease. Out of the studied three days in February 2020, significant information was not sought about the virus on the first day (day 1 = February 27, 2020, $n = 100$). The interest in understanding the virus started on February 28, 2020 ($n = 249$, $M = 41.50$) and was reduced on February 29, 2020 ($n = 166$, $M = 27.67$), three days after the index case was discovered. The expectation is that the media reports would also

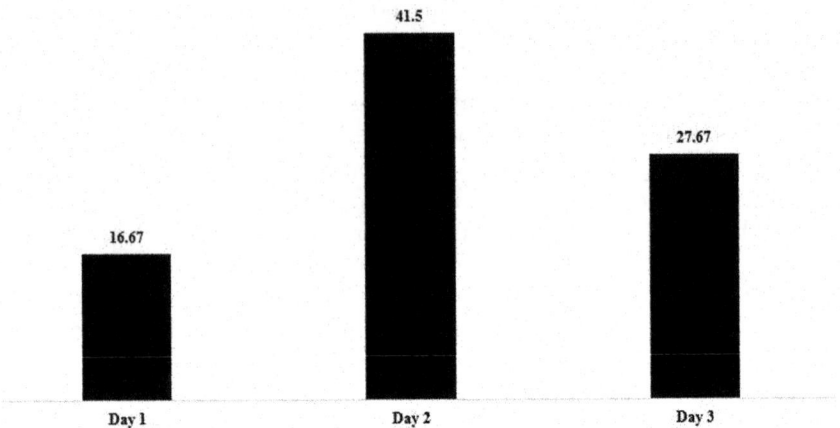

Figure 5.1 Mean score of total of topical issues or needs sought about the virus per day before media subsequent day publication in February 2020

Source: © Authors' Data Analysis

be significant during the days that the public developed significant interest in the virus in February 2020.

Figure 5.2 contains average (mean score) volume of information seeking (same with the earlier explanation about information seeking) about the virus in March and April, 2020. The figure shows that the public sought significant information about the virus on March 13 ($n = 408$, $M = 68$), March 27 ($n = 396$, $M = 66$), March 26 ($n = 245$, $M = 57.5$), March 29 ($n = 334$, $M = 55.67$), March 25 ($n = 330$, $M = 55$), March 16 ($n = 329$, $M = 54.83$), March 20 ($n = 322$, $M = 53.67$), March 22 ($n = 317$, $M = 52.83$), March 21 ($n = 316$, $M = 52.67$), and March 19 ($n = 301$, $M = 50.17$) 2020. In April 2020, the public mostly sought information about the virus on April 4 ($n = 327$, $M = 54.5$), April 6 ($n = 308$, $M = 51.33$), and April 3 ($n = 305$, $M = 50.83$). These results indicate that the public had significant interest in understanding the virus in March than in April. It has also emerged that public interest in any health issue of global importance could vary per day: they could be silent on an issue during some days and also be inquisitive about it on some days.

Table 5.1 entails aggregated daily and weekly sum of the issues or needs Nigerian public searched through the internet before media report the issues the following day or week. According to the data, it could be seen that public started having interest in the disease in week 2 ($M = 250$, SD = 217.13191). From the total average mean score for week 2, more than 150 average mean score was recorded for week 3 ($M = 350.5000$) and week 4 ($M = 388.3333$). It was dipped in week 5 to ($M = 321.8333$) and ($M = 257.667$) in week 6. Overall analysis indicates that public interest in the disease was high in five weeks out of eight weeks. This could be linked with the number of rising cases during the weeks than the earlier days of reporting index case. It could also be said that people were equipped

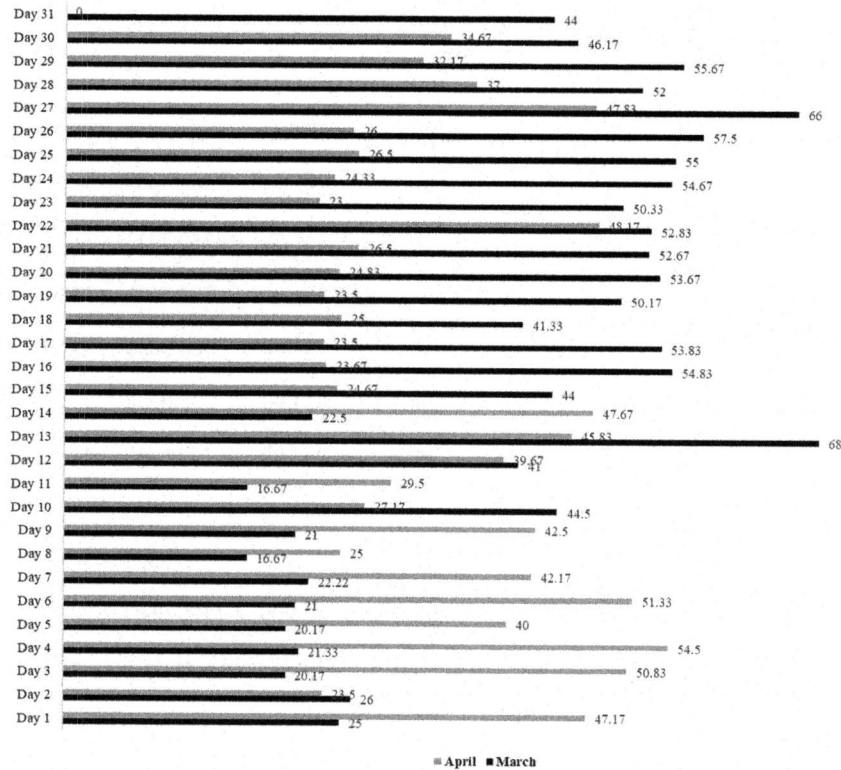

Figure 5.2 Mean score of total of topical issues or needs sought about the virus per day before media subsequent day publication in March and April 2020

with a lot of information which could cause lack of interest in the disease having understood the presence of the disease during the five weeks.

Since it is clear that the public sought knowledge about the virus in line with the data presented in Figures 5.1 and 5.2 and Table 5.1, we present the extent to which the media reported issues and needs around the virus (predominantly in 35 days out of the studied 64 days) in Table 5.2. Significant news reports were not published on the first day (February 27, 2020) and second day (February 28, 2020) of the index case. Analysis further reveals that significant publications were noticed between March 1 and March 12, 2020. Between March 13 and March 15, 2020, insignificant publications were discovered, which peaked on March 16. There was a dip in publication between March 17 and March 18, 2020; in the five days that followed, media publication on the virus was huge. There were no sizable reports about the virus on March 24, but publication rose on March 25 and was sustained till April 19, 2020. The observed silence on March 24, 2020, and other previous days was repeated on April 20 and April 21, 2020, until there was a change from

Table 5.1 Daily/weekly descriptive statistics of total of topical issues or needs sought about the virus before media subsequent day/week publication

Week/day	Timeline	N	Minimum	Maximum	Mean	Std. Deviation
3 Days	February 27–February 29, 2020	6	18.00	300.00	85.8333	109.38998
1	March 1–March 7, 2020	6	.00	661.00	205.0000	286.23906
2	March 8–March 14, 2020	6	**48.00**	**649.00**	**250.3333**	**217.13191**
3	March 15–March 21, 2020	6	.00	**918.00**	**350.5000**	**355.11787**
4	March 22–March 28, 2020	6	.00	949.00	388.3333	393.61385
5	March 29–April 4, 2020	6	.00	827.00	321.8333	341.09437
6	April 5–April 11, 2020	6	.00	**965.00**	**257.6667**	**417.23694**
7	April 12–April 18, 2020	6	.00	1031.00	230.0000	416.50018
8	April 19–April 25, 2020	6	.00	920.00	196.8333	366.48188
6 Days	April 26–April 30, 2020	6	.00	422.00	177.6667	207.30525

Source: © Lasisi and Oyedele 2021

Table 5.2 Extent of news reports about the virus by the media after information seeking the previous days

News report category	T	df	Sig (2-tailed)
February 28, 2020	.000	5	1.000
March 1, 2020	−17.000[b]	5	.000[a]
March 2, 2020	−8.000[b]	5	.000[a]
March 3, 2020	−11.180[b]	5	.000[a]
March 4, 2020	−7.319[b]	5	.001[a]
March 5, 2020	−17.000[b]	5	.000[a]
March 6, 2020	−17.000[b]	5	.000[a]
March 7, 2020	−17.000[b]	5	.000[a]
March 8, 2020	−5.000[b]	5	.004[a]
March 9, 2020	−2.928[b]	5	.033[a]
March 10, 2020	−8.000[b]	5	.000[a]
March 11, 2020	−12.649[b]	5	.000[a]
March 12, 2020	−17.000[b]	5	.000[a]
March 13, 2020	−1.567	5	.178
March 16, 2020	−17.000[b]	5	.000[a]
March 17, 2020	−.904	5	.408
March 18, 2020	−.259	5	.806
March 19, 2020	−7.000[b]	5	.001[a]

News report category	T	df	Sig (2-tailed)
March 20, 2020	**−8.000**[b]	5	.000[a]
March 22, 2020	**−3.993**[b]	5	.010[a]
March 23, 2020	**−17.000**[b]	5	.000[a]
March 24, 2020	−1.145	5	.304
March 25, 2020	**−8.000**[b]	5	.000[a]
March 26, 2020	**−5.000**[b]	5	.004[a]
March 27, 2020	**−8.000**[b]	5	.000[a]
March 28, 2020	**−4.719**[b]	5	.005[a]
March 29, 2020	**−17.000**[b]	5	.000[a]
March 30, 2020	**−8.000**[b]	5	.000[a]
April 9, 2020	**−12.649**[b]	5	.000[a]
April 10, 2020	**−8.000**[b]	5	.000[a]
April 12, 2020	**−11.180**[b]	5	.000[a]
April 13, 2020	**−5.000**[b]	5	.004[a]
April 14, 2020	**−3.313**[b]	5	.021[a]
April 15, 2020	**−7.319**[b]	5	.001[a]
April 16, 2020	**−3.162**[b]	5	.025[a]
April 17, 2020	**−7.319**[b]	5	.001[a]
April 18, 2020	**−12.649**[b]	5	.000[a]
April 19, 2020	**−8.000**[b]	5	.000[a]
April 20, 2020	.000	5	1.000
April 21, 2020	−.775	5	.474
April 22, 2020	**−5.398**[b]	5	.003[a]
April 23, 2020	.000	5	1.000
April 24, 2020	.373	5	.725
April 25, 2020	−.237	5	.822
April 26, 2020	−.553	5	.604
April 27, 2020	.493	5	.643
April 28, 2020	−.904	5	.408
April 29, 2020	**−12.649**[b]	5	.000[a]
April 30, 2020	−1.870	5	.120

Source: © Lasisi and Oyedele 2021

a News reportage during the day is significant at $P < 0.5$.
b Indicates greater magnitude of accepting alternative hypothesis.

April 22 to April 29, 2020. These results have indicated that media in Nigeria were not consistent in their quantitative coverage of the happenings about the virus.

Data in Table 5.3 further confirm our earlier position that the Nigerian newspapers did not report significantly about the disease during some days. According to the data, the size of the difference relative to the first three days (February 27 to February 29, 2020) was zero, which indicates that we can report that the media had insignificant publications during the days ($t = 0.000$, df = 5, $P > 1.000$). Examining the data further, it is clear that the level of publications in week 1 ($t = -1.035$, df = 5, $P > .348$) absolutely confirms our position than the publications we found in week 4 ($t = .484$, df = 5, $P > .649$), week 7 ($t = 0.498$, df = 5,

Table 5.3 Extent of news reports about the virus by the media after information seeking
the previous days/weeks

Day/week	Timeline	t	df	Sig. (2-tailed)
3 Days	February 27–February 29, 2020	**.000**	**5**	**1.000**
1	March 1–March 7, 2020	**−1.035**	**5**	**.348**
4	March 22–March 28, 2020	.484	5	.649
7	April 12–April 18, 2020	.498	5	.640
8	April 19–April 25, 2020	1.032	5	.349
5 Days	April 26–April 30, 2020	1.194	5	.286

Source: © Lasisi and Oyedele 2021

$P > .640$) and week 8 ($t = 1.032$, df $= 5$, $P > .349$) and last 5 days of April, 2020
($t = 1.194$, df $= 5$, $P > .286$). This is hinged on the fact that size of the difference
relative to the entire publications during the week was negative, indicating greater
magnitude of accepting the null hypothesis (the media did not publish significantly during the week).

Data in Table 5.4 are the outcomes of further exploration of the data presented
in Table 5.1. Out of the 44 models, 20 models (45.5% of the total) adequately
predicted media consideration of public information-seeking behavior in their
(media) news reportage on the following days. Our inference is that the variance of information seeking in the subsequent media reportage of what the public
sought as news in previous days differed significantly. The level of information
seeking about the virus on April 14, 28, 19, 24, 23, 26, 20, 15, 16, and 22 largely
determined media publication on April 15 (standardized coefficient $= 0.999$,
$R^2 = 0.999$), April 29 (standardized coefficient $= 0.993$, $R^2 = 0.985$), April 20
(standardized coefficient $= 0.990$, $R^2 = 0.980$), April 25 (standardized coefficient $= 0.990$, $R^2 = 0.980$), April 24 (standardized coefficient $= 0.988$, $R^2 = 0.976$),
April 27 (standardized coefficient $= 0.988$, $R^2 = 0.975$), April 21 (standardized
coefficient $= 0.981$, $R^2 = 0.961$), April 16 (standardized coefficient $= 0.966$,
$R^2 = 0.933$), and April 23 (standardized coefficient $= 0.864$, $R^2 = 0.747$). During
these days, one unit of interest in the virus through the internet by the public translated to over 80% and 90% of the media reportage of the topical issues or needs
searched (see standardized coefficient scores). Despite reported significant interest in the virus through internet searches and news publications in March, three
models in the month had a significant percentage of variation. The data showed
that information seeking on March 16, 10, and 18 largely determined media publications on March 17 (standardized coefficient $= 0.970$, $R^2 = 0.941$), March 11
(standardized coefficient $= 0.856$, $R^2 = 0.733$), and March 19 (standardized coefficient $= 0.775$, $R^2 = 0.601$).

Table 5.5 reveals aggregated variation that information seeking of the public
about the virus had in the news reported by the media the following days and
weeks. The data indicate substantial and significant variation in the news reportage in week 7 (standardized coefficient $= 0.963$, $R^2 = .926$, Sig. F change $P < .002$)

Table 5.4 Daily information seeking variation in news report about the virus

Model	Standardized coefficient (Beta)	R-square	Adjusted R-square	Std. error of the estimate	F change	Sig. F change
1	ISC and NRC, February 27 and February 28, 2020	-.533	.284	.105	2.608	1.588	.276
2	ISC and NRC, February 29 and March 1, 2020	-.215	.046	-.192	.446	.194	.683
3	ISC and NRC, March 1 and March 2, 2020	.744	.554^b	.443	.610	4.971	.090
4	ISC and NRC, March 2 and March 3, 2020	.205	.042	-.197	.599	.176	.697
5	ISC and NRC, March 3 and March 4, 2020	.977	.955	.943	.199	84.375	.001^a
6	ISC and NRC, March 4 and March 5, 2020	.081	.007	-.242	.455	.027	.878
7	ISC and NRC, March 5 and March 6, 2020	.489	.240	.050	.398	1.260	.324
8	ISC and NRC, March 6 and March 7, 2020	.701	.491	.364	.326	3.862	.121
9	ISC and NRC, March 7 and March 8, 2020	.632	.400	.250	1.061	2.667	.178
10	ISC and NRC, March 8 and March 9, 2020	.293	.086	-.143	1.789	.375	.573
11	ISC and NRC, March 9 and March 10, 2020	.701	.491	.364	.651	3.862	.121
12	ISC and NRC, March 10 and March 11, 2020	.856	.733	.666	.298	10.979	.030^a
13	ISC and NRC, March 16 and March 17, 2020	.970	.941	.927	.978	6.005	.000^a
14	ISC and NRC, March 18 and March 19, 2020	.775	.601^b	.501	3.336	.065	.811
16	ISC and NRC, March 22 and March 23, 2020	.492	.243	.053	.397	1.281	.321
17	ISC and NRC, March 23 and March 24, 2020	.355	.126	-.093	3.355	.576	.490
18	ISC and NRC, March 24 and March 25, 2020	.473	.223	.029	.804	1.151	.344
19	ISC and NRC, March 25 and March 26, 2020	.448	.201	.001	1.224	1.006	.373
20	ISC and NRC, March 26 and March 27, 2020	.290	.084	-.145	.874	.369	.577
21	ISC and NRC, March 27 and March 28, 2020	.211	.045	-.194	1.324	.186	.688
22	ISC and NRC, March 28 and March 29, 2020	.316	.100	-.126	.433	.442	.542
23	ISC and NRC, March 29 and March 30, 2020	.377	.114	-.108	.859	.513	.514
24	ISC and NRC, April 8 and April 9, 2020	.732	.536^b	.420	.393	4.617	.098
25	ISC and NRC, April 9 and April 10, 2020	.414	.171	-.036	.831	.826	.415
26	ISC and NRC, April 11 and April 12, 2020	.645	.416	.270	.468	2.848	.167
27	ISC and NRC, April 12 and April 13, 2020	.232	.054	-.183	1.332	.228	.658
28	ISC and NRC, April 13 and April 14, 2020	.577	.333	.166	1.463	1.993	.231

(Continued)

Table 5.4 (Continued)

Model	Standardized coefficient (Beta)	R-square	Adjusted R-square	Std. error of the estimate	F change	Sig. F change
29 ISC and NRC, April 14 and April 15, 2020	.999	.999	.998	.032	3313.500	.000[a]
30 ISC and NRC, April 15 and April 16, 2020	.966	.933	.916	.449	55.443	.002[a]
31 ISC and NRC, April 16 and April 17, 2020	.951	.905	.881	.289	37.896	.004[a]
32 ISC and NRC, April 17 and April 18, 2020	.739	.546[b]	.432	.389	4.809	.093
33 ISC and NRC, April 18 and April 19, 2020	.047	.002	-.247	.912	.009	.929
34 ISC and NRC, April 19 and April 20, 2020	.990	.980	.975	.889	195.796	.000[a]
35 ISC and NRC, April 20 and April 21, 2020	.981	.961	.952	.694	99.889	.001[a]
36 ISC and NRC, April 21 and April 22, 2020	.709	.503	.379	.775	4.050	.114
37 ISC and NRC, April 22 and April 23, 2020	.864	.747	.684	3.591	11.817	.026[a]
38 ISC and NRC, April 23 and April 24, 2020	.988	.976	.970	1.882	165.193	.000[a]
39 ISC and NRC, April 24 and April 25, 2020	.990	.980	.975	.815	197.179	.000[a]
40 ISC and NRC, April 25 and April 26, 2020	.248	.061	-.173	4.795	.262	.636
41 ISC and NRC, April 26 and April 27, 2020	.988	.975	.969	2.038	158.136	.000[a]
42 ISC and NRC, April 27 and April 28, 2020	.416	.173	-.034	3.676	.835	.412
43 ISC and NRC, April 28 and April 29, 2020	.993	.985	.982	.070	271.537	.000[a]
44 ISC and NRC, April 29 and April 30, 2020	.781	.610[b]	.513	1.676	6.260	.067

Source: © Lasisi and Oyedele 2021

* *ISC: Information Seeking Categories* (coronavirus Nigeria, coronavirus in Nigeria, coronavirus in Lagos, Kano coronavirus, coronavirus Symptoms, Is Coronavirus in Nigeria, Symptoms of coronavirus, coronavirus Update, coronavirus Cure).
* *News Report Categories* (coronavirus Nigeria, coronavirus in Nigeria, coronavirus in Lagos, Kano coronavirus, coronavirus Symptoms, Is coronavirus in Nigeria, Symptoms of coronavirus, coronavirus Update, coronavirus Cure).
a Indicates significant variation of information seeking in news reportage about the disease.
b Indicates above average variation but not significant in news reportage about the disease.

Table 5.5 Daily/weekly information-seeking variation in news reportage about the virus

Model	Standardized coefficient (beta)	R-square	Adjusted R-square	Std. error of the estimate	F change	Sig. F change
1 Week 3 information seeking and week 4 news reportage	.751	.563	.454	4.98105	5.163	.086
2 Week 6 information seeking and week 7 news reportage	**.963**	**.926**	**.908**	**1.74079**	**50.394**	**.002**[a]
3 Week 7 information seeking and week 8 news reportage	**.984**	**.968**	**.960**	6.33020	120.910	**.000**[a]
4 Week 8 information seeking and week 9 news reportage	.068	.005	−.244	17.16152	.018	.899

Source: © Lasisi and Oyedele 2021

Key: *Week 3 (March 15–March 21, 2020), Week 4 (March 22–March 28, 2020), Week 6 (April 5–April 11, 2020), Week 7 (April 12–April 18, 2020), Week 8 (April 19–April 25), Week 9 (5 days) (April 26–April 30, 2020).*

a Indicates significant variation of information seeking in news reportage about the disease.

and week 8 (standardized coefficient = .984, R^2 = .968, Sig. F change $P < .000$). For week 7, standardized coefficient of .963 signifies that one unit of public interest in the disease translated into 96.8% increase in news reportage during the week, while 92.6% of the interest in the virus could be explained from the media reportage during the week. The translation was also applicable to week 8, but it is 98.4% increase, an increase of more than 2%. Over 96% of the public information seeking in week 7 could be determined from the media reportage of the virus in week 8. This implies that the newspapers were only aligned with the public curiosity about the disease in two weeks out of five weeks of intensive information seeking about the disease (see Table 5.1).

Discussion of findings

The study has shown that mass media outfits in Nigeria did not consider as significant and useful, the quantum of leadings from what their potential audiences (online news consumers) search online about coronavirus to guide their reportage daily and weekly. Since there is a possibility of using online information-seeking behaviors of their audiences to set agenda for the society and serve the interests of their audiences, we hypothesize a situation where information seeking behavior predicts media coverage the following day. That this hypothetical prediction was true in few cases feeds into a possible conclusion that most of the questions or needs that pushed the audiences to search for information about coronavirus might have been fulfilled, answered, or met by other means and not through the media. As obtained in the studies by Petersen et al. (2017), Falade (2019), Collinson, Khan, and Heffeman (2015), Sell et al. (2018), and Majid and Rahmat (2013), the mass media in Nigeria provided information on corona virus to raise awareness, build knowledge, and encourage people to be pro-health and be conscious, they did not significantly maximize the opportunities provided by online search engines in knowing the needs of their audiences and planning to satisfy them. This is a gap in crisis and risk reportage that could affect the capacity of the media to effectively perform their responsibility of satisfying the needs of their consumers and lead them into taking recommended actions. The field or beat for news gathering has been shaped by the digital revolution; the digital environment affords media agencies that quick opportunity to know what online media audiences are discussing and interested in, leading to a win-win situation when both parties (mass media and news consumers) have their goals met.

This also limits the capacity of the nation to provide real-time and even delayed information for its ever-increasing online information users. There are millions of Nigerians in the digital space daily, netizens whose lives cannot be separated from their digital experiences. The nation may be leaving the information needs of this section of the society unmet and considering that they are millions of people, it is important that media reportage of critical issues feed into the gratifications and information needs of these people. This improves the capacity of the media and the nation in general to effectively perform during a disease outbreak, as they provide information, manage perception, and response to sudden disease outbreak.

Managerial and policy recommendations

Based on the foregoing, the study recommends that media industries in the nation should revitalize their capacity to appropriate the digital environment for news gathering, processing, and distribution. They need to devise means and train their reporters to acquire digital tools needed for turning the digital space into a news theater, field for gathering news, and satisfying the needs of netizens. The nation also needs to focus on what goes on in the digital space during a pandemic disease as this provides them needed arsenal to understand the dynamics of information generation, processing, and consumption, and also the bulk of discourses on the nation's performance and assessment during a crisis.

References

Champion, V. L., and C. S. Skinner. 2008. "The Health Belief Model." In *Health Behavior and Health Education: Theory, Research, and Practice*, edited by K. Glanz, B. K. Rimer, and K. Viswanath, 45–65. San Francisco, CA: Jossey-Bass.
Collinson, Shannon, Khan Khan, and Jane M. Heffeman. 2015. "The Effects of Media Reports of Disease Spread and Important Public Health Measurements." *PLoS One* 10, no. 11: 1–21. DOI journal.pone.0141423pp.:10.1371/.
Falade, Bankole. 2019. "Leveraging Media Informatics for the Surveillance and Understanding of Disease Outbreaks." *South African Journal of Science* 115, no. 3/4: 75–83. DOI:10.17159/sajs.2019/5290.

Kim, Louis, M. Fast Shannon, and Natasha Markuzon. 2019. "Incorporating Media Data into a Model of Infectious Disease Transmission." *PLoS One*,14, no. 2. DOI: 10.1371/journal.pone.0197646.

Majid, Shaheen, and Nor Ain Rahmat. 2013. "Information Needs and Seeking Behavior During the H1N1 Virus Outbreak." *Journal of Information Science Theory and Practice* 1, no. 1: 42–53. http://dx.doi.org/10.1633/JISTaP.2013.1.1.3.

McCombs, Maxwell, C., and Donald L. Shaw. 1972. "The Agenda-Setting Setting Function of Mass Media." *The Public Opinion Quarterly* 36, no. 2: 176–87.

Pavelka, Jiri. 2014. "The Factors Affecting the Presentation of Events and the Media Coverage of Topics in the Mass Media." *Social and Behavioral Sciences* 140: 623–629. DOI: 10.1016/j.sbspro.2014.04.482.

Petersen, Jakob, Hilary Simons, Dipti Patel, and Joanne Freedman. 2017. "Early Detection of Perceived Risk Among Users of a UK Travel Health Website Compared with Internet Search Activity and Media Coverage During the 2015–2016 Zika Virus Outbreak: An Observational Study." *BMJ Open; London* 7, no. 8. DOI: 10.1136/bmjopen-2017-015831.

Randle, Janet, Mark Nelder, Doug Sider, and Karin Hohenadel. 2018. "Characterizing the Health and Information-Seeking Behaviours of Ontarians in Response to the Zika Virus Outbreak." *Canadian Journal of Public Health; Ottawa* 109, no. 1: 99–107. DOI: 10.17269/s41997-018-0026-9.

Schiavo, R. 2007 *Health Communication: From Theory to Practice*. San Francisco, CA: Jossey-Bass.

Sell, Tara, K., Crystal Watson, Diane Meyer, Marissa Kronk, and Ravi Sanjana. 2018. "Frequency of Risk-Related News Media Messages in 2016 Coverage of Zika Virus." *Risk Analysis; Oxford* 38, no. 12: 2514–24. DOI: 10.1111/risa.12961.

Part II

Responses to regulation

Media as instruments of social control
or conflict/resistance

6 Imagining pandemic as a failure

Writing, memory, and forgetting under COVID-19 in China

Yawen Li and Marius Meinhof

Introduction

On March 10, the Chinese state-owned periodical Ren Wu, or *People* magazine, featuring lives of influential people in China, released an article featuring an interview with the Chinese doctor, Ai Fen, who was the first to warn others about the coronavirus, yet was immediately disciplined and silenced by the hospital. The article was deleted within hours of being released, only to be restored by netizens with seemingly unstoppable vigor, in at least 33 different languages and fonts, including emojis, braille, ancient inscriptions, morse code, and Mao's calligraphy, in order to circumvent censorship algorithms. It seems that, against a strong push of censorship and propaganda to erase accounts of chaos and suffering during the pandemic, netizens insisted on the memories of failure being voiced.

This chapter discusses the imagination of national failure by certain sections of the netizenry, especially with regard to state strategies of information control, as generating agency for the individual Chinese citizen while also establishing significant possibilities for both critical reflection and atavistic forms of patriotism. It will draw from online sources, mainly a telegram channel "2019 COVID-19 News Cyberpunk Graveyard,"[1] and focus on two case examples of international fame: debates about Doctor Li Wenliang and on Fang Fang's Diary. It will be argued that the narrative of national failure and that of national victory are equally based on an internationalized yet regulated structure of new media and the logic of such new media discourse. The advancement of new media and online platforms in present-day China is remarkably conducive to exposing sociopolitical realities that do not fit into official narratives, while disseminating reflexive commentary. Yet it also makes it equally convenient for these "truths" to be enrolled into an online propaganda discourse and allows the rise of cyber-nationalism.

Memories of national failure may imply a strive for improvement. Jing Tsu (2005) proposes that, in China, the experience of failures in invasive wars and semi-colonialism generated a mode of restless self-reproach and reflection among Chinese and thus gave birth to an intellectual nationalism based on self-critique that is ultimately productive to the project of nation-building. Meinhof (2018) suggests that an urge to prove Chinese modernity and a fear of lagging behind haunt Chinese nationalist discourse as a historical stigma from the colonial era, and trap Chinese youths in a dual power structure between critique of an imagined Chinese backwardness and a defense of China against perceived insults. In the course of this, however, doubt and discontent about China's success in creating a distinct modernity can become a source of strength: to mobilize agency for further improvement and to keep a state of constant critical self-reflection. However, the situation of COVID-19 in China with its increasingly stringent censorship also authorizes and empowers triumphalist news coverage and cyber-nationalists to suppress those voices in the name of patriotism and in defense against a perceived unfair critique from abroad.

Such a momentum of critique and defense can be seen very clearly in the unfolding of debates over COVID-19. In the initial stage of the pandemic, many construed the COVID-19 outbreak as a national "failure," attributable to officials' self-silencing at the Central Hospital of Wuhan. Yet, within two-month time, the memories of failure had been appropriated and transformed by some propaganda discourses into stories of a victory achieved through heroic sacrifices in a battle against a natural disaster. Cybernationalists, motivated by China's relatively successful containment compared to "the West," and the feeling of being threatened by accusations from the United States, joined to rewrite the memories of the early stages of the pandemic as accounts of triumphalism. On April 15, editor Qin Wu et al. (2020) from *The Paper* lamented that it seems all our past suffering was reduced to a footnote for structural superiority.

Netizens facing a growing erasure of their stories of failure and grief in China sometimes tried to use international infrastructures to preserve these stories outside of the control of the Chinese government. Plenty of archives were established on foreign platforms by netizens with VPN. A public Telegram group-chat—numbering 16,000 members—was created to migrate everything that has been said online about COVID-19 and deleted in China to servers abroad. Also, some Chinese netizens resorted to English language mass media to tell the stories prohibited to be told in Chinese.

This use of international infrastructures, however, happened in a global context where China-Watchers carefully observed Chinese online debates and often appropriated them into their own narrative: a neo-orientalist (Vukovich 2012) narrative of a struggle of liberalism, narrated as an imaginary alliance of "the West," Chinese dissident voices and the China-Watchers themselves, against a malign, authoritarian Other represented by "the Chinese communist party." However, the China-Watchers, too, appropriated Chinese popular memories to rewrite the story of the early pandemic in China as a neo-orientalist discourse.

The act of remembering

On February 20, Chinese writer Yan Lianke (2020) gave an e-lecture that foregrounds the importance of remembering and learning from history, while also alerting everyone to the collectivizing of cultural memories and the disappearance of individual accounts. Yan underscores the moral and pedagogical aspects of memory in times of COVID-19, and insists on the "incorporating" of mnemonic practice[2] in an era of digital media and localized censorship, which could also inform the resisting act of overseas archiving: "COVID-19—a national and global catastrophe—has not truly been contained; families are still torn apart and heart-wrenching cries ring out throughout Hubei, Wuhan, and elsewhere. Yet, songs of victory are already echoing all around. All because statistics are looking up" (Yan 2020).

In China like elsewhere, the confinement in lockdown made it almost impossible to bear witness to the real human suffering, and therefore drastically reshaped memory-forming processes regarding this event. Thus, the victims are represented as figures, names, photos, voices, interviewees, which distances their experiences from those who view them from afar. However, for Yan, there are failures that could not be told from the statistics and to remember them is a crucial act in acknowledging the particularities of individual suffering. Yan calls upon the audience to "have graves in their hearts, with memories etched in them" because he knows how sympathy can be translated to amnesia. This echoes with what Susan Sontag (2004, 102) asserts, "So far as we feel sympathy, we feel we are not accomplices to what caused the suffering. Our sympathy proclaims our innocence as well as our impotence." Transposed to the current situation in China, the insight has force for those who hastily consolidate a triumphalist nationalist narrative as well as for those who become too dependent on virtual memories and never reflect on the discourses: an impasse in memory, which precisely affirms the numbing effect of archives and their inadequacies in communicating trauma (Caruth and Hartman 1996, 646).

Nevertheless, the subjection to this particular collective amnesia that Yan is referring to cannot be simply ascribed to a universally physical plight, but also the media to which Chinese are exposed. Instead of suffering from the "hypertrophy of memory" (Huyssen 2003, 3–4), most Chinese are experiencing an "atrophy of memory" due to the tightening censorship and homogenized official narratives laced with triumphalist nationalism.

Li Wenliang and collective amnesia

At the end of December 2019, the ophthalmologist Li Wenliang warned some friends in a Chat Group about a strange, SARS-like pneumonia. After his post was shared with a broader audience on the internet, he was reprimanded for rumor-mongering, mainly for drawing parallels to SARS. When the extent of the COVID-19 pandemic became publicly known in China, he quickly became a symbol for the suppression of news and warnings by state institutions. Especially the young generations flew into a fury against the enforcers of the silencing act, and the rage peaked on February 7, 2020, when Li himself died of COVID-19.

Many online articles published after his death fixated on his "I think there should be more than one voice in a healthy society," declaring him a symbol of the suppression of freedom of speech. However, Li was no radical advocate of free speech in ordinary life and the interviews retrospectively affirm this as he did not express any form of displeasure against the reprimand (Qin et al. 2020). Neither was he a whistleblower. His death did sound the public alarm at COVID-19 yet his initial intention was to alert only his college classmates. It is precisely the fact that Li was a law-abiding, non-iconic citizen that compels almost every Chinese to identify themselves with him.

The initial cyber outrage was triggered by netizens' internalizing doctor Li's position and introjecting his truth-telling spirit to seek apologies and accountability from officials. A great majority of people posted pictures of official media news broadcasting on January 1 subtitled "An Unidentified Pneumonia Discovered in Wuhan. Eight Rumormongers were Investigated and Disciplined" and hashtagged "Wuhan Government Owes Doctor Li an Apology" on Weibo. Many others repeated phrases from the letter of reprimand that police made Li sign such as "Do you understand?" "I understand" to underscore the immense irony by performatively reenacting a simulacrum of the reprimand. Some made appeals for protecting citizens' right to question and supervise the authorities. The indignation was conjoined with confusion, when the twitter account of the People's Daily, China (@PDChina) announced the death of doctor Li, whereas Chinese people were told to wait while Li was being treated using ECMO. Many netizens suspected it as a staged rescue and a typical method to manipulate public opinions.

One day after Li's death, central authorities dispatched an investigation team to Wuhan. Many netizens had demanded and welcomed such an investigation. Unlike the national failures foregrounded in Jing Tsu's book that would lead to reforms and revolutions, most people in this situation were looking for accountability and the vindication of doctor Li's name. They continue to leave comments on Li's Weibo account (920,000+ pieces by April 27) after his death while anticipating the investigation result.

The anger at Li Wenliang's death and the subsequent calls for accountability, however, were either censored or implemented into a propaganda narrative, which reimagined Li as a national hero, part of a larger group of outstanding figures in the people's war against the coronavirus. The phrase "I understand" was banned and topics relevant to doctor Li dismissed. Despite netizens' growing caution with words, even allegorical phrases such as "each snowflake in an avalanche pleads not guilty" were removed. The asymmetric battle with censorship forced them to either assiduously record everything on foreign platforms or to self-censor.

At the same time, propaganda picked up and rewrote memories of Li Wenliang. The official investigation team found that the letter of reprimand, which had become a symbol of anger for Chinese netizens, was an "improper action" led to by the local police. Subsequently, the reprimand was revoked for Li postmortem. Li was conferred the title of a national martyr who sacrificed himself for the good of China, and enrolled into a narrative of national struggle against the coronavirus, led by the communist party and culminating in a victory.

In addition, stories focusing on Li's death caused by the natural disaster of a severe illness produced a mourning narrative that privileges privatized grief and melancholia, contributing to a normalization of grief within the nationalist narrative, and subsequently a collective amnesia of the initial narrative of national failure. Expression of a normalized grief devoid of its political edge became the only recognized form of mourning, gradually blunting the grievances against the authorities. This normalized grieving includes everyday greetings with weather updates; light-hearted thank-you notes; sharing daily grinds, incidents, secrets, personal troubles, good news, and seeking comfort; posting food pictures as doctor Li was a food enthusiast.

Domestic propagandists, however, were not the only ones appropriating the narrative on Li Wenliang: Foreign China-Watchers, especially in anglophone countries, closely observed the online outrage of Chinese netizens. Their narratives often followed a logic antagonistic to Chinese propaganda yet strikingly similar in their tendency to enroll Chinese public memories into a preestablished narrative of a grand battle of free speech versus the authoritarian regime. Newspapers romanticized Li as a promoter of free speech (*The Economist* 2020); later, right-winged politicians treated him as a symbol to blame China for lying (Rubio 2020). These stories portrayed Li and his admirers as part of a silent majority desiring Western democracy. They, too, invented Li as someone who suffered a heroic sacrifice: not for the nation but one for liberty and freedom of speech—a dissident, whose name would stand for resistance to the political system. Long before the Chinese government, some foreign media already considered Li a martyr, and asked if he would become the tank man—the protester who stopped moving tanks in front of the Tiananmen square—of the era of COVID-19 (Palmer 2020). His party membership and his general affirmative position toward the political system were often erased; netizens' demand for transparency and accountability were reshaped to a stereotype of the Chinese longing for Western democracy.

Thus, popular memories of Li had to navigate between antagonistic discourses, which both constructed Li as a hyperreal symbol enrolled into a greater narrative: either a narrative of the people's war against the coronavirus or of the liberal struggle against authoritarianism—narratives that ignore the complexity and ambivalence of the popular memories connected to him. As a result of these multilayered and asymmetric negotiations, there is left not one, but a multiplicity of memories of Li Wenliang, all of which can rightfully claim to be Chinese popular memories: Li as a victim of a disease, Li as a whistleblower, Li as a national hero, and so on.

All of these prepared the ground for a collective amnesia where the original narrative of failure and the connected demands for accountability were lost between competing narratives of systemic superiority or inferiority. The official acknowledgment of Li, together with an improving domestic situation and a steady increase in reports about failure to contain the pandemic abroad, quenched many people's rage at the authorities. Through the discourse of legitimate, normalized grief, the initial demands for accountability and anti-censorship were being gradually "reshaped" to melancholic identification and prolonged attachment, manifesting themselves in the netizens sustaining thoughts and fantasies about Li.

This transmutation is not necessarily a sign of the State's control over discourse, but could also connote netizens' way of coping with the realization that radical changes might not come into being. Before the investigation result came out on March 19, many netizens were still hopeful at some level. The day when the result was released a second smaller wave of digital resistance could be observed.

"Censors must have had a long day," said one of them. However, the subsequent erasure of politically charged posts and photos of worldwide mourning rituals for doctor Li marked the unlikelihood of structural changes. The remaining number of netizens voicing their thoughts and emotions tried to avoid sensitive words and critical details, and thus produced texts that turned out to be fairly vague, inducing little resonance.

Fang and the politics of individual memory writing

Chinese writer Fang has been recounting her experience of the lockdown in Wuhan since January 25 in daily articles published on Wechat. Her diary used to win millions of followers for its adherence to truth, thoughtful reflections, and deep care about people in Wuhan. From early on, she was the target of critique, but the critique could not gain momentum.

However, when Fang decided to publish her articles as a book in America titled *Wuhan Diary: Dispatches from a Quarantined City*, she was hit by a huge wave of aggressive responses, including insults and death threats. The rise of these aggressive critiques needs to be understood in the global context of the struggles between China and the United States. In the context of Trump's attempts to shift blame on China, her decision to publish abroad made her suspect and provoked her critics to label her as a traitor. Certainly, this belief that the overseas publication of Fang's individual account could be used by "Western" forces to harm the country's reputation and substantiate their claims for compensation confused her literary work with testimonies of an eye-witness. It was, however, not entirely baseless: like in the case of Li Wenliang, Fang and her critics were observed closely from abroad. In foreign media, her Diary was reinvented as the "true" yet hidden voice of China and the symbol of the battle against the oppressive regime (Y. Wu 2020).

This aroused the suspicions of many people. That her Diary went on presale in April was for many Chinese netizens suspiciously close to the time when the Trump administration needed to draw attention to China's wrongdoings in order to distract from its own mistakes. They started accusing Fang of exploiting Chinese misery for money or fame, and "giving ammunition" to the United States in their attempt to lay blame for the pandemic on China (Cao and Chen 2020).

This backlash against Fang was silently supported by institutional structures. Netizens who defended Fang often had their commentaries removed, and therefore turned to mimicry and ironic rhetoric to ridicule the logics of Fang's attackers. One blogger wrote a letter to one of the most acclaimed Chinese writers, Lu Xun, "criticizing" his speedy publication of *A Mad Man's Diary* in Japan, his "exploiting" Chinese people's "backwardness" as profit-making sources.[3] By using the arguments made against Fang on a writer highly regarded in China, the blogger made the fallacies currently imposed upon Fang obvious to the readers and suggested that time will test Fang's writing.

If nationalists label Fang's deviation from the narrative of national victory as a betrayal, they seem to have already forgotten doctor Li's appeal for multiple voices and unable to accept a public dialogue negotiated among heterogeneous memories on the lockdown. The fact that many cybernationalists declared that "domestic shame should not be made public" indicates a reassertion of the Chinese patriarchal tradition, which affirms the patriarchal power through its ability to manage problems within the household. This fear of being unfairly criticized, and the restlessness to prove how China has progressed in the course of modernization, resembles what Meinhof (2018) has described for debates on Chinese modernity. Now, however, this is not transformed into a collective passion to confront and deflect unfair allegations from abroad, but turns against fellow Chinese and silences self-critique. Ironically, this reproduces a silencing of divergent voices not entirely dissimilar to the silencing of Li Wenliang—however, not through official censorship and reprimanding, but through a grassroots nationalist discourse boosted by China seeming to have successfully contained the coronavirus.

What is striking here is the Chinese cybernationalists and foreign media experts' apparent inability or unwillingness to understand each other's logic. On the one hand, cybernationalists seem strangely oblivious to the fact that the intense, aggressive critique of Fang, especially labeling her as a traitor, makes her accounts in the eyes of the Western audience even more attractive and credible, and more likely to be perceived as a revelation of hidden events. They did not understand or ignore the fact that violent, sexist, dehumanizing critique of Fang would make it easier for foreigners to label China as an evil or aggressive power. On the other hand, few foreign media attempted to understand why Fang's decision to publish abroad could be suspicious to many Chinese. Critical comments directed at her were often reduced to the insulting and aggressive forms, making it seem to Western audiences as if only irrational nationalists or propaganda writers could find her decision to publish abroad objectionable.

Conclusion

If the initial handling of COVID-19 was imperfect in China, so was it in many countries that now reinvent Li Wenliang and Fang as fighters of liberal democracy. Cybernationalists' defense of a narrative of Chinese national victory is related to real concerns about China being unfairly depicted abroad. However, by attacking memories of failure and loss, Chinese cybernationalists show a superficial self-confidence, attained through the erasure of self-critique. They force a story of pride and sacrifice that leaves no space to articulate grief. Hailing the relative success of the lockdown in Wuhan as a manifestation of structural superiority and rejecting any criticism of the delay and application of the lockdown measures do not do justice to the freedom and convenience people had to give up. Justifying all losses with a sacrificial logic permits a closure to those who grieve over injustices and losses. Moreover, rejecting any hint of officials' mistakes out of fear to give "ammunition" to the United States is unlikely to stop Trump from blaming China. The attempts to erase memories of failure and calls for accountability in China create an image of China being in a state of siege, cornered by foreign critique so much so that Chinese do not dare to reflect on their own mistakes. This makes Chinese discourse seemingly controlled by (the fear of) foreign media opinions.

Chinese propagandists, cybernationalists, and Western China-Watchers alike claim to represent or listen to the "true" voice of China, yet all share an attempt to transform popular memories to make them fit better into a contrasting grand narrative—a narrative of national victory on the one hand or a narrative of Chinese desire for Western liberalism on the other. They both claim to stand on the side of Chinese people, yet each constructs a twisted discourse of blame shifting in which the loss cannot be addressed. Hence, with public memory suffering from amnesia, grief must be worked through individually.

For China, this amnesia may prove more harmful than the narrative of national failure would have been. The outrage on the internet was never directly threatening the system, but rather focused on specific events and demanded specific accountability. It called for changes but was not necessarily a call for liberalism and democracy. Given China's successful containment compared to Europe and the United States, it is likely that the negotiating of collective memories in public discourses would not have ended up in a push against the party-state, but in a narrative of failure, recovery, and learning from the past. However, censorship and aggressive attempts to defend China from foreign blaming have created a logic of amnesia, where memories of loss cannot come to a closure. Some Chinese netizens even experienced identity crises because the censorship regime has suppressed their capacity to articulate in their mother tongue.

The risk lurking in this moment of amnesia is the compulsion of nationalists to invent a victory: those who supported the lockdown hasten to prove that they have been right, which paradoxically reveals that they themselves are not so convinced. To disguise such insecurity, they begin to imagine their opponents according to their willingness to sing along with the victory songs. This predisposition is becoming increasingly absurd as can be seen in a popular Weibo blogger, who is leading his followers to believe that doctor Li died of being exhausted by journalists' frequent interviews.

To permit voices that would imagine the pandemic as a failure is important not only to resist a collective amnesia, but also useful in stifling the egregious Chinese triumphalist and nationalists. Such imagination intends for survivors and witnesses to remain alarmed, reflexive, and critical, to resist the collectivizing of memories, to refuse to come to terms with past traumas, so as to refrain from repeating them. As Adorno said, "the past will have been worked through only when the causes of what happened then have been eliminated" (1998, 103). This should be understood as an appeal to confront the causes that entail negative sides of the story, instead of taking excuses such as the current international tension for silencing or of forgoing the discussion altogether.

Maybe we need to remember that the countries most successful in fighting the pandemic were those that were alert because they remembered the failures of fighting SARS—and those who arrogantly believed to own a superior system or be superior modern were those who failed hardest (Meinhof 2020). But learning from mistakes now seems almost impossible when efforts are wasted in an obsession to prove the exact origin of COVID-19 and to battle over a macabre ranking of national death rates.

Notes

1 This is a Channel hosted outside of China, established by Chinese using VPN in order to preserve debates endangered to be censored from Chinese internet. We will refer to posts from the Chinese internet mostly censored already but are documented as screenshots in this channel. Since it is not possible to reference them in a conventional way, we have not attached references to statements on Chinese debates, but they can all be found at this Channel, which makes a secondary analysis of our arguments possible. Accessible via: https://t.me/wuhancensored.
2 Paul Connerton (1989, 72–104) terms "incorporating practice" as a fundamentally different way in which memory is sedimented in the body—"the transmission occurring only during the time that their bodies are present to sustain that particular activity"—from the "inscribing practice."
3 The original post by Ouyang Qian was removed. Accessible via: https://project-guten berg.github.io/Pincong/post/ed1521eafc66665bfcafdbd54fc5ffca/.

Works cited

Adorno, Theodor W. 1998. "The Meaning of Working Through the Past." In *Critical Models: Interventions and Catchwords*, edited by Theodor W. Adorno, translated by Henry W. Pickford, 103. New York: Columbia University Press.
Cao, Siqi, and Chen Qingqing. 2020. "Fans Disappointed as Wuhan Diary's Overseas Publication 'Gives Ammunition to Antagonist Forces'." *The Global Times,* April. 10. Accessed May 16, 2020. www.globaltimes.cn/content/1185246.shtml.
Caruth, Cathy, and Geoffrey Hartman. 1996. "An Interview with Geoffrey Hartman." *Studies in Romanticism* 35, no. 4: 630–52.
Connerton, Paul. 1989. *How Societies Remember*. Cambridge: Cambridge University Press.
The Economist. 2020. "Li Wenliang's Death Exposes the Costs of China's Authoritarianism." February 15, 2020. Accessed March 28, 2020. www.economist.com/china/2020/02/13/li-wenliangs-death-exposes-the-costs-of-chinas-authoritarianism.
Huyssen, Andreas. 2003. *Present Pasts: Urban Palimpsests and the Politics of Memory*. Stanford: Stanford University Press.
Meinhof, Marius. 2018. "Contesting Chinese Modernity? Postcoloniality and Discourses on Modernisation at a Chinese University Campus." *Postcolonial Studies* 21, no. 4: 469–84.
———. 2020. "Othering the Virus." *Discover Society*, March 21, 2020. Accessed March 28, 2020. https://discoversociety.org/2020/03/21/othering-the-virus/.
Palmer, James. 2020. "Wuhan Gets Its First Virus Martyr." *Foreign Policy*, February 6, 2020. Accessed May 16, 2020. https://foreignpolicy.com/2020/02/06/li-wenliang-corona virus-lies-wuhan-gets-its-first-virus-martyr/.
Qin et al. 2020. "Whistleblower Doctor Who Died Fighting Coronavirus Only Wanted People to 'Know the Truth'." *Caixin*, February 7, 2020. Accessed March 28, 2020. www.caixinglobal.com/2020-02-07/whistleblower-doctor-who-died-fighting-corona virus-only-wanted-people-to-know-the-truth-101512578.html.
Rubio, Marco. 2020. "Sen. Rubio: Chinese Official Spreads Virus Propaganda." *The Wall Street Journal*, May 14, 2020. Accessed May 16, 2020. www.wsj.com/articles/

sen-rubio-chinese-official-spreads-virus-propaganda-11589490481?redirect=amp#click
=https://t.co/sOwrNYr1AY.

Sontag, Susan. 2004. *Regarding the Pain of Others*. New York: Picador.

Tsu, Jing. 2005. *Failure, Nationalism, and Literature: The Making of Modern Chinese Identity, 1895–1937*. Stanford: Stanford University Press.

Vukovich, Daniel F. 2012. *China and Orientalism. Western knowledge Production and the P.R.C.* Milton Park and Abingdon, UK: Routledge.

Wu, Qin et al. 2020. "New World and Old Problems: The Unsettled Pandemic and Thoughts." *StochasticVolatility*, Episode 003, April 15. Accessed March 28, 2020. https://mp.weixin.qq.com/s/9Dd_I51IzBumd08-dtttDw.

Wu, Yuwen. 2020. "Chinese Propagandists Don't Want You to Read This Diary on the Coronavirus Lockdown in Wuhan." *The Independent*, March 2, 2020. Accessed May 16, 2020. www.independent.co.uk/voices/coronavirus-wuhan-lockdown-fangfang-diary-china-dr-li-a9368961.html.

Yan, Lianke. 2020. "When the Epidemic Ends, Let Our Memories Live." *ThinkChina*, March 9, 2020. Accessed April 15, 2020. www.thinkchina.sg/chinese-novelist-yan-lianke-when-epidemic-ends-let-our-memories-live?from=singlemessage&isappinstalled=0.

7 Arrest of the public interest or fight for public health in Serbia

Contrasting roles of professional and citizen journalists

Kristina Ćendić

Introduction

Journalists speak about matters of public interest and therefore play an important role in a democratic society. But new technologies changed the very definition of journalism by providing a variety of means of communication. The internet "lowered barriers of entry in the media" and "enabled citizens to become active participants in the communication process," so they have become not just receivers but coproducers of information, too (Kheny 2019, 1). Therefore, today we use terms such as "media actors," "citizen journalists," or "participatory journalists" in order to be able to cover actors providing information in a text, video, podcast, etc. (Thurman and Hermida 2010). Therefore, today we speak about "an increasingly diverse range of contributions to public debate, comprising a professional and largely institutionalized core, but also stretching to cover alternative forms of journalism located at and even beyond the periphery of traditional understandings of the term" (McGonagle 2013, 5). However, it seems that professional journalists are not so much at ease with citizens taking up these roles stating that "citizen posting news content has proved less valuable, with too little that is new or verifiable," (Noor 2017, 58). Moreover, citizen journalists have on some occasions been labeled as those "attacking the very idea that there is any sort of journalistic expertise at all" (Anderson 2008, 248)" because they are "amateurs pursuing the task without compensation (and) training" (Noor 2017, 58).

But despite different perspectives of citizen journalism, the safety of both professionals and citizen journalists is a matter of public concern and "essential for the wellbeing of media institutions, civil society, academia and the private sector" (Henrichsen, Betz, and Lisosky 2015). However, in the past few years, physical and verbal violence against journalists has been on the rise in member countries of the Council of Europe and threats against journalists, but these threats often remain uninvestigated (Noorlander 2020, 2). Such environment easily leads to a chilling effect, when journalists refrain from reporting on sensitive topics such as politics, organized crime, and corruption, in fear of possible consequences of their stories.

According to Reporters without Borders (RWB 2020), Serbia is unsafe for journalists and media landscape overall has deteriorated over the past few years. Since 2014, Serbia dropped for 40 places in RWB ranking: from 54th in 2014 to 93rd as of April 2020, which is a stunning decrease and illustrates the atmosphere in which media actors in Serbia operate. Bjelotomić (2020) stated that recently "the number of attacks on media has risen sharply, while officials increasingly use inflammatory rhetoric against journalists," whereas "most other investigations into attacks on media personnel have stalled or shelved." According to Freedom House (2020), "the Serbian authorities have created an environment in which attacks on journalists are allowed and critical reporting is shunned while media loyal to the president and government are rewarded." Moreover, it seems that all of these problems have intensified during the pandemic of COVID-19 (RWB 2020). The reason for this is that, much like everyone else, media actors shifted their activities online more than ever, which made them more prone to digital threats and attacks. However, it appears that citizen-journalists found themselves under attacks, too, when they exercised their right to freedom of expression, participated in a public debate, or spoke about issues of public interest. Not only were some citizens in Serbia arrested, but the support from other media actors may have been non-existent, too. This chapter will therefore ask: if Serbian citizen journalists wrote about matters of public interest, was there support from media actors who should be working for the same cause or was this support missing? Moreover, has the reporting about the arrests of citizen journalists in Serbia proven the polarization of media of which we so often speak—the pro-government ones and the independent ones?

In order to answer these questions, the paper analyzed media reporting on citizen's arrests for alleged "causing panic and disorder" during the state of emergency due to COVID-19 outbreak in Serbia. The analysis covered the period between March 16 and May 6 and in the preliminary analysis identified nine known cases of arrests of citizens for causing panic. Out of those cases, the chapter will focus on two most prominent ones which found themselves in the media most often, thus covering 74 articles in total.

Restrictions of freedom of expression

Media actors "inform the public about matters of societal interest, comment on them and hold public authorities and other powerful forces up to scrutiny"(McGonagle 2013). But, according to Miller-Carpenter (2019, 4), it often happens that it is the citizens who learn of certain events first, and "some active citizen journalists take pride in deviating from traditional reporting styles," believing "that they contribute to society by documenting important historical moments and people and by inspiring dialogue and action around issues often ignored by traditional newsmedia organizations." Citizen journalists can therefore also act as "public watchdogs" in a democratic society, and their protection matters, too, because punishing them often means having a criminal record, unfair convictions, and arbitrarily imposed restrictions, just like it happens with professional journalists (Ismayilova

v. Azerbaijan). But if citizen journalists in Serbia are now contributors to news, too, we wonder if they receive sufficient protection and support. In fact, according to Bjelotomić (2020), the authorities in Serbia have "used the state of emergency and the pandemic to strengthen their executive power and massively restrict freedoms," which affected not only professionals, but citizen journalists, too.

When the state of emergency was introduced, the authorities stated immediately that there would be criminal charges pressed to those who "carelessly use social networks and other means of providing public information" and that the punishments and will be very strict (Rogač 2020). But we wonder if such measures were in line with the standards of freedom of expression enshrined, among other by Article 10 of the European Convention on Human Rights and Fundamental Freedoms. In its paragraph 1, the Article guarantees freedom of expression to everyone without interference by public authority. On the other hand, paragraph 2 explains the restrictions that may be imposed in certain circumstances in the interest of, among others, public health. Although, "the practical and effective impact of Article 10 still differs from one member state to another" (Voorhoof 2014), the limitations are still to be applied restrictively. However, according to the Venice Commission (1995), in a state of emergency derogations from normal human rights standards are possible, but even in these times, restrictions on freedom of expression and other human rights must be approached only in exceptional cases.

But during the state of emergency, the Serbian Prosecutor's Office seemed to be paying special attention to the Criminal Code of Serbia in Article 343—causing panic and disorder. The Article states that "whoever by disclosing or disseminating untrue information or allegations causes panic, or serious disruption of public peace and order . . . shall be punished by fine or imprisonment up to one year" and if such offence "is committed through media or similar means or at public gathering, the offender shall be punished by imprisonment up to three years." However, this Article did not apply when the Crisis Staff that sent messages to all MTS[1] mobile network users saying: "The situation is dramatic. We are getting close to the Spanish and Italian scenario. Please stay at home." (European Western Balkans 2020). These messages were clearly aimed at disturbing and scaring the citizens while "motivating" them to stay at home, but they were not treated as "causing panic" at all.

Moreover, freedom of expression and information during the pandemic in Serbia suffered through the attempts to centralize the information on the pandemic, too. It was on March 28 when the Government of Serbia forbade anyone not in its Crisis Staff, from stating any information about the pandemic. This meant that information from "unauthorized persons" could not be considered "correct and verified," whereas those disseminating that information could be liable based on the Article 343 of the Criminal Code (European Western Balkans 2020). Finally, it was only a few days later, on April 2, that this decision on centralization of information was revoked after pressures received from international organizations (Article 19, 2020). But it was precisely in the first two weeks of the state of emergency—March 16–April 1 that citizens speaking about any COVID-19 topic suffered the most, as most arrests happened precisely then.

Serbian citizens have a low trust in media in general (Konrad Adenauer Stif-tung 2019), and at the very beginning the rules imposed by the state of emergency kept changing and the information coming through the media was ambiguous (Kosorić, 2020), which is why many started speaking about this on social net-works. It appeared that when official institutions do not offer enough information, citizen journalism takes over, and "as the readership of mainstream traditional media declines, the audience is looking for other alternatives to acquire their information" (Kheny 2019). It is important to note that freedom of expression includes not only "information" or "ideas" that are favorably received or regarded as inoffensive, but also those that offend, shock, or disturb which is in line with standards of pluralism and tolerance (Handyside v. UK).

But this principle seems to have been forgotten in Serbia during the state of emergency, because several people publicly speaking about the virus were arrested, too. The citizens of Serbia were arrested for posting information on social networks such as that post offices will not work, that the shops would work shorter than usual, that citizens were receiving bread-coupons,[2] that there would be a complete 24-hour lockdown, that only one person from a household would be allowed to leave their home every second day but only to go to a shop[3]; and others posting that a person may be infected,[4] or that they themselves may be infected.[5] At the same time, media outlets did not show much sympathy to the arrested citizens, instead differences between professional and citizen journalists emerged more than ever.

Little media support for public interest matters: lack of fuel

Numerous platforms today allow the emergence of citizen journalism, which could provide the information missing from traditional media reporting (Cengiz v. Turkey). The case with the biggest coverage was the one of a person from Belgrade arrested due to messages sent on Viber on March 19. These messages stated that there would be a lack of fuel, and that regular citizens would not be able to buy it, as well as that from March 20 it would be prohibited to go even to a store. In total, the analysis covered 41 articles about this case. There were 14 articles with a neutral tone purely copying the official statement from the website of the Ministry of Interior, but not showing support to the detainee either. Neutral articles showed up in local media outlets, and traditionally independent media— daily newspaper *Danas* and television N1 (Kosorić 2020), but also the public broadcaster: RTS, and the broadcaster of Vojvodina RTV.

On the other hand, 27 articles had a negative tone while reporting about this person. The tone is reflected in a wide use of exclamation points, capital letters, and relying on sensationalism by using phrases such as "He caused a chaos!," "He spread fake news on purpose!," "He spread falsehoods and caused panic!," "An incredibly fast reaction of the police!," "To jail, immediately!," "Now he can only regret!," "Lies about the fuel shortage!," "While waiting for a punish-ment, he can now think about what he has done!," "To jail!" More than half of the articles praised the police and quoted the president threatening with immediate imprisonment of all those who "spread panic." The media speaking particularly negatively about the case were *Kurir*,[6] *Alo*,[7] *Informer*,[8] *Srbija Danas*,[9] and *Pink*,[10] all of which are claimed to be affiliated with the ruling Serbian Progressive Party (SNS) (Strika 2020). However, although they continuously used words such as "lies," "lied," and "liar," some of these media outlets are precisely the ones who were connected with fake Twitter accounts deleted in March. Namely, Twitter removed 8,558 bot accounts in Serbia, but before this deletion, the content "found its way into the pages of pro-government tabloids disguised as the 'voice of the people'" (Nikolić and Jeremić 2020). The tweets were included in stories published by precisely *Kurir*, *Informer*, and *Srbija Danas*. Moreover, in 2019, *Kurir* published at least 142 fake news without any relevant sources or evidence (N1 info 2020), but in this case of a citizen arrest, they kept insisting that the person spread fake news and "lied."

The statements in question all referred to matters of public interest and public debate today is shaped by, among other, citizen journalists, NGOs, bloggers, whistleblowers, ordinary individuals, etc. (McGonagle 2019) It seems that in the state of emergency the role of citizen journalism rises more than ever, especially when there are the matters of public interest. A possible shortage of gas as a topic was certainly a matter of public interest and such statements usually have a greater protection (Tromsø and Stensaas v. Norway). Therefore, even if some statements are harsh or even partially untrue, it is still important to determine whether someone "acted in good faith." In this particular case, the standards could have been the same, because the citizen may have acted in a good faith and due to the urgency of the matter, did not have time to verify the information. In fact, non-professionals have some "flexibility in the exercise of professional standards," but it sometimes happens that "journalistic part of "citizen journalist" is overshadowed by the citizen part, hence emerging primarily as an activist, opinionator, or simply social media user (Darbo and Skjerdal 2019). This citizen did not get support from professional journalists either, and it remains unknown what happened with the detainee and whether he has been released.

Different media treatment of professional and citizen journalists: lack of medical equipment, staff, and space

Another prominent case involved a person from the city of Loznica who was accused for causing panic through social networks about the lack of equipment, staff, and space at the General Hospital in Loznica. An additional reason for his arrest is also the alleged insult to the ruling party. Out of the 33 articles on this case, 19 had an openly negative tone again copying the official Ministry statements, 13 were neutral, and only 1 article was supportive. This media outlet, N1,[11] showed sympathy toward this person and published an article containing both the official charges and the statements of the suspect stating that he would take his case to Strasbourg court if necessary, showing a rather positive tone toward him (N1 info 2020). This article showed a level of solidarity with a person who has been active on social networks, spread matters of public interest, and exercised his freedom of expression. The topic of the case and of the statements is rather similar to another case of arrest, but with much more media coverage, which only reiterated the difference between professional and citizen journalists and exposed the different treatment of the arrests, too.

On April 1, a journalist, Ana Lalić, was arrested, because of her article about the lack of equipment for protection such as masks and gloves at the Clinical Center of Vojvodina. This journalist was arrested on the very same day when the article was published, and her laptop and two phones were confiscated just as it happened with the person from Loznica. But in the case of a professional journalist, numerous media outlets, European Union bodies, and journalists' groups reacted on her detention, and there was a big pressure coming from international journalists associations and institutions (Mong 2020). Ana Lalić was released the next day and the authorities dropped the charges against her on April 27. However, the citizen from Loznica who spoke about a similar topic in another hospital, still waits for the trial, has spent 50 days in prison in total, and received almost no support from the public and media actors in general.

Citizen journalists therefore turned out to be regular people facing risks that could be greater than those of professionals (Nikkanen 2012). In fact, the lack of support to citizen journalists is found in media outlets, too, because they were rather condemning about the posts. And even when both groups of journalists speak about the public interest, there is rarely anyone standing behind citizen journalists. If a professional is arrested or sent to court, their media outlet will pay for the lawyers and if a professional is being threatened, numerous associations will react. On the other hand, citizen journalists seem not to be receiving support and "more vulnerable than professionals to violence, frivolous lawsuits and extrajudicial online takedowns" (Nikkanen 2012).

While the international associations and institutions, local associations of journalists, and the few independent media outlets insisted on the respect of freedom of expression, the pro-government media conducted smear campaigns against those who dared speaking about the situation in hospitals in Serbia. The titles on the citizens' arrest were as follows: "He spread panic through social networks," "Maliciously spread panic on social networks about coronavirus and ended up in detention for 30 days," "30 days behind the bars for causing panic!" etc. This case has not seen its epilogue yet, but the condemning media were again *Kurir*, *Informer*, *B92*,[12] *Pink*, and *Telegraf*.[13] *Kurir* labeled Ana Lalić as a liar, too, which shows that although working in the same field, professional journalists do not support each other when it comes to the matters of public interest. *Kurir* published texts accusing Ana Lalić of violating the journalistic code, but the Press Council of Serbia stated that *Kurir* violated the Code of Journalists of Serbia by writing about Ana Lalić instead. Moreover, according to the Press Council (2020), *Kurir* violated the Code of Journalists of Serbia 1106 times in the past six months. Even though smear campaigns against journalists are unacceptable in a democratic society, in Serbia, they seem to be happening often when journalists write about a sensitive topic. All these moves coming from media outlets were said to be a "demonstration of exercise intended to intimidate the public" (Vojinović 2020).

Conclusion

The cases of arrests of citizens raised many questions and seem to have exposed the lingering problems of Serbian media landscape even more clearly. In the state of emergency, the polarization of media to "friendly" and "unfriendly" has become even clearer because "all non-aligned journalists are openly labelled as enemies of the Serbian state and people" (Janjić 2020). In fact, the state of the "traitors" media became much worse with journalists being arrested, but citizen journalists were labeled as traitors and liars, too, both by the authorities and media outlets close to the government. Overall, it seems that those who dared speak even slightly negatively about the measures introduced during the state of emergency have had a hard time in the past two months and faced threats, criminal charges, and intimidation. Hence, it seems that Serbia saw interference in one's freedom of expression when media actors were detained, threatened, or intimidated for what they were saying, but if citizen journalists contribute to public debate then they should have the same protection as professionals (McGonagle 2013). Therefore, the restrictions placed on citizen journalists in Serbia seemed much stricter than it could be justified. According to Janjić (2020), authorities targeted those who asked "uncomfortable questions, that is, questions on subjects of public interest that should be brought to the attention of the public," and this included citizen journalists, too, who got arrested for speaking out.

Moreover, in most articles about citizens' arrests, media showed no support for others discussing matters of public interest. This also showed the different treatment of professional and citizen journalists in Serbia, because unlike in the case of citizen journalists, when a professional was arrested, there were reactions from certain media and international community. On the other hand, pro-governmental media were quite harsh when speaking about both types of arrest, some of them resorting to unprofessional journalism, according to the Press Council (2020). Serbia not only introduced strict measures "to curb press freedom and open the door to arbitrary prosecutions," but also saw independent journalists, and citizen journalists, too, harassed by smear campaigns conducted by politicians and other actors (RWB 2020). And so, both professional and citizen journalists in Serbia found themselves under attack while trying to provide the information on public interest in risky conditions (RWB 2020). However, while the few independent media remained mostly silent about the arrests, the authorities and pro-government media were, during the state of emergency, fighting on two fronts: one against virus, and the other against the freedom of speech of both professional and citizen journalists (Mong 2020).

Notes

1 MTS is a telecommunications company in Serbia majority-owned by the state.
2 A person from the town of Malo Crniće.
3 A person from Belgrade.
4 A person from the city of Kruševac.
5 A person from the city of Novi Sad.

6 *Kurir* is a daily newspaper a part of Adria Media Group (AMG), owned by Igor Žeželj (https://serbia.mom-rsf.org/en/).
7 *Alo* is a daily newspaper owned by Saša Blagojević, (https://serbia.mom-rsf.org/en/).
8 *Informer* is a daily newspaper owned by Insider Team Ltd, owner Dragan Vučićević (https://serbia.mom-rsf.org/en/).
9 Srbija Danas is a portal founded by Srbija Danas Ltd, owned by Aleksandra Martinović (https://serbia.mom-rsf.org/en/).
10 Pink, a part of Pink Media Group owned by Željko Mitrović, openly pro-governmental (https://serbia.mom-rsf.org/en/).
11 Cable television N1, the Balkan affiliate of CNN, a part of United Group (https://serbia.mom-rsf.org/en/).
12 B92 is a TV station owned by Kopernikus Corporation with individual owner Srđan Milovanović (https://serbia.mom-rsf.org/en/).
13 *Telegraf* is a daily newspaper with an online edition, too, published by Medijska mreza with four individual owners Saša Milovanović, Milan Lađević, Ljubomir Dabović, and Lazar Simić (https://serbia.mom-rsf.org/en/).

References

"Kurir prekršio kodeks novinara tekstom o Ani Lalić (Kurir Violated the Code of Journalists with Its Text About Ana Lalić)." *Press Council of Serbia*, May 14, 2020. Accessed May 20, 2020. www.savetzastampu.rs/latinica/press/93/2020/05/21/2296/kurir-prekrsio-kodekds-novinara-tekstom-o-ani-lalic.html.
"Optužbe rekordera lažnih vesti (Accusations of Fake-News Record Holders)." *N1 Info*, April 7, 2020. Accessed April 24, 2020. http://rs.n1info.com/Vesti/a586688/Optuzbe-rekordera-laznih-vesti.html.
"Repressive Laws, Prosecutions, Attacks . . . Europe Fails to Shield Its Journalists Against the Abuse of the COVID-19 Crisis." Reporters without Borders, *Ecoi.net*, April 8, 2020. Accessed April 29, 2020. www.ecoi.net/en/document/2027798.html.
"Serbia: Journalist Ana Lalić Arrested for Reporting on Inadequate Hospital Facilities for Coronavirus." *Article 19*, April 2, 2020. Accessed April 15, 2020. www.article19.org/resources/serbia-journalist-ana-lalic-arrested-for-reporting-on-inadequate-hospital-facilities-for-coronavirus/.
"Serbian Journalist Arrested for Reporting on Difficult Working Conditions of Medical Staff in COVID-19 Pandemic." *European Western Balkans*, April 2, 2020. Accessed April 15, 2020. https://europeanwesternbalkans.com/2020/04/02/serbian-journalist-arrested-for-reporting-on-difficult-working-conditions-of-medical-staff-in-covid-19-pandemic/.
Anderson, C. 2008. "Journalism: Expertise, Authority, and Power in Democratic Life." In *The Media and Social Theory*, edited by D. Hesmondhalgh and J. Toynbee, 248–65. New York: Routledge.
Bjelotomić, Snežana. 2020. "Der Spiegel: The Serbian Authorities Have Done Everything Possible to Restrict Rights and Freedoms." *Serbian Monitor*, April 29. Accessed May 23, 2020. www.serbianmonitor.com/en/der-spiegel-the-serbian-authorities-have-done-everything-possible-to-restrict-rights-and-freedoms/.
Criminal Code of Serbia, Official Gazette of RS, Nos. 85/2005, 88/2005, 107/2005.
Freedom House. 2020. "Serbia." Accessed June 5, 2020. https://freedomhouse.org/country/serbia/freedom-world/2020.
Handyside v. The United Kingdom, App no. 5493/72, European Court of Human Rights, 7 December 1976.
Henrichsen, Jennifer R., Michelle Betz, and Joanne M. Lisosky. 2015. "Building Digital Safety for Journalism: A Survey of Selected Issues." *UNESCO*. ISBN: 978-92-3-100087-4

(print/pdf), 978-92-3-100096-6 (epub). Accessed May 23, 2020. https://unesdoc. unesco.org/ark:/48223/pf0000232358.

Janjić, Dragan. 2020. "Željko Bodrožić: The State of Emergency Smothers the Serbian Media." *Osservatorio Balcani e Caucaso Transeuropa*, April 17. Accessed May 25, 2020. www.balcanicaucaso.org/eng/Areas/Serbia/Zeljko-Bodrozic-the-state-of-emergency-smothers-the-Serbian-media-201029.

Kheny, Eesha Bansal. 2019. "Media Accountability: Critical Analysis of Citizen Journalism." Paper presented at International Conference on Media Ethics at University of Applied Sciences Bonn-Rhein-Sieg.

Konrad Adenauer Stiftung. 2019. "Media Program South East Europe." Accessed May 19, 2020. www.kas.de/en/web/medien-europa.

Kosorić, S. 2020. "Nezavisni mediji se ovde tretiraju kao kovid 19 (Independent Media Here Are Treated as Covid-10)." *Danas*, April 10. Accessed June 2, 2020. www.danas. rs/drustvo/nezavisni-mediji-se-ovde-tretiraju-kao-kovid-19/.

McGonagle, Tarlach. 2013. "How to Address Current Threats to Journalism: The Role of the Council of Europe in Protecting Journalists and Other Media Actors." Expert paper presented at the Council of Europe Conference of Ministers responsible for Media and Information Society, Freedom of Expression and Democracy in the Digital Age, Opportunities, Rights, Responsibilities, Belgrade 7–8 November 2013.

———. 2019. "Safety of Journalists." Presented at OSCE Human Dimension Implementation Meeting, OSCE Office for Democratic Institutions and Human Rights (ODIHR), Warsaw, September 18, 2019.

Miller-Carpenter, Serena. 2019. "Citizen Journalism." Subject: Communication and Technology, Communication Theory, Communication and Social Change, Journalism Studies, Mass Communication Online Publication Date: Mar 2019. DOI: 10.1093/ acrefore/9780190228613.013.786.

Mong, Atilla. 2020. "Serbian Reporter Ana Lalić on Her Arrest and Detention Over COVID-19 Report." *Committee to Protect Journalists*, April 29. Accessed May 13, 2020. https://cpj.org/2020/04/serbian-reporter-ana-lalic-on-her-arrest-and-deten/.

Nerdalen Darbo, Karoline, and Terje Skjerdal. 2019. "Blurred Boundaries: Citizens Journalists Versus Conventional Journalists in Hong Kong." 4, no. 1: 111–124, Article first published online: March 25, 2019; Issue published: March 1, 2019. https://doi. org/10.1177/2059436419834633.

Nikkanen, Hanna. 2012. "They Shoot Citizen Journalists, Don't They? Curating or Outsourcing? Opportunities and Threats in Post-Gatekeeper Journalism." *International Federation of Library Associations and Institutions*, December 10, 2012. Accessed May 29, 2020. www.ifla.org/publications/they-shoot-citizen-journalists-dont-they-curating-or-outsourcing-opportunities-and-thre.

Nikolić, Ivana, and Ivana Jeremić. 2020. "Vox Populi': How Serbian Tabloids and Twitter Bots Joined Forces." *Balkan Investigative Reporting Network, Balkan Insight*, April 10. Accessed April 19, 2020. https://balkaninsight.com/2020/04/10/vox-populi-how-serbian-tabloids-and-twitter-bots-joined-forces/.

Noor, Rabia. 2017. "Citizen Journalism vs. Mainstream Journalism: A Study on Challenges Posed by Amateurs." *Athens Journal of Mass Media and Communications* 3, no. 1: 55–76.

Noorlander, Peter. 2020. "Background Paper on the Implementation of CM/rec(2016)4 on the Safety of Journalists and Other Media Actors." Paper presented at the Conference of Ministers Responsible for Media and Information Society. Nicosia, Cyprus, May 2020.

Press Council of Serbia. 2020. "Reports for 2019." Accessed on May 31, 2020. www.savet zastampu.rs/monitoring-postovanja-kodeksa-novinara-srbije.html.

Reporters Without Borders. 2020. "Serbia." Accessed June 5, 2020. https://rsf.org/en/serbia.

Rogač, Milijana. 2020. "Širenje panike: Virus probudio tužioce (Spreading Panic: Virus Woke Up Prosecutors)." *Istinomer*, March 18. Accessed April 5, 2020. www.istinomer. rs/analize/sirenje-panike-virus-probudio-tuzioce/.

Strika, Zoran. 2020. "Novac za oglašavanje projekata od izuzetne važnosti za Novosađane odlazi beogradskim tabloidima koji podržavaju vlast (Money for Advertising Special Importance Projects for Citizens of Novi Sad, Goes to Pro-Government Tabloids)." *Cenzolovka*, December 24, 2019. Accessed June 2, 2020. www.cenzolovka.rs/drzava-i-mediji/novac-za-oglasavanje-projekata-od-izuzetne-vaznosti-za-novosadjane-odlazi-beogradskim-tabloidima-koji-podrzavaju-vlast/.

Thurman, Neil, and Alfred Hermida. 2010. "Gotcha: How Newsroom Norms Are Shaping Participatory Journalism Online." In *Web Journalism: A New Form of Citizenship?* edited by S. Tunney and G. Monaghan, 46–62. Eastbourne, UK: Sussex Academic Press.

Venice Commission 1995, "Emergency Powers." In *Science and Technique of Democracy*, No. 12. Strasbourg: CDL-STD(1995) 012. Accessed May 14, 2020. www.venice.coe.int/webforms/documents/default.aspx?pdffile=CDL-STD(1995)012-e.

Vojinović, Milica. 2020. "Serbia's COVID-19 Lockdown Takes an Authoritarian Turn." *Krik*, April 2. Accessed April 15, 2020. www.krik.rs/en/serbias-covid-19-lockdown-takes-an-authoritarian-turn/.

Voorhoof, Dirk, "The Right to Freedom of Expression and Information under the European Human Rights System: Towards a More Transparent Democratic Society." *Inforrms Blog*, February 14, 2014. Accessed March 31, 2020. https://inforrm.wordpress.com/2014/02/14/the-right-to-freedom-of-expression-and-information-under-the-european-human-rights-system-towards-a-more-transparent-democratic-society-dirk-voorhoof/.

8 "We don't want to cause public panic"

Pandemic communication of the Indonesian Government responding to COVID-19

Dyah Pitaloka and Nelly Martin-Anatias

Introduction

On December 31, 2019, a novel viral pneumonia originating from Wuhan, China, was announced to the World Health Organization. On January 7, the World Health Organization (WHO) announced that they had identified a new virus, named 2019-nCoV. On January 11, China announced its first death from coronavirus in Wuhan and soon after that the first case outside of China was found in Thailand on January 13. In breathtaking speed, coronavirus began to spread across the world. As of March 23, 2020, COVID-19 quickly spread across the globe, infecting more than 294,110 people in 187 countries and killing 12,944 individuals. Highly contagious with the possibility of causing severe respiratory disease, this outbreak quickly impacted governments and public health systems. The fear intensified when Chinese health official warned the world that people who are carrying the virus but not showing symptoms (asymptomatic) may still be able to infect others. This means those seemingly healthy people who travel internationally and interact with others may pass the virus, thus making the disease much more difficult to control. Changes to daily life have been swift and unprecedented, forcing governments worldwide took drastic measures to prevent the contagion and slow down the spread of the disease.

Emerging public health threats such as COVID-19 create many psychological stressors. Millions of lives have been significantly altered, and a global, multilevel, and demanding stress-coping-adjustment process is ongoing. Scholars argue that the uncertainty inherent in crises can create a narrative space that is often filled by multiple interpretations about what is happening and what steps should be taken to resolve the crisis. To reach the level of crisis, events must occur as a surprise, pose an immediate threat, and demand a short response time (Hermann 1963). Mass tragedies, particularly ones that involve infectious diseases, often trigger waves of heightened fear, panic, and anxiety that are known to cause massive disruptions to the behavior and psychological well-being—such as anxiety, stress, and depression—of many in the population (Balaratnasingam and Janca 2006; Lee 2020; Wang et al. 2020; Xiang et al. 2020).

By their nature, crises cause considerable levels of uncertainty among various stakeholders and groups (Lofstedt 2006; Holmes et al. 2009). In extreme conditions, this uncertainty may create a sense of chaos where the perspective from which individuals have been deriving meaning is lost. People across the globe are experiencing something at an extreme that is new to them—coronavirus, and they do not fully understand what is happening, how to cope with the situation, and where they can turn for help. Pandemic brings wide-ranging socioeconomic disruption pushing those living at the margins to accept a higher risk of exposure (Quinn and Kumar 2014). The high death toll during the West Africa Ebola outbreak triggers expanded social and household economic impacts and lost wages due to inability to work or contagion fear, increased poverty and food insecurity, lost education and lost jobs. In a similar fashion, the impact of COVID-19 on socioeconomic aspects of life could also be as substantial.

The rapid spread of COVID-19 across the globe and the fact that no vaccine is available to treat the disease cause people to no longer able to comprehend and control their own destiny. Weick (1993) designates this consistent emotional response as a "cosmologic episode." During a crisis, people want to understand what is happening and why. They want to know what they can do to reduce their risk of offset the harm they experience or could experience. As such, a best practice of crisis communication is to tell the public what is happening and instruct them on the appropriate actions they can take for self and community protection (Seeger and Sellnow 2019). The stories told by organization spokespersons and news media to fill this narrative space during the early phrase of the crisis are critical to resolving the crisis successfully. The narratives of health crises are difficult to manage. Unlike reputational crises, where a specific, contained incident leads to a loss in credibility of confidence, health crises defy attempts at containment, require considerable time to develop vaccines, and threaten entire populations.

The uncertainty inherent in crises can create a narrative space that is often filled by multiple interpretations about what is happening and what steps should be taken by individuals and collective to resolve the crisis. Strategic planning and consistent narrative should fully consider how sociocultural, economic, psychological, and health factors can either jeopardize or facilitate public health interventions that require a cooperative public (Vaughan and Tinker 2009). In relation to coronavirus outbreak, the collective cosmology episode should include a consistent narrative to explain the nature of the disease, possible risks that may occur as consequences of the implementation of COVID-19 interventions, recommendation on appropriate protective action steps, and information that motivate a multitude of diverse stakeholders to actually follow the instructions.

Indonesia: brief background

Indonesia is an archipelago country that prides themselves with "Unity in Diversity" motto, due to its rich linguistic background and ethnolinguistic groups across the country. While it assigns only one national and official language, *Bahasa Indonesia* (Indonesian), the country has approximately 500–700 languages (Sneddon

2003). *De facto* a religious country, Indonesia acknowledges six religions from Islam, Catholics, Christianity, Hinduism, Buddhism, and Confucianism. Islam plays such an important role that it has impacted and influenced the country's regulations and laws (Hefner 2000). This background is essential to understand the upcoming analysis.

The initial zero case reported by Indonesia prior to the Global Pandemic declaration by the World Health Organization raised concerns and questions about what set Indonesia apart from other countries with confirmed cases. Despite reports of increasing numbers of infection from countries across the globe, Indonesia did not issue any form of travel restrictions and specific quarantines of travelers coming in/coming back to Indonesia, not even from China. A decree declaring COVID-19 a national disaster was finally announced on April 13. Echoing many health experts, President Joko "Jokowi" Widodo has suggested people to stay work and pray at home to prevent further spread of the highly contagious disease.

Multicultural and religious contexts, nonetheless, posed great challenges in efforts to combat the spread of COVID-19. Although the government has called on the public to stay at home and avoid the crowds (physical distancing), some religious groups still intend to hold gatherings involving many people. With the arrival of the fasting month of Ramadan and Eid festivals, the situation gets more complicated. Muslims face a new challenge. The usual practices, traditions, and habits such as Ramadan night prayers (*tarawih*) and breaking-of-the-fast (*iftar*) events, which normally are conducted in a collective form, are suddenly outlawed by the government due to physical-distancing rules. Lockdown policy as part of an effort to contain the virus spread ahead Ramadan and the Eid holiday is seen as crucial to prevent people from *mudik*. Mudik, an exodus to return to hometown, has become the epitome of observing Ramadan and celebrating Eid al-Fitr (*Idul Fitri*).

Not only Muslims but also all Indonesians have adopted *mudik* as an annual ritual of reconnecting, remembering, and recharging. A mixture of Islamic values and Javanese and other regional customs (Sairin 2010), *mudik* has become an Indonesian national tradition where people will return to their hometown, meeting their parents and the extended family member to asking for forgiveness. This tradition, however, would heighten the risk of a nationwide epidemic. Governments in some provinces of Indonesia, including Jakarta, have enforced large-scale social restrictions to reduce mobilization of people in their area. The central government has also issued a policy restricting intercity and interprovince travel to prevent people from going to their hometowns and increasing the possibility of a surge in COVID-19 cases across the country.

Government interventions aimed to stop the spread of coronavirus, such as through the implementation of "Large-scale Social Distancing" (in Indonesian: *Pembatasan Sosial Berskala Besar*, hereafter PSBB) and work from home policy had caused major disruption to those at the margins. Mass layoffs as seen everywhere in the world and increased stress on those in informal sectors, forcing them to return to their hometown or village (*pulang kampung*). This situation acting more as push factors than *mudik* pulled. It becomes more of a safety-net rather than tradition or celebration. For Indonesians living in economic precarity, staying on in Jakarta, where living expenses are considerably higher compared to other regions, loss of income and social support had become major concern for this people to return to their hometown. As of Thursday, May 21, Indonesia has recorded the total number of infections nationwide to over 16,000 with almost 3,000 recoveries and 1,000 fatalities.

The context has provided an entry gate for us to further discuss the government's response to coronavirus outbreak, especially during the early days of the pandemic. Both national and foreign media highlights the incompetency and incapability that the Indonesian government shows in responding to the coronavirus outbreak. At the end of April, the number of positive coronavirus cases surpassed 9,500 with recorded 773 deaths, including more than 40 doctors and nurses that the declaration of a national health emergency and social distancing measures were imposed in the nation's capital city and other affected regions.

Method

In approaching our data, we used an interpretive analysis, which we refer to as a discourse tracing analysis. Here we unpacked how discourse and other semiotic elements have contributed to the meaning-making process. Utilizing discourse tracing (Legreco and Tracy 2009), we explore the ways Indonesian government tackle coronavirus pandemic, communicating the risks, and how the communication process transforms over time. The development of discourse tracing is influenced heavily by Foucault's (1972) work on discursive formations and Fairclough's (1995) work on discursive practices. Similar to content analyses, discourse tracing involves practices, including an initial reading of data for emergent themes and codes, followed by a more systematic reading to lift out patterns (Altheide 1987; Berg 1995). However, different to content analysis, discourse tracing move from the *what* to the *how*, and examine how various levels of discourse interacted with one another to create of transform a certain phenomenon, policy, or action over time. In this current study, we select newspapers reports covering Indonesian government response to coronavirus outbreak, set them in chronology, and examine across time to better understand the transformation of pandemic communication related to the coronavirus outbreak over a certain time period.

Most crises can be traced as they evolve through three stages: pre-crisis, [acute] crisis, and post-crisis (Ulmer, Sellnow, and Seeger 2015).

During the pre-crisis stage, warning signs—some of them long-standing and some of them fleeting—are present. Failure to address these warning signs (whether they go unnoticed or are deliberately overlooked) potentially turn the pre-crisis stage into an acute crisis. For this study, we searched for all articles on COVID-19 via the Factiva database. We used several terms, including "COVID-19," "*virus corona* (coronavirus)," "Indonesia," "Jokowi," "Terawan," and "*kebijakan*" (policy) to identify the relevant articles. We included both in print and those published online. After running many searches, combining list of articles, and eliminating articles that were not relevant, we collected and examined 155 articles published in both English and Indonesian languages in Indonesian media from January 2020 to June 2020. These articles provide information regarding the three turning points in the coronavirus outbreak in Indonesia: (1) turning point one also marks the early phase of the coronavirus outbreak (January—February 2020), which we can consider as the pre-crisis; (2) turning point two, which can be identified as the first wave of the outbreak, starts right after President Jokowi announced the first coronavirus cases until the imposing of the first round of large-scale social restrictions (March–May 2020), which we can consider as the beginning of the crisis period; (3) turning point three, which can be identified as the second wave of the crisis occurs when President Jokowi made a public statement to make peace with coronavirus and that the large-scale social restriction will be soon been relaxed (early June–continuing). For turning point three, we will only cover news report up from early of June, considering the deadline of this publication. At the moment of writing this piece, Indonesia has hit 100,000 cases making it the country with the highest number of COVID-19 cases in Southeast Asia. It is obvious that the crisis has not yet over.

The newspaper articles that we examined contain statements made by President Jokowi and Indonesian Health Minister, Terawan Agus Putranto, and related officials such as national COVID-19 spoke person, which provide a backdrop for our discussion regarding government strategy and outbreak communication narrative in response to rapidly emerging COVID-19. To provide in-depth discussion on how public reacted to government's decision, we also pay attention to public comments to President Jokowi's Twitter @jokowi related to COVID-19 issues, and also comments posted by readers in reaction to the related articles.

Along with the examination, we simultaneously offer our interpretation in order to unfold what the sentences could actually mean and how they have impacted the intended communities, during this COVID-19 pandemic era. In the section to follow, we will discuss our set of data and offer our interpretations.

Discussion

Based on our observation, there are three turning points that occurred in Indonesia's COVID-19 crisis (see Table 8.1). The first turning point happened between early January until the end of February 2020, just before the first two positive coronavirus cases was announced. The second turning point occurred in early March, when Indonesian government announced its first two cases. President Jokowi's statement admitting government's lack of transparency had caused public who had already been living in uncertainty and confusion, questioning government's commitment in managing the crisis. The third turning point occurred in mid-May, soon after President Jokowi made a statement that public should make peace with coronavirus and calls on public to adapt to "new normal."

Our brief introduction to Indonesian context shows that culture plays a significant role in people's lives and responses toward the current coronavirus outbreak. Taking culture as our main perspective in looking at the government response to COVID-19 pandemic in each turning point, we will discuss how understanding

Table 8.1 Turning points: Indonesia's COVID-19

Turning point	Government responses	Sample of excerpt (authorial voices)	Public responses
Turning Point 1 (Beginning of January 2020– early March 2020) Pre-crisis stage	Authorial voices reflect Indonesian's government over self-confident. Laidback approach, which reflected through the use of words such as "relax," "enjoy" (*santai*), "we're immune" (*kebal*). Statements made by government officials during this pre-crisis state tend to underestimate and imply as if Indonesians are immune to coronavirus attack. *Impenetrable *doa* (prayer) and divine interventions to counter COVID-19 Crisis insensitive policy *Denials *Lack of empathy *Focus on dealing with the economic Lack of transparency *Conflict avoidance, managing harmony Lack of information about risks	Health Minister Terawan: *"The way to confront [the virus] is with immunity . . . what influences the latter ranges from food to thoughts," Terawan said on Monday (The Jakarta Post, January 27, 2020).* *"If there are other countries protesting [our approach], just let them; it is our nation's right to rely on the Almighty," he said. "Why should we be ashamed of relying on the Almighty? We should not be ashamed of praying." (The Jakarta Post, February 17, 2020)* President Joko Widodo: *"Indeed, we did not deliver certain information to the public because we did not want to stir panic. We have worked hard to overcome this, since the novel coronavirus outbreak can happen regardless of the country border," Jokowi said on Friday (The Jakarta Post, March 14, 2020)*	Questioning government policy Disappointment Disbelieve Concerns Responses to @jokowi Twitter: *"Force people to wear mask"* *"How come the government can be this ignorant?"* *"Clueless . . . typical of Mr Joko [Jokowi]"*
Turning Point 2 (March 2020– May 2020) Crisis period	Underestimate the severity and consequences of the disease Withhold the truth Misleading statements lead to false hope Economic-lead decision *Government opting for "large-scale social restrictions" instead of quarantine' Leadership ambiguity *The use of word "*himbauan*," which means appeal is perceived by public as confusing	Health Minister Terawan *"The theory is true that this is indeed a self-limiting disease that will heal itself. Disease that will heal itself" (The Asian Affairs, March 13, 2020)* President Jokowi *"The coronavirus and the economy are highly related. They both are important. If people don't eat, the economy would collapse" (The Straits Times, April 13, 2020)*	Lack of trust and confusion Public perceived government as downplaying the issue *Sharp increase in number of coronavirus positive cases from 2 cases in March 2, 2020, to 96 positive cases in March 13, 2020.

*In relation to *mudik* (exodus) during 2020 Eid holiday *Rather than "*melarang*" (ban, prohibit), Jokowi uses the word "*meminta*" (to ask, to advise) and "*menghimbau*" Balance, harmony	Jokowi said the government had advised people not to go back to their hometowns for Idul Fitri, a tradition locally known as *mudik*, and had ordered regional heads to find ways to discourage people from traveling. (The Jakarta Post, April 2, 2020) "We must coexist with COVID-19. Most importantly, people must stay productive and be safe from the virus." (The Jakarta Post, May 16, 2020)	"I'm not worry about the virus, but I'm worry because the government doesn't do proper socialization and sufficient preventive actions before the cases are detected" "Doesn't Jokowi realize that he's the one in charge?! He's the one who should clearly state that returning home endangers your family and community. People who feel healthy could be carrying the virus and can give it others." Social media movement #JokowiKingOfPrank #menolaklupa (refused to forget)
Turning Point 3 (June—continuing) Crisis period Easing restriction *Balancing economic recovery and public health Vague policy *Unclear and confusing "new normal" policy Uncertainty *False hope: calming, avoiding conflict *Everything is (will be) fine	Ahmad Yurianto (COVID-19 spoke person) "We understand that the COVID-19 pandemic is under control. The decrease can be seen not only within the city/municipality level, but also within the provincial level. Public response also getting more positive." Achmad Yurianto (Indonews.id, June 4, 2020) On June 9, 2020, Ahmad Yurianto made a statement that there is an increase of 1045 positive cases of COVID-19 per day	Concerns mount *Lack of awareness Criticism through jokes and language and sarcasm. #NewNormal "I've never had to open my mask for someone else this fast." "I accept this marriage with a dowry of praying sets, mask and rapid test kit." #IndonesiaTerserah (#Whatever Indonesia)

Source: © Dyah Pitaloka, Nelly Martin-Anatias 2021.

differences in cultural practices and beliefs are of vital importance in evolving successful risk and outbreak communication practices. We will also evaluate the role of media in framing the crisis and identify how the media affect the community.

Comforting or downplaying?

The advent of health risk situation brings about several challenges to be addressed, such as risk preparedness and clear information to reduce uncertainties. Recent study reported that global pandemic, such as 2014–2016 Ebola outbreak in West Africa, challenged the UK mass media because not all pandemic was deemed equal by the media. Exploring the coverage of Ebola on the UK national newspapers, the study found that the framing of the infection risk by the Western media played a crucial role in shaping audiences' perception toward the crisis, such as whether it should be deemed local epidemic or global pandemic (Pieri 2019). Within the Indonesian context, the main big question during the first three months of the outbreak was how to speak honestly to public about the disease and what to expect in the future comes. From the perspective of risk communication, during the time of an outbreak, disease is not the only aspect that a government should consider. Equally important is risks that embedded in the social system. The impacts that COVID-19 bring to human body and the disruptions it causes to the everyday life of the people create uncertainty, confusion, and fear—conditions that require careful response and attention.

As Hildred Geertz's (1961) argues, Javanese social life is marked by two principles of overwhelming significance. The first and most important is to avoid open confrontation in every situation. The objective of the principle of conflict avoidance is the establishment and maintenance of social harmony, calm, and unity (Magnis-Suseno 1981), ensuring that each party is at peace. What is interesting from this principle is that it is not so much a question of establishing a condition of social harmony, but, rather, of not disturbing the existing one. For the sake of maintaining peaceful and harmonious interactions with others, Javanese people are often concealing the truth and denying themselves. Truth and straightforwardness may sometimes not be desirable in interaction among people. Related to this cultural predilection to the concealment of feeling is the tendency toward indirectness or "indirection" in Javanese culture because people often do not say directly what they mean (Geertz 1976, 244).

When the novel coronavirus hit China most severely during the months of December 2019–February 2020, the first reaction that Indonesian public could observe from its government was denial. Similar to Trump in the early days of the pandemic (Tom McCarthy, "It will disappear: the disinformation Trump spread about the coronavirus-timeline," *The Guardian*, April 14, 2020, accessed April 14, 2020), Indonesian government gave false assurances to the public and had tried to downplay the potential severity of COVID-19. Indonesia reported no case of infection at all. In late January, for example, President Jokowi stated that Indonesia is well prepared and COVID-19 will never enter Indonesia as his government has distributed 135 thermal scanners to detect infections from visitors (Ihsanuddin,

"Presiden Jokowi Perintahkan Kemenkes Antisipasi Masuknya Virus Corona." *Kompas*/President Jokowi gives instruction to Ministry of Health to Anticipate the Spread of Coronavirus, January 24, 2020, accessed April 12, 2020). Supporting President Jokowi, Ministry of Health, Terawan, made a statement to convincing and comforting public that impenetrable prayer (*doa*) will protect the people from getting the coronavirus. He suggests that prayers would keep Indonesians safe from the virus ("Don't panic, stay healthy and pray, says minister in response to coronavirus fears," *The Jakarta Post*, January 27, 2020, accessed April 18, 2020): "Don't panic, don't be anxious. Just enjoy it. Eat well, live healthily. If you have a cough use a face mask. If we just sit all day without moving, our immunity will drop. Take a 15- to 30-minute walk. . . . Also don't forget to pray."

Calming, comforting, ensuring that everything is under control, framed Indonesian government early responses to COVID-19 outbreak. Interacting peacefully and not causing fear in Javanese culture is perceived as an important endeavor to repress social tension: a condition that was perceived differently by the public. Minister Terawan who was also brushed off concerns about the virus reacted with fury, attacking Harvard researchers who suggest that the Indonesian government was possibly underreporting the number of coronavirus cases (Karen McVeigh, and Emma Graham-Harrison, "Academic stands by research querying Indonesia's claim to be coronavirus-free," *The Guardian*, February 14, 2020, accessed April 18, 2020).

To approach this comment, one should understand that Indonesia is *de facto* a religious nation whose regulations and rules have been largely influenced by the Islamic values. In that regard, for Terawan to advice and encourage Indonesians to pray may sound normal and acceptable, and perhaps expected and out of necessity, while it may appear to be illogical and non-sensical if we see it from a scientific point of view. In other words, there are at least two layers being delivered in this context and statement: one is to treat Terawan as another fellow Indonesian who might be expected to be religious (and for many Indonesians, it is important to appear to be a religious leader and individual), and the other one he is also a Minister of the Ministry of Health with a medical degree and a doctoral philosophy under his belt. It is in the context of his academic and professional background that we see his statement belies his capacity as the prime figure who needs to deliver such as a firm and factual piece of information and knowledge to the citizens and residents of Indonesia. While being religious is not wrong, it is actually the context that may have been a problem: Indonesians are in such a desperate need to have more firm directives, particularly and especially during this difficult time. Additionally, to pray is something that is personal and for many Indonesians, it is something that they do on a regular basis.

In addition to Terawan's statement, Indonesian transportation minister Budi Karya Sumadi, who later was tested positive of coronavirus, also made a joke about the disease and stated that Indonesian people have the immune to the coronavirus because they eat "*nasi kucing*"—a popular dish among many Indonesians, consisting of a small portion of rice wrapped in banana leaves with anchovies, eggs, tempeh, and sambal, and usually sold by street food sellers. This statement does not only belittle the majority of Indonesians who live in poverty but is out of line and is not necessary, particularly coming from a minister, presumably a figure with its professional and academic credentials, who should have given such a factual and firm direction to the citizens.

In February, when Indonesia's neighboring countries such as Singapore and Vietnam started to restrict their territory from the entry of foreigners, Indonesia's government under the Presidency of Joko "Jokowi" Widodo (hereafter Jokowi) introduced the opposite policy that grounded in economic stability. In early February, President Jokowi announced that the government will provide a stimulus package for the Indonesian tourism industry to keep the economic impact of the coronavirus outbreak at bay (Lenny T. Tambun, "Jokowi Promises 30 Percent Discount for Foreign Tourists," *Jakarta Globa*, February 17, 2020, accessed February 17, 2020):

We might also be able to offer the 30% discount to domestic tourists, and maybe travel agencies can offer additional deals, take the discount up to 50%. We need to stimulate our tourism industry to withstand the impact of the coronavirus outbreak

The policy, as President Jokowi further stated, was designed not only to prevent the outbreak from damaging Indonesia's economy, especially its tourism industry, but also to calm public (Wahyudi Soeriaatmadja, "Jokowi says economy, social stability equally important; Indonesia to boost coronavirus testing capacity," *The Straits Times*, April 13, 2020, accessed April 28, 2020). The coronavirus and the economy are highly related. They both are important. If people don't eat, the economy would collapse. . . . If panic among the public ensues and all the people rush to hospital, even a country with the best health system would face a breakdown. We chose to remain calm but tackle the crisis seriously.

Further, on February 26, while many countries issued travel restrictions and began to impose some drastic policies to slow down the spread of coronavirus, Indonesian government launched initiatives to bolster tourism, including the widely derided IDR 72 billion funds (equals to approximately US$4,862,779) for influencers. This policy, which faced much criticism, was later being introduced as part of the government's strategy to promote Indonesia's tourist destinations (Marchio Irfan Gorbiano, "Govt to pay Rp 72 billion to influencers to boost tourism amid coronavirus outbreak," *The Jakarta Post*, February, 26, 2020, accessed February 26, 2020).

Indonesia eventually and officially recognized the outbreak of the COVID-19 on March 2, 2020, with the announcement of the first two patients by President Jokowi. Since then, number of COVID-19 positive patients have continued to increase. By the end of April, there were 12,438 people who were positively infected, 2,317 were cured and 895 people died. As the number of victims increases, public concerns regarding the way the government responds and handles COVID-19 also increase. People began to question, "when" and "how hard" COVID-19 would hit and disrupt their lives. By this time, many governments across the globe had ordered drastic measures. Schools and university campuses were shut down. Shops, restaurants, tourist objects, and companies were closed, and people in many different jobs were asked to work from home.

Following the confirmation of cases in Indonesia, President Jokowi has asked public to remain calm, and stay vigilant, and look only for information from credible sources regarding the coronavirus outbreak. In responding to President Jokowi's statement, Minister of Health, Terawan, described coronavirus is self-limited disease and those infected would heal by themselves ("Menkes: Virus Corona Penyakit yang Bisa Sembuh Sendiri," CNN Indonesia, March 2, 2020, accessed March 5, 2020). Less than three weeks since Indonesia announced its first case of the virus, its death toll had reached 25—higher than any other Southeast Asian Country. As of Thursday, March 19, Indonesia reported 82 new coronavirus cases, the biggest daily increase for the country.

The public was left hanging, not knowing for certain what happened, what would happen, and what was to expect. On March 13, President Jokowi made a shocking statement, admitting that the government has not made public all data concerning the spread of the coronavirus (Dyaning Pangestika, "We don't want people to panic': Jokowi says on lack of transparency about COVID cases," *The Jakarta Post*, March 14, 2020, accessed March 16, 2020)

Indeed, we did not deliver certain information to the public because we did not want to stir panic. We have worked hard to overcome this, since the novel coronavirus outbreak can happen regardless of the country border. . . . We will inform the public eventually. However, we have to think of the possibility that the public will react to it by panicking or worrying, as well as the effect on the recovered patients. Every country has different policies

In his supporting statement, Coordinating Minister for Human Development and Cultural Affairs, Muhadjir Effendy asserts (Purnomo 2020) the government's position of not wanting to cause unrest was already decided during a limited cabinet meeting at the Presidential Palace several days before the first cases were announced on March 2. The President said not to use the term "crisis" in handling coronavirus to avoid causing panic.

President Jokowi's sentence, "We will inform the public eventually. However, we have to think of the possibility that the public will react to it by panicking or worrying" convey a message that he is completely aware of the situation and had no intention to cover things up. By not fully disclosing the information regarding COVID-19 situation, he had taken necessary preventative measures to avoid conflict and to maintain harmony. This statement, however, contrasts to another Javanese cultural value which emphasizing honesty and that a person's word should be sufficient to engender trust (Mulder 1978). During a crisis context, transparency is an absolute condition to ensure public rights to know, to help them manage uncertainty, to suppress rumor, and to guide public to do protective action.

Hashtag movement

Table 8.1 provides information on how on each turning point, public frustration scales up. This is due to lack of trust, concerns, and disappointment to Indonesian government's administrative for not taking the issue seriously, for not being transparent, for not disclosing to the public the advent of COVID-19 cases, and for delivering misguided tourism promotion campaign. During the first turning point, mass media contributed widely in shaping public's perception toward COVID-19. Public are exposed to "jokes" made by officials that tend to downplaying the severity of the disease and the potential risks that it may hold. Health Minister Terawan, for example, mentioned that people should not get too worry and just "enjoy" and "relax." Terawan, as further quoted by various media, said that the key to immunity is a healthy mind and body. Minister of Transportation, Budi Karya Sumadi joked that "COVID-19 will not hit us, as we eat *nasi kucing* every day." From Javanese cultural perspective, the use of calming words and jokes is seen as positive politeness strategy (Brown and Levinson 1978, 1987) to lower the tension, to maintain balance, and to avoid public panic. These comments however, do not prepare public for consequences and risks that they may counter as the coronavirus begins to spread. In seeking for alternative information, public turned to social media.

Daily update provided by an independent organization, "*Kawal* COVID-19" (Guard COVID-19) shows that as of April 15, Indonesia had 5,136 confirmed cases and 469 deaths, the most COVID-19 deaths in any Asian country outside of China. This situation has caused public panic and widespread distrust of President Jokowi's government's ability to manage the outbreak. Through social media, such as Twitter, people began to promote and share hashtag #Lockdown-Now, which demands the government to immediately performing a lockdown, especially in Jakarta, and other focal points for the country coronavirus spread ("Korban Corona di RI Kian Tinggi, Lockdown Makin Menggema," CNN Indonesia, March 24, 2020, accessed April 12, 2020). Turning point three becomes the moment for social media users to deploy the hashtag #IndonesiaTerserah (#WhateverIndonesia) to express their frustration over the public's apparent disregard for physical distancing measures and the government's inconsistent COVID-19 policies. Members of the general public have since tweeted #IndonesiaTerserah in solidarity with medical practitioners who have continued risking their lives to treat COVID-19 patients on the front lines. The hashtag #IndonesiaTerserah became a trending topic on Twitter and as mid-May 2020 had been tweeted 27,000 times.

Conclusion

An outbreak, epidemic, and pandemic are a collection of issues of health risk that trigger media reportage. This study found that Indonesian government's pandemic communication is strongly guided by Javanese cultural values that focus on maintaining harmony and balance. During the first three months of the outbreak, media discourse strongly highlight the importance of ensuring that "everything" is under control and that government has everything prepared to prevent the coronavirus from entering the country. Contesting the absence of alternative narrative on COVID-19 in mass media, especially potential risks and the impact of government's policy/interventions to prevent the spread of COVID-19 toward various groups in society, public turned their heads on the social media platform. Public reaction during the second and third turning points of the outbreak reflect the need for reliable information and interventions that would address the uncertainty and answer public needs. More studies need to be done to learn and unpack how the Indonesian government's discourse and directives are, particularly during the "New Normal" period where Indonesians are advised to live with the virus, while it is not yet contained.

References

Altheide, David, and David Altheide. 1987. "Ethnographic Content Analysis." *Qualitative Sociology* 10, no. 1 (April 1): 65–77. http://search.proquest.com/docview/60939929/.

Balaratnasingam, Sivasankaran, and Aleksandar Janca. 2006. "Mass Hysteria Revisited." *Current Opinion in Psychiatry* 19, no. 2 (March): 171–74.

Berg, Bruce L. 1995. *Qualitative Research Methods for the Social Sciences*. Boston, MA: Allyn & Bacon.

Brown, Penelope, and Stephen S. Levinson. 1987. *Politeness: Some Universals in Language Usage*. Cambridge: Cambridge University Press.

Brown, Penelope, and Stephen S. Levinson. 1978. "Universals in Language Usage: Politeness Phenomena." In *Questions and Politeness: Strategies in Social Interaction*, edited by E. N. Goody, 1st ed. London, New York and Melbourne: Cambridge University Press.

Fairclough, Norman. 1995. *Critical Discourse Analysis: The Critical Study of Language*. London: Longman.

Foucault, Michel, and Michel Foucault. 1972. *The Archaeology of Knowledge and the Discourse on Language*. New York: Pantheon Books.

Geertz, Clifford. 1976. *The Religion of Java*. Chicago: Chicago University Press.

Geertz, Hildred. 1961. *The Javanese Family: A Study of Kinship and Socialization*. New York: Free Press of Glencoe.

Hefner, Robert. 2000. *Civil Islam: Muslims and Democratization in Indonesia*. Princeton: Princeton University Press.

Hermann, Charles F. 1963. "Some Consequences of Crisis Which Limit the Viability of Organizations." *Administrative Science Quarterly* 8, no. 1 (June 1): 61–82.

Holmes, Bev J., Natalie Henrich, Sara Hancock, and Valia Lestou. 2009. "Communicating with the Public During Health Crises: Experts' Experiences and Opinions." *Journal of Risk Research* 12, no. 6 (September 1): 793–807. www.tandfonline.com/doi/abs/10.1080/13669870802648486.

Lee, Sherman A. 2020. "Coronavirus Anxiety Scale: A Brief Mental Health Screener for COVID-19 Related Anxiety." *Death Studies* 44, no. 7 (July 2): 393–401. www.tandfonline.com/doi/abs/10.1080/07481187.2020.1748481.

Legreco, Marianne, and Sarah J. Tracy. 2009. "Discourse Tracing as Qualitative Practice." *Qualitative Inquiry* 15, no. 9 (November): 1516–43.

Lofstedt, Ragnar E. 2006. "How Can We Make Food Risk Communication Better: Where Are We and Where Are We Going?" *Journal of Risk Research* 9, no. 8 (December): 869–90.

Magnis-Suseno, Franz. 1981. *Javanese Ethics and Worldview: The Javanese Idea of the Good Life*. Jakarta: PT Gramedia Pustaka Utama.

Mulder, Niels. 1978. *Mysticism and Everyday Life in Contemporary Java*. Singapore: Singapore University Press.

Pieri, Elisa. 2019. "Media Framing and the Threat of Global Pandemics: The Ebola Crisis in UK Media and Policy Response." *Sociological Research Online* 24, no. 1: 73–92.

Purnomo, Wayan Agus. 2020. "Menyangkal Krisis Menuai Bencana." https://majalah. tempo.co/read/laporan-utama/159957/salah-langkah-jokowi-hadapi-wabah-corona.

Quinn, Sandra Crouse, and Supriya Kumar. 2014. "Health Inequalities and Infectious Disease Epidemics: A Challenge for Global Health Security." *Biosecurity and Bioterrorism: Biodefense Strategy, Practice, and Science* 12, no. 5 (September 1): 263–73.

Sairin, Sjafri. 2010. *Riak-riak pembangunan; perspektif antropologi*. Yogyakarta: Media Wacana.

Seeger, Matthew, and Timothy L. Sellnow. 2019. *Communication in Times of Trouble*. Hoboken, NJ: Wiley-Blackwell.

Sneddon, James. 2003. *The Indonesian Language: Its History and Role in Modern Society*. Sydney: University of New South Wales Press.

Ulmer, Robert R., Timothy L. Sellnow, and Matthew W. Seeger. 2015. *Effective Crisis Communication: Moving from Crisis to Opportunity*, 3rd ed. Thousand Oaks, CA: Sage.

Vaughan, Elaine, Timothy Tinker, and Elaine Vaughan. 2009. "Effective Health Risk Communication About Pandemic Influenza for Vulnerable Populations." *American journal of public health* 99, no. S2 (October 1): S324–S32. http://search.proquest.com/docview/67671192/.

Weick, Karl. 1993. "The Collapse of Sensemaking in Organizations: The Mann Gulch Disaster." *Administrative Science Quarterly* 38, no. 4 (December 1). http://search.proquest.com/docview/1301302435/.

Xiang, Yu-Tao, Yuan Yang, Wen Li, Ling Zhang, Qinge Zhang, Teris Cheung, and Chee H. Ng. 2020. "Timely Mental Health Care for the 2019 Novel Coronavirus Outbreak Is Urgently Needed." *The Lancet Psychiatry* 7, no. 3 (March): 228–29.

Wang, Yenan, Yu Di, Junjie Ye, Wenbin Wei, and Yenan Wang. 2020. "Study on the Public Psychological States and Its Related Factors During the Outbreak of Coronavirus Disease 2019 (COVID-19) in Some Regions of China." *Psychology, Health & Medicine* ahead-of-print, no. ahead-of-print (March 30): 1–10. http://search.proquest.com/docview/2384819041/.

9 Pathological borders

How the coronavirus pandemic strengthened depictions of the Cyprus partition in the media and by the government

Daniele Nunziata

The modern history of Cyprus has been marred by the violence of intercommunal conflict that led to partition by 1974. Following a failed coup by Greece, and military invasion by Turkey, the past decades have seen the island's two largest linguistic communities remain geographically divided. Speakers of Cypriot Greek live in the southern part of the island that remains under the control of the Republic of Cyprus while speakers of Cypriot Turkish live in the breakaway state of the "Turkish Republic of Northern Cyprus," recognized only by Turkey.

There were few changes until 2003 when border-crossings were opened in the Green Line between the two sides. This allowed Cypriots to travel across in unprecedented ways, opening up new possibilities for employment and dialogue. The moment was heralded in the international press as an inspirational deconstruction of the world's last remaining divided capital, and parallels were made with the fall of the Berlin Wall (Woollacott 2003).

On February 29, 2020, however, the border-crossings were closed for the first time in almost two decades. Reportedly due to fears of the spread of the burgeoning coronavirus outbreak, the border closures became associated with the so-called Cyprus problem. It fueled a rise in xenophobic attitudes toward Cypriots living on the other side of the partition as well as migrants from outside the island, inspired by increased bloodshed against refugees on the Greece–Turkey border earlier that same month. Protests in its capital by left-wing, anti-partition activists resulted in demonstrators being pepper-sprayed by the Republic of Cyprus police. Right-wing football hooligans waved anti-migrant placards in Nicosia while covering their faces. It was an exceptional escalation of violence on the border that eclipsed anything that had been observed in decades.

This chapter will analyze the ways in which coronavirus has remarkably entered into political debates surrounding the "Cyprus problem" and how various kinds of media have been used to engage with it. Of particular focus is how the (Greek-speaking) President of the Republic of Cyprus, Nicos Anastasiades, used Twitter, mere days after the border closure, to express his position that the Cypriot border ought to remain closed in the future due to the perceived threat of so-called illegal migration. As such, temporary measures in response to the coronavirus outbreak appear to have been co-opted to justify more permanent division on, and of, the island. Anastasiades has employed language that echoes international media coverage of events pertaining to migration and displacement on the (symbolically related) Greece–Turkey border and further afield to populist discourse in the EU and the United States. The chapter will compare Anastasiades' social media posts with those of his Turkish-speaking counterpart, the internally elected leader of the northern part of the island, Mustafa Akıncı, and the response by the United Nations Peacekeeping Force in Cyprus (installed in 1964).

Central to this investigation is an analysis of how politicians appropriate social media as legislative communication tools. It might well be suggested that social media enable a more democratic engagement in politics through the creation of "[o]nline communities that do not meet in a physical space" but in which each member has an equal voice and "can be effective agents of change" (Gordon 2017, xvi–xvii). In reality, however, Deborah Johnson (2003) has shown that the internet often only permits a unidirectional movement of ideas and values from a politician to their audience; the internet is routinely "used to facilitate a pattern of communication that predated it, namely one-to-many flow of information from candidates . . . to citizens and potential voters" (11). As such, a comparison can be made with Pierre Bourdieu's theory of "cultural reproduction" (Bourdieu and Passeron 1990) in ways that demonstrate how social media today have replaced preceding print media and education as instruments through which politicized ideas are reproduced throughout society in order to maintain dominant power structures and enable the socialization of a target audience. Social media posts are, by their very nature, the easiest form through which words can be reproduced verbatim (copied-and-pasted). This is even aided by immediate online translations that are sometimes automatically generated by the applications being used. Fuchs and Trottier (2015) note that "[a]ll computing systems, and therefore all web applications, and also all forms of media can be considered social because they store and transmit human knowledge that originates in social relations in society" (5). Crucial to this is the understanding that social media are part of an existing genealogy of media systems that share information socially and that help create societal structures themselves. Nonetheless, social media mark the apotheosis of this history by becoming the *most* social of already-social modes of media relations because of the immediacy, accessibility, and affordability of using applications like Twitter. As a consequence, social media are the most streamlined and effective way in which "cultural reproduction" can occur today, allowing for easy and unidirectional indoctrination from politician to citizen based on maintaining power. It, therefore, has unparalleled influence in shaping societies—either by creating substitute online communities or by insidiously impacting physical societies through mass-media indoctrination.

In the case of Cyprus, political uses of social media have not received adequate study. Twitter posts by politicians like Akıncı and Anastasiades are careful in their choices of language and translation in order to maximize the political impact of their words on citizens. Hubert Faustmann (2009) has observed how, on the island, political "parties have developed quite efficient mechanisms to control the electoral behaviour of their clientele," often through "personal contacts" (27–28).

While he is primarily alluding to established methods like labor unions and even practices akin to bribery, this assessment now needs to be extended to newer methods like social media as means of establishing "personal contacts" with a technologically savvy generation. Politicians enter people's residences through computers and smartphones. In novel ways, "social media enable both citizens and politicians to circumvent the media, and directly influence each other within this networked new media environment" (D'heer and Verdegem 2014, 82). Nonetheless, it is worth putting pressure on this argument to stress that the "influence" politicians have over citizens through online media is often more dominant, to the extent that politicians can "circumvent" *both* traditional media and the views of unverified, semianonymous internet users. For conservative politicians, like Anastasiades, social media can be used to reaffirm right-leaning positions on both the "Cyprus problem" and immigration, arguing for firmer closures of the Green Line. From its onset, the coronavirus pandemic has been appropriated, through the influence of social media, to control Cypriot citizens' views of the existing division and of ideas about globalization itself—despite the irony of the internet being the prime facilitator of today's globalized world.

Anastasiades and the use of social media to further national borders

At the end of February, four border-crossings were shut by the Republic of Cyprus as a preventative measure against the possible spread of coronavirus between the south and north. A military-guarded embargo on movement across the Green Line was set to last one week, but the remaining border-crossings were subsequently closed and the roadblocks were extended indefinitely.

The government's motives for this are a source of suspicion. Indeed, days after the closures were announced on medical grounds, Anastasiades released a statement on Twitter offering a coded sociopolitical reason for the decision. He announced his contentment toward the border closures and that he had conveyed to his norther counterpart, Akıncı, "our grave concern regarding the organised and increasing illegal flow of migrants through the Green Line, underlining that appropriate measures must be taken in order to prevent the further exacerbation of the situation" (@AnastasiadesCY, March 4, 2020a). The first person pronoun here refers to him and his parliament and not an act of collaboration between Akıncı and Anastasiades. The declaration is a gesture by the most senior member of the southern government to appropriate the coronavirus outbreak to promote explicitly anti-immigrant policies. The "increasing illegal flow of migrants" to which the president alludes appropriates negative imagery about globalization to posit tacit links between the pandemic and a right-wing view of migration. In other words, globalization, for Anastasiades, is a process producing "increasing [unwanted] flow[s]" of peoples (so-called illegal immigrants) and phenomena (a deadly virus). Migrants are here demonized as sources of (figurative) disease for the safety of the government-controlled part of the island. Notably, the use of the adjective "grave" and its connotations of death directly associate the movement of migrants and refugees with the ability of coronavirus to cause infection and fatality. This is subsequently internalized on the island in the form of "appropriate measures" to maintain nationalist boundaries and division.

This division is not simply between Cypriot citizens and non-Cypriot migrants, but also one which draws on the partition of Cypriots living on either side of the Green Line. The border closures denied movement between Greek-speakers and Turkish-speakers, reducing the hope of the 2003 openings as a stepping-stone for future reconciliation, and became a physical and symbolic reconsolidation of the existing partition. Moreover, the consciously vague reference to "migrants" allows it to be used as a catch-all term that includes refugees associated with the contemporary crises of the Mediterranean as well as the perceived threat of set-tlers from Turkey living in northern Cyprus. Since 1974, Ankara has been engaged in encouraging people from Turkey to settle in the northern part of the island, thereby altering its demographics by increasing the number of Turkish-speakers. Anastasiades, by drawing on anxieties associated with this process held by some in the south of the island, is implicitly suggesting that the decades-long process of Turkish settlers arriving on the island is a cause for reinforcing the division to prevent the possible movement of Turkish settlers from the north to the south. Panic surrounding coronavirus as a symbol of the worst outcome of globalization is elided with *externally based* fears about the Mediterranean "refugee crisis" disseminated by the international press and *internal*, preexisting fears about the security of the island as a consequence of the unresolved "Cyprus problem." One of two scenarios is the case here: either the borders were closed as a national-ist strategy disguised as a medically approved act of quarantine (before its true motives were revealed through social media) or a justified act of quarantine was immediately co-opted to promote xenophobic and divisive rhetoric with a view for these notions to inform future policy after the coronavirus pandemic subsides.

In addition, English translation opens the president's words up to an interna-tional audience, placing his anti-migrant rhetoric in parallel with existing right-wing, populist discourse disseminated from the United Kingdom and the United States. There is one interesting translation choice between the two versions of the tweet that indicates differences in intended interpretations by different linguis-tic audiences (of Greek-speakers and English-speakers). The English, as already noted, describes "our grave concern" (@AnastasiadesCY, March 4, 2020a). The phrase, alongside the connotations of death, allows the first-person plural to include the Anglophone reader—which might comprise those sympathetic to anti-immigrant populism outside the island—while also offering a confusing per-spective that appears to *almost* include the leader of the northern part of the island. This second motive attempts to illustrate, to the international community, Anasta-siades' influence over Akıncı and, thus, his tacit control over the policies affecting the north. This implication is misleading as Anastasiades has no *de facto* impact on the policies of northern Cyprus. In the original Greek version, however, Ana-stasiades uses the first-person plural to refer only and directly to southern Cyprus, in which Greek-speaking Cypriots are the only people included (as primary target readers and the effected citizens to whom he is referring). In Greek, he says that he has conveyed *to* Akıncı the "έντονη ανησυχία της πλευράς μας" (@Anasta-siadesCY, March 4, 2020b), or *the intense concern of our side* (my translation). What is important is his use of "our side" to refer to Greek-speaking Cypriots *in Greek*, while using the vague "our grave concern" that can incorporate a wider readership in English. In addition, while the English version describes "illegal" movements across the Green Line, the Greek describes the entering of migrants into the Republic of Cyprus ("Κυπριακή Δημοκρατία") itself (@AnastasiadesCY, March 4, 2020b). The same Greek word for migrants is sometimes applied to Turkish settlers in the north. The Greek-language post, therefore, is more loaded with nationalist signifiers that right-wing, Greek-speakers on the island would view as signaling a personal, existential threat. The English version, however, uses less precise terminology; on first reading, it is unclear who is included in "our" and which "migrants" are being alluded to. This allows it fade into general-ist anti-immigrant discourses appearing across the world that view "migrants" as a homogenized threat to any nation.

It is no surprise, given Cyprus' political history, that events in Greece and Turkey would inform its internal policies. Anastasiades' language came in the aftermath of increased violence inflicted on refugees moving between the territorial borders of Greece and Turkey. Indeed, the president's description of his "grave concern" for Cyprus echoes the words of Antonio Guterres, UN Secretary General, released days earlier (February 28) to express his "grave concern" for the heighted vio-lence in Idlib, northern Syria (BBC News 2020). The same day, Turkey responded to this accelerated threat to its own border with Syria by fast-tracking the move-ment of Syrian refugees northward into Greece, resulting in escalating bloodshed on this frontier with both Greece and the EU. The international press responded with headlines directly emphasizing this perceived impact on continental and national boundaries. *The Independent* published an article titled, "Turkey to Open Borders and Let Refugees into Europe" (Trew 2020), in which Gueterres' afore-mentioned statement—his "grave concern" about Idlib—was quoted. It also cites the similar lexis used by the UK's Foreign Secretary, Dominic Raab, to refer to events in Syria that week as "the gravest humanitarian crisis of the entire [Syrian civil] war." It is important to stress that it was the very next day, February 29, that the Republic of Cyprus began closing its own border. While nominally ascribed to the coronavirus outbreak, the proximity to events in neighboring Greece, Tur-key, and Syria suggest a political and existential motivation to safeguard southern Cyprus' own symbolic border with Turkey (via northern Cyprus) as a reaction against Turkey's ostensible affront to its boundaries with Europe and/or the EU. The widely reported "grave concern" felt by members of the international com-munity for Turkey's actions in response to the "refugee crisis" directly informed Anastasiades' similarly worded "grave concern" for the relationship between his republic and the Ankara-supported northern part of Cyprus.

That same phrase, "grave concern," also echoes other descriptions of Recep Tayyip Erdoğan's policies in the international press as well as populist motifs shared on social media. First, it reproduces language used by the EU's Euro-pean External Action Service (likewise shared on Twitter) to depict their "grave concern" about Erdoğan's decision to sanction drilling in and around Cyprus' exclusive economic zone (EEZ) in May 2019 (@eu_eeas, May 4, 2019). Anastasiades directly responded to this by describing Turkey's actions as a "grave violation" (Al Jazeera 2019) against Cypriot sovereignty—illustrating how the events of March 2020 are in direct continuity with those of the preceding year, with the president's description of the border closures inheriting the language he previously used to refer to Turkey almost a year earlier. The border closures do not mark an entirely new event based solely on coronavirus, but are part of an existing series of political moves between Cyprus and Turkey dating back years.

In addition, Anastasiades' 2020 message shows echoes of the social media accounts of other right-wing politicians. In March 2019, for instance, Trump declared on Twitter that "Mexico is doing NOTHING to help stop the flow of illegal immigrants to our Country" (@realDonaldTrump, March 28, 2019). Months later, he similarly tweeted that "Mexico should immediately stop the flow of people . . . to our Southern Border" (@realDonaldTrump, June 3, 2019). Anastasiades' tweet incorporates and reiterates this lexis: the "grave concern"; the use of the first-person plural to refer to "our" nation; and the claims about migrant "flows." The jingoist language about the US–Mexico border are echoed in Anastasiades' tweets to present a comparable nationalist reaction to migration and against the national *other* for his own state, Turkey—all of which is masked by claims that the closure was ordered solely as a reaction to the pandemic.

The UN's and Akıncı's responses to the renewed division

It is pertinent to observe that the UN Peacekeeping Force in Cyprus (UNFICYP) did not release a press statement about the border closures until the day *after* Anastasiades' tweets. On March 5, it published a short, English-language statement on its official website. It stated that the UNFICYP is "concerned by the ongoing disruption caused to people on both sides," recommending the two "sides preserve the dialogue and coordination they have displayed in mutually agreeing to the opening of the crossings which have been an important confidence building measure between both communities" (United Nations Peacekeeping 2020). Notably, the statement expresses skepticism toward the medical justification of the closures, imploring the Republic of Cyprus to consult the Technical Committee on Health shared by the north and south rather than simply its own, internal resources. It implies that the closure is a decision with political ramifications "on both sides" that exceed the given healthcare rationalization. An accusation is inferred that the southern government was working in a politically isolationist manner and acting on the interests of the south rather than "both communities," specifically by ignoring the advice of any bicommunal organizations. This, alongside the timing of the statement's release, suggests that the UNFICYP was motivated to act in response to the closures as a *political*, not medical, measure. The president's heavy "grave concern" is here reduced somewhat to the UN's status as similarly, but less dramatically, "concerned."

Anastasiades responded defensively. He stated, in no uncertain terms, that the UNFICYP "has no jurisdiction over this issue. The health of the inhabitants of Cyprus is exclusively the concern of the Government of Cyprus and UNFICYP has no right to issue such a statement" (*Financial Mirror* 2020). Again, however, the discursive choices here are telling. While healthcare reasons form the basis of this statement, the administrative language of "jurisdiction" suggests a preoccupation with the republic's sovereignty, which is at the heart of both the border closures and the subsequent rejection of any intervention by the peacekeeping force. The "Government of Cyprus" is referred to in order to bolster the sole authority of Anastasiades' administration in the south, repudiating the involvement of any ostensibly outside forces, thereby tacitly excluding Akıncı and his cabinet from having any say on the healthcare of Cypriots. What is not clear is whether Anastasiades is expressing any desire to protect Turkish-speaking Cypriots from COVID-19. All that remains are vague and unstable movements across Anastasiades' social media posts about protecting "our" Greek-speaking part of Cyprus from migrants on March 4, followed by statements about protecting those under the rule of the "Government of Cyprus" (possibly also only the Greek-speakers) from threats to their "health." The border closures concern, and are justified according to, a broad signifier of contagion that vacillates arbitrarily across possible significations—migration or a virus—which are chosen to suit Anastasiades' given agenda.

Prior to the release of Anastasiades' tweets, Akıncı posted his own Twitter response to his telephone conversations with his southern counterpart on the day the border was closed, February 29, foreshadowing many of the UNIFCYP's worries. Akıncı noted forthright that "the situation created was nothing but torture and that it had nothing to do with the coronavirus struggle," before suggesting that "the virus is being planted between the two communities and this should be stopped as soon as possible" (@MustafaAkinici_1, February 29, 2020a). Like the UN agency, Akıncı views the closure as a political maneuver being masqueraded as a measure against the virus, disregarding the interests of "the two communities" in favor of just one. Implicitly, the events in Cyprus are not directly part of "the coronavirus struggle" but the preexisting political "struggle" of Cypriot partition. Of particular interest is the fact that the English terms "struggle" and "torture" very closely echo the terminology used to depict the Cypriot anti-colonial resistance against the British Empire in the 1950s. Akıncı's lexis, therefore, contains a coded warning that the closure of the border will return Cyprus to the intercommunal violence of its past, and revert any recent progress (after 2003) back to the bloodshed before and after Cyprus gained its independence (in 1960). It is precisely this which the UNIFCYP fears when it reminds Cypriot politicians of the benefits gained from the opening of the crossings.

While Anastasiades went on to depict his "grave concern" about migration, Akıncı's imagery of the closures as something being "planted" uses comparable motifs of life and death to present the border as a living, organic entity that requires responsible nurturing. Although Anastasiades sees the border—and its 2003 opening—as something that has already figuratively died and needs speedy amputation, Akıncı's more hopeful phrasing suggests that new possibilities can, and should, be "planted" by those invested in maintaining steady relations between "the two communities." Despite the force of these words, Akıncı's tweets were not quoted in any English-language media, except one article by *In-Cyprus* (2020). His views on the Cyprus problem have been marginalized by the international community, reflecting the issue Turkish-speaking Cypriots have in representing themselves beyond the island, and beyond the filter of either the Republic of Cyprus or the Republic of Turkey. Indeed, Akıncı, in comparable ways to Anastasiades, posted his tweets in both English and Turkish. While both versions are relatively similar, the Turkish contains a promise not included in the English: "Konuyla ilgili Birleşmiş ve Avrupa Birliği makamları ile de temas halinde olmaya devam edeceğiz" (@MustafaAkinici_1, February 29, 2020b)—or, *We will continue to be in contact with the relevant authorities in the UN and the EU* (my translation). Omitted from the English translation, this reassurance for only Turkish-speaking Cypriots is shielded from English speakers outside northern Cyprus due to a lack of faith in these global bodies—for which English is their primary language—to actively help Akıncı's administration. Only the government of the Republic of Cyprus, and not the northern part of the island, is a member of the UN and the EU. It is telling that the English-speaking press did not report on Akıncı's diplomatic, anti-partition words.

Conclusions

The coronavirus pandemic has been co-opted in peculiar ways in relation to the "Cyprus problem." It has been used as an excuse to strengthen the line of partition across the island through the evocation of right-wing populist discourse on social media, coupled with fears of disease as a negative symbol of globalization. The calcification of the border is an action that was arguably a long time in the planning but for which the excuse of quarantine provided a less controversial justification. Counter to Anastasiades' desire for renewed division, the UN and Akıncı have also used online platforms to call for more nuanced negotiation and mutual understanding: words that, in the current political climate, have been left unobserved.

References

Print works

Bourdieu, Pierre, and Jean-Claude Passeron. 1990 [1970]. *Reproduction in Education, Society and Culture*. Translated by Richard Nice. New York: SAGE Publishing.
D'heer, Evelien, and Pieter Verdegem. 2014. "An Intermedia Understanding of the Networked Twitter Ecology." In *Social Media in Politics: Case Studies on the Political Power of Social Media*, edited by Bogdan Pătruţ and Monica Pătruţ, 81–96. New York: Springer.

Faustmann, Hubert. 2009. "Aspects of Political Culture in Cyprus." In *The Government and Politics of Cyprus*, edited by Hubert Faustmann and James Ker-Lindsay, 17–44. Bern: Peter Lang.

Fuchs, Christian, and Daniel Trottier. 2015. "Theorising Social Media, Politics and the State: An Introduction." In *Social Media, Politics and the State: Protests, Revolutions, Riots, Crime and Policing in the Age of Facebook, Twitter and YouTube*, edited by Christian Fuchs and Daniel Trottier, 3–38. Oxford: Routledge.

Gordon, Steven. 2017. "Preface." In *Online Communities as Agents of Change and Social Movements*, edited by Steven Gordon, xv–xxiii. Hershey, PA: IGI Global.

Johnson, Deborah G. 2003. "Reflections on Campaign Politics, the Internet, and Ethics." In *The Civic Web: Online Politics and Democratic Values*, edited by David M. Anderson and Michael Cornfield, 9–18. Oxford: Rowman & Littlefield Publishers, Inc.

Online works

"Akinci [sic]: Checkpoints Did Not Close Because of the Coronavirus." *In-Cyprus*, March 5, 2020. Accessed May 11, 2020. https://in-cyprus.philenews.com/akinci-checkpoints-did-not-close-because-of-the-coronavirus/.

"Crossings Stay Closed as UN Raises Concerns." *Financial Mirror*, March 5, 2020. Accessed May 11, 2020. www.financialmirror.com/2020/03/05/crossings-stay-closed-as-un-raises-concern/.

"Second Turkish Drillship Arrives off Cyprus Amid 'Grave Concern'." *Al Jazeera*, July 8, 2019. Accessed May 11, 2020. www.aljazeera.com/ajimpact/turkish-drillship-arrives-cyprus-grave-concern-190708142152149.html.

"Syria War: Alarm After 33 Turkish Soldiers Killed in Attack in Idlib." *BBC News*, February 28, 2020. Accessed May 11, 2020. www.bbc.co.uk/news/world-middle-east-51667717.

Trew, Bel. 2020. "Turkey to Open Borders and Let Refugees into Europe, After 33 Soldiers Killed by Syrian Regime." *The Independent*, February 28, 2020. Accessed May 11, 2020. www.independent.co.uk/news/world/middle-east/turkey-border-open-refugees-migrants-greece-europe-syria-strike-a9364696.html.

United Nations Peacekeeping. 2020. "Statement on Closure of Crossing Points along the Buffer Zone." Last modified March 5, 2020. https://peacekeeping.un.org/en/statement-closure-of-crossing-points-along-buffer-zone.

Woollacott, Martin. 2003. "Free Movement May Still Heal the Division of Cyprus." *The Guardian*, May 9. Accessed May 11, 2020. www.theguardian.com/world/2003/may/09/cyprus.comment.

Social media posts

Akıncı, Mustafa (@MustafaAkinici_1). 2020a. "Tonight I Once Again Made a Phone Call with Mr. Anastasiades in the Chaotic Situation I Saw at the Kermiya—Metehan Crossing Point. I Pointed Out That the Situation Created Was Nothing but Torture and That It Had Nothing to Do with the Coronavirus Struggle."; "In Fact, I Said That the Virus Is Being Planted between the Two Communities and That This Should Be Stopped as Soon as Possible. I Hope This Last Talk Will Lead to a Positive Development." February 29, 2020. https://twitter.com/MustafaAkinci_1/status/1233852503378272257; https://twitter.com/MustafaAkinci_1/status/1233852575721672707.

———. 2020b. "Şimdi daha da netleşti. Bu yanlışa bir an önce son verilmesi lazım. Konuyla ilgili Birleşmiş Milletler ve Avrupa Birliği makamları ile de temas halinde olmaya devam edeceğiz. Kimsenin keyfi olarak her iki topluma da bu eziyeti çektirmeye hakkı yoktur . . ." *Twitter*, February 29, 2020. https://twitter.com/MustafaAkinci_1/status/1233814120752959488.

Anastasiades, Nicos (@AnastasiadesCY). 2020a. "I Conveyed to the Turkish Cypriot Leader, Mr. Akinci, Our Grave Concern Regarding the Organised and Increasing Illegal Flow of Migrants Through the Green Line, Underlining That Appropriate Measures Must Be Taken in Order to Prevent the Further Exacerbation of the Situation." *Twitter*, March 4, 2020. https://twitter.com/AnastasiadesCY/status/1235135761814564864.

———. 2020b. "Επικοινώνησα σήμερα με τον ΤΚ ηγέτη κ. Ακκιντζί, όπου του μετέφερα την έντονη ανησυχία της πλευράς μας για την οργανωμένη και αυξανόμενη παράνομη ροή μεταναστών στην Κυπριακή Δημοκρατία, τονίζοντας παράλληλα πως θα πρέπει να ληφθούν μέτρα αποτροπής του εν λόγω φαινομένου." *Twitter*, March 4, 2020. https://twitter.com/AnastasiadesCY/status/1235124096234594305.

European External Action Service (@eu_eeas). 2019. "'We Express Grave Concern Over Turkey's Announced Intention to Carry Out Drilling Activities within the Exclusive Economic Zone of Cyprus.' Read @FedericaMog's Full Statement Here." *Twitter*, May 4, 2019. https://twitter.com/eu_eeas/status/1124624506826498048.

Part III
Responses to regulation
Media as instruments of cooperation and representation

10 Digital media and COVID-19 in the UK and India

Challenges and constructive contributions

Indrani Lahiri, Debanjan Banerjee, K. S. Meena, Anish V. Cherian, and Maryam Alsulaimi

Coronavirus disease 2019 (COVID-19) in India and UK: the problem statement

The world has faced a new global health threat in the last few months. COVID-19 caused by SARS-CoV-2 has created a stirring impact on the global landscape. The World Health Organization has declared it as a "Public Health Emergency of International Concern" within one month of its origin at Wuhan, China, and subsequently after two months, it was declared as pandemic. Nearly four million people have been affected worldwide and more than 3,00,000 succumbing to the infection, the numbers rising as we speak (WHO COVID-19 Situation report, as on May 18, 2020). International borders have been sealed, economies slashed, travel restricted, and billions locked down at their own homes in an attempt to contain the viral spread. Every nation with its unique socioeconomic and cultural milieu has faced specific challenges during this outbreak.

The first case of COVID-19 was detected in India on January 30, 2020. It took till March 2020 for the number of affected to reach three figures, which has increased to more than a million at present. The infection had claimed the life of more than 6000 in India (Dantewadia and Devulapalli 2020). However, for a populous and socioethnically diverse subcontinent, there is much more beyond these statistics. The long-lasting psychosocial impact, exhaustion of already constrained public health resources, economic fallout, mass hysteria, and misinformation can be the real problem statement of COVID-19 in India, apart from the fatality rates. Though the infection rate of 1.8 is lower than most other countries, the decreased rates of testing fail to make it an assurance (Singh 2020). The WHO has commended India for having "tremendous capacity" to fight the pandemic, but at the same time warned about the impact of fake health news and the media (*Hindustan Times*, March 24, 2020).

Similarly, COVID-19 appeared in the UK in late January 2020, with the first confirmed case of the coronavirus reported on January 31 in the *British Medical Journal* (Razai et al. 2020). In that month, the UK's chief medical officers declared the risk level to be moderate. Cases in the UK then started to increase in February 2020 (Razai et al. 2020). In March 2020, the total deaths due to

COVID-19 in England and Wales were 3,372 (Campbell and Caul 2020) and 60 in Scotland (BBC Scotland, 2020). Since May 28, the government in England has initiated the easing of some lockdown restrictions, despite the high death rates (Vaughan 2020). At some point, the UK had lost 40,465 (Worldometer 2020). The UK government and the prime minister were criticized for their slow reactions to the emergency situation (Cowper 2020), but, after the number of cases increased dramatically, the UK government changed its plan on March 23, 2020. Prime Minister Boris Johnson announced a lockdown and responded more proactively to the pandemic (Hunter 2020). Nevertheless, according to critics, the lockdown messages contributed and continue to contribute toward further tensions and confusions, which the government has failed to respond and address (Edgerton 2020; Horton 2020; The Guardian 2020; Walker and Carrell 2020).

A public health information campaign was launched on January 31, 2020, to advise the public as to how they could lessen the risk of spreading coronavirus. Public Health England (PHE) details on their website the social media policy enacted by the UK government to inform the public about health incidents relating to COVID-19 (Public Health England 2020). Social media was used to share information and engage with other social media users. The members of the public could post responses or questions to these social media feeds. This ability to engage came with a strict code of conduct: the posting of comments and questions was clearly monitored, and a list of behaviors that would not be tolerated and so posts deleted were detailed on the same page (e.g., personal attacks, offensive language) (ibid.). The UK government utilized several social media platforms: Twitter, Facebook, LinkedIn, YouTube, Instagram, SlideShare, and their own blog (Public Health Matters) to reach members of the public with specific health concerns. The devolved assemblies have also undertaken comparable strategies by linking to NHS social media platform usage (Scottish Government 2020; Public Health Wales 2020; Public Health Agency 2020).

Conspiracies surrounding COVID-19 were first detailed by academics monitoring social media traffic of fake news. On March 23, Fish (2020) detailed academic concerns over conspiracy theories about the pandemic, which were hindering the national strategy to combat the virus. Dr Marc Faddoul (UC Berkeley) was cited, warning that social media platforms must do more to tackle misinformation. *British Medical Journal* (BMJ) (Pollock et al. 2020c) detailed concerns over how different information regarding contact tracing was spread in the UK, particularly when it came to discrepancies in the UK government's advice on contact tracing and testing for coronavirus and that provided by the World Health Organization (Dearden 2020; Hamzelou 2020; Press Association 2020). In fact, the BMJ came close to suggesting that the UK government was providing misinformation themselves over the length of time a person needed to self-isolate (Cowper 2020).

Misinformation has been ubiquitous across social platforming, as detailed by Brennen et al. (2020) in early April for Reuters Institute. They provided a go-to guide on what type of misinformation was being shared and how to combat it online. It took the UK government almost another two weeks to provide their guide to tackling misinformation (Lally and Christie 2020), subsequently transferring it to social media for sharing, ensuring that the public join in the effort to ensure no one comes to harm because of misinformation, and to keep people updated.

Hence, the backbone of the UK's PR campaign came in the form of its WhatsApp information service (Cabinet Office 2020). This social messaging service was free to use, and aimed to "provide official, trustworthy and timely information and advice" about COVID-19 and was specifically designed to combat misinformation that had been spread about the virus and how to combat it (UK Government 2020). Despite initial technical issues, the service was deemed as effective in warning about fake news spread on social media regarding the virus (Baraniuk 2020).

Social media and the pandemics: a long association

"Content is fire, social media is gasoline."

Jay Baer (2012)

Research shows that health communication and public need for information increases during disasters (Medford-Davis, Laura, and Bobby Kapur 2014). Anxiety and panic related to situational crisis impact human thinking and behavior, and social connectedness as well as integrity are vital for the well-being during these times. Social media has served this purpose in the recent viral outbreaks of Ebola in Africa, Zika in Brazil, and Nipah in India (Hyvärinen and Vos 2016). Various community interventions for public health have utilized the penetration and consumption of social media for outreach and awareness. The greatest advantage of knowledge dissemination over platforms like Facebook, WhatsApp, and Twitter is that it is dynamic and interactional, rather than passive consumption of information. Personal updates and interpersonal communication have proven to be effective channels of communication during the twenty-first century, when events can be witnessed and shared live with millions.

However, it is the same virtue of social media that brings upon its flip side, misinformation, and rumor mongering. Studies on human reactions to disasters have shown exaggerated fear response, illogical reasoning, and acceptance of "fast" solutions, contrary to the authenticity of evidence (Gantt and Gantt 2012). At times when the world is gripped with uncertainty, all that it takes is one senseless social media forward in the wrong hands to snowball the spread of fake news. This can spread not only panic, but also hate, stigma, and prejudice, more so when the use increases due to the imposed lockdown. Such racial "othering" had been propagated during the Ebola outbreak in Africa and the recent H1N1 influenza in Europe (Wilson 2013). Also, there is a huge gap between the magnitude of Facebook or WhatsApp's size, reach, linguistic diversity, and influence on one hand, and the limitations of the oversight board to look into localized propaganda on the other. As of the first quarter of 2020, Facebook has 2.7 billion monthly active users, which crosses 3 billion if WhatsApp, Messenger, and Instagram are accounted for

(Mansoor 2021; Statista 2020). They are available in 101 languages. For example, if a polarizing or fake message gets circulated in a local Indian dialect, its detection and debunking can be potent challenges. Mechanical translation into English would not reveal the true essence, and thus often go undetected and propagated during crisis times. The simultaneous reach to millions can aid in snowballing misinformation. Also, the "need to know" and "ease to communicate" can lead to "information pollution" that floods social media during infectious outbreaks.

COVID-19 in that sense has emerged as a "digital infodemic." Not one day has passed since it was declared as a pandemic that the social media platforms were not bombarded with videos, memes, and messages about the origin, transmission, and statistics of the outbreak. The content has ranged from conspiracy theories about coronavirus being used as biological weaponry to its extraterrestrial origin and finally the plethora of "believed" treatments available to cure it (Depoux et al. 2020). The effects vary from panic, fear mongering, stigma, and faulty treatment or precautionary measures. Ironically, the virus has hacked into human lives via social media much more than it has invaded the lungs. The content of social media related to COVID-19 effects on human response to the outbreak are discussed further in the subsequent section.

As mentioned before, COVID-19 has created a huge public global health crisis across the globe that is going to have long lasting impact on the lives of the people. The uncertainties of the cause, treatment, and the repercussion that it is bringing has left people vulnerable and distressed. With various governments across the world putting up norms for social distancing, hygiene, and many other things, what could be the role of mass media houses like WhatsApp and Facebook as they have become primary source of information for the people?

COVID-19 on Facebook, WhatsApp, and Instagram: promising findings from the UK and India

As more and more people are at home during the lockdown, there is a surge in viewership on social media platforms for COVID-19-related information, but what is consumed is far from factual and does not generate a rational discourse (Singh 2020). Maybe the best thing that has happened across a variety of social media platforms is the number of professional athletes, actors, celebrities, and influencers speaking and urging people to strictly follow the Government's lockdown orders, both in India and in the UK. This has been classically described by Bandura in his "social cognitive learning theory" as a method of behavior change based on modeling (Nabavi 2012).

However, people use social media not only for information, but also to propagate the circulated fake news. Of late, it was seen that social media platforms took responsibility for announcing that they were providing reliable source of information from valid agencies. Instagram, for example, announced that it would only include COVID-19 related posts and stories in their recommendation section that are published by official health organizations. Instagram and WhatsApp had technical glitches, with data security being at threat. Facebook, not far behind, recently had a "bug" that marked posts with reputable news articles as spam. According to the CEO Mark Zuckerberg, it was an error caused by the platform's spam detection system, but such errors can be potential vulnerabilities during such crisis times.

In the UK, the tone employed by officials (government, charities, media) was often markedly different to that of individual users, tending toward informative lexis, devoid of emotion. That said, even when the tone was informative, the accompanying images could be alarming. The media often used direct quotations to stir emotion, thereby putting the instigation of worry in the mouths of those cited, not their journalists. Some media proved to be making false claims, giving people false hope of a cure or what products to avoid. Some chose to avoid emotional descriptors and produce simple lists of facts with basic graphics that could be easily understood and have less potential to trouble their audience. Increasingly, posts (usually individual) utilized humor to make their point, adding welcome moments of levity, often consciously referencing the impact social media was having on people's mental health. Those who highlighted the kindness of others offered moments of joy for those overwhelmed by negative news. Responsible behavior reinforced positive vibes on the digital public sphere.

In India, just before the announcement of the nationwide lockdown till April 14, 2020, Prime Minister Narendra Modi reportedly called upon the nation and the various media houses, both print and online to support government efforts in tackling the pandemic and also advised them to present "positive news" and success stories related to COVID-19 (Sagar 2020). Bollywood actors who were diagnosed with COVID-19 and cured, shared their positive stories to break the social stigma and reinforce basic health hygiene. The consequent effect on public reaction is more facilitatory when it comes from public figures. This again is in line with Bandura's social learning theory, which has been used time and again as "entertainment-education" for behavior change in the masses (Singhal and Rogers 1999).

The recent pandemic has taught us, social media is uniquely equipped as an integral tool for public health during pandemics. Community outreach, awareness, organizing healthcare, training, and research can all be aided by social media in an effort to control the outbreak. The various ways are summarized in Table 10.1.

Success in social media and healthcare collaboration

As mentioned before, social media can serve as a powerful and integral tool of public health infrastructure. Careful liaison between media and healthcare personnel has shown to be beneficial at times of disasters. In a recent study by Li et al. (2020), the retrospective search trends in Google were used to predict COVID-19 infections in China. Banerjee and Nair (2020) proposed a community-based psychosocial toolkit, which will be delivered to primary healthcare providers through social media. The social networking platforms (Facebook, Twitter), and allied blogs (Twitter), media sharing (YouTube), content production (Blogger), information aggregation (Wikipedia), and virtual reality (Second Life) can enhance

Table 10.1 Constructive roles of social media during pandemics

Role of the social media during pandemics	Processes involved
Fighting false news and misinformation	• Using diagnostic and referral health tool (example: Facebook Preventive Health tool) • Individualized approach for evaluation, testing, counseling based on reported symptoms • Highlighting and debunking rumors, providing relevant data • Integrating data from search engines (like Google QHub) to understand and study trends of misinformation • Prevent information-overload and content related to xenophobia, stigma, and prejudice
Enabling digital health literacy	• Videoconferences and webinars • Live platforms (like Facebook, Instagram) for awareness campaigns • Liaison between journalists and physicians
Helping research during crisis	• Search data can be pooled and studied to understand the unmet needs • Community public health research
Resource and psychological preparedness during pandemics	• Liaising with public health platforms (WHO, CDC, ICMR, etc.) and forums like "Worldometer" to update statistics and trends of ongoing infection • Integrating essential service location and contact tracing using special applications • Counseling, mental health crisis intervention, and suicide prevention
Crisis communication	• Identifying priorities, providing relevant facts, and precautionary measures
Fighting stigma	• Community awareness campaigns • Information-Education-Communication (IEC) activities • Socioculturally and linguistically sensitive infographics
Facilitating public and mental health needs	• Geo-location facilities for identifying hotspot zones and case loads • "COVID-free" content for recreational purpose • Special services for those in quarantine • Training and health—communication between tertiary and primary healthcare
Aiding healthy use of media	• Advocate healthy use of technology • Regulated timelines and content

Source: © Indrani Lahiri, Debanjan Bannerjee, K.S. Meena, Anish V. Cherian, Maryam Alsulaimi 2021.

professional networking, education, health communication and promotion, patient care, and public health programs. This is especially vital during present times when interaction and discussion are restricted by "social distancing."

Social media personnel and physicians can be mutually trained in detection and debunking of fake news, using authentic information from global and regional public health agencies. Both the WHO and Indian Council of Medical Research (ICMR) have stressed upon the importance of social media in fighting misinformation and improving the Knowledge-Attitude-Practice (KAP) gap related to awareness of COVID-19 (Park, Thwaites, and Openshaw 2020). Like any collaborative approach, this too is fraught with challenges, namely, potential threat to digital privacy of patient's data, distribution of poor-quality information, information-overload with "digital clutter," damage to professional image, violation of personal–professional boundaries, and licensing or legal issues (Ventola 2014).

Conclusion

Social media has played a crucial role in connecting grieving communities globally to helping people in need, locally. At the same time, issues around digital literacy, digital sociality, and community resilience have surfaced and dominated the public discourses around the pandemic (Lahiri 2020). The link between resilience, engagement, and digital participation is underdeveloped in research. The Community Resilience Development Framework (Cabinet Office 2019a, 3) defines community resilience as "working with civil society to create social value and achieve a more resilient UK." The recent pandemic has reinforced the need for developing the public mental health agenda, particularly focusing on individual and collective experiences of the community as a method of preventing mental illness and disorders.

Digital sociality like digital literacy has cultural influences. Therefore, contextualizing digital society in a cultural context (Dijk 2012) is a precondition to understanding the digital sociality and digital media literacy of a nation. Digital media literacy is at the heart of tackling fake news on social media. An individual to survive through any distraction requires a higher level of cognitive and emotional ability to distinguish between the noise and the signal emerging out of a message. The cognitive and emotional ability can be enhanced through training and education by providing individuals with tools to understand the perspective. This perspective is constructed through a sociocultural environment that shapes an individual's understanding of a message. In times of crisis, an individual's exposure to external messages remains high and can affect psychological health, impacting their thinking and behavior (Cohut 2020; Gregoire 2015; McNaughton-Cassill 2001; Miller and Grandjean 2019). Information, Education and Communication (IEC) materials, in the form of posters, videos, photographs, brochures, and infomercials on social media from official sources could provide the right information to the public and also aids in curbing the spread of misinformation and rumors.

Finally, as the societies continue to grapple with the pandemic onslaught, and the resultant devastation, there is a serious need to develop digital social responsibility policy by the governments at all levels, to break the pernicious trend and hold the social media giants accountable for helping to permeate fake news, as billions of people access them. The credibility assessment of the social media posts linked to either public health or other sociopolitical issues are crucial to make the global community more prepared and resilient in facing such catastrophes in the future.

References

Baer, Jay. 2012. "New Research: Americans Hate Social Media Promotions." *Convince and Convert*. Accessed May 19, 2020. www.convinceandconvert.com/social-media-research/new-research-americans-hate-social-media-promotions/.

BBC Scotland. 2020. "Number of Scottish Coronavirus Deaths Reaches 60." 2020. *BBC News*. https://www.bbc.co.uk/news/uk-scotland-52104031.

Banerjee, Debanjan, and Vasundharaa S. Nair. 2020. "Handling the COVID-19 Pandemic: Proposing a Community Based Toolkit for Psycho-Social Management and Preparedness." *Asian Journal of Psychiatry* 51: 102152. Accessed DOI: 10.1016/j.ajp.2020.102152.

Baraniuk, Chris. 2020. "Coronavirus: UK's WhatsApp Bot Working after False Start. UK's Covid-19 WhatsApp Bot Works after False Start." *BBC*, March 26, 2020. www.bbc.co.uk/news/technology-52049520.

Brennen, J. Scott, Felix Simon, Philip N. Howard, and Rasmus Kleis Nielsen. 2020. "Types, Sources, and Claims of COVID-19 Misinformation Types, Sources, and Claims of COVID-19 Misinformation." *Reuters Institute for the Study of Journalism*. University of Oxford. April 7, 2020. https://reutersinstitute.politics.ox.ac.uk/types-sources-and-claims-covid-19-misinformation.

Cabinet, Office. 2019. "Community Resilience Development Framework—GOV.UK." *Assets.Publishing.Service. Gov.Uk.* Accessed 11 May 2020. www.gov.uk/government/publications/community-resilience-development-framework.

———. 2020. "Government Launches Coronavirus Information Service on WhatsApp." *GOV.UK*, March 25, 2020. www.gov.uk/government/news/government-launches-coronavirus-information-service-on-whatsap.

Campbell, Annie, and Sarah Caul. 2020. "Dataset Deaths Involving COVID-19, England and Wales: March 2020." *Office for National Statistics. Office for National Statistics.* April 16, 2020. www.ons.gov.uk/peoplepopulationandcommunity/birthsdeathsandmarriages/deaths/datasets/deathsinvolvingcovid19englandandwalesmarch2020.

Cohut, Maria. 2020. "How to Cope If the News Is Making You Anxious." *Medical News Today*, January 16, 2020. www.medicalnewstoday.com/articles/327516.

Cowper, Andy. 2020. "Covid-19: Are We Getting the Communications Right?" *The BMJ*, March, m919. https://doi.org/10.1136/bmj.m919.

Dantewadia, Pooja, and Sriharsha Devulapalli. 2020. "Delhi Deaths Double In A Week – Much Faster Than India Average." *Mint*. https://www.livemint.com/news/india/mint-covid-tracker-delhi-deaths-double-in-a-week-much-faster-than-india-average-11591247899730.html.

Dearden, Lizzie. 2020. "UK Goes against WHO Call for Countries to Test Every Coronavirus Case." *The Independent. Independent Digital News and Media*, March 14, 2020. www.independent.co.uk/news/health/coronavirus-update-testing-news-herd-immunity-who-uk-cases-map-a9402051.html.

Depoux, Anneliese, Sam Martin, Emilie Karafillakis, Raman Preet, Annelies Wilder-Smith, and Heidi Larson. 2020. "The Pandemic of Social Media Panic Travels Faster Than the COVID-19 Outbreak." *Journal of Travel Medicine* 27: taaa031.

Dijk, Jan Van. 2012. *Network Society. Place of Publication Not Identified*. London: Sage Publications.

Edgerton, David. 2020. "When It Comes to National Emergencies, Britain Has a Tradition of Cold Calculation | David Edgerton." *The Guardian. Guardian News and Media*, March 17, 2020. www.theguardian.com/commentisfree/2020/mar/17/national-emergencies-britain-government-health-covid-19-1940s-and-50s.

Statista. 2020. "Facebook MAU Worldwide 2020 | Statista. 2021." *Statista*. https://www. statista.com/statistics/264810/number-of-monthly-active-facebook-users-worldwide/.

Fish, Tom. 2020. "Coronavirus Conspiracy: Academic Reveals Social Media Spreading Harmful COVID-19 Fake News." *Express.co.uk*, March 23, 2020. www.express.co.uk/news/science/1259245/coronavirus-conspiracy-theory-spread-social-media-coronavirus-fake-news.

Gantt, Paul, and Ron Gantt. 2012. "Disaster Psychology: Dispelling the Myths of Panic." *Professional Safety* 57: 42–49.

Gregoire, Carolyn. 2015. "What Constant Exposure to Negative News Is Doing to Our Mental Health." *HUFFPOST*, February 19, 2015. www.huffingtonpost.co.uk/entry/violent-media-anxiety_n_6671732?ri18n=true.

The Guardian. 2020. "The UK Government's Woeful Response to the Coronavirus Outbreak | Letters." *The Guardian. Guardian News and Media*, March 19, 2020. www.theguardian.com/uk-news/2020/mar/19/the-uk-governments-woeful-response-to-the-coronavirus-outbreak.

Hamzelou, Jessica. 2020. "UK's Scientific Advice on Coronavirus Is a Cause for Concern." *New Scientist*, March 23, 2020. www.newscientist.com/article/2238186-uks-scientific-advice-on-coronavirus-is-a-cause-for-concern/.

Horton, Richard. 2020. "Scientists Have Been Sounding the Alarm on Coronavirus for Months. Why Did Britain Fail to Act? | Richard Horton." *The Guardian. Guardian News and Media*, March 18, 2020. www.theguardian.com/commentisfree/2020/mar/18/coronavirus-uk-expert-advice-wrong.

Hunter, David J. 2020. "Covid-19 and the Stiff Upper Lip—The Pandemic Response in the United Kingdom." New England *Journal of Medicine* 382, no. 16. https://doi.org/10.1056/nejmp2005755.

Hyvärinen, Jenni, and Marita Vos. 2016. "Communication Concerning Disasters and Pandemics." *The Handbook of International Crisis Communication Research*, 96–107. https://doi:10.1002/9781118516812.ch10.

Iqbal, Mansoor. 2021. "Facebook Revenue and Usage Statistics (2021)." *Business of Apps*. https://www.businessofapps.com/data/facebook-statistics/.

J Ryan, Michael. 2020. "India Has Tremendous Capacity, Must Continue To Take Aggressive Action Against Covid-19: WHO." *Hindustan Times*. https://www.hindustantimes.com/india-news/india-has-tremendous-capacity-must-continue-to-take-aggressive-action-against-covid-19-who/story-QZztbYCVDcjai73BujH9FP.html.

Lahiri, Indrani. n.d. "Community Resilience Is the Way Forward: Critically Reflective Academic Commentary." *Journal of Mental Health Education*. Accessed July 24, 2020. http://jmhedu.org/special-edition/brief-commentary/community-resilience-is-the-way-forward-critically-reflective-academic-commentary/.

Lally, Clare, and Lorna Christie. 2020. "COVID-19 Misinformation. A Purple Portcullis Accompanied by the Words UK Parliament." *POST*, April 24, 2020. https://post.parliament.uk/analysis/covid-19-misinformation/.

Li, Cuilian, Li Jia Chen, Xueyu Chen, Mingzhi Zhang, Chi Pui Pang, and Haoyu Chen. 2020. "Retrospective Analysis of the Possibility of Predicting the COVID-19 Outbreak from Internet Searches and Social Media Data, China, 2020." *Eurosurveillance* 25, no. 10: 2000199.

McNaughton-cassill, Mary E. 2001. "The News Media and Psychological Distress." *Anxiety, Stress & Coping* 14, no. 2: 193–211. doi:10.1080/10615800108248354.

Medford-Davis, Laura N., and G. Bobby Kapur. 2014. "Preparing for Effective Communications During Disasters: Lessons from a World Health Organization Quality Improvement Project." *International Journal of Emergency Medicine* 7: 15.

Miller, Libby, and Alicia Grandjean. 2019. "The News and Mental Health: Would You Filter Out Bad News If You Could?." *BBC R&D*. https://www.bbc.co.uk/rd/blog/2019-08-news-mood-filter-mental-health.

Nabavi, R. T. 2012. "Bandura's Social Learning Theory & Social Cognitive Learning Theory." *Theory of Developmental Psychology* 1–24.

Park, Mirae, Ryan S. Thwaites, and Peter J. M. Openshaw. 2020. "COVID-19: Lessons from SARS and MERS." *European Journal of Immunology* 50: 308.

Pollock, Allyson M., Peter Roderick, K. K. Cheng, and Bharat Pankhania. 2020c. "Covid-19: Why Is the UK Government Ignoring WHO's Advice?" *The BMJ*, March, m1284. https://doi.org/10.1136/bmj.m1284.

Press Association. 2020. "Discrepancies in Covid-19 Deaths 'To Be Put Right', Says First Minister." *Oxford Mail*. https://www.oxfordmail.co.uk/news/national/18409055.discrepancies-covid-19-deaths-to-put-right-says-first-minister/.

Public Health Agency Northern Ireland. 2020. "COVID-19: What Is the Situation in Northern Ireland?" *HSC Public Health Agency*, April 2020. www.publichealth.hscni.net/news/covid-19-what-situation-northern-ireland.

Public Health England. 2020. "Coronavirus (COVID-19): Guidance And Support." *GOV. UK*. https://www.gov.uk/coronavirus.

Public Health Wales. 2020. "Social Media Assets." *Public Health Wales*. https://phw.nhs.wales/topics/latest-information-on-novel-coronavirus-covid-19/coronavirus-resources/social-media-assets/.

Razai, Mohammad S., Katja Doerholt, Shamez Ladhani, and Pippa Oakeshott. 2020. "Coronavirus Disease 2019 (Covid-19): A Guide for UK GPs." *The BMJ*, March, 368. https://doi.org/10.1136/bmj.m800.

Sagar. 2020. "Speaking Positivity to Power: Hours before lockdown." *The Caravan*, March 31. Accessed May 19, 2020. https://caravanmagazine.in/media/hours-before-lockdown-modi-asked-print-media-owners-editors-refrain-negative-covid-coverage.

Scottish Government. 2020. "Coronavirus (COVID-19): Social Distancing in Non-Healthcare Public Services." Scottish Government. www.gov.scot/publications/coronavirus-covid-19-social-distancing-in-non-healthcare-public-services/pages/further-information-and-how-to-reduce-risk-of-infection/.

Singh, Bhupen. 2020. "Media in the Time of COVID-19." *EPW Engage*, April 18. Accessed May 19, 2020. www.epw.in/engage/article/media-time-covid-19.

Singhal, A., and E. Rogers. 1999. *Entertainment-Education: A Communication for Social Change*. Mahwah, NJ: Lawrence Erlbaum (now Routledge): 98.

UK Government. 2020. "Social Media Use." *GOV.UK*. www.gov.uk/government/organisations/public-health-england/about/social-media-use.

Vaughan, Adam. 2020. "Why Have There Been So Many Coronavirus Deaths in the UK?" *New Scientist,* June 3, 2020. www.newscientist.com/article/mg24632853-300-why-have-there-been-so-many-coronavirus-deaths-in-the-uk/.

Ventola, C. Lee. 2014. "Social Media and Health Care Professionals: Benefits, Risks, and Best Practices." *Pharmacy and Therapeutics* 39: 491.

Walker, Peter, and Severin Carrell. 2020. "All UK Chief Medical Officers Rejected Lower Virus Threat Level, Source Says." *The Guardian. Guardian News and Media*, June 2, 2020. www.theguardian.com/uk-news/2020/jun/02/chris-whitty-vetoed-lowering-of-coronavirus-alert-level.

Wilson, Kalpana. 2013. *Race, Racism and Development: Interrogating History, Discourse and Practice*. London: Zed Books Ltd.

Worldometer. 2020. "United Kingdom." Accessed June 3, 2020. www.worldometers.info/coronavirus/country/uk/.

11 New Zealand's success in tackling COVID-19

How Ardern's government effectively used social media and consistent messaging during the global pandemic

Nelly Martin-Anatias

Introduction

The World Health Organization officially declared the emergence of COVID-19 as a global pandemic in March 2020. In Aotearoa New Zealand (hereafter NZ), which had been prepared to memorialize the mass shooting at a Christchurch mosque that took place a year earlier, March took on new significance this year, particularly after the Prime Minister's official announcement that the nation would be on lockdown that lasted for six weeks, starting March 25, 2020, 11:59 PM.

The country has decided to "go hard" and "go early" to fight the virus that was originated in Wuhan, China, and has spread globally due to human social mobility. In late March 2020, the epicenter of the virus had shifted from Wuhan to Italy; at the time of writing, it has shifted to the United States. By late April 2020, the pandemic had affected 210 countries and territories around the world (Google 2020; Worldometer 2020). Some nations are struggling to respond, while others appear to have responded better than others. Seeing and following how the NZ Prime Minister (PM) responded to the pandemic, the majority of New Zealanders (hereafter NZers) felt safe and confident that NZ would be able to eliminate the virus, as reported by the news (see Baker and Wilson 2020; *Coronavirus: How New Zealand Relied on Science and Empathy* 2020). This chapter looks at what kinds of linguistic, discursive, and semiotic choices Ardern (and her handlers and publicists) made that enable the NZers to feel safe during this challenging time.

To this end, the data was gathered from the PM's personal social media account, a government Instagram account (@unitedagainstcovid19), brochures distributed by the government, and NZ national newspapers from March 26 to April 26, 2020. This study draws inspiration from a number of studies that have problematized how language is being used in social media (KhosraviNik 2018; KhosraviNik and Sarkhoh 2017). Social media provides an open platform that enables a collaborative participation that minimizes or even reduces gatekeeping processes, compared to traditional media outlets. Thus, this study operates under the assumption that social media usage celebrates democratization and treats power as fluid and dynamic (KhosraviNik 2018; KhosraviNik and Sarkhoh 2017; Martin-Anatias 2019).

Moreover, this piece considers the PM's social media updates and @united-againstcovid19's discourse as political statements delivered either officially or informally. The study treats the PM's appearance as political discourse in the sense that the discourse is delivered by a *politician* who is engaged in the political events and process surrounding the crisis (Fairclough and Fairclough 2012). A critical discourse analysis (CDA) is employed to unpack how language is being used to make meaning and to approach language as a social practice (Fairclough 1989, 2013). The focus is on the linguistic output of the dominating group in NZ. This study argues that the dominating figure with their asymmetrical power can appear progressive and humanistic, aided with social media and other semiotic elements.

Furthermore, this study shows how the most powerful figure in NZ has used her social media appearance to reduce, if not eliminate, the hierarchical power gap between herself and her fellow NZers during the COVID-19 pandemic national lockdown. Also, it aims to unpack how the discourse used by NZ government has encouraged collectiveness and highlighted humanity, as opposed to economics, in tackling this global pandemic. To this end, this study regards the discourse from the CDA viewpoint in which it also highlights the writer's subjective perspective as an Indonesian writer currently living in NZ with some North American experience.

In the sections to follow, this chapter will start by giving a brief background of NZ and its government bodies, as the object of the current research. It is then followed by explaining the research methods and the data collection for this study. Next, the findings are presented together with the writer's interpretive analysis. Finally, the key points of the chapter are summarized and a recommendation for future studies is provided.

New Zealand: a background

Aotearoa or "the Land of the Long White Cloud" is one among several nicknames for NZ. The country is a constitutional monarchy with a parliamentary system of government, which means that the supreme figure head is the British Empire, currently ruled by Queen Elizabeth II. It is a progressive and democratic country whose government is formed by democratic election every three years (*New Zealand Government* 2020). Although NZ is still considered a "white-dominant" country, in which the European-descent NZers (locally referred to as Pākehā) comprise the majority, the indigenous Māori cultural group that made up about 1.4% of the total population is formally acknowledged and visible in NZ (Stats NZ 2020). Home to approximately 5 million NZers, NZ recognizes Māori and New Zealand Sign Language as its official languages. *De facto*, however, English is widely spoken by about 90% of NZers (Stats NZ 2020).

Multiple imaginative responses: Prime Minister Ardern and the government used digital and print media to launch a successful campaign

Jacinda Ardern is the 40th prime minister of NZ. Her leadership has been tested at least during two critical times. The first was in March 2019, when Ardern firmly acted by banning semiautomatic weapons only six days after the Christchurch massacre. As reported by many international media, she was highly praised for her humanistic approach, particularly toward the affected groups, the NZer Muslims (Lester 2019). A year after the tragedy, just when NZ was about to prepare to honor and celebrate the lives of 51 NZer Muslims whose lives were taken by a white supremacist man, NZ needed to take measures to face a different massive crisis: preparing for the Alert Level 4 national lockdown, a method implemented to flatten the curve of the COVID-19 spread. In the NZ perspective, the Alert Level 4 was when the strictest rules were applied in which NZers needed to stay 24/7 at home, while doing the essentials (grocery shopping and/or going to the pharmacy) and exercising at the nearby park (solitary or with their household members) were allowed.

In preparing for the national lockdown, the government had used several methods to deliver information related to it. First, at 6 PM on March 25, 2020, a text message was sent out to everyone in NZ, including temporary visitors, informing them of the national lockdown starting at 11:59 PM. A few hours before the lockdown, the PM appeared in an impromptu Facebook live session direct NZers about what they needed to do during the lockdown. On day 1 when the national lockdown went into effect, on March 26, 2020, a government brochure titled "Our plan" was delivered to NZers' residences around the country. In that brochure, the government detailed information related to COVID-19 together with descriptions of the alert levels (1–4, with Alert Level 1 as the most relaxed stage, while Alert Level 4 applied the most rigorous rules and restrictions). From the brochure, we learned that the Alert Level 4 means a disease was not contained and there was a high possibility of widespread outbreak and transmission in our communities.

Thus, NZers have been instructed to stay at home and to interact only within their own "bubbles"—their own immediate family members or partners who live with them. Essential businesses such as pharmacies and supermarkets stayed open, and NZers were instructed to practice a physical distancing of at least 2 meters when doing their essentials, such as going for a grocery shopping, buying some medicines, or going for a run or a walk. Within this period, NZers were asked to stay local when exercising. All educational facilities were closed. Police officers were visible in public areas to ensure no NZers violate the national lockdown regulations. A new phone line 105, together with an online form, were created to facilitate NZers reporting their one another violating the regulations.

Additionally, Ardern made her first formal and official appearance on March 26, 2020, broadcast via both national television and Facebook live. Her official announcement of the national lockdown for the NZers was clear and straightforward. She asked NZers to stay home, to save lives, to stay kind, and stay healthy (Covid19.govt.nz).

It was the first of many atypical communications from Ardern that are the object of this study. In this light, this study compares this non-typicality to other international leaders, particularly the Indonesian and the US presidents. This piece of information is relevant to understanding the following analysis and interpretation, which puts NZ and its PM's use and her social media discourse as the center of the study.

Data collection

This study collected about four hours of Ardern's Facebook Live feeds during the national lockdown starting March 25, 2020. It focused on Ardern's informal speeches delivered on Facebook Live. Another set of data was also collected from the newly created NZ's official Instagram account (@uniteagainstcovid19) together with the government brochures sent out to NZers' residence. The PM's statements reiterated by those who run @uniteagainstcovid19 and other governmental bodies were analyzed. As a way to crosscheck NZers' responses to the government discourse, this study has also gathered and analyzed data from NZ national newspapers, as well as international ones. It also utilized the pictures the writer has taken of public service announcements echoing the PM's statements on private and commercial buildings in Auckland. All data were collected from late March to early April, during the NZ national lockdown that lasted from March 26 to April 27, before NZ shifted to alert level 3, where the lockdown rules and restrictions were a bit relaxed.

This study views discourse as a social use of language or language in social contexts (Fairclough 1989, 2013; Fairclough and Fairclough 2012). In this way, this study perceives discourse as a way of thinking, feeling, acting, and making meaning in social practices that are reinforced and repeated due to unequal and negotiated power (van Dijk 2011, 2014). This study is then positioned language in the center of the study and analyzed it in the context of the sociocultural and political discourse (Fairclough 2013; van Dijk 2011, 2014). In doing so, it aims to unpack the ideology implanted in the discourse. Ideology in this study is understood as the way we see and understand the world and the ways we represent the world (Fairclough 2013).

This research analyzed the data in three steps. First, the linguistic features of the discourse were examined. In this particular data analysis, this study looked at the interpersonal statements that emerged from the discourse: the ways in which a statement was constructed and delivered and its ideological presupposition (Fairclough 2003, 2013). Second, other semiotic aspects or modalities used were deconstructed in making social meaning such as visual images, and the means used to deliver the message. Third, both these linguistic and semiotic lenses were utilized to develop a set of interpretive analysis (Fairclough and Fairclough 2012; Fairclough 2013; van Dijk 2011, 2014).

When interpreting the data, this piece took advantage of the writer's positionality as an Indonesian currently living in NZ, who has lived previously in the United States. In other words, in interpreting the discourse produced in the writer's current adopted country, she benefits from her layered understanding as an Indonesian who has been living in the Western world. In this light, the way the writer sees things may have been different from many Indonesians and also many other NZers, this different perspective, as she found it, has helped her ground an interpretive analysis. Looking at the data from her perspective as an Indonesian citizen and a New Zealand permanent resident, the writer offers a nuanced analysis from at least these two focal points.

Findings: what the data have revealed

The findings are presented in three sections: linguistic features; semiotic analysis; and interpretation and discussion. This exercise helps us understand the layers behind a statement and other semiotic elements.

Linguistic features: clear, consistent messaging communicating authority and compassion

The first section discusses PM's repetitive discourse in her informal and formal speeches, reiterated and frequently repeated by other governmental bodies and by many NZers. These phrases include the following:

Stay local
Stay with your bubble
Be calm
Be kind
Stay home
Save lives
Unite against COVID-19
Let's unite against COVID-19
Check-in on the elderly or vulnerable
We're in this together
Kia kaha (A Māori phrase, *stay strong*)

The majority of the repeated phrases are delivered in the imperative, while the last one, "We're in this together," is an assertive and affirmative sentence.

The majority of the terms adopt imperative mood, in which a bare infinitive is used, such as *be (kind)*, *be (calm)*, *stay (home)*, *save (lives)*, *unite*, and *check in*.

There are at least two ways that we can decode the use of imperative in this discourse: one is the interpersonal relation between Ardern and her fellow NZers. It unpacks how Ardern appears to position herself during her speeches and may simultaneously illustrate how the current NZ government views their fellow

NZers. Second, it also unpacks how NZ government leads their fellow NZers during this unsettling time.

Examining it through the lens of functional grammar, we see that imperative is a device that creates an interpersonal meaning that is very direct and indicates the asymmetrical power of the speaker. Imperative produces straightforward, strong statements that demand others do something (Fairclough 2003). Due to her political situation, Ardern's power may be automatically assumed, and imperative helps her construct, deliver, and reinforce the greater hierarchical power she holds compared to her NZer fellows. Given that the speech is delivered during the pandemic situation where NZers need more directions than ever, Arden's usage of imperatives supports strong directives. If it were delivered in the form of question, or an implicit request, such as "Could you please stay home?" it would have created a different sense. The implicit request would appear to give some optionality for the listeners, in this case, the NZers. In other words, via the use of imperatives, Ardern has set up the necessity and the obligation.

Additionally, while imperative reinforces Ardern's strong directives and asymmetrical power, the next message she has been trying to deliver is compassion, through the use of *(be) calm, (be) kind,* and *(check in) on the elderly or vulnerable.* Therefore, it may be safely assumed that while the PM is direct and straightforward when regulating NZers' behavior during the pandemic, she also asks them to be caring and compassionate and thus portrays herself as such as well.

In addition to the imperatives, Ardern and the official government bodies also frequently use the assertive declarative sentence, "We're in this together," when communicating to their fellow NZers. While this may function as the NZ government's way to shore up their higher position and expertise, they also include themselves in the pronoun "we" in this particular statement. The use of the inclusive we in "we're in this together" appeared to reduce the hierarchy and distance, hinting that everyone is in the same boat and all need to contribute to do their bits during this global pandemic. In this way, the government highlights both authority and inclusivity, where they position themselves as leaders who are part of the community they lead.

Another example of Ardern's emphasizing inclusivity comes from one of her afternoon daily reports to the country. When thanking NZers who have diligently followed the government's directives by staying at home, Ardern said, "Our team of 5 million has broken the chain of transmission and taken a quantum leap forward in our goal to eliminate the virus." Here, again, her NZer listeners together with the government are presented as united in one-ness via the use of "our team of 5 million." Ardern's use of *we* and *our* appears to highlight the sameness of NZers, suggesting that the government and the people are positioned to be one team (cf. Bucholtz and Hall 2005).

Via both the content and the types of statements she uses, Ardern positions herself as a powerful entity and the leader of her fellow NZers (cf. Fairclough 1989, 2003). However, this asymmetrical and authoritative power seems to be subdued through the inclusive pronouns and words showing compassion. Even as the NZ government affirms its standing as authoritative and behavior-regulating through their language selection, they are still advocating community and compassion. In other words, they are imposing power and authority not in a dictatorial, but rather in an inclusive and compassionate fashion. Here, we learn that the discourse that values positivity in order to make world a better place coming from a political figure with inherent power asymmetry exists.

On the other hand, her discourse is not without any presuppositions that overlook the circumstances of some citizens and residents. For example, statements like "stay home" and "stay with your bubble" assume that all NZers are well-sheltered and well-interacted, and may marginalize any single or solitary NZers. These two statements are existential presuppositions that seem to overlook the presence of homeless and solitary individuals in NZ (cf. Fairclough 2003). In other words, the term "bubble" itself is problematic and tends to come from such a rather simplistic definition of what a family is (Trnka and Davies 2020). However, Ardern also amends this oversight by asking NZers to check-in on the elderly and vulnerable—and both homeless and solitary individuals may fall into either category or both. This study reads these statements ("stay home," "stay with your bubble," and "check-in on the elderly and vulnerable") together as illustrating her tendency to treat the issue from the majority perspective, while acknowledging that social inequalities do exist in the country.

Ardern's Facebook live and daily appearances on media from a semiotic lens

Government is an organization that tends to exercise power toward individuals and the social distance between these two entities is high (Fairclough 2003). Social media as a democratic channel is able to facilitate participatory from the people, seemingly reducing the social distance between the two (Cf. Khosravinik and Sarkhoh 2017). In this study, via the live chats on her social media, the PM appears to invite the voice of the NZers to directly interact with her. In other words, the PM acknowledges the dialogicality between hers and the other voices (cf. Fairclough 2003) as opposed to monologicality.

On top of her statements, Ardern has also solidified her strong yet relaxed discourse through a number of informal live appearances before and during the national lockdown, usually on weekends as a way to catch up with her fellow NZers. Ardern's first such appearance was a few hours before the lockdown, dressed in pajamas or a sweatshirt after putting her baby Neve to bed. She apologized for her informal appearance. Her informal appearance corresponded with the live, impromptu form, in which her statements, in response to questions posed by followers, were unscripted and spontaneous. This impromptu appearance was not without risk. Given that her Facebook live feed is publicly accessible, it may have provided an open space for anyone to participate and voice their honest opinion, but the PM appeared to take that risk. Furthermore, the fact that she is a mother who tucks in her daughter and wears a sweatshirt may construct her image as someone who is relatable, especially with many NZ mothers and/or women. We can read this as a strategic move to deliver a people person image to her fellow NZers.

This humility and openness are mediated not only by semiotic elements, such as Ardern's choice to wear a sweatshirt, but also through her use of social media. This is especially true because she has chosen Facebook, one of the most popular social media platforms. With the openness that social media has offered, Ardern's use of Facebook live sessions, where the public can participate relatively freely, hierarchical power is implicitly reduced (Khosravinik and Sarkhoh 2017). Thus, Ardern's choice to do a series of impromptu and informal Facebook live sessions seems to be an effective way to reduce the hierarchical gap between a leader and their citizens/people. More than a communication platform, this study found that Ardern's social media use plays an important role in bridging the gap between her and the people of NZ. In brief, both the linguistic discourse and the social media use have helped construct the "people" image, which the PM might want to be perceived as.

Furthermore, Ardern's semiotics of less formality makes her more relatable for many NZers. This study interprets this as another effective strategy to reduce the perceived power gap between her, a leader in NZ, and her fellow NZers. The discourse produced by Ardern does show that asymmetrical power does not need to be threatening and dominating negatively. Ardern appears to have strategically displayed that a leader can be directive but humanistic, in which everyone needs to be protective but compassionate at the same time. This government discourse and strategy can be read as the NZ government is being visible, present and doing their job during this global pandemic—the qualities that seem to be missing from both the ongoing US and Indonesian governments (*Indonesia: Little Transparency in COVID-19 Outbreak* 2020; Pahnke 2020; *Why the United States Is Losing the War on COVID-19* 2020).

In addition to her live weekend appearances on social media, Ardern, together with the country's Director-General of Health, Dr. Ashley Bloomfield, consistently appears at noon on weekdays to formally brief the media; these briefs are also broadcast live on Facebook and have become a "lockdown regular" for many NZers (Cooke 2020). On the first day of the national lockdown, she appeared on another informal Facebook live, and apologized for being so present and visible during this unsettling and difficult time. Her goal was to keep NZers informed and updated with how the government handled the deadly virus. We may interpret her apology to be paradoxical, because during an unprecedented global pandemic, firm directives from a leader are undoubtedly a necessity. We may also approach Ardern's apology as a recognition that her regular "virtual" or social media appearance may have trespassed other people's personal (albeit digital) boundaries. This study reads this apology as illustrative of Ardern's humility or how she may have wanted to present herself, given her position as a PM, and the number one person in NZ.

Discussion: communicating compassionate collective identity

The earlier findings on Ardern's discourse illustrate at least two important qualities of the NZ government: *compassionate authority* and *collectivism*. First, it informs us that authority and humanity do not have to be conflicting. Through the use of imperatives and declaratives, the NZ government shows authority and power when delivering their messages to the people of NZ. However, this power also comes with a sense of humanity and compassion.

This discourse, at once authoritative and compassionate, is also implemented by NZ police officers. More visible during the national lockdown, police officers have largely approached NZers breaking the Alert Level 4 (by going outside to the non-essentials) in a compassionate, friendly, and caring fashion.

Moreover, through the discourse repeatedly used by the government, it is clear what the priority is: to safeguard NZers' lives. This study interprets the discourse as if the NZ government prioritizes their people, unlike the Indonesian or the United States governments who have put consideration more on the economy over their people's public health (Lindsey and Mann 2020; Pahnke 2020).

Second, the NZ government builds a sense of collectiveness and togetherness via slogans like "We're in this together" and "Unite against COVID-19," used frequently on the NZ government's official Instagram account for COVID-19 information (@uniteagainstCOVID-19) and the PM's social media coverage and live sessions. This piece interprets the government, an entity with power, is not attempting to reinforce the perceived gap between the government and the people, but rather it is establishing a sense of solidarity. This sense of solidarity is also built by virtue of *kia kaha*, a Māori phrase that unites NZers, which is used both by the government and its people alike. Te Reo Māori (the Māori language) is unique to NZ and the phrase may have been used to instill the one-ness of the NZers (Kiwiness).

Furthermore, this sense of unity and community in the midst of this crisis is much needed and is strengthened by Ardern's repeated statements to check-in on our neighbors, especially the elderly who are more susceptible to being affected by COVID-19. In this light, what the NZ government has done via both the language selection, social media usage, and other semiotic elements during this global pandemic appears to be carefully crafted to emphasize that the government can only do the work with the support of the people. As it has been argued throughout this chapter, the government discourses are beautifully crafted and at time of writing, they have been successfully productive in making NZ as one of the countries that has successfully stomped out the COVID-19. As of December 2020, NZ is COVID-19-free, while many countries, including the United States and Indonesia, are still battling against the virus.

Summary: what we can learn from Arden's leadership during the pandemic

From Ardern's impromptu and regular appearances on her Facebook Live feed, we learn that a government who leads can strategically appear to reduce a large perceived gap with their people and establish a sense of collectivity and solidarity. The government has achieved this through language selection and other semiotic elements, such as informal appearances online using social media to check on people and directly answer their questions. Through their discourse and the social media usage, the government appears to practice compassion and kindness while telling their people to do the same.

In this way, via their language selection, the impromptu social media appearance, and other semiotic elements, NZ may have set an example on how a government is still authoritative or holding some hierarchical power but delivers compassion at the same time. The two qualities are necessary during the global pandemic where people need to be directed but embrace simultaneously. Social media, in this context, is used as a means to deliver the message directly and to connect with their fellow people, in a synchronous way giving a space for people to communicate directly to their leaders, without any "unnecessary" boundaries or formal bureaucratic regulations. The unscripted and spontaneous check-ins done by the NZ PM seem to deliver the message of openness. The social media usage in this light appears to be an effective means that solidifies this democratic spirit. Seeing this as an Indonesian whose country values a rather rigid hierarchical rank, the writer found this type of leadership as novel and refreshing. Also, to learn that a government is represented by a body that walks the talk is reviving her trust toward national government. New Zealand indeed has set a high standard in tackling this global pandemic in a humanistic and firm way. A future study that will look into Ardern's both formal and informal social media usage pre-and post-New Zealand lockdown will create a more comprehensive discourse analysis on Ardern's way of communication while being at the helm.

References

Baker, Michael, and Nick Wilson. 2020. "Elimination: What New Zealand's Coronavirus Response Can Teach the World." *The Guardian*, April 10. Accessed April 21, 2020. www.theguardian.com/world/2020/apr/10/elimination-what-new-zealands-coronavirus-response-can-teach-the-world.

Bucholtz, Mary, and Kira Hall. 2005. "Identity and Interaction: A Sociocultural Linguistic Approach." *Discourse Studies* 4–5: 585–614. Accessed April 28, 2020. doi:10.1177/1461445605054407.

Cooke, Henry. 2020. "The End of the Ashley and Jacinda Coronavirus Show: 1pm Joint Press Briefings to Cease." *The Stuff*, May 18. Accessed December 21, 2020. www.stuff.co.nz/national/health/coronavirus/300015140/the-end-of-the-ashley-and-jacinda-coronavirus-show-1pm-joint-press-briefings-to-cease.

"Coronavirus: How New Zealand Relied on Science and Empathy." *BBC*, April 20. Accessed April 21, 2020. www.bbc.com/news/world-asia-52344299

Fairclough, Isabela, and Norman Fairclough. 2012. *Political Discourse Analysis: A Method for Advanced Students*. London: Routledge.

Fairclough, Norman. 1989. *Language and Power*. London: Longman.

———. 2003. *Analysing Discourse: Textual Analysis for Social Research*. London: Routledge.

———. 2013. *Critical Discourse Analysis: The Critical Study of Language*. London: Routledge.

Global Peace Index. 2020. "Global Peace Index." Accessed June 15, 2019. http://statistics times.com/ranking/global-peace-index.php.

Google. 2020. "Google News." Accessed April 20, 2020. http://news.google.com/covid-19/map?hl=en-NZ&gl=NZ&ceid=NZ:en.

"Indonesia: Little Transparency in COVID-19 Outbreak." *Human Rights Watch*, April 2. Accessed December 21, 2020. www.hrw.org/news/2020/04/09/indonesia-little-transparency-covid-19-outbreak.

KhosraviNik, Majid. 2018. "Social Media Techno-Discursive Design, Affective Communication and Contemporary Politics." *Fudan Journal of the Humanities and Social Sciences* 11: 427–42.

KhosraviNik, Majid, and Nadia Sarkhoh. 2017. "Arabism and Anti-Persian Sentiments on Participatory Web Platforms: A social Media Critical Discourse Study." *International Journal of Communication* 11: 3614–33.

Lester, Amelia. 2019. "The Roots of Jacinda Ardern's Extraordinary Leadership after Christchurch." *New Yorker*, March 23. Accessed April 21, 2020. www.newyorker.com/culture/culture-desk/what-jacinda-arderns-leadership-means-to-new-zealand-and-to-the-world.

Lindsey, Tim, and Tim Mann. 2020. "Indonesia was in Denial over Coronavirus. Now It May Be Facing A Looming Disaster." *The Conversation*, April 8. Accessed December 21, 2020. https://theconversation.com/indonesia-was-in-denial-over-coronavirus-now-it-may-be-facing-a-looming-disaster-135436.

New Zealand Government. 2020. "How Government Works." Accessed December 21, 2020. https://www.govt.nz/browse/engaging-with-government/government-in-new-zealand/

Martin-Anatias, Nelly. 2019. "*Pelakor:* An Un-just Discursive Term for 'the Other Woman'." *Language@Internet* 17, article 3. www.languageatinternet.org/articles/2019/martinanatias.

Pahnke, Anthony. 2020. "Trump is Priotising the Economy over the Vulnerable." *Al Jazeera*, March 28. Accessed December 21, 2020. www.aljazeera.com/opinions/2020/3/28/trump-is-prioritising-the-economy-over-the-vulnerable.

StatsNZ. 2020. "Population." Accessed April 21, 2020. www.stats.govt.nz/topics/population.

Trnka, Susanna, and Sharyn Graham Davies. 2020. "Bursting the Bubble Fallacy: Lockdown and the Problematic Concept of 'Home'." *The Spinoff*, April 29. Accessed May 1, 2020. http://thespinoff.co.nz/author/susannaxsharyn/.

van Dijk, Teun. 2011. "Multidiscplinary CDA: A Plea for Diversity." In *Methods of Critical Discourse Analysis*, edited by Ruth Wodak and Michael Meyer, 95–120. London: Sage Publications.

———. 2014. "Discourse, Cognition, Society." In *The Discourse Studies Reader: Main Currents in Theory and Analysis*, edited by Johannes Angermuller, Dominique Maingueneau, and Ruth Wodak, 388–99. Amsterdam: John Benjamins.

"Why the U.S. is Losing the War on COVID-19." *TIME*, August 13. Accessed December 21, 2020. https://time.com/5879086/us-covid-19/.

Worldmeter. 2020. "Coronavirus Cases." Accessed April 20, 2020. www.worldometers.info/coronavirus/#countries.

12 Coronavirus pandemic

A historical handshake between the mainstream media and social media in response to COVID-19 in Vietnam

Hang Thi Thuy Dinh and Hien Thi Minh Nguyen

Vietnamese media context

The media in Vietnam are under the control of the government and the rule of the Communist Party. The role of the media is to be the voice of the Party, the State, the social, political organizations, and the tribune of the people (Media Law 2016). In the last 20 years, despite the early sign of traditional media's downfall in the world due to the emergence of new media, the media in Vietnam have had a qualitative and quantitative development with improved content and presentation. By the end of 2019, there are 850 media organizations with more than thousand media outlets in Vietnam (Ngoc Truong 2019). Despite the fall of the socialist block in 1990s, the media in Vietnam up till now are still relying on Lenin's notion that the media must be a "propagandist, agitator and organizer," the first and foremost role of the mainstream media in Vietnam is to inform, educate, and direct people in accomplishing the revolutionary tasks and Party policies (Huu Tho 1997, 30).

In the turn of the twenty-first century, social media have grown unprecedentedly in Vietnam and has become a powerful tool for the public in transmission of information without limits of space and time. According to Internet World Stats (2020a), by the end of January 2020, in Vietnam, there are more than 68.5 million internet users compared with 200,000 in the year 2000. Vietnam is the 14th country in the world in terms of the percentage of people using the internet, and it is one of the 10 countries with the highest number of Facebook (close to 67 million users) and YouTube users in the world; among them teenagers account for a large percentage (Internet World Stats 2020b). According to a report of the Vietnamese Ministry of Information and Communications, up to now, there are 455 social networks. The most popular among them are Facebook, YouTube, Zalo (a social network "Made in Vietnam" since 2012), Instagram, Facebook messenger (Van Anh 2019). Social media in Vietnam have their own agenda, and they are independent of the government and party propaganda.

Social media have created a huge impact on the overall media landscape in Vietnam, however they also have been blamed by political leaders for "pushing to threats and negative impacts on social development of the country," affecting "social order and security" (Tran 2019). Nevertheless, the domination of social media cannot be ignored when the circulation numbers and advertising revenue of the print media have been gradually decreasing as readers move to online media and social media.

COVID-19 and the handshake

In the outbreak of the COVID-19 pandemic, the Vietnamese state-run media and social media have a reciprocal relationship in informing the public. The "handshake" of the mainstream media and social media in Vietnam could be seen in ways that social media has become an "extended arm" of the mainstream media. Social media have never participated as positively as this time in an effort to raise the people's awareness against epidemics. At the same time, Vietnamese government organizations, including media system have used social media as an important tool in disseminating updated information about the situation of the outbreak and medical advisories to the public. As pointed out by CNN, "The country's massive propaganda apparatus was also mobilized, raising awareness of the outbreak through loudspeakers, street posters, the press and social media" (Gan 2020).

The study demonstrates that social and mainstream media met and coordinated in informing the public about COVID-19, and the public took notice of the information. Drawing on recent examples of the interplay between the mainstream media and social media, questions of the role of the media in setting the agenda and facilitating public discussions about COVID-19 are considered. These questions also imply that in the time of shrinking mainstream media audiences and the spread of social networks, media consumers need information that is relevant and useful for their well-being.

Research methodology

To carry out this study, the authors used a content analysis method to study COVID-19 media coverage in the first quarter of 2020 from online and TV platforms, which were as follows: *The 7 pm News Bulletin on VTV1*—the National TV Channel; three online newspapers, including *VnExpress*, *Vietnamnet*, and *Tuoi Tre Online*, the most trafficked pages. The result of this research retrieval was a large number of stories, with 3412 online media articles and 718 news items from 7 PM News Bulletin on VTV1.

To serve the purpose of this study, the authors chose three social networking sites on Facebook, including *"Join hands to fight against fake news of COVID-19," "Connection between Community and Medical Fields to prevent and fight against COVID-19,"* and *"Citizen's Perspectives for the Press"* for three weeks in March, 2020. The reason for examining social media sites only in March was a huge number of posts on these three social networks from January to March. The first case testing positive with coronavirus (the 17th patient) was reported in Hanoi in March, and during this period, the number of Vietnamese people returning home from overseas was rising rapidly, triggering panic in the community about increasing risks of becoming infected. March was considered as a peak time when a high number of COVID-19 stories appeared in both mainstream and social media. To examine what kind of mainstream media stories were transmitted by social media, the authors chose to focus on articles with shared links or posted during March, resulting in a total of 2979 articles on these sites.

The authors randomly chose 20% of the aforementioned articles in both mainstream and social media. Subsequently, the total number of sampled articles are 685 from online newspapers, 143 from the 7 PM TV News Bulletin, and 598 from three social media sites used to code for content analysis. All news items were read or watched thoroughly in order to choose frequently recurring topics, which were then grouped into four main categories, including: (i) statistics on situation of COVID-19 outbreak; (ii) responses of the society; (iii) medical information; (iv) other related news about COVID-19. The authors also picked up the 10 most interactive articles on each online newspaper in order to examine topic contents that attracted the most attention from the public. The study generated 25 articles with shared links on three social networking sites having the highest number of comments and shares on both Facebook page and online newspapers. The purpose of the data collection was to examine how social media interact with mainstream media to extend audience reach.

Findings

The study showed that responses of "society" to the coronavirus pandemic were the most popular topic covered by the media in Vietnam. They were followed by news about situations of the coronavirus outbreak as well as new developments about the science and medicines behind the outbreak. Other news related to the COVID-19 was the least popular topic in which stories on fakenews, or situation of economic crisis after COVID-19 pandemic were reported. These statistics reflected attitudes of society when people have been impacted by social distancing and self-quarantine, contributing to the understanding that people were concerned and focused their attention on news about coronavirus spread and the science behind the outbreak (see Table 12.1).

Statistics on the spread of the coronavirus COVID-19 pandemic became the second most popular topic across all collected articles on mainstream and social media (see Table 12.2). Referring to articles on VnExpress, Tuoitre, 7 PM TV News Bulletin, more stories about statistics on the spread of COVID-19 outbreak in the world were covered than those in Vietnam, while Vietnamnet reported less about this topic. On three social networks, statistics on the spread of COVID-19 in Vietnam were the more frequently recurring topic compared to statistics about the world. As Da Trang, a Deputy General Manager of *Tuoi Tre* explained, from the beginning of January to the first week of March, Vietnam had only 16 patients who had returned from Wuhan, China, infected by the coronavirus, and the situation in Vietnam was very much under the control because of the government's drastic and serious measures. However, the quick spread of the virus and a rising

Table 12.1 Percentage of the coronavirus topics reported by mainstream media and transmitted by social media sites

Mainstream media	Statistics on situation of COVID-19 outbreak	Responses of society	Medical information	Other related news about COVID-19
VnExpress	29.92%	50.00%	18.56%	1.52%
Vietnamnet	39.81%	45.97%	13.27%	0.95%
Tuoitre	35.89%	38.76%	23.44%	1.91%
7 PM News Bulletin	24.83%	65.10%	10.07%	0.00%

Social media	Statistics on situation of COVID-19 outbreak	Responses of society	Medical information	Other related news about COVID-19
Press citizen's perspectives	28.05%	68.84%	3.12%	0.00%
Connection between community and medical fields to prevent and fight against COVID-19	39.67%	50.83%	8.68%	0.83%
Join hands to fight against fake news of COVID-19	22.22%	55.56%	22.22%	0.00%

Source: © Hang Thi Thuy Dinh, Hien Thi Minh Nguyen, 2021

Table 12.2 Percentage of articles about statistics on COVID-19 outbreak spreading in Vietnam and in the world reported by mainstream media and transmitted by social media

The mainstream media	Statistics on COVID-19 outbreak spreading in Vietnam	Statistics on COVID-19 outbreak spreading in the world
VnExpress	24.05%	75.95%
Vietnamnet	55.95%	44.05%
Tuoitre	33.33%	66.67%
7 PM TV News Bulletin	37.50%	62.50%

The social media sites	Statistics on COVID-19 outbreak spreading in Vietnam	Statistics on COVID-19 outbreak spreading in the world
Press Citizen's Perspectives	67.68%	32.32%
Connection between community and medical fields to prevent and fight against COVID-19	75.51%	24.49%
Join hands to fight against fake news of COVID-19	75.00%	25.00%

Source: © Hang Thi Thuy Dinh, Hien Thi Minh Nguyen, 2021

death toll in China, where the virus originated, and in European countries such as Italy and Spain required media to provide as much as possible updated information to the public (Da Trang 2020).

Among published stories, 65.10% of the stories on 7 PM News Bulletin on VTV1 were related to society's responses, making up the highest percentage of the total news items. As for online newspapers, the number of articles on society's responses to COVID-19 on VnExpress accounted for the largest proportion (50.00%) compared to those in other online newspapers. Following this trend, the most popular topic in all three social networks was also society's responses, in which the number of articles sharing links on *"Press Citizen's Perspectives"* occupied the highest percentage, with 68.84% (see Table 12.3).

During the COVID-19 pandemic, the social responses reflected in media consisted of responses from the country's leadership (the Party, the State, the Government body, including organizational representatives); responses from the public; and responses from business community. The responses of the country's leadership related to giving directions or announcing policies or ideas became the most popular topic compared to responses of other groups. Most of the articles published by mainstream outlets and transmitted by social networks emphasized Vietnamese leaders' speeches in response to the pandemic (see Table 12.4).

The number of articles sharing links on social networks showed how responses from the Vietnamese Party, State or Government bodies were the most frequently recurring topic. The page *"Join hands to fight against fake news of COVID-19"* had the largest proportion of stories, with 70%. By contrast, the page *"Press citizen's perspectives"* had the highest number of articles with shared links covering responses of the Party, State or Government body compared to the two other pages, followed by the page *"Connection between community and medical fields to prevent and fight against COVID-19"* and *"Join hands to fight against fake news of COVID-19,"* respectively (see Table 12.4).

During the spread of the COVID-19 outbreak, the topic of medical treatments and medicine development attracted attention from the public. The study showed

Table 12.3 Percentage of articles about society's responses reported by mainstream media and transmitted by social media

The mainstream media	Society's responses	The social media sites	Society's responses
VnExpress	50.00%	Press citizen's perspectives	68.84%
Vietnamnet	45.97%	Connection between community and medical fields to prevent and fight against COVID-19	50.83%
Tuoitre	38.76%	Join hands to fight against fake news of COVID-19	55.56%
7 PM TV news bulletin	65.10%		

Source: © Hang Thi Thuy Dinh, Hien Thi Minh Nguyen, 2021

Table 12.4 Percentage of articles about responses of different strata of society in Vietnam and in the world reported by mainstream media and transmitted by social media

The mainstream media	Society's responses in Vietnam			Society's responses in other countries		
	Country's leadership	Public	Business community	Country's leadership	Public	Business community
VnExpress	28.03	10.61	12.88	40.91	4.55	3.03
Vietnamnet	53.85	5.77	21.15	11.54	0.96	6.73
Tuoitre	38.27	22.22	7.41	16.05	13.58	2.47
7 PM News Bulletin	47.22	14.81	11.11	24.07	0.93	1.85
The social media sites	*Country's leadership*	*Public*	*Business community*	*Country's leadership*	*Public*	*Business community*
Press citizen's perspectives	33.06	27.76	9.80	17.55	7.35	4.49
Connection between community and medical fields to prevent and fight against COVID-19	56.35	25.40	2.38	9.52	6.35	0.00
Join hands to fight against fake news of COVID-19	70.00	10.00	10.00	10.00	0.00	0.00

Source: © Hang Thi Thuy Dinh, Hien Thi Minh Nguyen, 2021

that there was more coverage on Vietnam's media about what is going on with science in the world generally than in Vietnam. However, *Vietnamnet* countered this pattern with more stories about medical information in Vietnam. Similarly, the page "*Connection between community and medical fields to prevent and fight against COVID-19*"and "*Press citizen's perspectives*" showed a higher percentage of medical information in Vietnam than that in the world generally (see Table 12.5).

By looking at news sources used most frequently in news items on the COVID-19 outbreak, statistics showed that the dominant news sources were from the Party, State or Government body. Other news sources were professional experts, scientific researchers, WHO, news agencies, business community, ordinary people, and social media (see Table 12.6).

Discussion

This survey showed that during the coronavirus outbreak, stories about the coronavirus pandemic development both in Vietnam and in the world were the topic that media delivered, a topic that also interested and concerned the public. Among the most interactive articles from online newspapers and articles sharing links on social networks, stories on newly infected patients and deaths from COVID-19

Table 12.5 Percentage of articles about medical information related to COVID-19 outbreak in Vietnam and in the world reported by mainstream media and transmitted by social media

The mainstream media	Medical information in Vietnam	Medical information in the world
VnExpress	36.73%	63.27%
Vietnamnet	70.97%	29.03%
Tuoitre	38.78%	61.22%
7pm News Bulletin	26.67%	73.33%
The social media sites	*Medical information in Vietnam*	*Medical information in the world*
Press citizen's perspectives	72.73%	27.27%
Connection between community and medical fields to prevent and fight against COVID-19	80.00%	20.00%
Join hands to fight against fake news of COVID-19	36.36%	63.64%

Source: © Hang Thi Thuy Dinh, Hien Thi Minh Nguyen, 2021

Table 12.6 The news sources used in the articles reported by mainstream media and transmitted by social media

Mainstream media	From the Party, State, Government body	From the experts, scientific researchers	From the ordinary people	From WHO	From news agencies	From business community	From social media
VnExpress	188	72	16	5	17	38	11
Vietnamnet	163	29	11	28	50	45	4
Tuoitre	140	36	14	23	92	32	18
7pm News Bulletin	111	21	20	8	3	31	4
Social media	*From the party, state, government body*	*From the experts, scientific researchers*	*From the ordinary people*	*From WHO*	*From news agencies*	*From business community*	*From social media*
Press citizen's perspectives	240	29	45	9	81	74	12
Connection between community and medical fields to prevent and fight against COVID-19	171	36	32	6	34	77	5
Join hands to fight against fake news of COVID-19	12	3	1	2	5	5	0

Source: © Hang Thi Thuy Dinh, Hien Thi Minh Nguyen, 2021

attracted the highest attention from readers. For example, on March 6, VnExpress published "*The COVID-19 patient appeared in Hanoi*" (Chi Le et al. 2020) had the highest number of discussions with 1328 comments. The article attracted a huge number of readers since it described a woman in Hanoi returning from Italy and the United Kingdom being tested positive for the novel coronavirus. The 17th patient was also the first positive case recorded in Hanoi—the capital of Vietnam. Most comments showed anxiety and anger against this patient, blaming her for a lack of awareness of the critically ongoing pandemic and her responsibility to the community. The article also contained a response from the Ministry of Health about the situation, urging all citizens returning to Vietnam from a COVID-19 infected area to honestly declare their health status prior to entry for medical advice, guidance, and assistance.

Published on January 3, 2020, the *Vietnamnet* article "*Three first Vietnamese citizens tested positive for coronavirus*" (Thu Hang 2020) attracted the highest number of comments with 41,012 reactions. The story was about the first three Vietnamese cases of COVID-19 confirmed by the Ministry of Health. Topics on responses and directions by the country's leaders played an important role in media coverage, drawing substantial attention from the public. For example, the article titled "*Prime Minister Nguyen Xuan Phuc agreed to announce nationwide pandemic*" (Ngoc An 2020), published on January 30, 2020, was one of the articles attracting the most interactions on Tuoitre online newspaper, with 63 comments and 1145 likes. Most comments expressed the public's confidence in the decision by the Prime Minister that all political system and authorities at all levels of Vietnam should concentrate on prevention and the fight against the COVID-19 pandemic.

These comments occurred at a time when the Coronavirus outbreak was raging in China, the neighboring country of Vietnam. From the end of January, when both China's authorities and WHO maintained that the coronavirus disease was under the control, the Prime Minister of Vietnam warned that the disease would soon spread to Vietnam, declaring war on the virus "Fighting this epidemic is like fighting the enemy" in the media. When people saw that its government was treating the coronavirus seriously, they were on high alert and followed guidance from the government on how to prevent spread of the infection.

Another article on responses to COVID-19 attracting considerable discussion was "*Ministry of Education and Training issued an official document to deal with coronavirus*' on Vietnamnet" (Song Nguyen 2020). It reported that the Ministry of Education and Training of Vietnam requested schools restrict the spread of the infection by obeying strict environmental hygiene. This Ministry information led to many interactions and discussions during a significant time in the week after Tet New Year Holiday. Many discussions showed concern about a risk of coronavirus infection spread when students returned to schools after the holiday. Other stories offered statistics on COVID-19 spread in the world; Vietnamese agricultural products calling for help due to COVID-19; or a proposal to reduce electricity prices due to COVID-19, etc. also generated considerable discussion. These issues were close to the heart of the large low-income population in Vietnam.

The study showed that social and mainstream media in Vietnam interacted with each other to cover the COVID-19 pandemic, and that they both attracted huge attention from the public. Social media became an extension arm of mainstream media in transmitting stories about COVID-19 pandemic. For example, over three weeks in March, the number of news links shared on three social networking sites was 2979. Among those articles, the page *"Press citizen's perspectives"* had the highest number with the total of 1769 shared links (or articles sharing links) from Vietnamese online newspapers, equivalent to about 70 links per day.

By sharing links of articles from online news media, three Facebook pages helped to spread news to a wide range of audiences. The more these social networks shared links, the more audiences were able to access news stories on the COVID-19 pandemic. Interactions and comments on mainstream media stories increased from readers in social media. Nic Newman (2011, 6) stated that Facebook and Twitter are important social networks and significant tools for journalists. "(Social networks) ha(ve) spread rapidly through newsrooms, and now play(s) a central role in the way stories are sourced, broken and distributed—contributing to a further speeding up of the news cycle."

One of the best examples was an article from VnExpress titled *"Shipper surrounded the shop waiting to pick up goods'* posted on the page *"Connection between Community and Medical Fields to prevent and fight against COVID-19"* (Hoang Thanh 2020). This was a story about restaurants with dozens of shippers waiting to pick up meals for delivery to customers at home during rush hours. At a time when many shops were closed due to COVID-19, some shops were open and were receiving many orders from customers; however, the risk of coronavirus spread could increase because of the large crowds of people. Together with 26,000 reactions and 280 comments from the original article, the post of its link elicited another 1100 reactions, 533 interactions of comments, and shares. Most of the comments expressed anxiety about the high risk of community infection from COVID-19, anger over the people's lack of awareness about social distancing, and shared warnings about the increase in speed of COVID-19 spread.

This study pointed out that in the coronavirus media coverage, a significant percentage of news sources were representatives of party, state, and government bodies. For example, in the 7 PM TV News Bulletin, the top ten longest news items about the government's responses on COVID-19 were from 3 minutes 27 seconds to 9 minutes 6 seconds. Among those, the longest story contained quotations in a speech made by Prime Minister Nguyen Xuan Phuc on the government's controlling and fighting against COVID-19 while promising economic growth. When new coronavirus cases were discovered, the Prime Minister frequently appeared on VTV National News Bulletin. TV news coverage of the Prime Minister in events related to the Coronavirus pandemic was often longer than that given other issues. This pattern stressed the importance of government shaping of agenda-setting for national audiences through the 7 PM VTV News Bulletin. Subsequently, in articles sharing links on social networks, news sources that came from party, state or government bodies also became the most dominant sources.

As has been shown, both social media and mainstream media were quick to report on topics related to COVID-19. However, some differences between them emerged. For example, in regard to the topic "COVID-19 outbreak spreading statistics," the number of articles covering the statistics in the "world" occupied a dominant percentage in mainstream media, while social networking sites mostly focused on statistics in Vietnam. Similarly, regarding articles on society's responses, the number of articles transmitted by social media reporting the general public community's responses was higher than on the business community's responses. Generally, on mainstream media, depending on different online newspapers or TV, the business community's responses became the second most popular topic. Regarding medical issues, mainstream media reported more about them in the world while social networking sites were more interested and concerned about what happened inside Vietnam.

These differences can be explained by Vinh Quoc Le, a communication expert, who said that "mainstream media have a broader approach while social media are interested in the issues which are close and familiar to the community." Social media often shared issues that influence users—what people are directly interested in, and obviously, people were concerned about and discussed more often the COVID-19 situation inside the country. Unlike social media, mainstream media had a responsibility to provide the public a panorama of the world, and to compare how different countries have confronted the pandemic. These broad panoramas also helped the Vietnamese Government set the agenda on the COVID-19 pandemic for the public in Vietnam (Vinh Quoc Le 2020).

Conclusion

It is commonly acknowledged that social media have brought benefits to newsrooms. Social media also create multidimensional conversations and dialogue among newsrooms, journalists, and readers. Sometimes comments from social media users help reporters find new angles for their stories. Social media user-generated content has also become a significant contributor to numerous online media.

Nic Newman (2011, 6) concluded that mainstream media content is "the lifeblood of topical social media conversations" in the UK—"providing the vast majority of news links that are shared." This cooperative pattern fits mainstream and social media in Vietnam in the context of the COVID-19 pandemic, as the study pointed out that the mainstream media news stories have become topics for public discussions and engagement on social media.

The study's statistics demonstrated that Vietnamese party, state or government leaders were the most popular news sources related to COVID-19 media coverage. These findings raise some assumptions: first, during the pandemic, the voices of high-ranking officials were credible to the journalists and public; second, the party, state, and government bodies showed effective results in sending directions, policies, and opinions to communicate and inform the public about COVID-19 on all types of media. According to the latest statistics of YouGov (2020), 94%

of Vietnamese people believe that the government is handling the COVID-19 epidemic well, and 89% believe in the media reporting the epidemic (McCarthy 2020).

The handshake between social media and mainstream media during the COVID-19 was not a coincidence; it was a part of the government's multiple platform communication and propaganda strategy. This was a smooth coordination, sometimes with willful effects, other times with spillover effects. Overall, cooperation between social and mainstream media has been successful in fighting fake news and providing effective communication. By using all types of media in the campaign against the coronavirus spread, Vietnamese leaders understand that social media content is now becoming important for disseminating information throughout the population. At the same time, media organizations should not blame social media for losing their monopolist position as the only communication tool for the public. Mainstream media have to accept coexistence in parallel with social media in order to reach audiences.

References

Chi Le, Le Nga, Thuy Quynh, Thuc Linh, and Thuy An. 2020. "The COVID-19 Patient Appeared in Hanoi" (Benh nhan COVID-19 xuat hien o Ha Noi). *VnExpress*, March 6. Accessed May 1, 2020. https://vnexpress.net/suc-khoe/benh-covid-19-xuat-hien-o-ha-noi-4065478.html.

Da Trang. 2020. In-depth interview on "Differences on Statistics of COVID-19 Spreading in the World and in Vietnam on Vietnamese Mainstream and Social Media in the First Quarter of 2020" by Hang Thi Thuy Dinh, June 6.

Gan, Nectar. 2020. "How Vietnam Managed to Keep Its Coronavirus Death Toll at Zero." *CNN*, May 30. Accessed May 30, 2020. https://edition.cnn.com/2020/05/29/asia/corona virus-vietnam-intl-hnk/index.html.

Hoang Thanh. 2020. "Shipper Surrounded the Shop Waiting to Pick Up Goods" (Shipper vay quanh quan cho lay hang), *VnExpress*, March 29. Accessed April 18, 2020. https://video.vnexpress.net/tin-tuc/thoi-su/shipper-vay-quan-an-cho-lay-hang-4075855. html?fbclid=IwAR2S6aQg3D4o_lC0LJfXW2dUb7ootmQaQCV9rtfSEUNqke0uZIl 02wCZT8Q.

Huu Tho. 1997. "Thinking of Journalism" (Nghi ve nghe bao), *Educational Publications*: 30.

Internet World Stats. 2020a. "Internet Usage in Asia". Accessed April 19, 2020. www.internetworldstats.com/stats3.htm.

———. 2020b. "Top 20 Countries with the Highest Number of Internet Users." Accessed April 19, 2020. www.internetworldstats.com/top20.htm.

McCarthy, Niall. 2020. "COVID-19: Where Trust in Media Is Highest & Lowest." *Statista*, May 20. Accessed May 22,2020. www.statista.com/chart/21779/trust-in-corona virus-media-coverage-worldwide/.

Media Law. 2016. "Article 4." *Law Library*, April 5. Accessed April 18, 2020. https://thu vienphapluat.vn/van-ban/van-hoa-xa-hoi/Luat-Bao-chi-2016-280645.aspx.

Newman, Nic. 2011. "Mainstream Media and the Distribution of News in the Age of Social Discovery." *Reuters Institute for the Study of Journalism*, September. Accessed April 17, 2020. https://reutersinstitute.politics.ox.ac.uk/sites/default/files/2017-11/Main

stream%20media%20and%20the%20distribution%20of%20news%20in%20the%20 age%20of%20social%20discovery.pdf.

Ngoc An. 2020. "Prime Minister Nguyen Xuan Phuc Agreed to Announce Nationwide Pandemic" (Thu tuong đong y cong bo dich COVID-19 tren toan quoc). *Tuoitre*, January 30. Accessed April 15, 2020. https://tuoitre.vn/thu-tuong-dong-y-cong-bo-dich-covid-19-tren-toan-quoc-2020033019134255.htm.

Ngoc Truong. 2019. "In 2019: 18 Media Organisations in the Whole Media System Were Cut" (Năm 2019: Ca nuoc giam 18 co quan bao chi). *Dang bo Thanh Pho Ho Chi Minh*, December 28. Accessed April 18, 2020. www.hcmcpv.org.vn/tin-tuc/ nam-2019-ca-nuoc-da-giam-18-co-quan-bao-chi-1491860900.

Song Nguyen. 2020. "Ministry of Education and Training Issued an Official Document to Deal with Coronavirus" (Bo Giao duc ra cong đien ung pho voi dich virus corona). *Vietnamnet*, January 29. Accessed April 17, 2020. https://vietnamnet.vn/vn/giao-duc/ goc-phu-huynh/dich-virus-corona-hoc-sinh-co-duoc-nghi-hoc-612183.html.

Thu Hang. 2020. "Three First Vietnamese Citizens Tested Positive for Coronavirus" (3 nguoi Viet Nam đau tien nhiem virus corona), *Vietnamnet*, 30 January. Accessed April 15, 2020. https://vietnamnet.vn/vn/thoi-su/3-nguoi-viet-nam-dau-tien-nhiem-virus-corona-612482.html

Tran, Viet Khoa. 2019. "Proactively Prevent and Repel Danger from the Reverse of Social Networks" (Chu đong ngan chan day lui hiem hoa tu mat trai của mang xa hoi). *Nhan dan Newspaper*, November 5. Accessed 21 April 2020. www.nhandan.com.vn/chinhtri/ item/42135202-chu-dong-ngan-chan-day-lui-hiem-hoa-tu-mat-trai-cua-mang-xa-hoi. html.

Van Anh. 2019. "Vietnam's Social Media: Possibilities and Impossibilities" (Mang xa hoi cua Vietnam: Khong the va co the). *VOV*. Accessed April18, 2020. https://magazine.vov. vn/20190805/mangxh/index.html.

Vinh, Quoc Le. 2020. Indepth interview on "Simmilarities and Differences Between Mainstream Media and Social Media in Reporting COVID-19 in Vietnam" by Hien Thi Minh Nguyen, July 20.

YouGov. 2020. "Latest Round-up of YouGov's Coronavirus Survey Results". *YouGov*. May 18. Accessed May 20, 2020. https://yougov.co.uk/topics/international/articles-reports/2020/05/18/international-covid-19-tracker-update-18-may?fbclid=IwAR07Utz Sdjr3sBR2TV1DUy8Wbx_FGeH7eve6wZT2OAP4dpueMdpvyMGaAFo.

13 Bloggers against panic

Russian-speaking Instagram
bloggers in China and Italy
reporting about COVID-19

*Anna Smoliarova, Tamara Gromova,
and Ekaterina Sharkova*

Social media in emergency management

Civil unrest incidents, natural disasters, food contamination—in all emergency situations people nowadays rely on social media for rapid updates, psychological support, and guidance (e.g., review in Li et al. 2020). The horizontal nature of connections between social media users allows information to spread across them virally (Bruns and Liang 2012), but it has its own advantages and disadvantages. Together with useful and desirable messages, an excessive amount of unreliable information is spreading through social networks, microblogging services, and photo- and video-sharing platforms.

Previous research has shown that during epidemics, virus-related communication on social media might hamper an effective public health response and confuse the population (Panagiotopoulos et al. 2016; Kavanaugh et al. 2012). During a widespread epidemic of Zika fever in 2016, a significant share of Instagram posts about the virus was misleading or included unclear information about the virus (Seltzer et al. 2017). Many users expressed fear and negative sentiment through the images they posted. Major world health organizations were not highly active in combating misleading information on Instagram and Twitter, at least, in the middle of the Ebola outbreak (Guidry et al. 2017).

The problem of unreliable information spreading on social media turned out to be so high-powered that the World Health Organization labeled the current COVID-19 outbreak not only as pandemic but also as "infodemic" (Cinelli et al. 2020). The anxiety of governments is supported by first publications about COVID-19 discourse on Twitter demonstrating "the severe impact of misleading people and spreading unreliable information" (Mourad et al. 2020, 9; see also Li et al. 2020; Dewhurst et al. 2020). Instagram, a worldwide famous photo- and video-sharing social networking service owned by Facebook, has received little research attention in comparison with Twitter (Maares and Hanusch 2020, the first dataset for COVID-19 by Zarei et al. 2020).

Migrants as a social group that is marginalized in terms of national languages are even more vulnerable due to the lack of trustworthy information during disasters or epidemics. The lack of rapidly updated information in a native language and of a social environment that helps people to estimate the trustworthiness of information is crucial (Elias 2006; Chen, Tu, and Zheng 2017). Social media plat-forms allow them to generate rich situational information that also includes the special needs of the population with migration background.

In this chapter, we focus on the Russian-speaking minority in China and Italy during the COVID-19 outbreak in January–April 2020. While China was the epicenter, Italy got the largest number of cases outside of China by March 2020. Native Russian speakers migrate from different post-Soviet countries and embrace "the whole repertoire of migrant groups and identities" (Pechurina 2017, 39). In China, different sources estimate the number of immigrants only from Russia up to 50,000, moving mostly for educational or business reasons. In Italy Ukraine takes fourth place among all countries of origin with 240,000 immigrants (a significant share of which consume and produce content in the Russian language). Eighty thousand moved to Italy from Russia, and 30,000 from Belarus (Pew Research Center 2018). More than 40% of migration to Italy from Ukraine and Russia are based on marriage (ISTAT. Statistical Report 2019). By January 2020, there were more than 60,000 Instagram posts from China and almost 90,000 posts from Italy with hashtags #lifein(country) or #Russiansin(country).

Data and sampling

First, we searched for publications on Instagram hashtagged #coronavirusinchina and #coronavirusinitaly (both hashtags in Russian). We manually went through the publications marked as "best" by Instagram. In the second step, we excluded users who used this hashtag for commercial purposes without posting about COVID-19 or do not belong to Russian-language native speakers who moved to Italy or China before the pandemic. According to users' salience in the "best publications," we selected six bloggers for each country. We also deliberately checked that we included at least one blogger from Wuhan and Northern Italy. To download the data, we used Popsters, a Russian-language service developed for social media analytics. The dataset contains the following information: users' ID, the web link to the post, data of the post, the full text of each post, general estimation of users' engagement rate (ER). The final sample included 640 posts published from December 10, 2019, to April 25, 2020 (262 from China and 378 from Italy).

The codebook used for this study has been elaborated from previous research on patterns of blaming and responsibility in Twitter discussions (Bodrunova et al. 2018). It included the following categories: the topic of a post; sources of information; the presence of emotional tone and calls for action; actors that were blamed or criticized. Since we had to adapt the codebook for the COVID-19 case, all items in the codebook were pre-tested with a subsample of posts. We accepted the second version of the codebook and did an inter-coder reliability test (89%, Cohen's Kappa = .81).

The first post about COVID-19 in our sample was published by a Russian-speaking blogger from Tianjin, China, on 22nd January—two days after China's

Table 13.1 Russian-speaking bloggers from China and Italy included in the sample

Country	Blogger	N followers by April 26, 2020	Date of the first COVID-19-related post
China	aikin_s	11,169	23.01.2020
Italy	albinashepel	2,131	23.02.2020
Italy	alexandra.bazhanova	16,341	24.02.2020
China	dasha_buria	24,292	22.01.2020
Italy	irabokalova	31,306	24.02.2020
Italy	lara_rome	89,586	24.02.2020
China	lovimenja	62,224	29.01.2020
Italy	mi.chiao.tanya	27,009	24.02.2020
China	nadia.in.china	659	28.01.2020
Italy	olyosip_proitalia	79,233	23.02.2020
China	sasha_kitay	4,354	27.01.2020
China	twins_in_china	384,516	27.01.2020

Source: © Anna Smoliarova, Tamara Gromova, Ekaterina Sharkova, 2021

National Health Commission confirmed the human-to-human transmission. The blogger from Wuhan posted for the first time on January 23, others followed the trend four days later, from January 27 to 29. Russian-speaking bloggers in China began to write about coronavirus simultaneously with the increase of its coverage in Russian media. Number or COVID-19 related posts on Weibo also peaked during January 24–25 (Li et al. 2020).

Despite Italy declaring a state of emergency on January 31, Italian Russian-speaking bloggers in our sample have not mentioned coronavirus before the outbreak at the end of February. All six bloggers published their first posts related to the virus on February 23–24. On February 23, Italy took third place in the world by the number of cases (Table 13.1).

Findings: the informative role of bloggers in China and Italy

Have all 12 bloggers changed their content policy due to the pandemic, and if yes, to what extent? To answer this question, we coded all the posts as "fully dedicated to the COVID-19," "no connection to the COVID-19," "COVID-19 is slightly mentioned." The first one implicates that the main topic of a post is fully connected to the virus and its consequences. No connection to the coronavirus in a post means that this post can be easily published at any time before or in the far future and it will preserve its meaning. The exceptions were covered with the third option. For example, the user mentioned in the post that travels are restricted and told a story about their previous journey.

We calculated the share of each option in the content of each blogger. Our results revealed two possible strategies. One-half of the bloggers reported about COVID-19 in every third post on average (from 32% to 43% of all posts after the first virus-related publication). The second half recomposed the content policy: COVID-19 took more than 68.75% share of their posts. Within this group, significant changes are first visible for Chinese bloggers: the share of virus-related posts is higher than 75% in four of six Russian-speaking blogs. Between Italian bloggers, one completely changed her content policy, and the second one takes a place on the lowest level of this strategy with 68.75%. Therefore, Russian-speaking bloggers living in China were much more active in reporting about COVID-19.

@dasha.buria, the blogger from Tianjin, who published the very first post about the virus in our sample, changed her agenda completely—after that, all her posts were focusing on COVID-19. @sasha_kitay drastically changed the intensity of publications: she published only six posts after the outbreak, while before she was posting not less than once every two–four days. All her posts were related to the virus. The only male blogger in our sample, @aikin_s from Wuhan, has not mentioned COVID-19 at all only once since he first wrote about the Wuhan on January 23. @lovimenja, who wrote about the virus only on January 29, has not mentioned it only in 5% of her posts published after that date. In Italy, the major changes are also visible for the author with one of the first publications, @olyosip_proitalia: she covers COVID-19 in 94.5% of posts. @olyosip_proitalia (Olga Osipova) was even invited as a primary source by plenty of Russian media, starting with "First Channel."

To understand what happened to the user engagement during the pandemic, we evaluated median values of ER (engagement rate, automatically provided by Popsters for each post) for each blogger: before and after the first post about the virus, and fully dedicated to the COVID-19 / others after the first post about the virus. Only in two cases, the user engagement rate of posts after the outbreak was lower than before the first post about the virus has been published. @nadia.in.china visited Viet Nam in the first ten days in February, @sasha_kitay, as we already mentioned, published posts much less often. So, in both cases, the decrease of user engagement might be explained by side factors. Within this general trend, the increase of ER is most significant for those bloggers, whose content policy has been most significantly recomposed. ER doubled for @aikin_s and tripled for @olyosip_proitalia.

Thus, the significant share of bloggers in our sample changed their content policy to provide their followers with up-to-date information. In turn, the followers rewarded the efforts bloggers made to generate rich situational information. We interpret these findings as a confirmation that Russian-speaking bloggers from China and Italy were perceived by their audiences as reliable sources.

Emotional less often than informational coverage: Chinese and Italian bloggers differ

Instagram bloggers elaborate strong personal ties with their audiences, many of them constantly share emotions, thus strengthening these ties. Previous research has shown that fear and negative emotions might dominate in the public sentiment on an epidemic. Thus, we expected that the coverage of COVID-19 in Russian-speaking blogs in China and Italy should be quite emotional.

Coding 209 posts fully dedicated to COVID-19, we considered them to be "emotional" in several cases. If a post included exclamation points, words, written in capital mode, invective language, hysterical emoticons, three periods, rhetorical questions, or figures of speech, it was coded as "emotional." To be coded as "informative," the post had to include facts or to tell a personal story without explicit intention to trigger an emotional reaction among readers. It might be written in a style imitating neutral news coverage.

Contrary to our expectations, we revealed a substantial share of informative posts—44.5%, the median value of informative posts among bloggers is 50%. The share of emotional posts is much lower on average in China: among Chinese bloggers, the median value of the share of the emotional posts is 45%, while among Italian bloggers it is 63.8%. Interestingly, the biggest share of emotional posts (88,2%) has been published by @olyosip_proitalia who covered COVID-19 most actively. @aikin_s from Wuhan took first place by emotionality among Chinese bloggers (60%).

This result corresponds with the attitudes of users toward national governments in their countries. Chinese bloggers in our sample have shown more emotional support to the Chinese government than Italian users to their national authorities. Thirty-eight percent of emotional posts from China contain statements that blogger estimates acts performed by the national government as effective and adequate: "Should the Chinese apologize to the world? For me, they don't owe anything. They did what others are unlikely to do. . . . They really did much more than they could" (@twins_in_china, March 4, 2020). Only 17% of Italian posts share this attitude toward the Italian government. We assume that Chinese bloggers felt themselves safer and this might be the reason why they could perform as an informative source for their audiences. "That is why I fell in love with China even more. For how the state has taken care even of people like me" (@sasha_kitay, March 24, 2020).

In 54% of emotional posts in our dataset representatives of a host society were mentioned. The famous image of Italians singing was present in the bloggers' posts.

> Such a nation that does not lose heart. . . . People go to the balconies and begin to sing and to play musical instruments. The whole city is singing. Incredibly touching. . . . And the Italians are trying to look around for the positive side.
>
> (@irabokalova, March 15, 2020)

Bloggers from China mentioned discipline, wrote about people welcoming those who recovered from COVID-19 with flowers and applause (@nadia.in.china, March 16, 2020) or shared admiration for kindergarten teachers who successfully supported children online (@twins_in_china, February 17, 2020). Chinese bloggers expressed admiration for local people much more often than bloggers from Italy. Fifty-two percent of Chinese posts mentioning local people were written in a highly positive tone, while only 31% of Italian posts expressing attitudes toward Italians were coded as highly positive.

Based on these findings, we assume that bloggers were not only perceived by their followers but performed an informative role. They contributed to the psychological support since they acted as ambassadors of the host society. In China, bloggers even actively spread positive attitudes toward governmental actions.

According to Russian-speaking bloggers in China and Italy: who is to blame and what to do? Calling for WHO obedience and avoiding panic

While reporting about the COVID-19, bloggers might attribute responsibility to some actors or powers or criticize the activities of institutional politicians, organizations, ordinary people. Actors responsible for the pandemic were mentioned only in 21% of all posts fully dedicated to COVID-19. Critical statements telling people how to behave properly were found twice as often than accusations (45% of all posts fully dedicated to COVID-19).

Bloggers mostly blamed individuals predicting that their behavior might result in exponential growth dynamics and lead to an increase of numbers COVID-19 deaths. People were accused of not following the instructions of the World Health Organization, of spreading panic or urging not to believe in the virus.

Russian-speaking bloggers in our sample have not accused the Chinese government of hiding information at the very beginning of a new epidemic. The story of Li Wenliang from Wuhan Central Hospital who warned about new unrecorded pneumonia cases by the end of December 2019 has been mentioned once by twins_in_china (@twins_in_china, February 10, 2020). A direct anti-Chinese sentiment has been registered only once ("I just want to cry from resentment and anger. And yes, to hate the Chinese" (@irabokalova, April 9, 2020). On the contrary, @olyosip_proitalia even criticized President of Veneto Luca Zaia for a xenophobic speech against Chinese people (@olyosip_proitalia, February 29, 2020).

The major cases of criticism relate to other people: locals and people living in Russia and other countries (see Figure 13.1). Bloggers actively criticize those who do not follow recommendations of the World Health Organization. As @olyosip_proitalia puts it: Their own interests are more important than security in the whole city/in the whole country. Who still believes that he is not at risk, and the risk of infecting others is not a problem for him, because "it's them who should stay at home, not me" (@olyosip_proitalia, April 4, 2020)? The rhetoric of the bloggers' claims is remarkably similar to what Dunbar (2004, 105) described as "policing of free riders." Policing "free riders—those who take the benefits of sociality without paying the costs" is one of four ways how language is "used for social exchanges in everyday life."

Besides those who violate the guidelines of the World Health Organization, bloggers constantly wrote about people who were spreading rumors, denying the coronavirus threat, or expressed conspiratorial views. This criticism could be

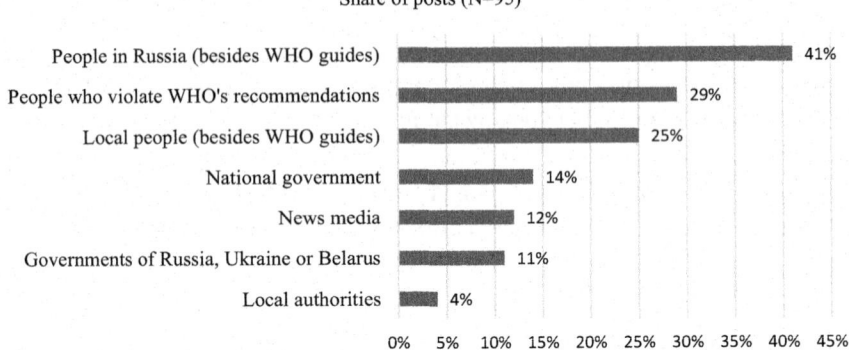

Figure 13.1 Objects of criticism in posts fully related to COVID-19

Source: © Anna Smoliarova, Tamara Gromova, Ekaterina Sharkova, 2021

quite emotional: we have already mentioned that bloggers even were afraid that denying the danger of coronavirus might lead to a tragedy. @olyosip_proitalia was most critical: she called such people "WhatsApp analysts" and "sofa-sitting virologist-political scientists" (people with absolutely zero expertise in a subject of discussion). Every tenth post contains criticism toward the news media: "I try not to watch TV, not to read newspapers with sensational lines, not to give way to panic" (@lara_rome, March 10, 2020). In general, 46% of posts include a call for action—mostly, to follow recommendations of the World Health Organization. Bloggers also explicitly called not to panic and to spread posts that are trust-worthy: "Do not follow the gossip and pseudo-truths that might be beneficial to someone else" (@twins_in_china, February 20, 2020).

Contrary to the more typical behavior of social media users during COVID-19(Li et al. 2020), Russian-speaking bloggers in China and Italy actively refuted rumors and stood against misleading people and spreading unreliable informa-tion. They did fact-checking, criticized destructive behavior, and made efforts to raise awareness of their followers.

Did the bloggers themselves rely on trustworthy information sources? Bloggers as primary sources

Bloggers in our sample referred to mass media in every tenth post. Every sec-ond post does not rely on any explicitly mentioned information source. Usually, bloggers just told their readers that they share official information from qualita-tive news media in different languages. In some cases, bloggers posted screen-shots from the news media websites. In every sixth post, they explicitly stated that they were not a primary source without mentioning media outlets or people. Authorities were mentioned only in 8% of posts, for example, a decree of the

Italian government. We have not expected that the World Health Organization and healthcare experts will be almost absent as information sources: they were present less than in 5% of posts. Telling their personal stories bloggers could mention, for example, an announcement from a local shop or an official statement of the company the blogger's husband is working for.

We observed several acts of participatory hashtagging connecting Russian-speaking migrant communities around the globe. In such an act, a blogger mentioned five more bloggers who live in other countries and invited their audience to find out about life during the quarantine. Such posts are united by a hashtag, for example, "coronavirus—the situation in my country," "appreciate life" or "the day will come." Posts with the last hashtag told about ideas and dreams what bloggers are going to do on the very first day after the end of quarantine.

Instagram users share much less content from the news media accounts than Twitter users. Russian-speaking bloggers in China and Italy were no exception. Instead, they created a global network and motivated their followers to get familiar with observations or information shared by bloggers from other countries.

Conclusion: fighting conspiracies and panic

Based on the findings already described, we can conclude that Russian-speaking bloggers from China and Italy performed the role of an informative source for their audiences. Bloggers constantly reacted to questions and comments they got from their audience, changed their content strategy, and included the news in blogs that before pandemic usually did not follow news agenda at all.

Russian-speaking bloggers served as fact-checkers and news curators for their audiences—living in China, Italy, Russia, and many other countries. They actively criticized rumors and conspirological ideas—such behavior we might expect from quality media. Although they communicate with their audience in an interactive and emotional manner following the style of the platform, we believe that bloggers in our sample did not contribute to the infodemic during COVID-19.

Their potential as an information source is mostly based on their own experience (and only for a few of them—on studying carefully and critically other news media) and their sense of responsibility to the audience. Bloggers positioned themselves as primary sources who were constantly asked to comment on the situation. We might assume that such statements legitimized changes in the editorial policy and might be used as a tool to demonstrate unique ties with the audience.

Contrary to the news media, bloggers focused their monitoring on other ordinary people. They not only shared guidelines of the World Health Organization but reported negatively about people who violate these guidelines, as well as swore at people who threaten the joint efforts to stop the exponential growth during the pandemic spreading panic or misinformation about the level of danger. Thus, they fulfilled the function of policing "free riders" and called their audience to follow the rules that will allow our society to minimize the threat and consequences of the pandemic.

Acknowledgments

The research has been supported in full by Russian Presidential Grant for Young Ph.D. Scientists, research grant MK-1448.2020.6.

References

Bodrunova, Svetlana, Smoliarova, Anna, Achkasova, Vera, and Ivan Blekanov. 2018. "Who Is to Blame? Patterns of Blaming and Responsibility Assignment in Networked Discussions on Immigrants in Russia and Germany." *Journal of Social Policy Studies* 16, no. 4: 627–44.

Bruns, Axel, and Yuxian Eugene Liang. 2012. "Tools and Methods for Capturing Twitter Data During Natural Disasters." *First Monday* 17, no. 4: 1–8.

Chen, Wenhong, Fangjing Tu, and Pei Zheng. 2017. "A Transnational Networked Public Sphere of Air Pollution: Analysis of a Twitter Network of PM2.5 from the Risk Society Perspective." *Information, Communication & Society* 20, no. 7: 1005–23.

Cinelli, Matteo, Quattrociocchi, Walter, Galeazzi, Alessandro, Valensise, Carlo Michele, Brugnoli, Emanuele, Schmidt, Ana Lucia, Zola, Paola, Zollo Fabiana, and Antonio Scala. 2020. "The COVID-19 Social Media Infodemic." *arXiv preprint*, arXiv: 2003.05004.1–18.

Dewhurst, David Rushing, Alshaabi, Thayer, Arnold, Michael V., Minot, Joshua R., Danforth, Christopher M., and Peter Sheridan Dodds. 2020. "Divergent Modes of Online Collective Attention to the COVID-19 Pandemic Are Associated with Future Caseload Variance." *arXiv preprint*, arXiv:2004.03516.1–16.

Dunbar, Robin I. 2004. "Gossip in Evolutionary Perspective." *Review of General Psychology* 8, no. 2: 100–10.

Elias, Nelly. 2006. "The Role of the Media in the Cultural and Social Adaptation of Immigrants from the CIS in Israel." *Diasporas* 4: 85–100 (in Russian).

Guidry, Jeanine P., Jin, Yan, Orr, Caroline A., Messner, Marcus, and Shana Meganck. 2017. "Ebola on Instagram and Twitter: How Health Organizations Address the Health Crisis in Their Social Media Engagement." *Public Relations Review* 43, no. 3: 477–86.

ISTAT. Statistical Report. 2019. "Non-EU Citizens in Italy | Years 2018–2019." Accessed October 17, 2019. www.istat.it/it/files//2019/11/Report-Cittadini-non-comunitari-2018-EN.pdf

Kavanaugh, Andrea L., Fox, Edward A., Sheetz, Steven, Yang, Seungwon, Li, Lin Tzy, Whalen, Travis, Shoemaker, Donald, Natsev, Paul, and Xie Lexing. 2012. "Social Media Use by the Government: From the Routine to the Critical." *Government Information Quarterly* 29, no. 4: 480–91.

Li, Lifang, Zhang, Qingpeng, Wang, Xiao, Zhang, Jun, Wang, Tao, Gao, Tian-Lu, Duan, Wei, Kam-fai Tsoi, Kevin, and Fei-Yue Wang. 2020. "Characterizing the Propagation of Situational Information in Social Media During COVID-19 Epidemic: A Case Study on Weibo." *IEEE Transactions on Computational Social Systems* 7, no. 2: 556–62.

Maares, Phoebe, and Folker Hanusch. 2020. "Exploring the Boundaries of Journalism: Instagram Micro-Bloggers in the Twilight Zone of Lifestyle Journalism." *Journalism* 21, no. 2: 262–78.

Mourad, Azzam, Ali Srour, Haidar Harmanani, Cathia Jenainatiy, and Mohamad Arafeh. 2020. "Critical Impact of Social Networks Infodemic on Defeating Coronavirus COVID-19 Pandemic: Twitter-Based Study and Research Directions." *arXiv preprint*, arXiv:2005.08820v1.1–11.

Panagiotopoulos, Panos, Barnett, Julie, Bigdeli, Alinaghi Ziaee, and Steven Sams. 2016. "Social Media in Emergency Management: Twitter as a Tool for Communicating Risks to the Public." *Technological Forecasting and Social Change* 111: 86–96.

Pechurina, Anna. 2017. "Post-Soviet Russian-Speaking Migration to the UK: The Discourses of Visibility and Accountability." *Post-Soviet Migration and Diasporas*: 29–45.

Pew Research Center. 2018. "Origins and Destinations of the World's Migrants, 1990–2017." Accessed February 28, 2018. www.pewresearch.org/global/interactives/global-migrant-stocks-map/.

Seltzer, Emily, E. Horst-Martz, M. Lu, and Raina Martha Merchant. 2017. "Public Sentiment and Discourse About Zika Virus on Instagram." *Public Health* 150: 170–75.

Zarei, Koosha, Farahbakhsh, Reza, Crespi, Noel, and Gareth Tyson. 2020. "A FIRST INSTAGRAM Dataset on COVID-19." arXiv preprint arXiv:2004.12226.1–4.

@irabokalova. Instagram. March 15, 2020. www.instagram.com/p/B9v4-g0qbGA (in Russian).

@irabokalova. Instagram. April 9, 2020. www.instagram.com/p/B-wD0_uqznt (in Russian).

@lara_rome. Instagram. March 10, 2020. www.instagram.com/p/B9itM49qxWa (in Russian).

@nadia.in.china. Instagram. March 16, 2020. www.instagram.com/p/B9yDz5Pndp3 (in Russian).

@olyosip_proitalia. Instagram. April 4, 2020. www.instagram.com/p/B-jS86yoPcP (in Russian).

@sasha_kitay. Instagram. March 24, 2020. www.instagram.com/p/B-G2wJnnOfu/ (in Russian).

@twins_in_china. Instagram. February 10, 2020. www.instagram.com/p/B8X-obcgfm7 (in Russian).

@twins_in_china. Instagram. February 17, 2020. www.instagram.com/p/B8qAdWoAxfH (in Russian).

@twins_in_china. Instagram. February 20, 2020. www.instagram.com/p/B8xulTxgsgU (in Russian).

@olyosip_proitalia. Instagram. February 29, 2020. www.instagram.com/p/B9KdslWozRw (in Russian).

@twins_in_china. Instagram. March 4, 2020. www.instagram.com/p/B9TM2oxgc_v (in Russian).

14 Reimagined communities in the fight against the invisible enemy

Soccer and the national question in Spain

Alberto del Campo Tejedor

Introduction

Soccer has often been compared to a ritual war (Ramonet 1999), and since the days of Mussolini at least, Nation States have used this popular sport not only to fuel patriotic sentiment, but also to infuse this sentiment with singular propagandistic messages. In Spain, the fascist dictator Francisco Franco, in power between 1939 and 1975, elevated the mighty Real Madrid soccer team as a national symbol, especially following five straight wins of the European Championships between 1956 and 1960. Peripheral ethno-nationalisms also had their respective teams (Llopis 2008): Athletic de Bilbao only recruited Basque players, Celta de Vigo wore the colors of the banned Galician flag, and F.C. Barcelona became "més que un club" (more than a club)—its main motto—because going to the stadium was essentially seen as an act of rebellion and collective self-affirmation against a centralist dictator. Particularly the derby matches between Barça and Real Madrid (known as "el Clásico") have been largely perceived and experienced as a clash between those who identify with Spain as one nation and those who identify with Catalonia as a nation, a symbolic connotation that has grown alongside the rise of Catalonia's separatist movement in recent years.

In Spain, the coronavirus crisis erupted in the midst of another social and political crisis revolving around nationalism. It is widely known that, at critical moments, including wars and, in general, any event in which an external enemy is identifiable, collective identifications are activated, particularly "imagined communities" (Anderson 1983). This chapter focuses on soccer as a field in which we can observe how Spanish and Catalan nationalist narratives, sentiments and symbols are constructed but also debated at this critical time during which, paradoxically, soccer matches have been suspended. The analysis focuses on the 50 days of lockdown between the declaration of the State of Emergency on March 14 and May 2, studying the media production, reception, and circulation of different communicative events within the world of soccer. These are inserted into a context of dual tensions: on the one hand, tension derived from how to fit ethno-nationalisms into the Nation State; and on the other hand, simultaneously, the tension driven by different political and ideological forces with regard to the governance of a nation, whose conceptualization and symbols are a matter of ongoing debate.

The world of soccer offers a magnificent arena to understand how the current healthcare, social and economic crisis is fueling battles and controversies around the very idea of Spain. But also how meanings created around the Nation State, country, nationalities, or government are not constructed beyond the reach of citizens, as mere consumers of messages fabricated by institutions and the media; rather, citizens discredit, resemanticize, and generate alternative narratives, particularly through social media, which have during this time of lockdown become a privileged forum for political communication.

The war against coronavirus in the state of self-governing communities

The Spanish Constitution of 1978 enshrines the notion of a unitary regional State known as the "Estado de las Autonomías" or State of Self-Governing Communities, an intermediate model between the Central State and the Federal system. Spain's 17 Self-Governing Communities are not sovereign and they do not have Constituent power, but they do have legislative and executive powers through their own regional parliaments and governments in the areas stipulated by their respective Statutes. The State of the Self-Governing Communities originated in response to the need to find a fit for regional/national singularities within the Nation State, but there is by no means consensus in this regard (Balfour and Quiroga 2007; Humlebaek 2015). A section of the Spanish population, particularly within the conservative and liberal spectrum, label themselves "constitutionalist" because they believe that the Constitution preserves the unity of Spain and is already sufficiently decentralized with regard to the "regions." Others, however, believe that Spain is a "nation of nations" and, therefore, from largely left-wing positions, they propose a Federal State. Others still are openly "secessionist," in favor (from different ideological positions) of opening up processes that would lead to a disconnection from the Central State and would allow the "nationalities" recognized in the Constitution to become independent Nation States, following a referendum.

On March 13, 2020, when there were 3860 confirmed cases of COVID-19 and 90 dead, the Spanish President announced that the country would enter a "State of Emergency" the following day, meaning that the Self-Governing Communities would be subject to a single chain of command from central government, personified in the figure of the President himself. With successive extensions, voted on every 15 days in Congress, the State of Emergency was prolonged for more than three months. Throughout this time, the pro-independence Catalan government interpreted the maneuver as an attempt by the State to annul Catalonia's autonomy. Since 2012, the Catalan government has been driving a process of sovereignty supported by approximately 50% of Catalans. One landmark moment in this process was the independence referendum held in 2017, declared illegal by the Constitutional Court. Consequently, the Supreme Court charged various nationalist leaders with sedition, sentencing them to up to 13 years in prison.

Pedro Sánchez, the Spanish president, has an ambivalent relationship with separatists: on the one hand, his party (*PSOE*) is clearly opposed to an independence referendum, but it cannot forget that it got into power first due to the support given by separatists to the vote of no confidence launched against the previous president, Mariano Rajoy (from the conservative *PP* party), and then that Sánchez was sworn in as president on January 7, 2020, which allowed him to form a minority government with *Unidas Podemos*, the communist grass roots party led by Pablo Iglesias. Sworn in as Vice President, Iglesias supports federalism and advocates a referendum agreed between the State and the *Generalitat de Catalunya* (Catalonia's institution of self-government), which places him in a diametrically opposed position not only to conservative and nation state parties but also to the majority of Spanish citizens, who oppose any process of self-determination that would lead to the secession of any region.

In return for their support, Catalan separatists opened up a process in which the governments of Spain and Catalonia would sit down at the negotiating table, a move that received harsh criticism from right-wing opposition led by the *PP*. The sudden eruption of the coronavirus crisis paralyzed this process after just one meeting, but both governments understand that they must take advantage of this exceptional situation to strengthen their position. If the fight against the virus is described in Europe as the greatest challenge since the end of World War II, in Spain, the government has on numerous occasions deployed the narrative that Spanish citizens are facing a genuine "war" in which the State binds together the different forces of king and country: doctors and other healthcare workers are fighting "on the front line"; the army is deployed on the streets to disinfect spaces; even citizens are considered "soldiers" who must show "sacrifice" and "heroism." as the President solemnly declared during his announcement of the State of Emergency, emulating the words of Churchill after the fateful Dunkirk landing[1]: "In the war on the virus, we shall never be defeated, we shall fight back, we shall win . . . We shall leave no one behind."

The war on the virus is being waged in parallel to the battle for information in a dual showdown between state nationalism and ethno-nationalism, and the national government (socialist-communist ideology, closer to the federal model) versus the right-wing opposition, associated with centralism interpreted through a lens of pro-Spanish patriotism. During lockdown, Spanish people en masse followed the daily press briefings held by a crisis committee made up of government ministers, senior military officers and scientists. The Chief of Staff of the *Guardia Civil* (military body that performs policing functions) unleashed controversy at one of these briefings, one month after the State of Emergency had been declared: as he was explaining the actions being taken by the police authorities to combat fake news being spread on social media about the coronavirus, the general stated that "one of the tasks is also to minimize the climate that is contrary to the government's handling of the crisis."[2] The government and the general himself rushed to clarify that this had been a "slip," although the conservative opposition and separatist parties deemed this declaration to be proof of an illegitimate and orchestrated plan on the part of the government to control the narrative on the handling of the crisis. One day after this "slip," the spokesperson of the *Generalitat* sparked yet more controversy when she stated that, in an independent Catalonia, "there would not have been as many dead or infected."[3] Meanwhile, the leader of *VOX*, the ultra-right-wing and ultra-nationalist Spanish party, called Sánchez a *"matasanos"* (which roughly translates as a "quack," but literally means "killer of healthy people"), and blamed his government for promoting "ferocious euthanasia" against the elderly.[4] When the death toll due to the coronavirus reached 25,000, the term "genocide" was bandied about widely on social media to criticize government handling.

Heroic feats in the national game

The battle to sway public opinion began the moment the State of Emergency was declared, and subtle strategies were deployed in areas that are not explicitly political, such as soccer. Soccer is undoubtedly the most popular sport in Spain: half the population over the age of 15 declare themselves to be soccer fans (Llopis 2008, 56). Unsurprisingly, therefore, as in other countries, the national soccer team has fostered imaginary national collectives. Following two consecutive wins at the European Championships (2008 and 2012) and one World Cup victory (2010), for the first time in history, these soccer players helped to build a feeling of patriotism, bolstered significantly by the media, Spain's two major political parties (*PSOE* and *PP*) and certain sporting celebrities (Resina and Limón 2014). The Spanish public celebrated these victories with unusual euphoria: for the first time in Spain's democratic era, the red and gold Spanish flag no longer invoked the legacy of the military dictatorship (which appropriated it as a symbol of Franco's regime), the heritage of the military and the most conservative wing of society.

With the outbreak of the COVID-19 pandemic, and under the pretext that all sporting events were cancelled and that the public demanded sporting entertainment during lockdown, *Televisión Española* (*TVE*), the public state TV network, decided to broadcast some of the country's greatest national sporting triumphs of the past. The match chosen to launch this programming, four days after the State of Emergency had been declared, on prime time television, was Spain's 12–1 defeat of Malta at the end of 1983. In the last qualifying game for the 1984 European Championships, Spain needed to beat its rivals with a goal difference of at least 11 if it wanted to finish the qualifying round above Holland. The Spanish Soccer Federation decided to play the match in Seville, whose fans have always considered themselves "the 12th player" in the national side. It was the right decision: the players always acknowledged that the public "lifted them up."

Why did the public state television network choose a game from 1983 against a lower ranking rival instead of one of Spain's more recent victories in the European Championships and the World Cup? These later victories were achieved with a style of play known as "tiqui-taca" (or "tiki-taka"), characterized by highly skilled short and precise passing. It is the Spanish version of a style of play implemented by Cruyff at Barça, which spurred the development of technical mid-fielders such as Guardiola, and later Xavi and Iniesta, who, together with other players from Barça, were the lynchpins in the Spanish national soccer side, during its golden age between 2008 and 2014.

The memory of Spain's heroic victory over Malta spurred the "recovery" of "la furia española" or Spanish Fury, the nickname given to the national side at the time, an allusion to Sack of Antwerp in 1576. A far cry from and even antithetical to the "tiki-taka" style of play, developed in Barcelona by the team's Dutch manager at the time, the Spain-Malta game is considered the epitome of an idiosyncratic approach to soccer that is rooted more in honor and pride than in technique, based on epic feats of heroism, which makes it even more emotive within the context of a pandemic. In this match, the enemy was not Malta (a weak rival), but rather Spain itself, its proverbial fatalism and its lack of unity following a civil war and 40 years of dictatorship. The Spain-Malta game is a symbol of an old nation that fights bravely and in unity to claim victory against the odds, just as Barça symbolizes a national project based on the values of the Catalan bourgeoisie, which is played out with a precise and elegant style of play. This re-run of the match, 36 years on, was a nostalgic nod to a time when Spaniards, having emerged from the Dictatorship in 1975 and survived an attempted Coup in 1981, achieved a difficult and unexpected consensus, putting general interest above their differences, as showcased in the Constitution of 1978.

In the war against the coronavirus, victory would not come from the Market (which sold face masks to the highest bidder) or from the European Union (which was dubious about the Spanish President's pleas to create a "Marshall Plan"[5]). Only a strong nation of unity and solidarity could vanquish the invisible foe. Following the reshowing of the Spain-Malta game, social media were abuzz with comments. Patriots called for unity and epic resistance against the virus. Immediately, an old song from 1988, by *Dúo Dinámico*, entitled precisely "Resistiré" (encapsulating the meanings of withstanding, surviving, and fighting back), became an anthem in this struggle. However, as one might expect, social media was also awash with comments that mocked how a nation could feel represented by a soccer defeat over a country 1600 times smaller than Spain and 6 times smaller than the smallest of Spain's 50 provinces.[6]

The war of the flags

With the slogan "Legendary moments in Spanish sport," *TVE* showed some of the most iconic sporting victories achieved by Spanish athletes and sports players, including the cyclist Miguel Induráin and tennis player Rafa Nadal. This programming helped to shift the focus onto sports players, who were progressively called upon to be "soldiers," given their financial capacity to show solidarity and support the nation through this "war." "Where are our sports stars?" demanded one Twitter user, whose post went viral.

Twelve days after the State of Emergency was declared, the media covered a patriotic initiative: the tennis player Rafa Nadal and basketball player Pau Gasol (one from Mallorca, the other from Catalonia, both sporting icons in Spain), launched an initiative on Twitter with the Spanish Red Cross to raise money to fight the coronavirus. "You, the people of Spain, have never let your sports players down. . ., and we cannot let you down now either," said Nadal in an emotive message posted on his official account. Soon, hundreds of professional sports players and athletes came on board and made their respective donations to the project. Some, such as Formula 1 racing driver Fernando Alonso, published their actions on Twitter, adding the hashtag *#NuestraMejorVictoria* (our finest victory), with a biceps emoji and a Spanish flag emoji, as did the rally racing driver Carlos Sainz, the athlete Orlando Ortega and various soccer players.

The national flag has ambiguous significations in Spain and is still burdened by connotations derived from its instrumental use by Franco's regime. Today, it is still largely the political right—and particularly leaders and followers of *VOX*— that makes the greatest use of the flag, bringing together the idea of country, centralism of the State, and conservative ideology. During the democratic period up until the pandemic, the flag had only appeared en masse among citizens in two circumstances: in the celebrations of the national soccer side's victories (2008, 2010, and 2012) and during the uproar over the independence referendum held in Catalonia in 2018, which led many Spaniards, not just on the right of the political spectrum, to hang the national flag from their balconies. Now, once again, in the war against the coronavirus, and in alliance with sport and the media, the flag once again became a symbol of victory to be achieved through patriotic union. Many professional sports players and athletes used it on their official accounts, its use was widespread on WhatsApp messages, and Spanish flags were once again draped on balconies and outside houses. Some citizens even played the national anthem with the quarantine clapping initiative that took place at 8 o'clock every evening, as if this was the time to stand proudly together in unity.

However, the ambivalent and polysemic Spanish flag, like other national symbols, can be used with very different political intentions. On March 18, left-wing organizations and separatist political parties, particularly from Catalonia, organized a mass banging of pots and pans during the televised speech given by King Felipe VI, whose father (Juan Carlos I) was being investigated for receiving 100 million euros in commissions from the Saudi Arabian monarchy. The next day, in clear response to this movement, the conservative *Unión Monárquica de España* association urged citizens to hang a flag with a black ribbon on their balconies. The three right-wing constitutionalist parties (*PP*, *VOX*, and *Ciudadanos*) copied the initiative, hanging national flags in mourning at their headquarters. At *Ciudadanos* party headquarters, a banner with the flag and the black ribbon was hung alongside two slogans: "Juntos venceremos" (Together we shall prevail) and "Somos España" (We are Spain). The purpose of these staged manifestations was to seize back control from the socialist-communist government over the patriotic narrative and symbols, usually controlled by the right wing. They achieved it. On April 24, more than 40 days after the State of Emergency had been declared, the video of a giant 48-meter flag with a black ribbon, draped from a centrally located building in Seville, went viral. The flag was owned by a beer company that usually used it for Spanish national soccer games, and had been voluntarily loaned to a right-wing voter who wanted to "show indignation over the handling of this crisis, which has given rise to this non-conformist and patriotic spirit."[7] The national flag, spurred on by the memory of great sporting achievements, was soon turned against the government, which rejected the use of the black ribbon. However, it would be a mistake to think that citizens have simply accepted and reproduced the ideas promoted by political parties and the media.

Guardiola and Messi, good soldiers

With the goal of "uniting all Spanish sport," during the crisis, the show of solidarity launched by Pau Gasol and Rafael Nadal received huge coverage in the written press, on the radio, throughout social media and on public and private television channels.[8] However, public television did not just stop with the news story that had hit the headlines in the daily press: the former player and manager of Barça, Pep Guardiola, known for his pro-independence activism, donated a million euros to a foundation run by the *Colegio de Médicos de Barcelona* to buy healthcare equipment. That same day, March 24, the media reported on an identical gesture of solidarity by Messi, who also donated a million euros, which he spread between Argentina and the *Hospital Clinic de Barcelona*.

The figure of Guardiola is atypical, since he contravenes an unwritten law in Spanish soccer that sports professionals should abstain from expressing political ideas. Born in Sampedor, a municipality in Barcelona, Guardiola was the captain of the Barça soccer team for many years in the 1990s, and later became the club's manager between 2008 and 2012. His role as a symbol for Catalan nationalism gradually grew, and many still remember his clashes with Mourinho, the manager of Real Madrid. Spurred on by the *pròces soberanista* (movement for sovereignty), Guardiola has increased his activism in support of independence. Not only on social media, but also in official campaigns, the current Manchester City manager has used his media platform to proclaim internationally that Catalan separatism is not "xenophobic or selfish: it is a movement that bases its strength on recognizing pluralism and diversity," while criticizing that "Spain is drifting into authoritarianism, under which anti-terrorism laws are used to criminalize dissidence."[9]

As a result of his unequivocal separatist activism, Guardiola is vilified not only by ardent Real Madrid fans, but also in general by the majority of pro-centralist Spaniards. Unsurprisingly, Guardiola's donation to a hospital in Catalonia was interpreted by separatists as a sign of his patriotic commitment to Catalonia, whose powers had been usurped by the State. More surprisingly, he was flooded with praise on social media, even in spaces such as *ForoCoches*, a virtual forum used mostly by right-wing pro-centralist Spanish men, nicknamed *ForoVox* by its detractors in reference to the ultra-nationalist Spanish conservative party. Analysis of such unusually favorable comments reveals that Guardiola, in a single gesture, broke the deeply entrenched stereotype of Catalans as being miserly and penny-pinching. But above all, his generosity stood in stark contrast with the players of Real Madrid. While Madrid players only agreed to take a 10% pay cut, Messi announced on his official account that the entire team would take a 70% pay cut. Messi's announcement, which ended with "Visca el Barça i visca Catalunya!" (Long live Barça and long live Catalonia), received one million "likes,"[10] not only from separatists. When Guardiola's mother died weeks later from coronavirus, there was widespread condolence and praise throughout Spain, regardless of political color.

Conclusions

The media undoubtedly wield a great deal of power in shaping public opinion. During the economic crisis of 2008, the media enthusiastically praised the successes of the Spanish soccer side at the European Championships and World Cup. They brandished slogans that associated soccer with war: "¡A por ellos!" (Go get 'em). Spanish fans celebrated their wins noisily on the streets waving flags and singing "¡Yo soy español, español, español" (I am Spanish, Spanish, Spanish). The economic hardships and political discrepancies seemed to dissipate.

The language of war, patriotism, soccer, and political and economic crisis became intertwined once again with the coronavirus crisis, in a context in which "the nationalist problem" had been further accentuated, as had the gloomy forecasts about the Spanish economy and general mistrust toward a minority government. In that context, figures such as Nadal play a prominent role as national icon, just like the army or public television. The Spanish public TV network chose the Spain-Malta game as a "reminder of nationality," an example of "banal nationalism" (Billig 1995) that calls to unity, historic achievement, and national epic, showing that, at critical times, the people of Spain, just like the soccer players and fans of that legendary match, would be ready to play their part. Reviving the glory of that day—not on the field, in the bars or out in the streets, but at home with the family—meant recreating and maintaining a compelling sense of national community from the comfort of the armchair.

Initially, the declaration of the State of Emergency and the battle between the State and the *Generalitat* allowed the Spanish government to present itself as a guarantor of unity in a situation comparable to that of war. The Spain-Malta game, and in general the broadcasting of past national sporting triumphs, was yet another propagandistic action to create a climate of affiliation and commitment, to which citizens responded. Sports players and athletes, like many citizens, brandished their Spanish flags: emojis on social media; physical flags hanging from balconies and windows. However, criticism of the government's handling of the crisis soon escalated. On the one hand, pro-separatists moved to create the narrative of an ineffective Spain, in which only "government by Catalans for Catalans" could save lives. The right-wing opposition also cashed in. Flags went into mourning and came to symbolize the government's guilt for the thousands of neglected compatriots, now dead.

The donations made by Messi but above all Guardiola (and the subsequent death of his mother) stoked feelings and declarations of empathy and recognition, even though certain sectors of the media and the public tried in vain to interpret the action of the separatist icon as another partisan and ethno-racial act, which only favored his own kind. Social media passed judgment, either interpreting the donations as an act that transcended politics (applauding a humanitarian effort that dilutes ideological differences), or reaching an explicitly political interpretation: the two Barcelona players were more patriotic than the Real Madrid players, traditional symbols of the Spanish nation.

The political wielding of soccer—in terms of the way in which institutions and the media use soccer to generate images and narratives that have an impact on the population and affect their ideas and behaviors—is not as simple or as monolithic in times of crisis. Although broadcasting an epic past victory can easily arouse patriotic feeling, there are other actors besides the State also vying to use national symbols and discourses for political ends. Furthermore, the public reacts differently to the behaviors of soccer icons. Undoubtedly, the support voiced by pro-centralist Spaniards toward Guardiola was shaped by a singular climate that favors the magnification of generous acts of solidarity, especially from soccer players, called upon to act as leaders and to set an example to others. But also, in the battle between government and opposition to highlight or discredit the handling of the crisis, citizens also stopped looking at Catalonia and laid the blame squarely with the government itself.

Although an exceptionally critical moment fosters identarian affiliations and the partisan use of soccer and sport in general, it also promotes tension and disputes in a scenario that throws into sharp relief the fragmentation, polarization and debate raging around the issue of the State, nation, country, and government. Political institutions and traditional media (television, radio, press) each displayed their customary bias and partisan leanings. But neither soccer players nor the general public, through social media, stuck to the established script, demonstrating the difficulty in times of crisis of unequivocally instrumentalizing the *us* versus *them* dialectic in the terrain of a disputed Spain.

Notes

1 www.lamoncloa.gob.es/presidente/actividades/Paginas/2020/130320-sanchez-declaracio.aspx
2 www.rtve.es/alacarta/videos/telediario/jose-manuel-santiago-explica-como-se-combaten-bulos/5560331/
3 www.economiadigital.es/politica-y-sociedad/coronavirus-la-generalitat-vincula-la-independencia-y-el-numero-de-muertos_20055285_102.html
4 www.elmundo.es/espana/2020/04/13/5e944cddfdddffdbbd8b45b7.html
5 https://elpais.com/economia/2020-03-22/sanchez-pide-a-la-ue-un-plan-marshall-y-eurobonos-contra-la-crisis-del-virus.html
6 https://twitter.com/RTVE_Com/status/1240261676114403342
7 https://sevilla.abc.es/sevilla/sevi-cuelgan-gran-bandera-espana-crespon-negro-edificio-plaza-salvador-202004241750_noticia.html
8 www.rtve.es/noticias/20200326/nadal-gasol-unen-deporte-espanol-para-recaudar-once-millones-euros/2010862.shtml
9 https://cadenaser.com/ser/2019/10/14/deportes/1571081255_155077.html
10 www.mundodeportivo.com/futbol/fc-barcelona/20200330/48174204973/fc-barcelona-barca-comunicado-messi.html

References

Anderson, Benedict. 1983. *Imagined Communities: Reflections on the Origins and Spread of Nationalism*. London: Verso.

Balfour, Sebastian, and Alejandro Quiroga. 2007. *The Reinvention of Spain: Nation and Identity since Democracy*. Oxford: Oxford University Press.

Billig, Michael. 1995. *Banal Nationalism*. London: Sage.

Humlebaek, Carsten. 2015. *Spain. Inventing the Nation*. London: Bloomsbury.

Llopis Goig, Ramón. 2008. "Identity, Nation-State and Football in Spain: The Evolution of Nationalist Feeling in Spanish Football." *Soccer & Society* 9, no. 1: 56–63.

Ramonet, Ignacio. 1999. "El fútbol es una guerra." In *Fútbol y pasiones políticas*, edited by Santiago Segurola, 131–38. Madrid: Temas de Debate.

Resina, Jorge and Pedro Limón. 2014. "Del consenso al tiki-taka: Redefiniendo el nacionalismo español desde la prensa escrita a través del fútbol." *Política y Sociedad* 51, no. 2: 297–336.

15 US nationwide COVID-19 newspaper coverage of state and local government responses

Community structure theory and community "vulnerability"

John C. Pollock, Miranda Crowley, Suchir Govindarajan, Abigail Lewis, Alexis Marta, Radhika Purandare, and James N. Sparano

Introduction

In just a few months, a novel coronavirus, COVID-19, from Wuhan, China, brought the world to a complete standstill. The World Health Organization tracked the respiratory disease from a national crisis in China, to a global health emergency, and now a global pandemic (World Health Organization 2019, 1). In the United States, the Centers for Disease Control and Prevention (CDC) confirmed cases in every state (CDC 2020, 2), leading governors to close most businesses and almost all states to issue "shelter in place" guidance for residents. Despite national guidance on "reopening," President Trump acknowledged that ultimate decisions are the domain of governors (BBC 2020, 3). Because of variations in political identity, income disparities, ethnic diversity, and healthcare access, it is assumed that coverage of each state and local response to COVID-19 may vary across communities.

This chapter will examine newspaper coverage of state and local COVID-19 responses in multicity coverage throughout the United States by exploring prevailing media "frames." Framing can be defined as "the activity of organizing events into a coherent story, presenting some perspectives as more reasonable than others" (Pollock 2007, 1). Two media frames will be investigated. Coverage will be considered "favorable" if the state and local COVID-19 responses are described in a positive, respectful way, or "unfavorable" if the measures are criticized or questioned.

This study will utilize the mass medium of newspapers, valuable sources of information read by well-educated and by political and economic elites, and notorious intermedia agenda setters for other news platforms such as television, radio, and the internet. Newspapers are also easily accessible to the public, serving as community forums.

Community structure theory will be employed to analyze COVID-19 coverage in major cities across the United States, best defined as "a form of quantitative content analysis that focuses on the ways in which key characteristics of communities, such as cities, are related to the content coverage of newspapers in those communities" (Pollock 2007, 23). Two questions guide this study: how much disparity across cities occurs in news coverage surrounding the COVID-19 outbreak in the United States? To what extent are community demographic differences associated with any variation in coverage of state/local responses to COVID-19?

Community structure theory

While media coverage of COVID-19 appears massively relevant for communication studies/journalism research, the discipline has only begun to investigate this or related topics, such as Severe Acute Respiratory Syndrome (SARS) or Middle East Respiratory Syndrome (MERS). Community structure theory provides a useful, bottom-up lens to understand how newspapers frame these health narratives. Community structure theory is defined by Funk and McCombs (2017) as the "conceptual inverse" of agenda setting. The theory focuses on demographic characteristics of communities shaping news instead of news as a driver of public perception; furthermore, "it provide[s] a powerful framework for analyzing society's influence on media coverage" (Wikipedia 2019). The approach was first utilized in the early twentieth century by Robert Park at the University of Chicago, who advocated that scholars examine society's influence on the media, and not only media's influence on society (1922).

Three University of Minnesota scholars—Tichenor, Donohue, and Olien—further explored "structural pluralism" (1973, 1980), suggesting that newspapers in larger cities were more progressive due to socially diverse populations. Though pioneering, structural pluralism studies generally confined their focus to one or two cities or one state, Minnesota, and emphasized media's role as an instrument of "social control" reinforcing interests of political and economic elites.

Next-generation structural scholars uncovered more media willingness to accommodate social change. Hindman (1999) found that media in a few cities could reflect the interests of dominant ethnic groups instead of political elites. McLeod and Hertog (1992, 1999) found that favorable media coverage in cities could reflect the size of specific protest groups. Demers and Viswanath concluded that "mainstream mass media are agents both of social control for dominant institutions and value systems" and also of social change (1999, 34). Jeffres concurred about the capacity of media to accommodate social change, accompanied by excellent empirical work from younger scholars such as Armstrong, Funk, Nah, Watson, and Yamamoto, together publishing articles in a special 2011 "community structure" issue of "Mass Communication and Society" (Pollock 2013a).

In the twenty-first century, Pollock and colleagues introduced three advances to the structural approach. First, through use of the first highly varied nationwide and cross-national samples, they associated multiple city or national level structural characteristics with variations in newspaper coverage of critical events. In addition, they created a "Media Vector," a sensitive composite score that combines measurements of article "content" and "prominence." Finally, despite the "guard dog" hypothesis of Donohue, Tichenor, and Olien (1995), emphasizing media protection of political and economic elite interests (Pollock 2007, 24), Pollock and colleague studies, including three books (2007, 2013a, 2015) and an annotated bibliography (Pollock 2013b), often conclude that media can reflect the interests of society's most "vulnerable" citizens.

Hypotheses

To analyze media coverage of the COVID-19 state/local pandemic response in the United States, three umbrella hypotheses are utilized: buffer, vulnerability, and stakeholder (Pollock 2007, 2013a, 2015).

Buffer hypothesis

The "buffer" hypothesis expects that the higher percentage of privileged groups in a city, the more likely a city's newspaper will cover human rights issues favorably (Pollock 2007, 52). Pollock's 2007 book, *Tilted Mirrors*, argues that "the more individuals in a city who are 'buffered' from scarcity or uncertainty, the more likely they are to accord legitimacy to those who articulate their concerns in human rights frames" (2007, 62). Larger percentages of privileged individuals in a city, particularly in professional/technical occupations, were aligned with coverage favoring Anita Hill in her 1991 sexual harassment charges against Clarence Thomas (Pollock 2007, 66–75). Higher metropolitan levels of education and family income were also associated with favorable coverage of accepting same-sex marriage (Vales et al. 2014, 2015), as was percent college-educated with positive coverage of those living with HIV/AIDS prior to "Magic" Johnson's announcement that he was HIV-positive in 1991 (Pollock 2007, 211–29).

Since the current COVID-19 pandemic disproportionately affects underprivileged populations and creates an unsustainable burden on state/local government, it can be surmised that the greater percentage of privileged or "buffered" individuals in a community or city, the greater the favorable coverage of state/local government responses. Accordingly:

> *H1: The greater the proportion of privileged groups "buffered" from uncertainty (measured by college education, family income $200,000+, or occupational status—management/business/science/art), the more favorable the coverage of state/local government responses to the COVID-19 outbreak (Gaquin and Ryan 2019).*

Healthcare access

The buffer hypothesis was also used to trace connections between healthcare access and variations in coverage of state/local responses. Pollock operationalizes healthcare access as "the proportion of the municipal budget that a city spends on healthcare, in addition to the availability of hospital beds and physicians" (2007, 99). Since COVID-19 is predicted to strain healthcare capacity throughout the United States, it is expected that high levels of healthcare access will be associated with negative coverage of state/local responses to the pandemic.

Previous studies have generally encountered a "buffer" pattern, associating healthcare access with progressive reporting on health or human rights claims. Cities with more physicians/100,000 residents manifested favorable newspaper coverage of stem cell research (Pollock 2007, 97), physician-assisted suicide (Pollock and Yulis 2004), and pediatric immunization (Trotochaud et al. 2015); and media emphasized "authoritative responsibility" for rape culture and rape on campuses (Pollock et al. 2017a), less media support for solitary confinement (Pollock et al. 2017b), and greater media emphasis on government responsibility for gun safety (Patel et al. 2017).

The pandemic has encumbered healthcare capacity across the United States. The CDC projects that between 2.4 million and 21 million people in the United States who contract COVID-19 will need hospitalization (Human Rights Watch 2020, 2), whereas an annual survey estimated only about 924,107 total staffed hospital beds are available in the nation (American Hospital Association 2020). Disparities in the US healthcare system will yield increased numbers of untreated cases and excess deaths. Therefore:

H2: The greater the healthcare access (measured by number of physicians per 100,000, hospital beds/100,000 or municipal spending on healthcare) the less favorable the coverage of state/local government responses to the COVID-19 outbreak (Gaquin and Ryan 2019).

Vulnerability hypothesis

The "vulnerability hypothesis" predicts connections between economically disadvantaged groups who are vulnerable, unemployed, live in high-crime areas, etc. and favorable media coverage of their interests (Pollock 2007, 137). Although the "guard dog" hypothesis of Donohue, Tichenor, and Olien advocates that media will primarily reflect political and economic elite concerns (1995), recent studies find that coverage often reflects the interests of the economically disadvantaged (Pollock 2007, 137).

The 1973 Supreme Court decision legalizing abortion discovered more favorable coverage in cities with higher percentages of African Americans or those below the poverty level (Pollock, Robinson, and Murray 1978). Higher poverty levels were linked to favorable coverage of a Patient's Bill of Rights (Pollock 2007, 151), immigration reform (Pollock et al. 2014, 2015), and genetically-modified food (Pollock et al. 2010, 51–75); and less favorable coverage of capital punishment (Pollock 2007, 138–46). Higher percent uninsured were linked to media emphasis on government responsibility for gun regulation (Sparano et al. 2020). Moreover, higher percentages of Hispanics correlated with media support for universal healthcare (Kiernicki, Pollock, and Lavery 2013).

Overall, newspaper coverage often represents the interests of vulnerable populations. They face disparities in healthcare access and accurate COVID-19 prevention information. Strikingly "(T)he cost of inpatient admissions for COVID-19 treatment could top $20,000" per person (Rae et al. 2020, 2). Vulnerable populations also face workforce barriers, suspension from jobs without pay, or compulsion to work in close quarters or while sick. Therefore:

H3: *The greater the proportion of "vulnerable" city residents (percent below the poverty level, unemployed, uninsured, single-parent families, African American, or Hispanic), the more favorable the coverage of state/local government response to the COVID-19 outbreak (Gaquin and Ryan 2019).*

Stakeholder hypothesis

The stakeholder hypothesis expects a connection between stakeholder percentages (e.g., political identity, belief system, and generation) and favorable coverage of stakeholder concerns (Pollock 2007, 172). Since political identity and generation were not found significantly connected to variations in coverage of state/local COVID-19 responses (reported in Table 5), only the belief system category is elaborated.

Belief system

Various religious beliefs and values could contribute to differing newspaper coverage of crucial issues. Pearson correlations yielded insignificant results for percent Evangelicals and Catholics, reported in Table 5 and are not elaborated. Regarding Mainline Protestant membership, the American Association of Religion Data Archives (ARDA) offers the following:

Mainline Protestant denominations typically emphasize a proactive view on issues of social and economic justice and a tolerance of varied individual beliefs. While mainline Protestantism is usually seen as more theologically and socially liberal than evangelical Protestantism, there obviously is variation among mainline denominations, congregations and individuals. Examples of Mainline Protestant denominations include the Presbyterian Church (USA), the United Methodist Church, the Reformed Church in America, the Episcopal Church, the United Church of Christ and the Evangelical Lutheran Church in America.

(Association of Religion Data Archives 2006, para. 1–2)

Previous community structure studies found greater percentages of Mainline Protestants linked to favorable coverage of the Occupy Wall Street movement in New York (Pollock 2013a, 1–30) and detainee rights at Guantanamo Bay (Zinck et al. 2014, 2015), and less favorable coverage of solitary confinement (Pollock et al. 2017b). By contrast, a greater percentage of Mainline Protestants were linked to less government responsibility for opioid abuse (Cruz et al. 2018). Often associated with progressive positions addressing inequality, Mainline Protestants may be dismayed by indecisive or confusing state/local government responses that diminish the capacity for "self-reliance." Therefore:

H5: *The greater the percentage of Mainline Protestants in a city, the less favorable the coverage of state/local government responses to the COVID-19 outbreak (Association of Religion Data Archives 2019).*

Methodology

To systematically study coverage of coronavirus, a sample of 23 prominent metropolitan newspapers from four major regions was selected from the NewsBank database. The search terms "coronavirus" OR "COVID-19" "AND "gov*," including all articles in the sample period with 250+ words on local/state government responses to COVID-19, yielded 336 articles. A larger sample of newspapers was initially drawn, but newspapers with fewer than ten articles were excluded. The following publications emerged: *Albuquerque Journal, Atlanta Journal-Constitution, Charlotte Observer, Chicago Sun-Times, Denver Post, Houston Chronicle, Las Vegas Sun, New Hampshire Union Leader, Sacramento Bee, San Diego Union, San Francisco Chronicle, Star Tribune (MN), St. Louis Post, The Buffalo News, The Detroit News, The Hartford Courant, The Oregonian, The Orlando Sentinel, The Philadelphia Inquirer, The Pittsburgh Post-Gazette, The Plain Dealer (OH), The State (SC)*, and *Wisconsin State Journal*. Newspapers that target nationwide rather than local audiences were excluded, including: *The New York Times, USA Today, The Wall Street Journal, The Los Angeles Times*, and *The Washington Post*.

The data collection inception date was January 23, 2020, when Illinois reported the first laboratory-confirmed case of COVID-19 in the United States. The data collection end date was April 3, 2020, when the Food and Drug Administration (FDA) announced several comprehensive coronavirus actions.

Article prominence

Each article was assigned two assessments. The first score evaluated "prominence," measuring an article's significance to an editor. Each article was evaluated with a number between 0 and 4 based on each of four elements: placement, headline size, article length, and any photos/graphics (Table 15.1).

Article direction

In addition to prominence, articles were evaluated for direction, representing how they were framed. Articles were assigned categories based on whether media emphasized "favorable," "unfavorable," or balanced/neutral" (neither favorable/unfavorable, or simply offering facts/statistics) coverage of coronavirus. Of 336

Table 15.1 Prominence score

Dimension	4	3	2	1
Placement	Front page, front section	Front page, inside section	Inside page, front section	Other
Headline size (# of words)	10+	9–8	7–6	5 or less
Article length (# of words)	1000+	750–999	500–749	250–499
Graphics/photos	2 or more	1		

Source: © John C. Pollock, 1994–2021

Table 15.2 Media Vector formula

f = sum of the prominence scores coded "favorable"
u = sum of the prominence scores coded "unfavorable"
n = sum of the prominence scores coded "balanced/neutral"
$r = f + u + n$
If $f > u$ (the sum of the supportive prominence scores is greater than the sum of the opposition prominence scores), the following formula is used:
Favorable Media Vector:
FMV = $(f^2 - fu)/r^2$ (Answer lies between 0 and +1.00)
If $f < u$ (the sum of the supportive prominence scores is greater than the sum of the opposition prominence scores), the following formula is used:
UMV = $(fu - u^2)/r^2$ (answer lies between 0 and −1.00)

Source: © John C. Pollock, 2000–2021

articles, 167 (50%) were double-coded, resulting in a Scott's Pi coefficient of inter-coder reliability of .7313.

Calculating a media vector

Examining 23 newspapers, a "Media Vector" was calculated using the Janis-Fadner Coefficient of Imbalance. Each newspaper's article prominence was combined with its directional scores into a single composite measure called a "Media Vector" of article "projection" onto audiences (Pollock 2007, 49). Scores lie on a spectrum from −1.00 to +1.00. A Media Vector score between 0 and +1.00 reflected favorable coverage of local/state government responses to coronavirus. A score between 0 and −1.00 represented unfavorable coverage (Table 15.2).

Results

This study examined coverage of state/local coronavirus responses comparing Media Vectors from 23 cities in a sample period from January 23, 2020 to April 3, 2020 using Pearson correlations and regression analysis. The highest Media

Vector composite score was San Francisco, CA (+0.4082), while the lowest was Pittsburgh, PA (−0.0713) for a range of .4715, with 14 of 23 newspapers (61%) manifesting favorable coverage of state/local government coronavirus responses (Table 15.3).

Media Vector scores for newspapers in each of four regions were averaged and rank-ordered from highest to lowest (Table 15.4). Results reveal the West had the most favorable coverage of state/local coronavirus efforts (0.2528), while

Table 15.3 Media vector scores

City	Newspaper	Media vector
San Francisco, CA	*San Francisco Chronicle*	0.4082
San Diego, CA	*San Diego Union*	0.3306
Denver, CO	*Denver Post*	0.3228
Sacramento, CA	*Sacramento Bee*	0.3022
Las Vegas, NV	*Las Vegas Sun*	0.2608
Columbia, SC	*The State*	0.142
Albuquerque, NM	*Albuquerque Journal*	0.1159
Cleveland, OH	*The Plain Dealer*	0.1143
Detroit, MI	*The Detroit News*	0.0844
Houston, TX	*Houston Chronicle*	0.0763
Manchester, NH	*New Hampshire Union Leader*	0.038
Portland, OR	*The Oregonian*	0.0293
Atlanta, GA	*Atlanta Journal-Constitution*	0.0272
Hartford, CT	*The Hartford Courant*	0.0017
Charlotte, NC	*Charlotte Observer*	−0.0026
Minneapolis, MN	*Star Tribune*	−0.0094
Orlando, FL	*The Orlando Sentinel*	−0.012
Chicago, IL	*Chicago Sun- Times*	−0.0208
Madison, WS	*Wisconsin State Journal*	−0.0263
Philadelphia, PA	*The Philadelphia Inquirer*	−0.0263
St. Louis, MO	*St. Louis Post*	−0.0345
Buffalo, NY	*The Buffalo News*	−0.0469
Pittsburgh, PA	*The Pittsburgh Post-Gazette*	−0.0713

Source: © John C. Pollock, Miranda Crowley, Suchir Govindarajan, Abigail Lewis, Alexis Marta, Radhika Purandare, James N. Sparano, 2021

Table 15.4 Media vector scores regional averages

Region	Media vector
West	0.2528
South	0.0372
Midwest	0.018
Northeast	−0.021

Source: © John C. Pollock, Miranda Crowley, Suchir Govindarajan, Abigail Lewis, Alexis Marta, Radhika Purandare, James N. Sparano, 2021

Table 15.5 Pearson correlations

City characteristics	Pearson correlation (R)	Significance (P)	Category
Mainline Protestant	−0.567	0.002**	BS
Hospital beds/1000	−0.515	0.007**	HA
Percent family income $200,000+	0.471	0.012*	P
Percent unemployed	−0.323	0.067	V
Ages 65+	0.318	0.69	A
Percent Hispanic	0.305	0.079	V
Percent ages 25–44	0.273	0.104	A
Percent Catholic	−0.219	0.158	BS
Percent voting Republican	−0.215	0.163	PI
Percent voting Democratic	0.174	0.214	PI
Percent ages 18–24	−0.171	0.218	A
Percent African American	0.162	0.230	V
Municipal spending on healthcare	0.158	0.236	HA
Percent below poverty level	−0.133	0.273	V
Occupational status (Management/ Business/Science/Arts)	0.123	0.289	P
Percent college educated	0.121	0.291	P
Percent Evangelical	−0.115	0.301	BS
Physicians/100,000	0.103	0.341	HA
Percent uninsured	−0.075	0.367	V
Percent ages 45–64	0.014	0.474	A

Source: © John C. Pollock, Miranda Crowley, Suchir Govindarajan, Abigail Lewis, Alexis Marta, Radhika Purandare, James N. Sparano, 2021

**significant at .01 level
* significant at .05 level
KEY: BS = Belief System, HA= Healthcare Access, P = Privilege, V = Vulnerability, A = Age, PI = Political Identity,

other regional averages were close to zero. SPSS was used to measure correlations between city characteristics and variations in newspaper coverage (Table 15.5).

Discussion of significant results

Mainline Protestants strongly associated with disapproval of state/ local responses to COVID-19; other belief systems not significant

It was hypothesized that community Mainline Protestant membership would be associated with negative coverage of state/local COVID-19 responses, partly because of historic associations with progressive issues. It was also expected that long term declines in Mainline Protestant membership, beginning in the 1960s, might contribute to a sense of shrinking relevance. Although members of Mainline Protestant denominations played leading political and economic roles in founding the United States and in business enterprises until around World War II, this prominence declined in the twenty-first century, evidence of increasing social "vulnerability."

Mainline Protestant membership was the study's most important city characteristic associated with negative coverage of state/local responses to COVID-19 ($r = -0.567$, $p = 0.002$). Although percent Catholic in communities, like percent Mainline Protestant, is often associated with progressive media, coverage of state/local COVID-19 responses did not reveal significant connections ($r = -0.219$, $p = 0.158$), nor did percent Evangelical ($r = -0.115$, $p = 0.301$). These findings regarding coverage of state and local responses to COVID-19 are unlike the findings of a similar nationwide community structure study of "federal" responses to the virus, finding that percent Catholic were significantly associated with "negative" coverage of government responses, while percent Evangelical were strongly associated with "positive" coverage of federal actions to counteract the virus (Pollock et al. 2020).

Healthcare access (hospital beds/100,000) significantly associated with negative coverage of state/local COVID-19 responses; another indicator of "vulnerability," percent unemployed, "directionally" consistent

Equipment shortages and lethal risks borne by healthcare workers transformed healthcare access, traditionally a repository of hope, into a crucible of despair, indicative of health "vulnerability." Consistent with that pessimistic expectation, higher numbers of hospital beds/100,000, significantly associated with higher poverty levels ($r = 0.507$, $p = 0.001$) and percent uninsured ($r = 0.276$, $p = 0.049$), correlated with negative coverage of state/local COVID-19 responses ($r = -0.515$, $p = 0.007$). Other indicators of "healthcare access," percent municipal spending on healthcare and physicians/100,000, were not significantly linked to variations in COVID-19 coverage. Percent unemployed, a traditional indicator of "economic" vulnerability, was "directionally" consistent and negatively linked to COVID-19 state/local response coverage ($r = -0.323$, $p = 0.067$).

"Buffered" economic privilege (family income $200,000+) associated with favorable coverage of state/local COVID-19 responses

Family income of $200,000+ was the only indicator of a category "buffered" from economic uncertainty significantly connected to positive coverage of state/local COVID-19 responses ($r = 0.471$, $p = 0.012$). Other indicators of "buffered" economic privilege, high occupational status (management/business/science/arts) and percent college-educated, were not significantly linked (respectively, $r = 0.123$, $p = 0.289$; $r = 0.121$, $p = 0.291$).

Unexpected findings

Although multiple media platforms and opinion polls emphasize political partisanship in COVID-19 coverage, political polarization was not encountered. Higher percentages voting Democratic or Republican in the 2016 presidential

Table 15.6 Regression analysis

Model (predictors)	R	R² cumulative	R² change	F change	Sig. F change
Mainline Protestant	0.552	0.305	0.305	8.779	0.008
Mainline Protestant, family income $200,000+	0.672	0.452	0.147	5.098	0.036
Mainline Protestant, family income, hospital beds/100,000	0.718	0.516	0.064	2.364	0.142

Source: © John C. Pollock, Miranda Crowley, Suchir Govindarajan, Abigail Lewis, Alexis Marta, Radhika Purandare, James N. Sparano, 2021

election were not associated significantly with coverage of state/local COVID-19 responses (respectively: $r = 0.174$, $p = 0.214$; $r = -0.215$, $p = 0.163$). Despite the disproportional risk of infection and mortality in seniors, different age categories had no significant connection with COVID-19 response coverage.

Regression analysis

Regression analysis revealed that communities with higher percentages Mainline Protestant (30.5% of the variance) and hospital beds/100,000 (6.4%) collectively accounted for 36.9% of the variance associated with negative coverage of state/ local COVID-19 responses. By contrast, communities with higher percentages with family incomes of $200,000+, linked to positive coverage of state/local COVID-19 efforts, only accounted for 14.7% of the variance. "Vulnerable" community indicators of negative coverage (Mainline Protestant and hospital bed density) were more than two times more potent than a "buffered" indicator of positive coverage (family income $200,000+) (see Table 15.6.).

Conclusion

Overall results confirmed a robust "vulnerability" pattern (Media "mirror" the interests of economically or socially marginal or disadvantaged groups: Pollock 2007, 137.). A "vulnerability" pattern was encountered with higher proportions of hospital beds/100,000 connected to "less favorable" coverage of state/local responses to COVID 19. Another measure of economic vulnerability, percent unemployed, was "directionally" consistent. By contrast, at the other end of the economic spectrum, the higher the percent family income $200,000+ in a city (more "buffered" from economic uncertainty), the "more favorable" the reporting on government responses.

The most powerful predictor of "vulnerable" coverage, "Percent Mainline Protestant," associated strongly with negative coverage of state/local responses to the virus ($r = -0567$, $p = 0.002$), accounted for 30.5% of the regression variance, compared to less for family income (14.7%) and hospital beds (6.4%). Previous research found Mainline Protestant membership, declining for decades, linked to progressive reporting (positively) on the "Occupy" movement and detainee rights at Guantanamo, and (negatively) on solitary confinement.

The category "Mainline Protestant" cannot be reduced to a proxy or "mask" for other indicators. Although this belief system is significantly associated with hospital beds/100,000, the same city comparison reveals no significant association between Mainline Protestant and voting Republican/Democratic, nor with percent college-educated or occupational status or family income $200,000+, nor with indicators at the other end of the economic ladder (unemployed, poverty, or uninsured). Informal content analysis of unfavorable coverage of state/local responses to the pandemic suggests that it is linked to perceived government failure to offer protection against health risks or economic dislocations, either of which can prevent individuals from acting with a sense of agency or efficacy. That reporting pattern is consistent with previous community structure research linking Mainline Protestants with support for progressive perspectives. Confronting the coronavirus and inadequate government responses, perhaps the iconic "self-reliance" of the Protestant Ethic Max Weber celebrated in "The Protestant Ethic and the Spirit of Capitalism," has met a challenge so vast that the belief system itself is in jeopardy, potentially unraveling political, social, economic, and even spiritual contracts, generating a "crisis of faith."

Empirically, media coverage of federal COVID-19 responses confirmed it as a national issue associated with community "vulnerability." Methodologically, combining measures of both "prominence" and "direction," Media Vectors reflected community measures of "belief system" and "vulnerability." Theoretically, emphasizing the influence of local demographics, community structure theory complements agenda-setting theory at the national level, reconfirming the findings of a founder of agenda-setting (Funk and McCombs 2017), that both nationally prominent newspapers (agenda setting) and local community characteristics/concerns (community structure) can affect coverage of critical local issues.

References

American Hospital Association. 2020. "Fast Facts on U.S. Hospitals, 2020." Accessed March 20, 2020. www.aha.org/statistics/fast-facts-us-hospitals.

Association of Religion Data Archives (ARDA). 2006. Accessed March 30, 2020. www.thearda.com/.

BBC News. 2020. "Coronavirus: Trump Unveils Plan to Reopen States in Phases." Accessed April 17. www.bbc.com/news/world-us-canada-52314866.

CDC. 2020. "Situation Summary." Accessed April 19, 2020. www.cdc.gov/coronavirus/2019-ncov/cases-updates/summary.html.

Cruz, Brittany, Sabrina Garcia, Chris Moncada, Morgan Tarrant, John C. Pollock, Nolan DeVoe, and Patrick Moore. 2018. "Nationwide Newspaper Coverage of Opioid Abuse: Testing Community Structure Theory." Paper presented at the biannual Kentucky Health Communication Conference, Lexington, Kentucky, April 12–14.

Demers, David, and Kasisomayajula Viswanath, eds. 1999. *Mass Media, Social Control, and Social Change: A Macrosocial Perspective.* Ames, IA: Iowa State University Press.

Donohue, George A., Phillip J. Tichenor, and Clarice N. Olien. 1995. "A Guard Dog Perspective on the Role of Media." *Journal of Communication* 45: 115–32.

Funk, Marcus J., and Maxwell McCombs. 2017. "Strangers on a Theoretical Train: Intermedia Agenda Setting, Community Structure, and Local News Coverage." *Journalism Studies* 18: 845–65.

Gaquin, Deirdre, and Mary Meghan Ryan, eds. 2019. *County and City Extra. 2019: Annual Metro, City, and County Data Book*, 27th ed. Lanham, MD: Bernan Press. Accessed April 20, 2020. https://tcnj.primo.exlibrisgroup.com/discovery/fulldisplay?context=L& vid=01COLLNJ_INST:TCNJ&docid=alma999426819105191.

Hindman, Doug B. 1999. "Social Control, Social Change and Local Mass Media." In *Mass Media, Social Control, and Social Change: A Macrosocial Perspective*, edited by David Demers and Kasisomayajula Viswanath, 99–116. Ames: Iowa State University Press.

Human Rights Watch. 2020. "US: Ensure Affordable COVID-19 Treatment Cost of Coronavirus Care Could Lead to Crushing Medical Debt." Accessed March 20. www.hrw.org/news/2020/03/20/us-ensure-affordable-covid-19-treatment.

Kiernicki, Kristen, John C. Pollock, and Patrick Lavery. 2013. "Nationwide Newspaper Coverage of Universal Health Care: A Community Structure Approach." In *Media and Social Inequality: Innovations in Community Structure Research*, edited by John C. Pollock, 116–34. New York: Routledge.

McLeod, Douglas M., and James K. Hertog. 1992. "The Manufacture of Public Opinion by Reporters: Informal Cues for Public Perceptions of Protest Groups." *Discourse and Society* 3:259–75.

———. 1999. "Social Control, Social Change and the Mass Media's Role in the Regulation of Protest Groups." In *Mass Media, Social Control, and Social Change: A Macrosocial Perspective*, edited by David Demers and Kasisomayajula Viswanath, 305–31. Ames: Iowa State University Press.

Park, Robert. 1992. *The Immigrant Press and its Control*. New York: Harcourt.

Patel, Amit, Michael Ruggiero, Kelly Ver Haeghe, Michael DiBlasi, John C. Pollock, and Melissa Morgan. 2017. "Nationwide Newspaper Coverage of Gun Safety: A Community Structure Approach." Paper presented at the Biannual DCHC (DC Health Communication) Conference, Fairfax, Virginia, April 25–27.

Pollock, John C. 2007. *Titled Mirrors: Media Alignment with Political and Social Change: A Community Structure Approach*. Cresskill: Hampton Press.

Pollock, John C. 2013a. *Media and Social Inequality: Innovations in Community Structure Research*. New York: Routledge.

Pollock, John C. 2013b. "Community Structure Research." In *Oxford Bibliographies Online,* edited by Patricia Moy. New York: Oxford University Press.

Pollock, John C. 2015. *Journalism and Human Rights: How Demographics Drive Media Coverage*. New York: Routledge.

Pollock, John C., S. Govindarajan, A. Marta, J. N. Sparano, M. Crowley, A. Lewis, and R. Purandare. 2020. "US Nationwide Coronavirus Newspaper Coverage of Federal/National Government Responses: Community Structure Theory and a 'Violated Buffer'". *Trípodos*, 47, no. 1, 27–47, July.

Pollock, John C., Stefanie Gratale, Kevin Teta, Kyle Bauer, and Elyse Hoekstra. 2014. "Nationwide Newspaper Coverage of Immigration Reform: A Community Structure Approach." *Atlantic Journal of Communication* 22: 259–74.

———. 2015. "Nationwide Newspaper Coverage of Immigration Reform: A Community Structure Approach." In *Journalism and Human Rights: How Demographics Drive Media Coverage*, edited by John C. Pollock, 125–140. London and New York: Routledge.

Pollock, John C., Michelleslie Maltese-Nehrbass, Patricia Corbin, and Pamela B. Fascanella. 2010. "Nationwide Newspaper Coverage of Genetically-Modified Food in the United States: A Community Structure Approach." *Ecos de la Comunicación* 3: 51–75.

Pollock, John C., Brielle Richardella, Amanda Jahr, Melissa Morgan, and Judi P. Cook. 2017a. "Nationwide Newspaper Coverage of Rape and Rape Culture on College Campuses: Testing Community Structure Theory." *Human Rights Review* 19: 51–75.

Pollock, John C., James L. Robinson, and Mary C. Murray. 1978. "Media Agendas and Human Rights: The Supreme Court Decision on Abortion." *Journalism Quarterly* 53: 545–48.

Pollock, John C., Andrew Street, Madison Moran, Ashley Van Riper, Christopher Minick, Theresa Soya, Melissa Morgan, K. Morgan, and Emma Streckenbein. 2017b. "Nationwide Newspaper Coverage of Solitary Confinement: A Community Structure Approach." Paper presented at the DC Health Communication Conference, Fairfax, Virginia, April 27–29.

Pollock, John C., and Spiro G. Yulis. 2004. "Nationwide Newspaper Coverage of Physician Assisted Suicide: A Community Structure Approach." *Journal of Health Communication* 9: 281–307.

Rae, Matthew, Gary Claxton, Nisha Kurani, Daniel McDermott, and Cynthia Cox. "Potential Costs of COVID-19 Treatment for People with Employer Coverage." Peterson-KFF Health System Tracker. Accessed March 9, 2020. www.healthsystemtracker.org/brief/potential-costs-of-coronavirus-treatment-for-people-with-employer-coverage/

Sparano, James, Olivia DeGirolamo, Hayley Martin, Dana Corvil, and John C. Pollock. 2020. "Nationwide Newspaper Coverage of Government Gun Safety Regulation: Community Structure Theory and Community 'Vulnerability.'" Paper presented at the Kentucky Conference on Health Communication, Lexington, Kentucky, April 2–3.

Tichenor, Philip J., George Donohue, and Clarice Olien. 1973. "Mass Communication Research: Evolution of a Structural Model." *Journalism Quarterly* 50: 419–25.

———. 1980. *Community Conflict and the Press*. Beverly Hills: Sage.

Trotochaud, Marc, Lydia Huang, Craig Dietel, Lauren Longo, Stephanie Agresti, and John C. Pollock. 2015. "Nationwide Coverage of Pediatric Immunization in the US: A Community Structure Approach." Paper presented at the DC Health Communication Conference, Washington, DC, April 16.

Vales, Victoria, John C. Pollock, Victoria Scarfone, Carly Koziol, Amy Wilson, and Patrick Flanagan. 2014. "Nationwide US Newspaper Coverage of Same-Sex Marriage: A Community Structure Approach." *Atlantic Journal of Communication* 22: 229–44.

———. 2015. "Nationwide Newspaper Coverage of Same-Sex Marriage: A Community Structure Approach." In *Journalism and Human Rights: How Demographics Drive Media Coverage*, edited by John C. Pollock, 95–110. London and New York: Routledge.

Wikipedia. 2019. "Community Structure Theory." Accessed October 13, 2019, https://en.wikipedia.org/wiki/Community_Structure_Theory.

World Health Organization (WHO). "Coronavirus disease (COVID-2019) R&D." Accessed March 26. www.who.int/blueprint/priority-diseases/key-action/novel-coronavirus/en/.

Zinck, Kelsey, Maggie Rogers, John C. Pollock, and Matthew Salvatore. 2014. "Nationwide US Multicity Newspaper Coverage of Detainee Rights at Guantanamo Bay." *Atlantic Journal of Communication* 22: 245–58.

Zinck, Kelsey, Maggie Rogers, John C. Pollock, and Matthew Salvatore. 2015. "Nationwide US Multicity Newspaper Coverage of Detainee Rights at Guantanamo Bay." In *Journalism and Human Rights: How Demographics Drive Media Coverage*, edited by John C. Pollock, 111–24. London and New York: Routledge.

16 Exploring the COVID-19 social media *infodemic*

Health communication challenges and opportunities

Carolyn A. Lin

Introduction

In time of a global health crisis such as the current COVID-19 pandemic, media play the most important role in keeping the public informed and educated about the scientific facts and government responses related to this crisis. If correctly educated by reliable media sources, individuals will be better equipped to take appropriate actions to avoid subjecting themselves and others to the COVID-19 virus. The current information flow associated with the COVID-19 pandemic has been nicknamed an *infodemic*; the implications of this *infodemic* could have serious consequences, due to the ongoing infection cases and fatalities around the world.

From the perspective of risk communication, the current COVID-19 *infodemic* has created confusion about science-based information and distrust in such information, due to the spread of misinformation, disinformation, and rumors. Specifically, the World Health Organization appears to be fighting a losing battle against the COVID-19 *infodemic*—to protect those who could more easily fallen victim to the false information—as it spreads through the internet. Social media companies such as Facebook and Twitter have intensified their effort to identify and remove Russian troll accounts and the like. Their progress appears to be both insufficient and ineffective, as new trolls are quickly repopulated much like an uncontained COVID-19 virus itself.

The objective of this chapter is to help risk communication researchers, public policymakers, and health professionals gain a better understanding of how the public perceives and responds to the myths, misinformation, disinformation, and rumors amidst an *infodemic*, alongside science-based facts and recommendations. To elucidate the potential social influence of this *infodemic* could have on the current pandemic communication, this chapter will review how it relates to COVID-19 information access and knowledge—as well as key health behavior theories and models—applicable for studying the adoption of COVID-19 preventive behaviors.

Background

In time of a global health crisis such as the current COVID-19 pandemic, media play the most important role in keeping the public informed and educated about the scientific facts and government responses to the crisis. The spread of misinformation and disinformation about a pandemic could lead to public misperceptions about how to prevent the spread of the virus, protect themselves from being infected, and treat the symptoms. If correctly educated by reliable media sources, individuals will be better equipped to take appropriate actions to avoid subjecting themselves and others to the COVID-19 virus. The current information flow associated with the COVID-19 pandemic has been nicknamed an *infodemic*; the implications of this *infodemic* could have serious consequences, due to the ongoing infection cases and fatalities around the world.

The *infodemic* in question here has been acting as a form of viral communication, which is contagious, continuous, and widespread just like the COVID-19 pandemic itself. The objective of this chapter is to help risk communication researchers, public policymakers, and health professionals gain a better understanding of how the public perceives and responds to the ongoing COVID-19 infodemic, alongside science-based facts and recommendations. To elucidate the potential influence this *infodemic* could have on pandemic communication, this chapter will review how it relates to COVID-19 information access and knowledge—as well as key health behavior theories and models—that are applicable for studying the adoption of COVID-19 preventive behaviors.

Infodemic **and COVID-19 communication**

According to the United Nations, an *infodemic* is a phenomenon where there is an excessive amount of information about a problem, which hinders the identification of a solution to the problem (United Nations 2020). From the perspective of risk communication, the current COVID-19 *infodemic* has created confusion about science-based information and distrust in such information, due to the spread of misinformation, disinformation, and rumors. Nielsen et al. (2020) found that one-third of US citizens on social media reported seeing misinformation about COVID-19.

The current COVID-19 *infodemic* might have also contributed to social divisions or instability in American society. For instance, individuals armed with assault rifles were seen protesting against their respective state's COVID-19 "stay home" mitigation order across the country. Cybersecurity research indicates that these protests were organized by pro-gun rights groups, state Republican Party organizations, conservative think tanks, religious groups, and the like (Chandler 2020). As Russian trolls have been discovered online to stir up vaccine debate in the United States in 2018 (Pierre 2020), it is plausible that these trolls could have been helping to fan the flame in these groups' social media activities (Friedman 2020).

It is important to note that semi-government entities or political leaders could also spread misinformation, disinformation, and rumors, aside from domestic or international groups that promote conspiracy theories. For instance, the Islamic Revolutionary Guard Corps stated that the United States might have developed COVID-19 as a biological weapon to first strike China, followed by Iran and other parts of the world; Russian media soon began to spread the Iranian conspiracy theories and Chinese media also alleged that the CIA created COVID-19 to keep China from continuing its economic growth (State of New Jersey 2020). In the case of the falsehood circulated by China, it was a retaliation against an US Senator and the US State Secretary—who had claimed that the virus was either manufactured by or accidentally released from a Wuhan laboratory—even though U.S Intelligence agencies found no evidence to back up their claim (Walcott 2020).

Donald Trump, the US President, touted non-science based COVID-19 treatments such as sunlight exposure, disinfectant injection, and hydroxychloroquine (a drug that treats malaria) (Sarkis 2020). Following Trump's suggestion of self-injection of household disinfectant to kill the COVID-19 virus, calls to the Kentucky Poison Control Center rose from an average of 150 per day to 1000; the same occurrence also took place in different states across the country (Aitken 2020). Tragically, due to social media accounts that falsely promoted whiskey and honey as an effective COVID-19 treatment from a British tabloid story, nearly 300 Iranians were dead and more than 1000 were sickened by ingesting methanol (because it is illegal to consume alcoholic beverages in Islamic Iran) (Associated Press 2020).

Social media companies such as Facebook and Twitter have intensified their effort to identify and remove Russian troll accounts; yet their progress appears to have been both insufficient and ineffective, as new trolls are quickly repopulated much like the uncontained and fast-moving COVID-19 virus itself (Ward et al. 2020). This viral disinformation momentum suggests that a lack of cybersecurity in a public information domain could allow Russian trolls or the likes to infiltrate the ongoing discourse about COVID-19 to undermine both social stability and civil society domestic and abroad.

The COVID-19 social media *infodemic:* its extent and audience effects

The World Health Organization has mobilized cybersecurity experts and has been working with major social media and digital information search companies—including Facebook, Twitter, YouTube, Pinterest, Google, Tencent and Tiktok, among others—to battle the continuing dissemination of falsehood. Specifically, WHO describes four types of COVID-19 misinformation that could be found online. These include: (1) the cause and origin of the virus and disease; (2) its symptoms and transmission patterns; (3) available treatments, prophylactics, and cures; and (4) the effectiveness and impact of interventions by health authorities or other institutions (WHO 2020).

Even so, WHO appears to be fighting a losing battle against the COVID-19 *infodemic* to protect those who could more easily fallen victim to the false information, as it spreads through the internet. For example, Richtel (2020) reported that wildly untrue claims have been transmitted or retransmitted by "the unwitting and the devious" on the internet (especially social media)—alongside medical disinformation pedaled by anti-science ideologues who distrust science (e.g., anti-vaxxers)—and profiteers (including some evangelical preachers) who sell miraculous cures to their believers. This report also indicated that even though the internet company *Google* did launch an "SOS alert" to direct those who search for COVID-19 news and information to the WHO website/social media account, numerous people from around the world had already been exposed to all kinds of falsehoods that continue to flourish online.

The constant stream of misinformation disseminated by Trump and others appears to have had an impact on public perception of the trustworthiness of science-based COVID-19 information. For instance, a recent national poll (Jones 2020) suggested that while 36% of the American public felt overburdened by the onslaught of COVID-19 information, 68% and 54% mentioned social media and the Trump administration as the "main" and "next most common" misinformation source, respectively. This poll also revealed a sharp political divide in public perceptions, with 85% Democrats versus 4% Republicans naming the Trump administration as the main source of misleading information.

These polling results are consistent with a series of COVID-19 studies published in medical journals, which painted a picture of a public displaying both expected and unexpected patterns in their responses to the information overflow. For instance, a national survey of 718 American adults in early February of 2020 reported that a majority (69%) preferred scientific and public health experts to lead the US response to the pandemic, relative to a small minority (14%) that favored having politicians (i.e., the president or Congress) to lead the effort instead. Additional results from another large-scale survey showed that public perception of the COVID-19 risks was low (median = 50%), even though they trusted the information presented by health officials and professionals (McFadden et al. 2020).

A survey of 3000 adults each in the United States and the United Kingdom (Geldsetzer 2020) showed that people in both countries expressed their suspicions of and distrust in COVID-19 risk, due to their perceptions of individuals of East-Asian descent. In particular, participants overestimated infection cases in the East-Asian communities; a substantial majority stated that they should avoid Chinese restaurants, refuse Uber rides for East-Asian looking individuals, and consider a package arrived from China as posting an infection risk. In addition, while over 25% of participants chose ineffective remedies posted on social media (e.g., rinsing nose with saline, using a hand dryer, taking antibiotics, and gargling with mouthwash) that are identical to those published on WHO's "myth busters" webpage, most did not foresee a high fatality rate by the end of 2020.

Another national study of 1034 US adults (in March, 2020) demonstrated that less COVID-19 knowledgeable individuals spent more money, participated in large gatherings (>50 people), and wore a mask less often during their outings (Clements 2020). Findings also indicated that baby boomers (relative to their younger counterparts) and individuals with higher income were more knowledgeable about COVID-19; while black participants' knowledge scores were 75% lower than those of whites, Democrats and independents respectively had knowledge scores 113% and 76% higher than that of Republicans. These results seem to echo the findings of another study, which analyzed 167,073 unique tweets (Abd-Alrazaq et al. 2020) related to coronavirus (between February 2 and March 15). Study findings describe that among the 12 topic categories analyzed, the most and least followed tweets were about "increased racism" and "economic loss," in that order. Moreover, the tweets that garnered the highest and lowest means for "likes" fell in the categories of "economic loss" and "travel bans and warmings," respectively.

By and large, the empirical research results have demonstrated that the current *infodemic* has had an impact on the public's awareness, knowledge, beliefs, attitudes, and actions in terms of how they have responded to the COVID-19 threat. Summarily, these findings show a consistency in demarcating the public response pattern by socioeconomic, cultural, and political-ideological factors. Low SES populations who have suffered most from the pandemic also have the lowest COVID-19 knowledge. Politically conservative individuals likewise demonstrate much lower knowledge than their more liberal counterparts. Culturally intolerant groups display their attitudinal and behavioral tendencies through social prejudice and discrimination against people of East Asian descent. Those who believe in the myths, instead of scientific facts, also exhibit behaviors that endanger their health, either through non-compliance with prevention/mitigation measures or adoption of reckless home remedies.

Infodemic and digital health divides: unequal internet access, knowledge gaps, and mistrust in officials

As of this writing (July 25, 2020), the novel Coronavirus has infected over 4 million Americans and caused about 146,000 fatalities since tracking began on February 29, 2020. These statistics show that the United States has claimed more than 26% of the 15.8 million infected cases and nearly 23% of the 641,003 deaths reported worldwide (Pettersson, Manley, and Hernandez 2020). Among the infected cases and fatalities in the United States, the majority have been identified to fit the following demographic profile: elderly, African Americans, Hispanic Americans, and native Americans as well as low-income and hourly-pay workers. According to a *Washington Post* report, "The pandemic is striking members of minority groups, especially African Americans, at dramatically disproportional rates" (e.g., 14% of the population in that demographic group represented 44% of victims in Michigan) (Daniels and Morial 2020, para. 1). Another report also suggested that African Americans had accounted for fully 80% of COVID-19 hospitalizations in the state of Georgia in April (Silverstein 2020).

This pandemic has thus exposed a long-standing health disparity crisis among the economically disadvantaged and disenfranchised minority communities, as a large percentage of them have inadequate access to health services, low health literacy, and high rates of chronic diseases (e.g., Daniels and Morial 2020; Zanolli 2020). With online channels emerging as a primary source of health information (e.g., Dobransky and Hargittai 2012), many individuals from these economically and socially marginalized communities often lack either the basic skills to conduct effective health information searches or the resources to purchase a computer to engage in internet search activities (Lin et al. 2015). Study findings also indicated that these disadvantaged groups may be less able to access such information, due to their lack of motivation or knowledge-based media habits (Dobransky and Hargittai 2012; Whitten, Kreps, and Eastin 2009), even though their need for health information is as great as in privileged communities (e.g., Wyatt et al. 2005).

As approximately 27% of the US households are estimated to be without a high-speed internet connection, racial and economic divides continue to define the new digital divides (Watkins et al. 2018). Examples of the devastation that COVID-19 has impacted on the African community have been unveiled in plain sight among cities such as New Orleans, New York, and Detroit (Evelyn 2020). According to a recent report, 23–33% of New Orleans household lacked home internet access via a broadband service and nearly 21% of them did not own a computer (Mackie 2020). A 2018 study about New York City's broadband access suggested that about 56% of New Yorkers from the lowest-income households had no home internet subscription; the same was true for 32% of Black New Yorkers (City of New York 2018). As for the City of Detroit, a 2019 news release revealed that nearly 40% of its residents were also without broadband access at home (Frank 2019). While approximately 80% and 78% of African Americans and Hispanics are smartphone users nationwide, 25% and 23% of them rely on their smartphones to access the internet, respectively. By comparison, 82% of the Whites are smartphone users and 12% of them rely on their smartphones for internet access (Perrin and Turner 2019).

Underscoring the changing nature of the digital divide, past research has considered the impact of different forms of information and knowledge gap—stemming from a lack of broadband access—in economically disadvantaged communities (e.g., Floberg 2019; Pew 2018). For instance, a study about the H1N1 pandemic (Hutchins et al. 2009) suggested that minority populations had a high risk for pandemic exposure, greater susceptibility to infection, lower access to healthcare and treatment, and less ability to adopt pandemic mitigation actions. A systematic review of the H1N1 literature (Lin et al. 2014) also concluded that the less educated, young, and the indigent were more likely to perceive the risk to be low and not know enough about the threat, in addition to being less likely to follow proscribed behaviors. These authors also found that adoption of recommended infection practices was related to levels of (1) knowledge and worry about the disease, (2) trust in public officials and source of information, (3) information-seeking behaviors, and (4) routine media exposure.

A lack of trust could also play an important role to lessen the willingness to access or accept the pandemic information that individuals received from the governments and public health agencies. For example, Plough et al.'s (2011) study of the H1N1 response (in L.A. County) showed that African Americans were the least vaccinated group (3%), compared to Hispanics (47%) and Asians (28.5%). Their findings also noted that when interpreting the risk messages, African Americans (1) expressed greater concern that the vaccine would have adverse effects; (2) received information running counter to that of health professionals; and (3) thought "the vaccine was not safe" and thus "mistrust in government." This mistrust in the H1N1 information is particularly alarming and damaging, when faith-based leaders and even popular disk jockeys in the African community reportedly advised the followers to avoid receiving the H1N1 vaccine, due to perceived safety concerns (Ordway 2020).

By implication, as digital information divide has helped contribute to the health knowledge gap and systemic health disparities in American society, the COVID-19 pandemic has thus brought to light a digital health divide in American society. In this digital health divide, economically disadvantage individuals who are primarily African Americans, Hispanics, Native Americans, and immigrants either do not have sufficient access to the healthcare system or have no access to such system at all. This lack of access to healthcare is also a common phenomenon associated with many hourly workers, who do not receive any employer-subsidized health insurance; their limited access to healthcare providers thus has a side effect of sustaining a low health literacy rate as well.

The contributions of health behavior theories to pandemic response

The key public risk communication goals of the CDC involve facilitating adherence to a set of guidelines for mitigation strategies—such as staying home whenever possible, washing hands frequently, wearing a mask in public, and physically distancing from others—as well as practicing self-isolation if non-symptomatic, after testing positive or being exposed to a test-positive individual (CDC 2020). Evidence suggests that remaining home and practicing social distancing (or maintaining a safe physical distance between individuals outside)—as well as washing hands and wearing a face mask—have been able to help prevent COVID-19 transmission and save lives (Li et al. 2020; Benito and Forte 2020).

Parallel work on infectious diseases demonstrated that exposure to media coverage can encourage individuals to limit interpersonal contacts with others; as a result, such exposure could also shorten the duration of an outbreak (Sun et al. 2011). Likewise, a study that examined the role of risk communication in influencing infectious disease outbreaks—including SARS (of 2003), H1N1 (of 2009), and H7N9 (of 2013)—also confirmed that when people are exposed to a variety of communication sources, they are more likely to correct the misconceptions about the disease in question and become more knowledgeable about the updated status of that disease (e.g., Frost, Moolenaar, and Xie 2019). In the present context, outcomes that reflect increasing awareness and hence adoption of COVID-19 risk-mitigation behaviors are thus expected to involve effective risk communication that could successfully recommend science-based protective behaviors.

While the preventive behaviors recommended by the CDC do not seem difficult to implement, questions arise about the psychological factors that could affect the effectiveness of risk communication in triggering the adoption or non-adoption of those behaviors. As the preceding discussion of this chapter has addressed how the system, demographic, SES, and *infodemic* factors could influence the access to and knowledge about COVID-19 risk communication, it is important to examine the relevant psychological and behavioral factors that could contribute to the effects of such communication.

A logical starting point to address disease-outbreak related psychological factors would involve explicating the role of risk knowledge in influencing health protection motivation and behavior. Based on the H1N1 pandemic research literature, pandemic knowledge is likely a necessary but insufficient factor for triggering health motivation that could help enact the subsequent protective behaviors. The extant literature has shown that the effect of H1N1 knowledge on vaccination uptake is mixed (Lin et al. 2014). In particular, this literature reveals that knowledge was found to be a significant factor (Ravert, Fu, and Zimet 2012) or a non-factor (Yang 2015) in explaining H1N1-related health motivation. H1N1 knowledge was also identified as a negative predictor of vaccination intention, as the influence of perceived descriptive norm was established as a positive predictor (Lin, Xu, and Dam 2020). This finding associated with the influence of perceived social norms on H1N1 vaccination intention is consistent with past work, which indicated that interpersonal influences could change an individual's initial attitude toward an object or event (Friedkin and Johnsen 1999). In a pandemic context, such interpersonal influences could involve perceived descriptive and/or injunctive norms in relation to the adoption of COVID-19 preventive behaviors.

A systematic literature review also suggested that psychological determinants such as utility (or perceived benefits), risk perception, subjective norm (or injunctive norm), perceived behavioral control, self-efficacy, attitude, cues to action, prior behavior, and past vaccination experience could all be factors for consideration, alongside knowledge (Schmid et al. 2017). This review also concluded that lower H1N1 risk perception (via lower perceived severity of and susceptibility to the virus)—as well as higher risk perception of adverse H1N1-vaccine effects—helped contribute to decrease vaccine uptake.

This systematic review (Schmid et al. 2017) thus unfurls a set of theoretical constructs affiliated with such behavioral theories as the Health Belief Model (HBM) and Theory of Planned Behavior (TPB) to help explain the H1N1-vaccination behavior. The HBM is a framework that links beliefs to behaviors, as it asserts that risk perception (vulnerability and severity), cost/benefit analysis (perceived barriers and benefits), cues to action (a motivational trigger), and self-efficacy are relevant to explaining health behavior adoption (Glanz, Rimer, and Viswanath 2008). By comparison, the TPB is a typology that considers how the combined influences of attitudes, subjective norms, and perceived behavior control (or efficacy) will help determine behavioral intentions, which will lead to adoption of health behaviors (Ajzen 1991).

In the current COVID-19 pandemic context, the Protection Motivation Theory (PTM) could also be useful in explaining how people are motivated to adopt preventive measures. The thesis of the PTM considers that people's threat appraisal (perceived susceptibility and severity) and coping appraisal (perceived self-efficacy and response efficacy) will help facilitate their protection-motivation, leading to the adoption of preventive behaviors (Rogers 1975; Maddux and

Rogers 1983). A meta-analysis (Floyd, Prentice-Dunn, and Rogers 2000) examining how well the PTM explains health behavior reported a moderate overall effect size ($d+ = .52$) across 20 different health issues. The study also found that when perceived threat and coping appraisal levels increase, adaptive intentions or behaviors also increase. Consistently, the opposite is also true, when threat and coping appraisal levels decrease, there is an increase in maladaptive response.

Preliminary research has suggested that protection motivation theory is a useful framework for explaining adoption of pandemic preventive behaviors. For instance, a study of US adults indicated that appraisal of severity and susceptibility as well as appraisal of efficacy and response benefits of receiving a vaccine were significant predictors of H1N1 vaccination intention, but perceived vaccination cost (or response cost) was irrelevant to H1N1 vaccination intention (Ling, Kothe, and Mullan 2019). Likewise, both threat appraisal results (i.e., perceive severity and susceptibility) and coping appraisal outcomes (i.e., perceived self-efficacy and response efficacy to evaluate protective actions)—were found to be significant predictors of protection motivation (intention) to adopt and then the subsequent adoption of the recommended preventive behaviors (Barati et al. 2020).

With the ongoing *infodemic* overwhelming the virtual landscape, constant exposure to COVID-19 news and information could cause mental stress in society. According to a review of 3166 published papers, the psychological toll resulting from experiencing quarantine due to COVID-19 (Brooks et al. 2020) include "emotional stress, depression, irritability, insomnia, fear, confusion, anger, frustration, boredom and stigma" (913). Pfefferbaum and North (2020) suggested that providing psychosocial support to individuals in emotional distress triggered by COVID-19 is essential, in order to prevent depression and other mental health issues. Social support for coping with the pandemic notwithstanding, past research has also contended that health disparities and income inequality have long contributed to heath behavior adoption barriers in American society (Artiga, Garfield, and Orgera 2020).

Vaux (1988) maintained that social support could include three key aspects: support network resources, supportive behavior, and subjective appraisals of support. These different aspects of social support could communicate both emotional and informational support from sources such as members of one's social network, community leaders, and/or healthcare providers. Both types of support could also share positive social norms that reflect adoption of preventive measures to help facilitate others' engagement in pandemic communication, knowledge formation, and threat/coping appraisal, in addition to developing protection motivation and adopting preventive behaviors.

Outside of the context of chronic diseases, the extant literature generally suggests that online and offline social support espoused from strong-tie network members, could be effective in increasing an individual's well-being. For examples, past research has found that social support could be helpful for individuals who otherwise lacked the communication competence to deal with mental health issues (e.g., Wright 2016) as well as reduce stressful life experiences and psychological distress (e.g., Hashimoto et al. 1999). Walther and Boyd (2002) define social support in the form of emotional support as "statements of affection, emotional understanding, and statements geared toward relieving pain and stress" (158). Additional research has reported that online paralinguistic social support cues (e.g., "likes") posted by members of a strong-tie network could positively increase an individual's perceived well-being (Burke and Kraut 2016; Hayes, Carr, and Wohn 2016).

The concept of social capital, as proposed by Putnam (2000) as well as Astone et al. (1999) and others, emphasizes that interpersonal networks with strong ties and weak ties are beneficial for individuals who seek information, social influence, and social support. Pollock, Borges, and Cook (2020) conceptualized social capital as the relationship resources that could support healthy behavior and reduce disease prevalence. In particular, they stressed the importance of considering social capital for health promotion in different community contexts—including "poverty, education, working conditions, housing conditions, social support, stress, and neighborhood context" (p. 958)—that encapsulate the core reasons for health disparities. They further recommended activating social capital by connecting social cohesion, social trust, and individual and social responsibility at the community-level for health decision-making.

Conclusion

In the digital information age, public health professionals that utilize internet resources could benefit from technological affordances—characterized by interactive features, engaging images, and social presence—to conduct risk communication more effectively in a rich media environment. However, the openness of this virtual landscape also enables numerous entities to spread false information about how not to interpret, believe or accept scientific facts. The current COVID-19 *infodemic* is the best testament to how challenging it is for scientists and public health experts to counter the spiraling misinformation and disinformation campaigns online.

In the year 2020, social media is the most efficient communication vehicle for waging a COVID-19 information war—from those who spread conspiracy theories and falsehoods—for different political and ideological reasons. The lessons that we have learned from the current *infodemic* suggest that the only way to reduce the negative public health consequences of this information war is to counter it with effective risk communication and media placement strategies. As such, risk communication researchers, scientists, and health professionals should consider joining forces to craft a compelling science-based narrative that could cleanse and outlast the toxic sludge polluting the COVID-19 *infodemic* swamp.

References

Abd-Alrazaq, Alaa, Dari Alhuwai, Mowafa Househ, Mounir Hamdi, and Zubair Shah. 2020. "Top Concerns of Tweeters During the COVID-19 Pandemic: Infoveillance Study." *Journal of Medical Internet Research* 22, no. 4: e19016. doi:10.2196/19016.

Aitken, Peter. 2020. "States See Spike in Poison Control Calls Following Trump's Comments on Injecting Disinfectant." *Fox News*, April 25. www.foxnews.com/us/states-spike-poison-control-calls.

Ajzen, Icek. 1991. "The Theory of Planned Behavior." *Organizational Behavior and Human Decision Processes*, no. 50: 179–211.

Artiga, Samantha, Rachel Garfield, and Kendal Orgera. 2020. "Communities of Color at Higher Risk for Health and Economic Challenges Due to COVID-19." The Kaiser Family Foundation, April 7. www.kff.org/disparities-policy/issue-brief/communities-of-color-at-higher-risk-for-health-and-economic-challenges-due-to-covid-19/.

Associated Press. 2020. "In Iran, Hundreds Die Ingesting A Poison They Wrongly Believed Could Fight Coronavirus." *Los Angeles Times*, March 27. www.latimes.com/world-nation/story/2020-03-26/in-iran-false-belief-a-poison-fights-virus-kills-hundreds.

Astone, Nan Marie, Constance A. Nathanson, Robert Schoen, and Young J. Kim. 1999. "Family Demography, Social Theory, and Investment in Social Capital." *Population and Development Review* 25, no. 1: 1–31.

Barati, Majid, Saeed Bashirian, Ensiyeh Jenabi, Salman Khazaei, Akram Karimi- Shahanjarini, Sepideh Zareian, Forouzan Rezapur-Shahkolai, Babak Moeini. 2020. "Factors Associated with Preventive Behaviours of COVID-19 Among Hospital Staff in Iran in 2020: An Application of the Protection Motivation Theory." *Journal of Hospital Infection*. https://doi.org/10.1016/j.jhin.2020.04.035.

Benito, Marcelino, and Janel Forte. 2020. "New Data Suggests Staying Home, Social Distancing Is Saving Lives." *KHOU TV-11*, April 7. www.khou.com/article/news/health/coronavirus/new-data-suggests-staying-home-social-distancing-is-saving-lives/285-880fefea-a7ed-4aad-9d8b-13e8930eeb73.

Brooks, Samantha K., Rebecca K. Webster, Louise E. Smith, Lisa Woodland, Simon Wessely, Neil Greenberg, and Gideon James Rubin. 2020. "The Psychological Impact of Quarantine and How to Reduce It: Rapid Review of the Evidence." *Lancet* 395: 912–20.

Burke, Moira, and Robert E. Kraut. 2016. "The Relationship Between Facebook Use And Well-Being Depends on Communication Type and Tie Strength." *Journal of Computer Mediated Communication* 21: 265–81.

CDC. 2020. "How to Protect Yourself & Others. Coronavirus Disease 2019 (COVID-19)." Centers for Disease Control and Prevention, April 24. https://Covid.cdc.gov/coronavirus/ 2019-ncov/prevent-getting-sick/prevention.html.

Chandler, Simon. 2020. "Security Researchers Say the Reopen America Campaign Is Being Astroturfed." *Forbes*, April 24. www.forbes.com/sites/simonchandler/2020/04/24/security-researchers-say-the-reopen-america-campaign-is-being-astroturfed/#475e76426506.

City of New York. 2018. "Truth in Broadband: Access and Connectivity in New York City." April 28. https://tech.cityofnewyork.us/wp content/uploads/2018/04/ NYC-Connected-Broadband-Report-2018.pdf.

Clements, John M. 2020. "Knowledge and Behaviors Toward COVID-19 Among US Residents During the Early Days of the Pandemic: Cross-Sectional Online Questionnaire." *JMIR Public Health Surveill* 6, no. 2: e19161, April–June.

Daniels, Ronald J., and Marc H. Morial. 2020. "The covid-19 racial disparities could be even worse than we think," *The Washington Post*, April 23. https://www.washingtonpost.com/opinions/2020/04/23/covid-19-racial-disparities-could-be-even-worse-than-we-think/

Dobransky, Kerry, and Hargittai, E. 2012. "Inquiring Minds Acquiring Wellness: Uses of Online and Offline Sources for Health Information." *Health Communication* 27, no. 4: 331–43.

Evelyn, Karin. 2020. "It's a Racial Justice Issue: Black Americans Are Dying in Greater Numbers from Covid-19." *The Washington Post*, April 8, www.theguardian.com/world/2020/apr/08/its-a-racial-justice-issue-black-americans-are-dying-in-greater-numbers-from-covid-19.

Floberg, Dana. 2019. "The Truth About the Digital Divide." *Free Press*. https://Covid-19.free-press.net/our-response/expert-analysis/insights-opinions/racial-digital-divide-persists.

Floyd, Donna L., Steven Prentice-Dunn, and Ronald W. Rogers. 2000. "A Meta-Analysis of Research on Protection Motivation Theory." *Journal of Applied Social Psychology* 30, no. 2: 407–29.

Frank, Annalise. 2019. "New Detroit Director Aims to Improve Internet, Computer Access Across City." *Crain's Detroit Business*, April 10. www.crainsdetroit.com/people/new-detroit-director-aims-improve-internet-computer-access-across-city.

Friedkin, Noah, and Eugene Johnsen. 1999. "Social Influence Networks and Opinion Change." *Advances in Group Processes* 16: 1–29.

Friedman, Wayne. 2020. "Russian Trolls Are Still Contaminating." *MediaPost*, April 3. www.mediapost.com/publications/article/349447/russian-trolls-are-still-contaminating-media.html.

Frost, Melinda, Richun Li, Ronald Moolenaar, Qun'an Mao, and Ruiqian Xie. 2019. "Progress In Public Health Risk Communication In China: Lessons Learned From SARS To H7N9." *BMC Public Health* 19, no. 3: 475.

Geldsetzer, Pascal. 2020. "Use of Rapid Online Surveys to Assess People's Perceptions During Infectious Disease Outbreaks: A Cross-sectional Survey on COVID-19." *Medical Internet Research* 22, no. 4: e18790, April. doi: 10.2196/18790: 10.2196/18790.

Glanz, Karen, Barbara K. Rimer, and K. Viswanath, eds. 2008. *Health Behavior and Health Education: Theory, Research, and Practice*, 4th ed. San Francisco, CA: Jossey-Bass.

Hashimoto, Kimik, Hiroshi Kurita, Takashi Haratani, Ken Fuji, and Tomoaki Ishibashi. 1999. "Direct and Buffering Effects of Social Support on Depressive Symptoms of the Elderly with Home Help." *Psychiatry and Clinical Neurosciences* 53: 95–100.

Hayes, Rebecca A., Caleb T. Carr, Donghee, and Yvette Wohn. 2016. "It's the Audience: Differences in Social Support Across Social Media." *Social Media and Society* 4: 1–12.

Hutchins, Sonja S., Kevin Fiscella, Robert S. Levine, Danielle C. Ompad, and Marian McDonald. 2009. "Protection of Racial/Ethnic Minority Populations During an Influenza Pandemic." 99, no. S2: S261–70. https://ajph.aphapublications.org/doi/pdf/10.2105/AJPH.2009.161505.

Jones, Jeffrey. 2020. "Americans Struggle to Navigate COVID-19 Infodemic." *Gallup Poll*, May 11. https://news.gallup.com/poll/310409/americans-struggle-navigate-covid-infodemic.aspx.

Lin, Carolyn A., Xiaowen Xu, and Linda Dam. 2020. "Information Source Dependence, Presumed Media Influence, Risk Knowledge and Vaccination Intention." *Atlantic Journal of Communication*. https://doi.org/10.1080/15456870.2020.1720022.

Lin, Carolyn A., David J. Atkin, Celeste Cappotto, Carrie Davis, Julie Dean, Jennifer Eisenbaum, Kenyetta House, Robert Lange, Alexandra Merceron, Jacqueline Metzger, Ariane Mitchum, Heidi Nicholls, and Simona Vidican. 2015. "Ethnicity, Digital Divides, and Uses of the Internet for Health Information." *Computers in Human Behavior* 51: 216–223.

Lin, Leesa, Elena Savoia, Foluso Agboola, and Kasisomayajula Viswanath. 2014. "What Have We Learned About Communication Inequalities During The H1N1 Pandemic: A Systematic Review of the Literature." *BMC Public Health* 14: 484. https://doi.org/10.1186/1471-2458-14-484.

Ling, Mathew, Emily J. Kothe, and Barbara A. Mullan. 2019. "Predicting Intention to Receive a Seasonal Influenza Vaccination Using Protection Motivation Theory." *Social Science & Medicine* 233: 87–92.

Mackie, Calvin. 2020. "STEM and Coronavirus: The Crisis within the Crisis." *Forbes*, April 21. www.forbes.com/sites/calvinmackie/2020/04/21/stem-and-coronavirus-the-crisis-within-the-crisis/#53eb1de8e662.

Maddux, James E., and Ronald W. Rogers. 1983. "Protection Motivation and Self-Efficacy: A Revised Theory of Fear Appeals and Attitude Change." *Journal of Experimental Social Psychology* 19, no. 5: 469–79.

McFadden, Sarah Ann M., Amyn A. Malik, Obianuju G. Aguolu, Kathryn S. Willebr, and Saad B. Omer. 2020. "Perceptions of the Adult US Population Regarding the Novel Coronavirus Outbreak." *PLoS One*. https://doi.org/10.1371/journal.pone.0231808.

Nielsen, Rasmus Kleis, Richard Fletcher, Nic Newman, J. Scott Brennen, and Philip N. Howard. 2020. "Navigating the Infodemic: How People in Six Countries Access and Rate News and Information About Coronavirus." *Reuters Institute for the Study of Journalism*. www.politico.eu/wp-content/uploads/2020/04/Navigating-the-Coronavirus-info demic.pdf.

Ordway, Denise-Marie. 2020. "How We Can Improve Public Health Messaging About COVID-19." Harvard Kennedy School's Shorenstein Center, April 28. https://journalist-sresource.org/studies/society/public-health/public-health-messaging-coronavirus/.

Pettersson, Henrik, Byron Manley, and Sergio Hernandez. 2020. "Tracking Coronavirus' Global Spread." *CNN*, July 24. www.cnn.com/interactive/2020/ health/corona virus-maps-and-cases/.

Perrin, Anderson, and Erica Turner. 2019. "Smartphones Help Blacks, Hispanics Bridge Some—But Not All—Digital Gaps With Whites." *Pew Research Center*, August 20. www.pewresearch.org/fact-tank/2019/08/20/smartphones-help-blacks-hispanics-bridge-some-but-not-all-digital-gaps-with-whites/.

Pew Research Center. 2018. "Internet/Broadband Factsheet." December 12. http://Covid-19.pewinternet.org/fact-sheet/internet-broadband/.

Pfefferbaum, Betty, and Carol S. North. 2020. "Mental Health and the Covid-19 Pandemic." *The New England Journal of Medicine*, April 13. doi:10.1056/NEJMp20 08017.

Pierre, Joe. 2020. "Make America Open Again: Grassroots Protest Or Astroturfing?" *Psychology Today*, April 30. www.psychologytoday.com/us/blog/psych-unseen/202004/make-america-open-again-grassroots-protest-or-astroturfing.

Plough, Alonzo, Benjamin Bristow, Jonathan Fielding, Stephanie Caldwell, and Sinan Khan. 2011. "Pandemics and Health Equity: Lessons Learned from the H1N1 Response in Los Angeles County." *Journal of Public Health Management and Practice*, January–February. doi:10.1097/PHH.0b013e3181ff2ad7.

Pollock, John C., Carolina M. Borges, and Judi Puritz Cook. 2020. "Converging Innovations in Health Communication and Public Health: The Vibrant Role of Social Capital." In *The Handbook of Applied Communication Research*, edited by H. Dan O'Hair, Mary John O'Hair, Erin B. Hester, and Sarah Geegan, 955–70. Hoboken, NJ: Wiley.

Putnam, Robert D. 2000. *Bowling Alone: The Collapse and Revival of American Community*. New York: Simon & Schuster.

Ravert, Russell D., Linda Y. Fu, and Gregory D. Zimet. 2012. "Reasons for Low Pandemic H1N1 2009 Vaccine Acceptance within a College Sample." *Advances In Preventive Medicine,* November 28. doi:10.1155/2012/242518.

Richtel, Matt. 2020. "W.H.O. Fights a Pandemic Besides Coronavirus: An 'Infodemic'." *The New York Times*, February 6. www.nytimes.com/2020/02/06/health/coronavirus-misinformation-social-media.html.

Rogers, Ronald W. 1975. "A Protection Motivation Theory of Fear Appeals and Attitude Change." *The Journal of Psychology* 91, no. 1: 93–114.

Sarkis, Stephani. 2020. "Trump Touts Treatments for COVID-19 Without Evidence." *Forbes*, April 23. www.forbes.com/sites/stephaniesarkis/2020/04/23/trump-touts-treatments-for-covid-19-without-evidence/#4e58650c3549.

Schmid, Philipp, Dorothee Rauber, Cornelia Betsch, Gianni Lidolt, and MarieLuisa Denker 2017. "Barriers of Influenza Vaccination Intention and Behavior—A Systematic Review of Influenza Vaccine Hesitancy, 2005–2016." *PLoS One*, January 26. doi:10.1371/journal.pone.0170550.

Silverstein, Jason. 2020. "More Than 80% of Hospitalized COVID-19 Patients in Georgia Last Month Were Black." *CDC Study Finds. CBS*, April 30, 2020. www.cbsnews.com/news/georgia-coronavirus-patients-black-covid-19/.

State of New Jersey. 2020. "Iranian, Russian, and Chinese Media Drive COVID-19 Disinformation Campaign. *Covide-19 Rumor Control and Disinformation Update.*" *Office of Homeland Security and Preparedness*, March 17. https://static1.squarespace.com/static/54d79f88e4b0db3478a04405/t/5e70e05c9cd60200a7e0e240/1584455774872/Iranian+Russian+and+Chinese+Media+Drive+COVID-19+Disinformation+Campaign.pdf.

Sun, Chengjun, Wei Yang, Julien Arino, and Kamran Khan. 2011. "Effect of Media-Induced Social Distancing on Disease Transmission In A Two Patch Setting." *Mathematical Biosciences* 230, no. 2: 87–95.

United Nations. 2020. "UN Tackles 'Infodemic' Of Misinformation and Cybercrime in COVID-19 Crisis." The Department of Global Communications. www.un.org/en/un-coronavirus-communications-team/un-tackling-%E2%80%98infodemic%E2%80%99-misinformation-and-cybercrime-covid-19.

Vaux, Alan. 1988. *Social Support, Theory, Research, and Intervention.* New York: Praeger Publishers.

Walcott, John. 2020. "How the Trump-China Rivalry Has Hampered U.S. Intelligence on COVID-19." *Time*, May 1. https://time.com/5830420/trump-china-rivalry-coronavirus-intelligence/.

Walther, Joseph B., and Shawn Boyd. 2002. "Attraction to Computer-Mediated Social Support." in *Communication Technology And Society: Audience Adoption And Uses*, edited by Carolyn A. Lin and David J. Atkin, 153–88. Cresskill, NJ: Hampton Press.

Ward, Clarissa, Katie Polglase, Sebastian Shukla, Gianluca Mezzofiore, and Tim Lister-and. 2020. "Russian Election Meddling Is Back—Via Ghana And Nigeria—And In Your Feeds." *CNN*, April 11. www.cnn.com/2020/03/12/world/russia-ghana-troll-farms-2020-ward/index.html.

Watkins, S. Craig, Alexander Cho, Andres Lombana-Bermudez, Vivian Shaw, Jacqueline Ryan Vickery, and Lauren Weinzimmer. 2018. *The Digital Edge: How Black and Latino Youth Learn, Create, and Collaborate Online.* New York: New York University Press.

Whitten, Pamela, Gary Kreps, and Mathew Eastin. 2009. *The Advent of Online Cancer Information Systems.* Cresskill, NJ: Hampton.

WHO. 2020. "Coronavirus Disease 2019 (COVID-19) Situation Report—85." World Health Organization, April 15. www.who.int/docs/default-source/coronaviruse/situation-reports/20200415-sitrep-86-covid-19.pdf?sfvrsn=c615ea20_2.

Wright, Kevin. 2016. "Social Networks, Interpersonal Social Support, and Health Out-comes: A Health Communication Perspective." *Frontiers in Communication*: 14. https://doi.org/10.3389/fcomm.2016.00010.

Wyatt, Sally, Flis Henwood, Angie Hart, and Julie Smith. 2005. "The Digital Divide, Health Information and Everyday Life." *New Media & Society* 7, no. 2: 99–218.

Yang, Z. Janet. 2015. "Predicting Young Adults' Intentions to Get the H1N1 Vaccine: An Integrated Model." *Journal of Health Communication* 20, no. 1: 69–79.

Zanolli, Lauren. 2020. "Data from US South Shows African Americans Hit Hardest by Covid-19." *The Guardian*, April 8. www.theguardian.com/world/2020/apr/08/black-americans-coronavirus-us-south-data.

Part IV
Risk, space, and cyberattacks

17 Manufacturing fear

Infodemics and scaremongering about coronavirus and Ebola epidemics on social media platforms in West Africa

Paul Obi and Floribert Patrick C. Endong

Introduction

Since its advent in December 2019, the coronavirus has profoundly inspired the social, political, and media discourse across the world. However, many mysteries surrounding it have remained unraveled till date. In many respects, the level of information dissemination, conspiracy theories, fake news, misinformation, disinformation, and propaganda associated with the pandemic have all combined to overwhelm experts' advice and evidence-based information about coronavirus. The rise of misinformation and disinformation occasioned by the disruption of global health communication on coronavirus has also led to a two-pronged form of pandemics—one on information epidemic and the other on the main virus. Amuta (2020) holds that the constant inflow and outflow of news about deaths, threats, and the uncertainty surrounding COVID-19 surreptitiously create a fertile ground for disruption and epidemic of pessimism.

This disruption poses great challenges on how information and communication on a pandemic like COVID-19 is disseminated. Facing these difficulties in combating the pandemic and information epidemic in an era of viral modernity (Peters et al. 2020), the World Health Organization (WHO 2020) has likewise been compelled to declare this superimposing information disruption on global health as Infodemics. By definition, infodemic is an overt inflow and outflow of disruptive and distorted information, fake news, misinformation, and propaganda about a disease, virus, epidemic or pandemic. Such disruptive information poses a bigger challenge than the main disease itself (WHO 2020). With the outbreak of coronavirus, Infodemics have also posed equal measure of challenges as COVID-19 (Zarocosta 2020).

Historically, the flow of infodemics during outbreak of pandemics is not new to the world. From the Spanish Influenza, HIV/AIDS, to SARS, Zika and Ebola in Africa, the avalanche of misinformation has also formed part of the complications in tackling diseases and viruses around the world. Aderet (2020) highlights cases of the Spanish Influenza and the spiral information warfare and misinformation in Spain, United States, China, Russia, Japan, Italy, and Great Britain. While Infodemics were observed in nations and states in the early nineteenth century, they were not as fierce as today. In effect, the emergence of disruptive technologies—such as the internet and social media in the twenty-first century—has made the spread of Infodemics to be more rapid and phenomenal today, compared to previous times. Thus, in today's twenty-first century, Infodemics are spread across different spectrum of information and communication platforms that cannot even be tracked. Such spread of Infodemics have been at the root of waves of fear and panic particularly in recent cases of Ebola virus disease outbreak and the ongoing COVID-19 pandemic in West Africa.

Scholars have attempted to interrogate the extent to which Infodemics fuel fear and scaremongering, derailing the smooth flow of public health communication around the globe (Beck 1992; Cushion et al. 2020; Moeller 1999; Gray and Ropeik 2002). Loveday (2020) for instance argued that even the media narrative on coronavirus has tended to invoke fear and panic with words such as invisible enemy, killer virus, threat to world order among other numerous scaremongering clichés. This seeming way of narrativizing COVID-19 can create a climate of fear and disrupting the consumption of authentic information on coronavirus and other health-related crises. Fuchs (2020) maintained that the atmosphere of crisis, uncertainties, shocks, and collective fear of death on coronavirus provides a veritable platform for fake news and misinformation on the virus.

Further, Mejova and Kalimeri (2020) contend that information around COVID-19 has created a strong competing zeal among politics, news, and business, such that the main objective is no longer accurate information dissemination but to feed into the culture of fragmentation of coronavirus narrative. This fragmentation of information on COVID-19 in most cases might also be geared toward creating panic and deflecting attention about the virus by foreign powers, (Barnes et al. 2020; Emmott 2020; Farraresi 2020). Critically, the contest for control of information on pandemics both at transnational and national spheres raises the bar for Infodemics. The use of the internet and the social media by "agents" of Infodemics has made the whole situation worse. In effect, because public discourse on pandemics on social media platforms inadvertently makes everyone an expert, the degree to which wrong information is disseminated becomes a significant part in addressing public health challenges. A basic part of the challenge is that Infodemics create a culture of fear and scaremongering among the populace during pandemics, disrupting scientifically proven and evidence-based health communication.

This chapter seeks to illustrate the scenario already mentioned using the 2014–2016 Ebola epidemic and the current COVID-19 pandemic in West Africa as case studies. The chapter specifically seeks answers to the following research questions: how does Infodemic on coronavirus and Ebola epidemic applies to West Africa and how has it given rise to fear and scaremongering? What form(s) does Infodemics operate or have taken on social media platforms in West Africa and what are the implications for public health communication? What then are the most cogent and pragmatic steps and strategies to address this communication gap because of Infodemics on Coronavirus and Ebola epidemic?

Ebola, COVID-19, and social media driven infodemics in West Africa

Most—if not all—of the major epidemics that have rocked West African countries brought with them information crises or tsunamis of mis/disinformation. This is not too surprising as "every time you have an epidemic of disease, you have an epidemic of rumours as well" (Reid Wilson 2019). This epidemic of rumors generally leads to an "epidemic of fear" and/or an "epidemic of panic" (World Bank Group 2019). The information crises brought about by epidemics of disease in West Africa have however been more than mere "epidemics of rumours." In fact, they have most often been characterized by at least three findings:

(i)   Citizens' predominant reliance on hear-and-say or spurious myths as source of information about the epidemics.
(ii) Citizens' tendency of suspecting official sources of information—which most often are government-owned organs of communication or "authoritative" foreign health organizations—even when the latter are disseminating accurate and pertinent information.
(iii) The proliferation (through social networking sites) of false information that undermine medical advice, proffer fake or fraudulent cures, incite panic, and that is used for political point scoring.

In effect, West Africans have over the years developed the tendency of mistrusting government communications or official sources of information. In the popular fantasy, government officials' pronouncements and information strategies are at best, kinds of well calculated lies and mere instruments of propaganda. Politicians are popularly regarded as entities that will not hesitate to manipulate (health) information for specific political agendas. In the same popular fantasy, foreign health agencies such as the World Health Organizations, UNICEF, UN, Unites States Centre for Disease Control and Prevention (CDC), and USAID among others are not to be totally trusted (Idayat 2020). Thus, people tend to believe that, most often, these agencies are sociopolitical forces whose communications about epidemics are often aimed at some imperialist or neocolonialist goals (Georgetown University Medical Centre 2018).

This arguable myth is even complicated by the fact that the foreign agencies already mentioned most often fail to share or provide concordant information about the epidemics, thereby creating conditions favorable for the emergence and proliferation of all manner of rumors, fake news, and misinformation about epidemics. During the 2014–2016 Ebola epidemics in Guinea, Liberia, and Sierra Leone, for instance, data-sharing barriers were observed between health ministries, NGOs, and other major parties involved in the mitigation of the epidemics (Georgetown University Medical Centre 2018; Kinsman et al. 2017). In some situations, the information published by one health organization was not supported or concurred by others. This did not only hamper the effective dissemination of similar information about the causalities and severity of the epidemics; but also led the public to give credence to all manner of conspiracy theories, citizen journalists, rumor mongers, and opinion leaders/molders so long as the latter were deemed sufficiently eloquent.

In deeply religious countries such as Nigeria, Sierra Leone, and Ghana, for instance, one observes that, during epidemics, religious leaders seem to have greater powers to win the hearts of the populace compared to health experts and government officials. People in these countries tend to unquestionably digest health-related information emanating from religious leaders or religious myths than trusting credible sources of information. During the Ebola outbreak in Sierra Leone for instance, health information emanating from experts and government sources were strongly competing with a plurality of spurious religious myths and rumors in the sociopolitical and media landscape of the country. Rumors attributed the outbreak of the Ebola virus disease either to witchcraft, government-instigated genocide or water poisoning; thereby challenging genuine sources of health information that could have helped in sensitizing the people and in equipping them with relevant knowledge to ensure their safety during the epidemic (Kinsman et al. 2017; Kirsh et al. 2017; Koroma and Ly 2015; Roy et al. 2020).

The advent of the social media has made the situation even worst. This is so as social media networking has among other things, facilitated the dissemination of half-truths, fake news, and misinformation about epidemics. These half-truths, fake news and misinformation have represented one of the major challenges to the effective sensitization of the public during advents of epidemics in West African countries. Indeed, with the continuous saturation of West African countries with cell-phones coupled with the proliferation of social media networking sites as Twitter and Facebook, fighting diseases most often entails fighting misconceptions or fake news, one tweet or Facebook comments after the other. Fake news or misinformation through online platforms often causes a paradoxical situation where the public (particularly communities at risk) develop an unjustified fear for doctors and health organizations that are trying to contain a disease. In such situation, bad information is often worse than the total lack of information.

The aforementioned can be illustrated by the fact that, during the 2014–2016 Ebola outbreak in Liberia, Guinea, Sierra Leone, and Nigeria, many West Africans created Facebook groups and hashtags such as #KickEbolaOut to share information about the Ebola virus disease (EVD). They created awareness and mount a strong online-based activism in favor of the mitigation of the disease. Although these platforms assumed a key role in the discourse around the Ebola virus disease and its mitigation, they served as a double-edge sword: on one hand, they facilitated the dissemination of expert information about the Ebola virus and, on the other hand, appeared to be the sites of misinformation, fake news, and unsubstantiated solutions to the outbreak. For instance, it was not uncommon to find such online platforms replete with posts which simultaneously spread useful and misleading information about the Ebola virus. As noted by Sarmah (2014) "for every post pushing true information, you [could] find another about saltwater baths and kola as supposed cures" and rumors claiming that poisoned water wells, instead of Ebola, are sickening the population in Liberia and Sierra Leone.

The advent of the coronavirus in December 2019 and its subsequent propagation in West African countries have led to the emergence of social media platforms where the good, the bad, and the ugly about the COVID-19 cohabit. Wrong information about coronavirus and Ebola pandemic can be broadly divided into four categories: (i) fake or fraudulent cures, (ii) loose news, (iii) exaggerations aimed at instilling fear, anxiety, and panic among West Africans, and (iv) spurious myths about "genuine" vaccines and vaccinations.

Fake cures

An example of fake and fraudulent cures "advertised' through online rumors was observed in 2015 when a diversity of social media networking sites relayed Professor Maurice Iwu's unsubstantiated claims that Kola nut (an African fruit which is bitter in taste and rich in caffeine) is a suitable cure for Ebola. Another unsubstantiated claim that went viral on social media was the saltwater baths and consumption purported to be an infallible cure for the Ebola virus disease. This myth in particular went viral on social media after a Nigerian state leader twitted that saltwater baths have some magical virtues working against the Ebola virus. All these fraudulent cures were debunked by the World Health Organization. In a communication released on August 8, 2016, the WHO warned pointedly saying: "all rumours of any other effective products or practices are false. Their use can be dangerous. In Nigeria, for example, at least two people have died after drinking salt water, [which was] rumoured to be protective" (cited in Sifferlin 2014, 18). Recently, another similar online rumor claimed Chloroquine is an ideal cure for COVID-19. This rumor motivated many COVID-19 infected West Africans to riskily take overdoses of the medicine with the hope of recovering their health. Idayat (2020) has reviewed cases of such rumor mongers who rather complicated their conditions by overdosing chloroquine.

Other online rumors have propagated the faulty myth that African blood is immune to the coronavirus and recommended sitting on the sun or constant sex as magic cures for the COVID-19. It is thus observed that day by day, new and strange cures are popularized on social media challenging the health information released by health experts or heath organizations such as the WHO and *Médecins Sans Frontières*. The pushing on social media of these cures and rumors which have no medical basis creates confusion in the domain of health information dissemination and public health. The cures are however bound to be regarded as tempting and pertinent in West African societies where the fear of the unknown and a weak communication between the governing elites and the governed prevail; and where the healthcare system is near collapse.

Loose news

An example of loose news on Ebola virus that has been rampant on social media is the series of controversial myths that have attributed the massive deaths recorded in Sierra Leone and Liberia to genocide instigated by government, witchcraft, and/or poisoned water (Koroma and Ly 2015). These rumors have not only been spread on social media, but they have in several contexts been reported by the traditional media in Liberia, Guinea, and Sierra Leone making many West Africans to believe in their veracity (Sarmah 2014; Koroma and Ly 2015). According to the director of Liberian organization called Youth in Technology Arts Network, Donnish Pewee, these myths have reduced public awareness of the virus. Pewee writes that the aforementioned myths have created various misconceptions about the Ebola virus "some people are now taking the virus seriously [while] others don't. When we ask them 'do you believe Ebola exists?', some say no" (cited in Sarmah 2014).

Information aimed at inciting fear and panic

As earlier said, bad news spread on social media about epidemics also take the form of exaggerations and sensationalist comments aimed at inciting fear and panic among West Africans. A case in point is the plurality of online rumors which predicted that there will be hecatombs in different West African countries because of the COVID-19 outbreak. On March 31, 2020, for instance, an audio clip emerged on WhatsApp where a "fake heath expert" delivers an exposé hinged on a presumed WHO prediction that the COVID-19 pandemic is going to claim the lives of at least 45 million Nigerians. In other similar online messages, specific political activists, political ideologues, and self-styled orators are seen discussing various conspiracy theories related to West African countries' management of the COVID-19 crisis. Some of these orators pretend to be revealing classified information about the coronavirus in their continent of origin. In line with this, the controversial Nigerian blogger Kemi Olunloyi tweeted that Nigerian President Muhammadu Buhari is in an extremely critical health situation. The tweet also claimed that the president has a persistent cough and is under intensive medical care at the presidency. This tweet went viral as it was liked 3300 times within few hours and was retweeted more than 2000 times as coronavirus (Idayat 2020, Elumelu 2020). Much of the bad news spread on social media is the design of bloggers seeking to grow their followership. This however does not cancel the fact that their sensational and transactional comments and posts contribute to inciting fear, confusion, and panic among members of the public.

Conspiracy theories around COVID-19 vaccines and vaccinations

In West Africa, the history of vaccines and vaccination has not been received by the public genuinely. There is a great level of suspicion wherever vaccines are involved in the prevention of diseases. The situation is complicated when such vaccines are manufactured in the West; there is a constant mill of rumors and speculations about an alleged hidden agenda by the West to reduce Africa's population. In Senegal, fake news on social media about COVID-19 vaccination of seven children, resulting to the dead of all seven sparked a national uproar (Reuters 2020). The case of Pfizer and the missteps in the Meningitis drug trials in Kano, Nigeria, often echo negative implications (Ahmad 2001).

Table 17.1 Showing cases of fake conspiracy theories and cures on pandemics and epidemics in West Africa

S/No.	Propagator of fake news	Fake news item	Source of factual news	Factual news item
1	IPOB	Centre for Global Human Population Reduction	Gates Foundation/ Reuters	Bill and Melinda Gates Foundation
2	Igala King (Nigeria)	Salt Water Bath as Cure for Ebola	Nigeria's Ministry of Health	Disapprove Salt Water Bath as Ebola Cure
3	Social Media (Senegal)	Black people immune from COVID-19; heat prevents coronavirus and neem leaves cure coronavirus	#Fagarungirmuccu Initiatives	Debunked all fictitious claims; initiate a national response mechanism to fight online mechanism on COVID-19

Source: © Paul Obi, Floribert Patrick C. Endong, 2021

With the outbreak of COVID-19 and the various controversies that have characterized the pandemic, public discourse on vaccines on COVID-19 on social media in West Africa have dwelt extensively on suspicion, dispelling and labeling the anticipated vaccines as a product of population reduction in Africa. While social media discourse has in most cases fueled campaigns to reject such vaccines whenever they are discovered, Bill Gates' clamor for a vaccine for COVID-19 has rather faced the highest level of misinformation and fake news.

Leading the pack of campaign against any COVID-19 vaccine is the Indigenous People of Biafra (IPOB) Twitter account. IPOB, a South-East Nigeria based separatist group with branches across the world has used its Twitter account to bombard Bill Gates' calls for vaccines with fake news and misinformation (see Plates 1 and 2). On IPOB's Twitter account, a Twit is posted showing Bill and Melinda Gates Foundation's Centre for Global Human Population Reduction in Seattle, Washington. Though the information is fake news and propaganda, its intention is clearly to discourage Africans from accepting any COVID-19 vaccine from the West or any form of COVID-19 medicine. Such peddling of misinformation, while, in some cases can be said to be an error or mistake, most fake news and misinformation on coronavirus have been audacious and deliberate. Despite several reports by international media that the photo of the fake Centre for Global Human Population Reduction is fictitious, most online platforms in West Africa have refused to take them down. This gives credence to the deliberate manufacturing of fear, risk, and panic through misinformation (Table 17.1).

The unintended consequences of infodemics and bioinformational warfare on social media

The study has, in the preceding sections, established different layers of Infodemics and misinformation across West Africa during the Ebola epidemic and coronavirus pandemic. It identifies four patterns of Infodemics and misinformation, including fictitious cure claims; loose news and propaganda; deliberate manufacturing of fear and panic, and dispelling and negatively labeling anticipated vaccines for prevention of pandemics and diseases. In real sense, the manufacturing of fear seemingly becomes the greatest challenge in time of pandemics and outbreak of diseases.

Although Beck (1992) and Cottle (2006) theoretically harped on the "complexities of media performance" and "manufactured uncertainties" in relation to industrial, environment, and ecological risks, today's technological risk feeds into the present dis/misinformation pandemic on COVID-19 and Ebola with regard to social media. In addition, the current (bio)informational warfare on coronavirus and Ebola epidemic add to risk communication theatrics that the world is now confronting. The summation of these risks and information war on pandemics create a communication of fear. A predominant thread of the public health communication in West Africa by both citizens and authorities at the forefront both on social media and mainstream media indicated the displacement of standardized and science-based public health communication to the buzzification of Infodemics and misinformation.

Further, reasons for the high rate of misinformation, fake news, and propaganda on COVID-19 could be traceable to the sloppy communication approaches by China, WHO, and political leaders. Again, lockdown and social distancing have also helped to spur citizens to engage in banal information sharing. Because of COVID-19 social distancing and lockdown, a wide gulf appears to have been created; as distance conditioned citizens to resort to uncoordinated form of sharing unfiltered information, which often pans out as fake news and misinformation. This in turn feeds into our daily fears; a situation that raises both the public's fear level and confusion on public health communication.

The trajectory of fear, panic, and scaremongering create several layers of fears induced by Infodemics, whereby one form of fear is chasing another form of fear. The sum total which often snowballed into an array of fear versus fear, resulting in citizens being gripped by viral fear. At the center of this phenomenon is the media influence in manufacturing fear, spreading it, creating a web of fear in the midst of a pandemic. No doubt, during this outbreak of coronavirus, there has been a corresponding rise in media campaigns supporting citizens to keep off from overdose consumption of news and information. Such media campaigns have stemmed from the justified fear that Infodemics are capable of injecting panic into the psyche and psychology of the people.

Conclusion

Strategically, this study has shown how nearly all forms of information dissemination have been caught up in the (bio)informational warfare during the 2014–2016 Ebola crises and the current coronavirus pandemic in West Africa. The study argues that during these two crises, information sharing and dissemination, were not geared toward explicitly communicating the real issues about public health and the mitigation of pandemics and epidemics. The sharing of information has among other things, also fueled a feast of fear. Across all the social media platforms in West Africa observed, the sharing of data and numbers of Coronavirus victims—fatality, confirmed cases, recovered cases was not about the science behind-the-numbers, but an infotainment game deliberately or inadvertently aimed at generating and spreading fear.

Because of fear, citizens and *internautes* have been quick to share dis/misinformation with the intent to educate and inform others. Conversely, such sharing of information in many cases led to the spreading of distorted information. Thus, overt consumption of news and information has sometimes inadvertently created an atmosphere of fear and uncertainty.

In a world of pandemics and Infodemics, certainty becomes uncertain; uncertainty in turn breathes fear and panic. In a society where Infodemics is endemic, well-entrenched, and unchallenged; chances are that manipulation of information and fake news tend to set the pace on communication about public health among the populace. In the research, this phenomenon was pervasive among citizens in West Africa outside the corridors of power, governmental and trusted health institutions. Overall, Infodemics during the coronavirus and Ebola epidemic in West Africa was intense and severely affected the mitigation of the pandemics.

While the global battle to confront Infodemics may be a tough order, there are critical steps that have become imminent if Infodemics are ever to be tamed. A probable way of addressing Infodemics is to ensure that anti-infodemics platforms and channels are immediately opened once there is an outbreak of pandemics or any disease. There is also the need to establish fact-checking apps and models to track Infodemics and expose them. Also, there is an urgency to prohibit states and governmental institutions from spreading Infodemics and propaganda or withholding information for political gains during pandemics. That way, the world can position itself better in communicating the underpinning exigencies associated with public health, and also end Infodemics.

References

Aderet, Ofer. 2020. "A Terrible New Weapon of War: The Spanish Influenza Had Its Own Share of Conspiracy Theories." *Israel News*. Accessed May 8, 2020. https://www-haaretz-com/s/www.haaretz.com/amp/israel-news/.premium-the-spanish-flu-had-its-own-share-of-conspiracy-theories.

Ahmad, Khabir. 2001. "Nigerian Government Investigates Pfizer Drug Trial Allegations." *The Lancet* 357, no. 9250: 125–32.

Amuta, Chidi. 2020. "Pessimism as an Entitlement." *This Day*, March 26.

Barnes, Julian E. Rosenberg, Mathew and Wong, Edward. 2020. "As Virus Spreads, China, Russia See Openings for Disinformation." *New York Times*, March, 28.

Beck, Ulrich. 1992. *Risk Society: Towards a New Modernity*. London: Sage.

Cottle, Simon. 2006. *Mediatized Conflict: Issues in Cultural and Media Studies*. Maidenhead: Open University Press.

Cushion, Stephen, Maria Kyriakiduo, Marino Morani, and Nikki Soo. 2020. "Coronavirus: Study Shows People Want More Scientific Experts Analysis and—Less of Boris Johnson." *The Conversation*. Accessed May 6, 2020. https://theconversation.com/amp/coronavirus-study-shows-people-want-more-scientific-expert-analysis-and-less-boris-johnson.

Elumelu, Tony. 2020. "Making Impact during Covid-19 Pandemic." Accessed May 23, 2020. www.tonyelumelufoundation.org/making-impact-during-covid-19-pandemic/how-olasupo-abideen-is-battling-fake-news-during-covid-19.

Emmott, Robin. 2020. "Russia Deploying Coronavirus Disinformation to Sow Panic in West, EU Document Says." Accessed May 21, 2020. https://mobile.reuters.com/article/amp/idUSKBN21518F?__twitter_impression=true.

Farraresi, Mattia. 2020. "China Isn't Helping Italy: It's Waging Information Warfare." Accessed May 8, 2020. https://foreignpolicy.com/2020/03/31/china-isnt-helping-italy-its-waging-information-warfare/.

Fuchs, Christian. 2020. "Everyday Life and Everyday Communication in Coronavirus Capitalism, Triple C." *Communication, Capitalism and Critique* 18, no. 1: 1–9.

Georgetown University Medical Centre. 2018. *Data Sharing During the West Africa Ebola Public Health Emergency: Case Study*. Georgetown: Georgetown University.

Gray, George M., and David P. Ropeik. 2002. "Dealing with the Dangers of Fear: The Role of Risk Communication." *Health Affairs* 21, no. 6: 106–16.

Idayat, Hassan. 2020. "Nigeria: The Other Covid-19 Pandemic—Fake News." *African Arguments*, March 20.

Kinsman, John, De Bruljne, Kars, Jalloh Alpha, Haris Muriel, and Abdullah Hussainatu. 2017. "Development of a Set of Community-Informed Ebola Messages for Sierra Leone." *PLoS: Neglected Tropical Diseases* 11, no. 8: 1–20.

Kirsh, Thomas, Heidi Moseson, Massaquoi Moses, Nyenswah Tolbert, and Goodermote Rachel. 2017. "Impact of Interventions and the Incidence of Ebola Virus Disease in Liberia—Implications for Future Epidemics." *Health Policy and Planning* 32: 205–14.

Koroma, Mohamed and Ly, Shan. 2015. Ebola Wreaks Havoc in Sierra Leone. *Infectious Diseases of Poverty*, 4, no.1: 4–10.

Loveday, Heather. 2020. "Fear, Explanation and Action—the Psychosocial Response to Emerging Infection. *"Journal of Infection Prevention* 21, no. 2: 44–46.

Mejova, Yelena, and Kyriaki Kalimeri. 2020. "Advertisers Jump on Coronavirus Bandwagon: Politics." *News and Business*, January 28.

Moeller, Susan D. 1999. *Compassion Fatigue: How the Media Sell Disease, Famine, War and Death*. New York: Routledge.

Peters, Michaels A., Petar Jandric, and Peter McLaren. 2020. "Viral Modernity? Epidemics, Infodemics and 'Bioinformational' Paradigm." *Education Philosophy and Theory* 18: 23–56.

Reid, Wilson. 2019. "Ebola Outbreak in Africa Spreads Fake News in America." *The Hill*. Accessed May 8, 2020. https://thehill.com/policy/international/448197-ebola-outbreak-in-africa-spreads-fake-news-in-america.

Reuters. Seven Children Killed in Senegal after Receiving Covid -19 Vaccine, *Mobile Reuters*, Accessed July 15, 2020, https://mobile-reuters-com.cdn.amproject.org/v/s/mobile.reuters.com/article/

Roy, Melissa, Nicholas Moreau, Cècile Rousseau, Arnaud Mercier, Andrew Gordon Wilson, and Laëtitia. 2020. "Ebola and Localized Blame on Social Media: Analysis of Twitter and Facebook Conversations During the 2014–2014 Ebola Pandemics." *Culture, Medicine and Psychiatry* 44: 56–76.

Sarmah, Satta. 2014. "Fighting the Endless Spread of Ebola Misinformation on Social Media." *Fast Company*. Accessed May 9, 2020. www.fastcompany.com/3034380/fighting-the-endless-spread-of-ebola-misinformation-on-social-media.

Sifferlin, Alexandra. 2014. "Fake Cures and Ebola—Drug Sensationalism. Need to Stop, WHO Says." *Time Magazine*, August 15.

World Bank Group. 2020. *Lessons Learned in Financing Rapid Response to Recent Epidemics in West and Central Africa*. New York: World Bank Group.

Zarocosta, John. 2020."How to Fight Infodemics." *The Lancet* 395, no. 10225: 676–83.

18 Space matters in narrating the catastrophe

Relational riskscapes of COVID-19, dominant discourses, and the example of Turkey

Şemsettin Tabur

The first quarter of the year 2020 in Turkey was saturated with the news of natural disasters of different sorts, fatal accidents along with a serious military crisis with one of its neighboring country: the earthquake on January 24 hit a small town in Elazig and caused 41 people to die and around 1000 to be injured, a catastrophic event that was followed by an avalanche which took again 41 lives and many more people to get stuck under large piles of snow in a notoriously cold and mountainous region in the country. The news of both calamities struck the nation for several days as the search and rescue works were televised all day long on numerous channels. The situation got only worse with the news of more earthquakes from other regions, a passenger plane's fatal crash and breaking into pieces while landing at Sabiha Gökçen Airport in Istanbul, and the escalating conflict between Turkey and Syrian regime forces.

While these already sufficed to keep people immersed in mass media, the news of then-local coronavirus breakout in China became another crisis to be faced. Starting from mid-January, a scientific advisory board composed of specialists was set up, international flights with some countries were suspended, the borders with Iran were closed, and many other preemptive measures were taken by the authorities. It was however on March 11 when the first positive case of infection was officially confirmed in Turkey that all the other news began to be overshadowed by the novel coronavirus. Since then, the COVID-19 pandemic has taken the center stage not only in various forms of media but also in people's everyday lives, as of the beginning of June 2020.

Considering its representation, management, and impact on people's everyday lives, this new phenomenon has already distinguished itself from the aforementioned hazards and crises of the preceding months especially with regard to its ontologically uncertain, causally complex, socially constructed, global, anticipatory and catastrophic features, because of which it, I argue, needs to be considered in terms of a global risk, in the way the term has been conceptualized in the social sciences. Although the pandemic has largely been approached as an externally caused, ongoing catastrophe that needs to be fought back in the ways earthquakes or military conflicts require, I contend that what is needed at this point is to admit that we are facing a new, global phenomenon that defies old ways of framing and action.

Through the concept of "riskscape" as an interpretive tool, the present study will examine how physical spaces and spatial practices have been shaped by the ways the pandemic has been defined, represented and managed by institutions such as mass media and the state. Pointing toward the "dark irony" the dominant, institutional risk assessment has caused, I argue that a more ambivalent, complex, long-term "dwelling in crisis," to borrow Frederick Buell's formulation (2003, 76), unlike a linear, progressivist narrative with a beginning, a climax and a closure, characterizes the current situation.

Neither risk nor risk-related phenomena such as chance, uncertainty and the limitedness of knowledge about future are new to humanity, yet the word is of premodern origin, employed primarily "as a navigational device used by sailors entering uncharted waters" (Mythen 2014, 11). Within time however, this spatial aspect in the term's early usage was replaced with a more temporal emphasis, and risk, starting especially from the late seventeenth century was associated with future threats that could be estimated and controlled. However, more recent scholarship on the term, beginning in the late 1970s and 1980s and especially with the works of scholars, such as Douglas, Luhmann and Beck, has referred to its socially and culturally constructed aspects. In contrast to the modern usages of the term which emphasized that risks could actually be calculated, ruled, and even avoided, thanks to scientific and industrial advancements, the risks in the twenty-first century, or what Beck calls world risk society, are uncertain, complex, anthropocentric, anticipatory, and catastrophic. Mastering today's risks goes beyond the capacity and control of science, which, in turn, leaves people more anxious and perplexed with a sense of doubt and distrust in modern institutions such as state and technology. In this context, they govern our lives, for human beings no longer "choose to take risks [but] we have them thrust upon us" (Beck 1998, 12). Living in world risk society and opening up new opportunities of action amid the destructiveness of faced global risks, Beck suggests, is possible only through leaving the denial or past epistemes aside and acknowledging that such new risks require novel ways of framing and action.

The processes of assessment, representation and management are co-constitutive and vital for the social construction of risks because they are what make risks "real":

> Risk is *not* synonymous with catastrophe. Risk means the *anticipation* of catastrophe. . . . Risks are always *future* events that *may* occur, that *threaten* us. But because this constant danger shapes our expectations, lodges in our heads and guides our actions, it becomes a political force that transforms the world.
>
> (Beck 2009, 9–10, emphasis in original)

More precisely, in what Beck calls "world risk society," risks are no longer just about "objective," probability calculations, but they are socially and culturally constructed, that is, they become "real" as they are anticipated, "stag[ed]" (Beck 2009, 16) and acted upon. Beck's distinction between risk and catastrophe accentuates the issue of power: the questions such as who has the capacity to define certain phenomena as risk and how certain risks to be managed and represented to create risk awareness in people make risk definition fundamentally a "power game" (Beck 2006, 333).[1] Similarly, Garland suggests: "Objective versus subjective risk is a false opposition. The contrast is more often between different conventions for observation, measurement and evaluation" (2003, 56).

With Beck's distinction in mind and having no interest in questioning the "reality" or objectivity of coronavirus, I, as a humanities scholar working on the sociospatiality of human life, seek to investigate how the discursive construction of pandemic, functioning as symbolic space, has been a driving force in shaping physical spaces, spatial practices and thus people's everyday lives. To me, a spatial perspective in the enquiry of sociocultural phenomena is highly relevant and urgent because space is never neutral nor innocent,[2] and it, unlike the linearity of time, reveals multiple experiences and perspectives simultaneously. My choice of bringing these two concepts, namely, space and risk, is not random at all.[3] Müller-Mahn et al. contend that "[t]he spatial dimension is essential for the social construction of risk, including risk governance and moral judgements about risk taking and risk distribution" (2013, 202). Examining the contested spatiality of COVID-19 above all demonstrates that the recent pandemic is a new, global risk in the sense Beck defines the term, and sheds light on the lived experiences of individuals as well as alternative risks definitions that are largely overlooked in the institutionalized risk discourse.

The concept of riskscape, in this regard, is a useful frame of reference in investigating the recent pandemic through physical and symbolic spaces, and vice versa.[4] For Müller-Mahn et. al, the concept "links the material dimension of potential physical threats, the discursive dimension of how people perceive, communicate and envision risks, and the dimension of agency, i.e., how people produce risks and manage to live with them" (2018, 197). Among other issues such as the question of power and temporality, their account emphasizes the relevance of point of view and the "sociospatial" nature of riskscapes. More precisely, the conception and perception of a territory at being risk depends partly on individual perspective. While a given physical space, for instance, can be experienced in terms of certain risks or risky by some individuals, other people may experience it differently. This emphasis on one's perspective in experiencing risks and riskscapes is significant in terms of calling institutionalized, mainstream risk assessments into question. The "sociospatial" nature of riskscapes, on the other hand, stresses that individuals perceive and conceive riskscapes as the members of a social group, and their experience of a landscape as risky or not is shaped by socially produced knowledge as well. Based on these premises, Müller-Mahn and Everts further point toward the significance of performance and practice: "Riskscapes are practiced and constituted in practice" (2013, 26). Approaching riskscapes as multiple and produced out of human practice highlights that they are "partially overlapping, intrinsically connected and at the same time often controversial sociospatial images of risk" (Müller-Mahn and Everts 2013, 26). Correspondingly, my examination of the ways the recent pandemic has shaped space and spatial practices, its discursive construction as well as individuals' divergent experiences as represented and practiced in virtual space, social media in particular, will address the overlapping riskscapes based on various factors.

Within a relatively short period of time, the COVID-19 pandemic has become a major driving force in social, cultural and spatial change, affecting people's physical spaces and everyday practices with varying levels. Ranging from bodyspaces and houses to workplaces and cityscapes, a wide spectrum of physical spaces have participated in the process in which the idea that "we are all in danger" has been staged, represented, and communicated to people. Indeed, it is hard to think of any physical space which has not been pervaded with the discourse that assesses the recent pandemic in terms of a fatal disaster with even more catastrophic outcomes unless acted upon immediately. Only one day after the confirmation of the first positive case on March 11, 2020, did the Turkish state, as the primary agent in managing the crisis, implement measures that included the closing of public places such as schools, universities, restaurants and shopping malls. Curfew for those who are 65 and under 20 years of age, two-weeks-long quarantining of evacuated citizens as well as restrictions in domestic travels between cities left public spaces empty to a large extend. People started wearing face masks and avoided touching everyday objects such as banknotes and elevator buttons voluntarily.

As a prime example of the risk's shaping power in social and cultural life, mosques nationwide were closed on March 19, 2020, an event that would be unimaginable to the country's Muslim majority population under any other circumstance.[5] While most of Turkey's mosques, constituting a central place in Muslims' daily routine, remained extraordinarily quiet, some actually became part of the riskscape, thanks to the scripts reading such as "Cleanliness is Half of Faith" and "Be Responsible and Stay Home" written on their *mahya*, a centuries old tradition of decorating mosques with an illuminated, celestial message hung between two minarets especially during Ramadan month. Similarly, the public announcements on protection from coronavirus taking place right after *adhan*, the Islamic call to prayer recited from every mosque for five times a day, have linked the public space acoustically to the COVID-19 discourse. Gradually, cities have been imagined as risk zones in which everyone has been encouraged to suspect others of being a risk for herself, no matter in the streets or in public transportation. Cities, like houses, mosques, and hospitals, have been perceived as container-like structures, and measures, such as the suspension of intercity travels and spraying streets with disinfectants, the efficiency of which is doubtful yet it creates a feeling that the authorities take action, have been imposed to stop the spread of coronavirus and sanitize public sphere. In short, the whole discourse on COVID-19 as assessed and managed by institutions such as the state and mainstream media has been embedded in physical settings, and issues such as safety, the ubiquitous danger of infection have shaped people's sociospatial practices significantly. Such measures have gradually turned multiscalar physical spaces into the riskscape of pandemic on a material level.

It would however be misleading and redundant to think the role of spatial structures only in terms of being passive, static background for risk action. On the contrary, space is both the product and producer of social practices. Correspondingly, everyday spaces, such as homes and workplaces have rapidly turned into risk sources, contributing to people's risk awareness and their further immersion in the risk discourse. In other words, physical spaces and spatial practices not only have been shaped by the discursive construction of pandemic but also have actively functioned as wild cards promoting that very discourse.

Since its outbreak in China in December 2019, institutions, such as media and the government, have played a pivotal role in the discursive construction of the pandemic, and thereby have functioned as the symbolic, relational riskscape of COVID-19. Despite its claim to provide individuals with an orientation in the uncharted spaces of the pandemic, mass media, news media in particular, have caused them to cope with vast amounts of information circulating easily and rapidly not only within the nation but also across the world. Almost all sorts of pandemic-related, globally circulated (mis)information have been influential in media's agenda-setting role. The broadcasted programs, ranging from news bulletins to live stream interviews held with risk professionals such as epidemiologists, economists, and security experts, have not only covered what's going on but also provided the public with information regarding how this crisis can be assessed, controlled and overcome ultimately.

The representation of the pandemic, concerning its nature, spread, and possible treatment, in Turkish media is ironically both divergent and monolithic. To name only few examples concerning its "genesis," the following speculations have been addressed as the "cause" of coronavirus: bat-soup eating Chinese people's transgression against the divine laws, Zionist plot against all humanity, implementation of 5G technology, the deglobalization of the world as well as the globalists' plans for a global socialism. With the official affirmation of the first positive case on March 11, 2020, the coronavirus' "entry" and its spread across the nation have pointed toward equally divergent reasons: Turkey's allegedly unexamined borders with Iran, citizens coming back to Turkey after their visits of the holy sites in Saudi Arabia, and "irresponsible" senior citizens who disregarded the government-implemented measures. Moreover, Islamic emphasis on hygiene, a so-called Turkish gene, traditional lamb soup, Turks' obsession with tea and Turkish cologne have found their ways to the mainstream media as potentially effective guards against COVID-19. While scientific-technological approach and the testimony of scientists have been accepted as the main authority in assessing the pandemic, scientific explanations and projections have been varied and sometimes contradictory concerning issues such as the efficiency of face masks, life span of the coronavirus on surfaces, its symptoms, the implementation of 14-day quarantine, the measures taken by the state, and the pandemic's potential outcomes, with regard to economy and public health and safety in particular, in "the post-COVID-19" world. Despite such differences however, some narrative commonalities can be identified in the coverage of COVID-19 in Turkey's media, mainstream news media in particular.

First, there has been an emphasis on uncertainty concerning the genesis, spread and outcomes of pandemic, but this has largely been associated with an epistemological one. More precisely, epistemological uncertainty, as Russell and Babrow suggest, "is rooted in characteristics of our information about or knowledge of the world" (2011, 250). In most cases, news stories identify what is not known and claim to explain "the emerging threat so that the audience is equipped to make informed, reasoned, risk mitigating choices" (Russell and Babrow 2011, 251). The news reporting of the earthquake happened in Elazig on January 24, 2020 was simple in the sense that a hazard happened, and the media provided audience with "the five Ws and one H" as the story unfolded. The new coronavirus has however marked a challenge, for it, as I contend, has defied "readily ascertainable dimensions of event structure" (Russell and Babrow 2011, 251). The uncertainty with global risks such as international terrorism is rather an ontological one, which "arises when the cause or consequence of some event cannot be known with certainty" (Russell and Babrow 2011, 251). The global, anthropomorphic, causal complexity and irreparably catastrophic features of COVID-19 are the very facts that make it an ontologically uncertain risk, which has required a different sort of reporting highlighting "unknown unknowns" (Beck 2006, 335), ambivalence and the acts of choice and decision-making in order to avoid redundant conclusions concerning the "not yet known" of COVID-19.

Second, and closely related to the first issue, a linear, progressive narrative has been adopted in representing the pandemic in mainstream Turkish media. The pandemic, as a global risk, has disrupted not only the sense of order in our everyday lives but also the conventional storyline with an identifiable beginning, rising action, climax, falling action, and an end. It thus defies simplistic explanations about causal and temporal relations. However, mass media, mainstream news media in particular, have represented the pandemic based largely on the past events as a frame of reference. For instance, positioning the coronavirus as a deadly enemy, citizens as warriors and risk management as an all-out fight,[6] and covering the whole process in a progressive, linear fashion have provided people with a narrative to make sense of what is going on and with a sense of control over the unknown yet anticipated catastrophe(s).[7] It should however be emphasized that mapping past, present and future, and ordering events into a meaningful or familiar structure are still processes of selection. Following Beck, risks are nothing but the *anticipation* of future catastrophes. Our present projections remain independent from what will actually happen in the future, which makes risks, including the media discourses, socially constructed narratives rather than "objective" accounts of a "danger out there."

Third, in an effort to explain and communicate the "danger" of COVID-19 as a meaningful story to ordinary citizens, expert opinions have been given a privileged status in constructing causal relationships and meaningful narratives about the pandemic. The testimony of scientists and experts has been vital in speculating about the temporal and causal explanations, yet they, too, are far from being objective explanations about the "deadly risk" of COVID-19. Despite media's emphasis on expert opinions as a benchmark or the only trustworthy source of knowledge about the coronavirus, "risk assessments depend for their validity upon a prior system of categorizations and metrics, which are, in turn, grounded in specific conventions, or institutions, or ways of life" (Garland 2003, 56). Therefore, any attempt to assess an ongoing event and its possible outcomes is by no means a value-free endeavor, and the different ways in which individuals, scientists and experts can interpret facts cannot escape their beliefs and commitments of various sorts. An emphasis on human agency and processes of selection and evaluation in assessing risks, in this regard, is significant and a more responsible way of media coverage.

Lastly, news media have made extensive use of emotions, fear and anxiety in particular, in representing the pandemic in Turkey. Sensationality is a significant criterion in selecting events as newsworthy or not, and thus hyperbolic language, including phrases such as the "killer virus," "all-out war," and dystopian images and catastrophic risk scenarios have turned the media into a machine imagining the nation a battle ground on different spatial scales and instilling fear, anxiety in individuals whose lives have been driven by the questions of risk, safety and security in order to prevent the worst. This has been nothing like the times of crises happened in the first quarter of 2020. Such moments of heightened uncertainty, anxiety and fear of everybody and everything are only comparable to the horrible times of the suicide bombings that happened repeatedly in different Turkish cities especially at the first half of 2016. As in the atmosphere of fear and uncertainty caused by international terrorism back then, the mediated risk discourse has supported and even justified the state's particular choice in assessing, managing certain risks as well as implementing precautionary policies. Therefore, the issues I have raised about the media coverage of the pandemic can also be read as the arguments for Beck's idea that risk definition is essentially a "power game."

In spatial terms, the institutionalized risk discourse can be seen as a dominant, symbolic space shaping physical spaces and spatial practices, which, in turn, suggests that riskscapes are produced not only physically but also discursively. The dominant discourse shaped largely by the government and mass media have been closely related to the practice and experience of riskscapes, for they have attempted to control the domestic and public spaces with the promise of fighting the coronavirus and protecting the citizens. This, in turn, has contributed to the monolithic representation of physical spaces as static, empty container-like structures. Yet, this particular conception of the threat and consequent measures conjure up what Beck calls the "dark irony" (Beck 2006, 330). It is ironic because the media have so far attempted to narrate a meaningful story out of the inherently ambivalent, causally complex "nature" of this new global risk, and the state, framing the new uncertain, global risk in terms of "old dangers," has required citizens to fight against an ambivalent, unknown threat. It is surely understandable that such times of crisis necessitate immediate action, but that the whole process has been framed as a linear narrative of fighting against an enemy and the legitimization of measures to prevent the anticipated catastrophe can not only create more fear and anxiety by bringing social and cultural life to a standstill, but also overlook other risks and thereby other, overlapping riskscapes based on different points of view.

At such times of quarantine, self-isolation, limited social interaction, and heightened anxiety about viral infection, virtual space has gained more prominence and enjoyed a central role in people's everyday lives. The sharp transition to distance education with the closing of schools and universities, video conferences with personal and professional contacts and digitalized forms of social collaboration and coordination are only some examples that have linked large numbers of people to each other. Virtual environment is by no means a risk-free zone, and vast amount of (mis)information, manipulation, hate speech and trolls have possibly caused individuals to get more anxious and fearful during the whole process. However, it, being a simultaneously real and imagined space, has also functioned as a dynamic, enabling space in which individuals' lived experiences and alternative perspectives are represented and even put into practice. In contrast to the either dystopian or falsely optimistic representations of physical spaces, social media sites, for instance, have proven to be the potential domains of resistance and multiplicity where both the flow of information complementing risk scenarios of mainstream news media and counter perspectives can be found and contested. For instance, concerns such as the limitation of individual rights, the expansion of digital surveillance via "contact-tracing apps" and the danger of state authoritarianism have been raised by many non-experts. Furthermore, myriad impacts of institutionalized risk discourse on individuals have been expressed in virtual environment, which has revealed alternative, overlapping and simultaneously both supporting and undermining riskscapes. This, I believe, has enabled a more complex and intersectionalist examination of the pandemic. As Giritli Nygren and Olofsson suggest, institutionalized practices of risk assessment and management depend on "a particular conception of the self, an assumption that people have the same potential to protect themselves, and that to be responsible in relation to COVID-19 does not expose you to other risks" (2020, 4). Contesting such pre-set assumption and imagination of the self, as in the narrative construction of "responsible citizen" for instance, and emphasizing class, gender, culture, space-based differences in negotiating risks is indeed very urgent. All in all, unlike the dominant risk discourse of mainstream media, virtual environment can be characterized with ambivalence, individualized forms of coping with uncertainty, novel forms of cosmopolitanism, and the need for collaboration and "communication across all differences and borders" (Beck 2006, 338). Virtual space should neither be celebrated nor maligned, and it is by no means a homogeneous space. Yet, it has marked a new beginning and functioned as contact zones, enabling people across different social groups and nations to interact with each other in the face of this new, global risk and adding to its alternative, albeit conflicting, definitions and representations by bringing suspicion, imagination and lived insights.

In conclusion, the COVID-19 pandemic, differing from natural hazards and "old dangers" that could be mastered and avoided, needs to be considered in terms of a global risk, and living with it, because of its uncertain, complex, anticipatory and catastrophic characteristics, can be characterized with "dwelling-in-crisis"

(Buell 2003: 76), which requires new forms of framing and action instead of denial and sticking to old certainties. As Beck avers, "rationality, that is, the experience of the past, encourages anticipation of the wrong kind of risk, the one we believe we can calculate and control, whereas the disaster arises from what we do now know and cannot calculate" (2006, 330). The institutionalized risk discourse has constructed COVID-19 as a risk in the modern sense or a threat that could be averted through safety measures, yet this "choice" runs the danger of creating other risks and instilling more anxiety and fear in individuals. My central proposition has been that space matters in the processes in which risks are socially constructed, staged and represented. In contrast to the monolithic representation and practice of multiscalar spaces as passive, empty backgrounds for institutionalized risk discourse, virtual environment has been examined as a more contested, enabling space, *in* and *through* which lived experiences and alternative riskscapes have been represented and practiced by individuals. In so doing, it has been suggested that an emphasis on uncertainty, human agency, intersectionality, causal complexity, and collaborative action in dealing with global risks is necessary.

Notes

1 This point about the centrality of power in thinking about global risks conjures up the so-called governmentality approach to risk. As Mythens argues, the thinkers who follow governmentality approach "have been especially keen to bring to the fore the political quality of risk" (*Understanding* 36) and demonstrated "the rising prevalence of the language of risk and its broader usage as a way of individualising social problems and responsibilizing citizens" (2014, 37).
2 Similarly, Soja argues: "We must be insistently aware of how space can be made to hide consequences from us, how relations of power and discipline are inscribed into the apparently innocent spatiality of social life, how human geographies become filled with politics and ideology" (1989, 6).
3 For more about this, see Müller-Mahn et al. (2013, 2018) and November (2008). Elsewhere, I explored the relations between space and risk as represented in literary and cultural studies in greater detail (2017, 183–223).
4 The term riskscape belongs to Susan L. Cutter who first used the term for her research entitled "Toxic Riskscapes: The Geography of Acute Airborne Releases." Especially with the anthropologist Arjun Appadurai's bringing the suffix -scape to five words and coming up with the terms finansescapes, ideoscapes, mediascapes, ethnoscapes, and technoscapes, there is an inflationary use of words ending with -scape that mostly stress the relations between spatiality and various social phenomena. Müller-Mann and Everts' is the earliest comprehensive use of the term riskscape in risk research.
5 On May 29, 2020, mosques were reopened partially for collective prayers on condition that people would obey the measures such as bringing one's own prayer mat, not using ablution rooms, and distancing themselves from others at the time of praying.
6 The Turkish word "seferberlik," which means mobilization in a military sense, has been used extensively in the pandemic-related discourse throughout the whole process. For instance, Turkish Minister of Health, at a press conference on May 20, 2020, reemphasized the individual responsibility and praised Turkish people's "fight against the coronavirus" as the nation's "most significant mobilization." At the same conference, Koca addressed homes as the safest place and recommended citizens to continue watching out the rules especially during the holiday time so that "we can be more free after." For more about this, see Koca (2020).

7 For instance, since its outbreak, the question "when will the coronavirus end entirely?" has become one of the most commonplace headlines in media, suggesting a narrative closure to the story. Especially, with the government's recent call for "normalization" starting from June 1, 2020, there has been an increasingly strong emphasis on the resolution of the trouble.

References

Beck, Ulrich. 1998. *Democracy without Enemies* Cambridge: Polity Press.
———. 2006. "Living in the World Risk Society." *Economy and Society* 35, no. 3: 329–45. Accessed May 1, 2020. doi:10.1080/03085140600844902.
———. 2009. *World at Risk*. Cambridge: Polity Press.
Buell, Frederick. 2003. *From Apocalypse to Way of Life: Environmental Crisis in the American Century*. New York: Routledge.
Garland, David. 2003. "The Rise of Risk." In *Risk and Morality*, edited by R. V. Ericson and A. Doyle, 48–86. Toronto: University of Toronto Press.
Giritli Nygren, Katarina, and Anna Olofsson. 2020. "Managing the Covid-19 Pandemic through Individual Responsibility: The Consequences of a World Risk Society and Enhanced Ethopolitics." *Journal of Risk Research*. Accessed May 29, 2020. doi:10.1080/13669877.2020.1756382.
Koca, Fahrettin. 2020. "Our Fight Against the Coronavirus Will be the Most Important Mobilization." *Turkish Ministry of Health*, May 21. Accessed May 20, 2020. www.saglik.gov.tr/EN,65640/quotour-fight-against-the-coronavirus-will-be-the-most-important-mobilizationquot.html.
Müller-Mahn, Detlef, and Jonathon Everts. 2013. "Riskscapes: The Spatial Dimensions of Risk." In *The Spatial Dimension of Risk: How Geography Shapes the Emergence of Riskscapes*, edited by Detlef Müller-Mahn and Jonathon Everts, 22–36. London: Routledge.
Müller-Mahn, Detlef, Jonathon Everts, and Martin Doevenspeck. 2013. "Making Sense of the Spatial Dimension of Risk." In *The Spatial Dimension of Risk: How Geography Shapes the Emergence of Riskscapes*, edited by Detlef Müller-Mahn and Jonathon Everts, 202–7. London: Routledge.
Müller-Mahn, Detlef, Jonathon Everts, and Christiane Stephan. 2018. "Riskscapes Revisited—Exploring the Relationship between Risk, Space and Practice." *Erdkunde* 72: 197–213. Accessed May 15, 2020. doi: 10.3112/erdkunde.2018.02.09.
Mythen, Gabe. 2014. *Understanding the Risk Society: Crime, Security and Justice*. Basingstoke: Palgrave Macmillan.
November, Valerie. 2008. "Spatiality of Risk." *Environment and Planning A* 40, no. 7: 1523–27. Accessed May 16, 2020. doi: 10.1068/a4194.
Russell, L. D., and A.S. Babrow. 2011. "Risk in the Making: Narrative, Problematic Integration, and the Social Construction of Risk." *Communication Theory* 21: 239–60. Accessed May 26, 2020. doi:10.1111/j.1468-2885.2011.01386.x.
Soja, Edward. 1989. *Postmodern Geographies: The Reassertion of Space in Critical Social Theory*. London: Verso.
Tabur, Şemsettin. 2017. *Contested Spaces in Contemporary North American Novels: Reading for Space*. Newcastle upon Tyne: Cambridge Scholars Publishing.

19 Risk society in the age of pandemics

Disaster reporting in the media—Ebola and COVID-19

DeMond Shondell Miller and Nicola Davis Bivens

Introduction

Threats to individual biosecurity via localized viral outbreaks or global pandemics mark a generational event that connects the macro (global) to the micro as a highly impactful personal event that defines a generation—much like the fourteenth-century plague or "Black Death", during the Middle Ages or the 1918 Spanish Influenza Pandemic. In each pandemic instance, information to influence judgments regarding the severity of risk via public perceptions became a way to assess one's susceptibility. Recently, the omnipresence of risk offers a paradigmatic shift from modernity to a "second modernity," which represents an epochal break and paradigm shift characterized by a distinct set of values and beliefs and a unique set of aspirations and expectations (Ekberg 2007, 345). According to Beck, man-made and unwanted side effects of modernity, produce growing uncertainties, resulting in a new age where people must come to terms with the consequences of their own actions. This ongoing process is reflexive modernization. Ultimately, society in the "second modernity" becomes more concerned with the way it handles risks than the stratification of power and wealth. This influences the definition of social groups as well; as Beck describes in *Risk Society*, problems such as ecological risks are not distributed according to wealth, social milieus, and strata—they affect society as a whole. However, the ability to avert risk is highly dependent on knowledge and information—*here, mass media and journalism come into play by making these risks visible* [emphasis added] (Wimmer and Quandt 2006, 337).

Theoretical framework: Beck's risk society

In his seminal work, *The Risk Society*, Beck (1999) asserts that

> wealth creation that characterized industrial modernity has been overshadowed by an ethos of risk avoidance, class consciousness . . . displaced by a risk consciousness, and the increased awareness of living in an environment of risk, uncertainty, and insecurity has become a major catalyst for social transformation.

> (Ekberg 2007, 344)

The key pillars on which Beck's risk society thesis rests are:

(1) the development of new, manmade, mega risks that threaten the existence of humanity on a global scale; (2) globalization with a world risk society; (3) expert dependence: the insensibility and complexity of risk that leave both politicians and the individual dependent on scientific knowledge; (4) individualization: old social structures such as social class are replaced, or at least hidden by, a new political self-fulfilling subject; and (5) risk positions: although social class and other social structures diminish, inequality remains but in the shape of risk positions.

(Nygren and Olofsson 2020, 4)

The assessment of risks rests on the assumption that people have accurate information to make decisions to protect themselves and others, in response to COVID-19 exposure. However, decades of social science risk and crisis research have shown that the ability to manage risks and crises by conduct is largely related to social inequality. This inequity can also be in reference to the inability to access reliable information. Ekberg (2007, 337) notes that previous "research on the perception of risk consistently shows that the perception of risk is influenced by sociodemographic variables including gender, ethnicity, age, education, occupation, and prior experience." She continues by building on the work of Slovic (1986) as she notes risk perception, in combination with *fright factors* such as whether risk exposure is voluntary or involuntary; whether exposure is equally or unequally distributed; whether the risk can be avoided by taking personal precautions; whether the risk arises from a familiar or unfamiliar source; whether the risk is natural or manufactured; and how well the origin and effects of the risk are understood by experts.

Amplification or attenuation of risks by their overrepresentation or underrepresentation in the mass media via the 24 hours, 7 day a week news cycle or "breaking news" reports, and regional/cultural bias, is dependent on their human impact, signal value, visual impact, their capacity to evoke conflict, or their link with existing high profile issues (Kasperson et al. 1988). For example, the visual imagery of dead bodies morgues, overrun hospital systems, or visual images of mass graves, place in plain view the suffering of those experiencing the infection either directly as a patient, healthcare provider, or vicariously as a silent witness. Finally, perceptions of risk may be influenced by cognitive illusions and heuristics such as an availability bias or optimistic bias (Joffe 1999). Such heuristics including empty store shelves, quarantine, national lockdowns, or shelter in place and social distance are a shorthand way of signaling impending doom. Each represents a specific level of risk to one's safety and security. As Ekberg (2007, 357) examines, in her work *The Parameters of the Risk Society A Review and Exploration.*

As a consequence of these fright factors, media triggers, and cognitive heuristics, there is greater spatial and temporal variability and more disagreement with perceived risks than there is with actual risks. Individuals will often perceive a similar risk, regardless of location in time or space. Individuals perceive risks that operate beyond the natural limits of human sensory perception. They perceive something microscopic, subatomic, electromagnetic, transparent, concealed, or disguised. They perceive a concept rather than a physical object, event, or entity. According to Beck (1999, 55), "technologically induced hazards, such as those associated with chemical pollution, atomic radiation and genetically modified organisms, are characterized by an inaccessibility to the human senses."

Previous risk and crisis communication studies also emphasize the importance of considering social, cultural, and economic differences, especially regarding the functional ability and language skills needed to understand and interpret risks (Kvarnlof and Montelius 2020).

Media: averting, assessing, and portrayal of risk

The framework put forth by Kasperson et al. (1988) asserts that there are two primary sources of information regarding risks and how risks are accessed by individuals include the mass media and interpersonal networks (Frewer, Miles, and Marsh 2002, 701–2). While the media are framed by a number of social, cultural, economic, timing and immediacy, and bias factors, Young, Norman, and Humphreys (2008, 1) maintain that "[i]nterpersonal networks are, by their nature, idiosyncratic; thus, individual variation of available information should not lead to the systematic trends in estimation seen in these studies. By contrast, the information provided through media sources may well lead to systematic over- or underestimates at a population level." Furthermore, Combs and Slovic (1979, 837; Young, Norman, and Humphreys 2008, 1) argue that an individuals' estimates of mortality rates were not correlated with actual mortality statistics, but that the participants' estimates correlated highly with the frequency of print media reporting about any particular subject. Thus, in a society highly characterized by risks, the fear of the spread of viral contagion is both framed and reified to serve as a seminal force for understanding risks, determining social behavior, serving as a catalyst for social change as a framework to avert and manage risks in a risk-filled society.

Media reporting is a powerful tool to influence public opinion as understood from prior outbreaks (Brooks et al. 2020, 917). Pandemics and other crises have been covered in the media as far back as the 1918 Influenza Pandemic (Garret 2007, 19). However, John Barry (2004, 221, 339) criticizes the lack of newspaper coverage of the pandemic, noting that they provided little coverage of the pandemic, and intentionally downplayed the extent of the virus by failing to report daily death accounts and offering little advice on avoiding infection except maintaining cleanliness and dining habits. Thomas Garret, however, posits that media accounts provided statistics on the number of persons who were sick and deceased, as well as reports about closings of schools and houses of worship. In some instances, remedies and alleged cures for the flu were published in newspapers across the nation (Garret 2007, 19). Applying Barry's lens of the lack of media coverage, people's lack of knowledge and fear of being infected with influenza, prompted them to isolate family members and neighbors, resulting in those infected not receiving care or basic necessities of food and water and being isolated and abandoned (2004, 331, 462). Garret's assertion (2007, 19) allows one to conclude readers could assess their risk based on the portrayals of influenza and its impacts as well as determine strategies to avert the same. Risk is perceived based on how it is depicted in the media and news coverage where individuals determine the perception and estimation of the hazard-based on limited information and within the limits of social systems. (Mileti 1999, 39; Sell et al. 2017, 108).

While mainstream media, newspapers, etc. are primarily relied upon for information, the internet and social media have gained prominence as an additional means of information about epidemics and other critical incidents (Haddow and Haddow 2013, 19, 25). Haddow and Haddow (2013, 4) posit that Hurricane Katrina was one of the first critical incidents where individuals sought information using social media platforms, specifically Facebook. The 2014 Ebola outbreak (which will be examined in further detail later in this chapter) was the first pandemic to occur amid prevalent social media use (Morin, Mercier, and Atlani-Duault 2019, 2).

Media reporting contributes to knowledge acquisition in the general public; the media are powerful influences on public attitudes and dramatic headlines and fear-mongering have been shown to contribute to stigmatizing attitudes in the past (Person et al. 2004, 358–63). This issue highlights the need for public health officials to provide rapid, clear messages delivered effectively for the entire affected population to promote an accurate understanding of the situation. Also, in a time of fear and uncertainty, the belief in unverified information from social media and standalone content consumption tendencies could create another harmful *infodemic* (Matteo et al. 2020). The term infodemic (Zarocostas 2020, 676) has been coined to outline the perils of misinformation phenomena. So pervasive is misinformation that WHO's risk communications and "infodemic" management team actively track misinformation, in multiple languages (World Health Organization 2020). Moreover, misinformation could even speed up the disease transmission process by influencing and fragmenting social response (Kim, Fast, and Markuzon 2018, 2). In other words, the information spreading out from a volume of (questionable) platforms should not be assumed conclusively.

Ebola — "Africa's epidemic"

In December 2013, the first case of Ebola Viral Disease (EVD) was reported in December 2013 in a small village in Guinea, and on March 23, 2014, the World Health Organization had declared an outbreak of EVD (Centers for Disease Control 2020). By July 2014, EVD had spread through Guinea to its capital, as well as to Liberia and Sierra Leone (Centers for Disease Control 2020). In the United States, a total of 11 persons contracted EVD during the 2014–2016 outbreak, with the first case confirmed September 30, 2014 (a travel-related case). Of these 11 confirmed cases, there were 2 fatalities (Centers for Disease Control 2020). Globally, there were a total of 28,652 cases in a total of 10 countries (of which all were reported in 6 African countries, except 1 case each in Spain, Italy, and the United Kingdom, and those 11 cases in the United States) (Centers for Disease Control 2020).

Although EVD was initially discovered in 1976, the virus did not generate intense media attention until the 2014 outbreak (Seidu 2018, 203). Media and communications are a viable resource to disseminate information about infectious diseases, reduce fears, and aid in decision-making about avoiding infection, etc. (Basch, Basch, and Redlener 2014, 247), news media in the United States was criticized for causing unnecessary fear by sensationalizing the Ebola outbreak (Sell et al. 2017, 108). Mainstream media's coverage of Ebola further heightened public fear of the virus as newspaper coverage of the virus primarily focused on the number of cases, the outbreak in Africa, the number of deaths, travel bans, and the emotional responses to EVD (panic, fear, etc.) (Basch, Basch, and Redlener 2014, 248).

Then Presidential candidate Donald Trump tweeted, erroneously, about the dangers and risk of Ebola to the American public (Salek and Cole 2019, 22), with other media citing the risk factors of foreign travelers bringing the virus into the country (Sell et al. 2017, 108). Given that there were so few cases in the United States, a heightened sense of fear was unwarranted. Despite the Ebola outbreak in West Africa with 1,400 confirmed cases and a 50% mortality rate, there was minimal mention of the outbreak in the US media for the first 8 months of 2014 (Yusuf, Yahaya, and Qabli 2015, 2). Within 24 hours of the first Ebola diagnosis in the United States on September 30, 2014, there was a spike in tweets about the virus (Morin, Mercier, and Atlani-Duault 2019, 4). Further, despite only two Ebola-related deaths in the United States, Americans reported that Ebola was in the top three of the greatest health problems facing the country at that time (Morin, Mercier, and Atlani-Duault 2019, 4) based on how it was portrayed as apocalyptic in the media (Salek and Cole 2019, 22).

There is little question that social media exacerbated the fear of EVD (Yusuf, Yahaya, and Qabli 2015, 1) given the prevalence of tweets, posts, etc. about the virus. In turn, images and pictures tweeted during the outbreak often showed doctors wearing full, ultra-protective suits, means of transmission (i.e. semen, sweat, etc.), and graphics of the virus in and of itself (Morin, Mercier, and Atlani-Duault 2019, 6–9). This is no doubt a result of American media about EVD being risk-elevating (Sell et al. 2017, 108), thus creating a heightened sense of fear and risk in the United States. Despite EVD being a challenge for West African countries, it became a global health panic with PolitiFact naming the Ebola "crisis" in America the "Lie of the Year" (Salek and Cole 2019, 22).

Despite only one confirmed EVD case diagnosis in the United Kingdom, persons in the United Kingdom, France, Germany, Denmark, Sweden, Finland, and Norway reported fears and concerns similar to that of Americans as already described (Prati and Pietrantoni 2016, 2000). In Italy, where there was only one confirmed case per the Centers for Disease Control (2020), xenophobic views against African immigrants indicate that it was not a widespread fear of risk; it is limited only to said immigrants. Rumors, myths, and misinformation likely fueled these negative social consequences (Prati and Pietrantoni 2016).

In Ghana, newspapers typically covered EVD as either news, in featured columns, editorials, or opinion articles. Seidu (2018, 4) found that in the news coverage of EVD was either depicted as (1) concerns about Ghana's preparedness to handle the epidemic and criticisms of the same, (2) support for and assurances about the country's preparation for the outbreak, (3) education about Ebola, (4) the extent of the outbreak and suspected cases, (5) the effects of the virus, and (6) misinformation about EVD.

Although news and information related to health should promote good health, prevent illnesses, and protect the public, Maria Ballester and Paloma Villafranca (2016, 247) contend that communications in Spain have not accomplished those objectives. As was the case in the United States, despite the World Health Organization issuing a global warning about Ebola, it was not until the first case was confirmed in Spain, that Spanish media began to cover the virus. When Ebola was covered in the media, the terms deaths, dead, epidemic, victims, crisis, and danger were used in the stories (Ballester and Villafranca 2016, 257), which no doubt created an unfounded sense of fear among residents. In fact, news coverage in Spain generated anxiety about the virus (Ballester and Villafranca 2016, 260).

COVID-19—risk, uncertainty, and bias in the media

In the capital of Hubei province, Wuhan, China, a new infectious disease was identified in December 2019 by scientists, health experts, and government officials. COVID-19 first appeared in the European nations in January 2020 when three persons were confirmed in France (Gianfranco 2020). The highly infectious disease, commonly named COVID 19, quickly spread globally and was declared a pandemic on March 11, 2020, by the World Health Organization. By then, the virus had spread throughout Europe (Mavragani 2020). The virus is transmitted primarily when people are in close contact and one person inhales small droplets produced by an infected person (Hamner et al. 2020, 606). Early guidance regarding infection risks published and widely disseminated by the by the United States Centers for Disease Control (CDC) in the media asserted that contaminated droplets on surfaces and uninfected people that touch contaminated surfaces and then their eyes, nose, or mouth with unwashed hands have a greater chance of contracting the virus. Later, that advice changed and stated that on surfaces, the amount of active virus decreases over time until it can no longer cause infection, and surfaces are not thought to be the primary route of viral spread (CDC 2021).

While media can help provide relevant timely available information to improve knowledge, increase awareness, and help modify behavior in the general public, they play a key role in communication among researchers, scientists, public health experts, and funding agencies, for an effective and rapid global response (Gralinski and Menachery 2020; Ippolito et al. 2020). The emergence of the COVID-19 outbreak grabbed the attention of media news, press, and social media pages worldwide. However, there are many credible and non-credible sources through which anyone can obtain information that is difficult to distinguish its veracity. Thus, the public must be able to access non-bias, non-political and trustworthy sources for timely information regarding COVID-19 to help citizens perform their risk assessments based on technical risk communication to respond to the ever-increasing rumors and myths that define the evolving risk landscape in the wake of viral pandemics.

During the CODIV-19 pandemic, the daily detection rates, along with information regarding the complex clinical course of the virus in each country was presented as it changed daily. At best, the accuracy of these calculations of the case fatality rate has also been challenged for its underestimation and overestimation (Rajgor et al. 2020, 1; Rahman and Jahan 2020, 2). When these numbers are in the forefront of the discussion of the spread of COVID-19—in addition to the shocking images of regional food shortages or countries in "lockdown," the reification of these statistical metrics, no matter how inaccurate or accurate they may be based on counting errors or labeling errors, becomes a real value and often rarely understood. In reality, as noted by Rahman and Jahan (2020, 2), "the impacts of media reporting that influence public sentiments toward the outbreak such as panic buying, food hoarding, and behaviors toward the risk groups including isolation from grandparents." The outbreak in Italy shocked European political leaders, who initially were slower to implement public health measures (The Lancet 2020, 755). Italy was the first of many European countries to announce nationwide travel limits—which also prompted the European Union to impose travel limits as well, shortly after the virus appeared. The virus's spread impacted millions of people. In Italy, media attention and the early understanding of the 'new" virus prompted the cancellation of part of the carnival in Venice, closures of educational intuitions, local curfews, and canceled sporting events. Country-wide outbreaks easily overwhelmed the Italian healthcare system and put on display the fears of the virus amplified by the nature of uncertainty, shifting information and statistics, and ill-prepared healthcare systems in the wake of this pandemic.

Germany

Germany is one European country that seemingly showed some success in its progress to mitigate the COVID-19 outbreak. According to Wieler, Rexroth, and Gottschalk (2020), the preparedness and response framework focused on prevention, detection (testing; contact tracing), containment (travel bans), and treatment (the benefit of national healthcare). The National Pandemic Plan was also implemented, delegating the roles of the various subnational governments in the country. COVID-19 was first diagnosed in Bavaria on January 27, 2020, and it has managed to contain the spread of the virus in a relatively short amount of time. As of July 2020, the country had the lowest mortality rate of all European countries (Farr 2020). Media depiction of the virus in the country focused on data-driven reporting and the implications of the virus on the economy. Chancellor Angela Merkel is often commended for her leadership and messages in the media, and her ability to explain complex concepts to the masses and the Minister of Health was prominent in conveying messages about the virus through the media (Farr 2020; Tran 2020). Germany's focus on scientific communication and the scientific-medical community conveyed facts via podcasts, children's television programming, and other media, empowering citizens to scrutinize facts from fiction about the virus (Farr 2020).

Serbia

As cases in nearby Italy skyrocketed, leading Serbian officials did not take the virus or its threat to the country seriously. During a February 26, 2020, press conference, Serbian President Aleksandar Vučić, flanked by public health experts, officials, and doctors, laughed at pulmonologist Branimir Nestorovic's remark that Serbian women should "go shopping in Italy" and take advantage of the discounts given the retail closures in that country. Public Officials also cited that the virus was "nearing its end" and minimized the seriousness and risks of COVID-19 (Stojanovic 2020). By the time the World Health Organization declared COVID-19 a pandemic on March 11, 2020, the first case of the virus had been diagnosed in Serbia the week prior. The initial response from the Serbian Health Minister was that there was not any need for panic and that citizens should abide by the recommendations of authorities (Medical Express 2020). According to Global Voices (2002), Serbian officials made a number of false claims about COVID-19, including the virus was less mild than seasonal influenza, that officials could not reveal information about the number of ventilators as it was an international "state secret," banning mass gatherings would prevent parliament from a meeting, and that women were less susceptible to the virus as a result of their estrogen levels.

On March 26, 2020, President Vučić blamed the increase of COVID-19 cases on Serbian citizens, displaced from other European countries, who were now returning to Serbia for free healthcare, and failing to abide by quarantine rules (Stojanovic 2020). Not only did Serbian officials downplay the seriousness of the virus, assign blame for the spread, and fail to be proactive in mitigating the impact of COVID-19, government influence on the media may have been implicit in the failed response and exacerbated the infodemic of misinformation (Serbian Media 2021). According to Tomić (as cited in Serbian Media 2021), Serbian media are subject to political influence, and is of poor quality, as there is a "low level of implementation of professional standards." Tomić argues that the public interest is not a primary concern and Serbian media are seeking a political agenda, and presents information about COVID-19 based on said agenda misinformation (Serbian Media 2021).

On June 3, 2020, Dr. Predrag Kon of Crisis Staff of the Government of Serbia, declared the pandemic was over (European Western Balkans 2020). Yet the day after the June 21, 2020, Serbian elections (scheduled for April 26, 2020, but postponed as a result of COVID-19), Kon stated that the virus again posed a risk (European Western Balkans 2020). Although President Vučić assured that the government would not cover up the number of casualties in a May 1, 2020, press conference, in July 2020, Serbian public officials have been accused of under-reporting the extent of the COVID-19 data, prompting some media and organizations to file a complaint with the Commissioner for Information of Public

Importance and Personal Data Protection to demand access for official information about the virus (European Western Balkans 2020; Maksimović 2020).

Conclusion

More and more, people are forced to shoulder a multitude of burdens placed on individuals, families, and entire societies regarding risk assessment and navigating a "new normal" using the information presented in the media regarding the realities of risks in daily life. From the risk society perspective, how we perceive and understand risk and risk production from a transnational perspective and respond to pandemic disasters such as COVID-19 within specific, social, political, and cultural contexts continues to unfold. Global pandemics cross national borders to encircle the globe with few open borders (or at least borders without restrictions). Both the United States and the European Union have seriously restricted or closed their land and air border traffic. However, with modern media, information and international organizations can communicate rapidly and effectively in crisp detail with vivid images to illustrate the risks and consequences associated with COVID-19. Facts, the framing of facts, and the politics of risk within a risk society leave data presented in the media open to any number of interpretations. This is evident in the current COVID-19 crisis. "Questions such as the danger of the virus, the interpretation of the death rate or the question of why the number of deaths in Italy is so high compared to the infection rate can only be answered by experts" (Schmidt 2020). Many around the world rely solely on media reports to formulate a risk assessment.

However, this constant barrage of new information, new cases, and new advice has been challenging to keep up with. It not only makes the story difficult to keep up with from a journalist's perspective, it makes it confusing for anyone trying to follow the story. A news piece you read one day could be entirely out-of-date by the next morning, and this has meant there have been many questions from the public surrounding the outbreak and the virus. In addition, as more information has emerged over the past weeks, experts and public health officials have revised their opinions, advice, and recommendations in line with this, and it has been suggested that these updates have made it hard to build trust (Powell 2020).

As a critical interface between the scientific community, government, and the public with a responsibility to strike a careful balance between raising awareness of issues of public concern, building and promoting trust among media consumers—as new or changing information emerges, and irrationally alarming the public. Because "[v]iewers will purposefully tune in to a news program to see a story about a health topic that interests them" (Cooper and Roter 2000, 337), the mass media have an awesome job in an everchanging info-technological landscape. During times of disaster, the news medias' role in informing and protecting the public, cannot be underscored enough as it mediates between multiple stakeholders within the ever-evolving disaster landscape with public health issues.

Media coverage of both COVID-19 and Ebola clearly illustrate how these are not merely "fright factor" health stories, but rather, stories about the global disruption of travel and tourism (Powell 2020), stories about the economic impacts (Powell 2020), the cancelation/postponement of sports seasons have made the coverage of COVID-19, and to a lesser extent Ebola, a sports story (Powell 2020), and multiple stories about life in a post-COVID risk society or a post-Ebola risk society. However, incidents such as COVID-19 or Ebola, when viewed for their potential risks are rarely understood and difficult to control bring forth great public concern. Herein lies "[t]he challenge that confronts health advocates is framing news stories to appeal to both media gatekeepers and the public" (Cooper and Roter 2000, 336). Despite variances in the manner in which people consume media, there is little question that people assess and avert risk based on media portrayals of the same.

During times of disaster, such as the COVID-19 pandemic and the spread of Ebola, the risk society is at its zenith and information is critical. Beck (1992; see also Cottle 1998, 7) argues that

> [t]hey [risks] can thus be changed, magnified, dramatized or minimized within knowledge and to that extent they [risks] are particularly open to social definition and construction. Hence the mass media and the scientific and legal professions in charge of defining risks become key social political positions.

So critical that the inevitability of how we conceptualize the media provides the mass media a privileged position of mediation between government elites, the scientific community, and others who produce knowledge, shape, and socially construct messages in the media.

Evidence of the media's position framing, amplifying, constructing, and deconstruction messages included: the spread of disease, protection of disease, or even the start and end of the pandemic, as illustrated by the German approach (which employed a more strategic focus on scientific communication in the form of podcasts, children's television programming, and other media, empowering citizens to scrutinize fact from fiction about the virus) in the Serbian example, or the daily news briefings issued by the President of the United States, or the framing of Ebola. The German example stands in contrast with the Italian, US, and Serbian examples. Thus, the German example offers a model to be explored as opposed to other examples of media constructions that posit the affected against the very organizations and leaders (WHO, US-CDC, political leaders) engaged in macro and micro risk management within the risk society—the *knowledge creators*, the *knowledge disseminators*, and the *knowledge consumers*. As Beck (1992, 46) notes:

> As the risk society develops, so does the antagonism between those *afflicted* by risks and those who *profit* from them. The social and economic importance of knowledge grows similarly, and with it the power of the media to structure *knowledge* (science and research) and disseminate it (mass media). The risk

society in the since is also the *science, media, and information* society. Thus, new antagonisms grow us between those who *produce* risks definitions and those who consume them.

The presentation of both Ebola and COVID-19 in an age of pandemics forces us to reflect on the role of the media in a capitalist society and how these messages relate to risk-perception to support individual risk assessment and decision-making when faced with ambiguity during public health crises in a world of uncertainty. The examples from Italy, Germany, Serbia, and the United States remind us of the privileged position the mass media hold as knowledge is disseminated for consumption by people who rely upon its accuracy to make informed decisions for themselves and their families.

While there is more work to be done in this area, this analysis contributes to the extant literature by presenting, understanding, and demystifying extreme uncertainty, ambiguity, xenophobia, and Western bias in the content of messages promoted in United States' media with regard to risk for both Ebola and COVID-19. In the age of pandemics, risk and the value of information will continue to increase. The duty of social scientists and media professionals remains—provide clear, accurate, and timely information that can be trusted to aid in the risks in a society straddled with visible and invisible risks.

References

Ballester, M. C., and Paloma Villafranca. 2016. "The Impact of the Ebola Virus and Rare Diseases in the Media and the Perception of Risk in Spain." *Catalan Journal of Communication & Cultural Studies* 8, no. 2: 245–63. doi:10.1386/ cjcs.8.2.245_1.
Barry, John. 2004. *The Great Influenza*. London: Penguin Books.
Basch, Corey, Charles Basch, and Irwin Redlener. 2014. "Coverage of the Ebola Virus Disease Epidemic in Three Widely Circulated United States Newspapers: Implications for Preparedness and Prevention." *Health Promotion Perspectives* 4, no. 2: 247–55. doi:10.5681/hpp.2014.032.
Beck, Ulrich. 1992. *Risk Society—Toward a New Modernity*. London: Sage.
———. 1999. *World Risk Society*. Cambridge: Polity Press.
Brooks, Samantha, Rebecca Webster, Louise Smith, Lisa Woodland, Simon Wessely, Neil Greenberg, and Gideon Rubin. 2020. "The Psychological Impact of Quarantine and How to Reduce It: Rapid Review of the Evidence." *The Lancet* 395, no. 10227: 912–20, February. doi:10.1016/s0140-6736(20)30460-8.
Centers for Disease Control (CDC). 2021. Science Brief: SARS-CoV-2 and Surface (Fomite) Transmission for Indoor Community Environments. Accssed June 4, 2021. https://www.cdc.gov/coronavirus/2019-ncov/more/science-and-research/surface-transmission.html.
Centers for Disease Control (CDC). "2014–2016" Ebola Outbreak in West Africa." Centers for Disease Control. Accessed June 6, 2020. www.cdc.gov/vhf/ebola/history/2014-2016-outbreak/index.html#:~:text=Ebola%20in%20the%20United%20States,-Overall%2C%20eleven%20people&text=On%20September%2030%2C%202014%2C%20CDC,died%20on%20October%208%2C%202014.

Combs, Barbara, and Paul Slovic. 1979. "Newspaper Coverage of Causes of Death." *Journalism Quarterly* 56: 837–843, December.

Cooper, Crystale, and Debra Roter. 2000. "If It Bleeds It Leads? Attributes of TV Health News Stories That Drive Viewer Attention." *Public Health Reports* 115, no. 4: 331–38, July–August.

Cottle, Simon. 1998. "Ulrich Beck, 'Risk Society' and the Media: A Catastrophic View?" *European Journal of Communication* 13, no. 1: 5–32, March. doi:10.1177/026732319 8013001001.

"Director-General's Remarks at the Media Briefing on 2019 Novel Coronavirus on 8 February 2020." World Health Organization. Accessed June 7, 2020. www.who.int/dg/speeches/detail/director-general-s-remarks-at-the-media-briefing-on-2019-novel-coronavirus-8-february-2020.

Ekberg, Merryn. 2007. "The Parameters of the Risk Society: A Review and Exploration." *Current Sociology 55*, no. 3: 343–66, May. doi:10.1177/0011392107076080.

European Western Balkans. "Serbia Covered Up the Real Number of COVID-19 Cases Before Elections, Claims BIRN." *European Western Balkans*. Accessed July 24, 2020. https://europeanwesternbalkans.com/2020/06/25/serbia-covered-up-the-real-number-of-covid-19-cases-before-elections-claims-birn/.

Farr, Christina. "Germany's Coronavirus Response is a Master Class in Science Communication." *CNBC*. Accessed July 22, 2020. www.cnbc.com/2020/07/21/germanys-coronavirus-response-masterful-science-communication.html.

Federal Reserve Bank of St. Louis. 2007. *Economic Effects of the 1918 Influenza Pandemic: Implications for a Modern-Day Pandemic*, Thomas A. Garrett. St. Louis: Federal ReserveBank of St. Louis. Accessed June 6, 2020. www.stlouisfed.org/~/media/files/pdfs/community-development/research-rch-rts/pandemic_flu_report.pdf.

Frewer, Lynn J., Susan Miles, and Roy Marsh. 2002. "The Media and Genetically Modified Foods: Evidence in Support of Social Amplification of Risk." *Risk Analysis: An Interdisciplinary Journal* 22, no. 4: 701–11, October.

Gianfranco, Spiteri, Fielding James, Diercke Michaela, Campese Christine, Enouf Vincent, Gaymard Alexandre, Bella Antonino, Sognamiglio Paola, Sierra Moros Maria José, Riutort Antonio Nicolau, Demina Yulia V., Mahieu Romain, Broas Markku, Bengnér Malin, Buda Silke, Schilling Julia, Filleul Laurent, Lepoutre Agnès, Saura Christine, Mailles Alexandra, Levy-Bruhl Daniel, Coignard Bruno, Bernard-Stoecklin Sibylle, Behillil Sylvie, van der Werf Sylvie, Valette Martine, Lina Bruno, Riccardo Flavia, Nicastri Emanuele, Casas Inmaculada, Larrauri Amparo, Salom Castell Magdalena, Pozo Francisco, Maksyutov Rinat A., Martin Charlotte, Van Ranst Marc, Bossuyt Nathalie, Siira Lotta, Sane Jussi, Tegmark-Wisell Karin, Palmérus Maria, Broberg Eeva K., Beauté Julien, Jorgensen Pernille, Bundle Nick, Pereyaslov Dmitriy, Adlhoch Cornelia, Pukkila Jukka, Pebody Richard, Olsen Sonja, Ciancio Bruno Christian. "First cases of coronavirus disease 2019 (COVID-19) in the WHO European Region, 24 January to 21 February 2020." *Euro Surveillance*. 25, no. 9 :pii=2000178. https://doi.org/10.2807/1560-7917. ES.2020.25.9.2000178.

Global Voices. 2002. "Six False Statements by Serbian Government Officials on COVID-19." *Global Voices*. Accessed July 24, 2020. https://globalvoices.org/2020/04/22/six-false-statements-by-serbian-government-officials-on-covid-19/#.

Gralinski, Lisa E., and Vineet Menachery. 2020. "Return of the Coronavirus: 2019 nCoV." *Viruses* 12, no. 2: 135. https://doi.org/10.3390/v12020135

Haddow, George D., and Kim S. Haddow. 2013. *Disaster Communications in a Changing Media World*. Oxford: Elsevier.

Hamner, Lea, Polly Dubbel, Ian Capron, Andy Ross, Amber Jordan, Jaxon Lee, Joanne Lynn, Amelia Ball, Simranjit Narwal, Sam Russell, Dale Patrick, Howard Leibrand. 2020. "High SARS-CoV-2 Attack Rate Following Exposure at a Choir Practice—Skagit County, Washington, March 2020." *Morbidity and Mortality Weekly Report* 69, no. 19: 606–10, May.

Ippolito Giuseppe, David S. Hui, Francine Ntoumi, Markus MAeurer, and Almuddin Zumla. 2020. "Toning down the 2019-nCoV hype – and restoring hope." *The Lancet Respiratory Medicine* 8, no. 3: 230–31. https://doi.org/10.1016/S2213-2600(20)30070-9

Joffe, Hélène. 1999. *Risk and "the Other"*. Cambridge: Cambridge University Press.

Kasperson, Roger, Ortwin, Renn, Paul Slovic, Halina Brown, Jacque Emel, Robert Goble, Jeanne Kasperson, and Samuel Ratick. 1988. "The Social Amplification of Risk: A Conceptual Framework." *Risk Analysis* 8, no. 2: 177–87.

Kim, Louis, Shannon Fast, and Natasha Markuzon. 2019. "Incorporating Media Data into a Model of Infectious Disease Transmission." *PLoS One* 14, no. 2: e0197646, February. doi:10.1371/journal.pone.0197646.

Kvarnlof, Linda, and Elin Montelius. "Militariseringen av Covid-19/The Militarization of Covid 19" Dagens Arena/Todays Arena. Accessed May 16, 2020. www.dagensarena.se/essa/militariseringen-av-coronapandemin/.

The Lancet. 2020. "COVID-19: Too Little, Too Late?" *The Lancet* 395, no. 10226: 755, March. doi:10.1016/s0140-6736(20)30522-5.

Maksimović Sandra. 2020. "Serbian CSOs and Media Demand Access to Official COVID-19 Information." *European Western Balkans*. Accessed July 24, 2020. https://europeanwesternbalkans.com/2020/07/22/serbian-csos-and-media-demand-access-to-official-covid-19-information/.

Matteo, Cinelli, Walter Quattrociocchi, Alessandro Galeazzi, Carlo Michele Valensise, Emanuele Brugnoli, Ana Lucia Schmidt, Paola Zola, Fabiana Zollo and Antonio Scala. The COVID-19 social media infodemic. 2020. *Scientific Reporting* 10. https://doi.org/10.1038/s41598-020-73510-5

Mavragani, Amaryllis. 2020. "Tracking COVID-19 in Europe: Infodemiology Approach." *JMIR Public Health Surveillance* 6, no. 2. https://publichealth.jmir.org/2020/2/e18941.

Medical Express. "Serbia Announces First Coronavirus Case: Ministry." *Medical Express*. Accessed July 24, 2020. https://medicalxpress.com/news/2020-03-serbia-coronavirus-case-ministry.html.

Mileti, Dennis. 1999. *Disasters by Design: A Reassessment of Natural Hazards in the United States*. Washington, DC: Joseph Henry Press.

Miura, Lully. 2020. "It's Time to Face the Real Risks Posed by COVID-19." *Japan Times*. Accessed July 25, 2020. www.japantimes.co.jp/opinion/2020/05/24/commentary/japan-commentary/time-face-real-risks-posed-covid-19/.

Morin, Celine, Arnaud Mercier, and Laetitia Atlani-Duault. 2019. "Text-Image Relationships in Tweets: Shaping the Meanings of an Epidemic." *Societies* 9, no. 12: 1–18, January.

Nygren, Katarina, and Anna Olofsson. 2020. "Managing the Covid-19 Pandemic Through Individual Responsibility: The Consequences of a World Risk Society and Enhanced Ethopolitics." *Journal of Risk Research*, April. doi:10.1080/13669877.2020.1756382.

Person, Bobbie, Francisco Sy, Kelly Holton, Barbara Govert, Arthur Liang, Brenda Garza, Deborah Gould, Meredith Hickson, Marian McDonald, Cecilia Meijer, Julia Smith, Liza Veto, Walter Williams, and Laura Zauderer. 2004. "Fear and Stigma: The Epidemic

Within the SARS Outbreak." *Emerging Infectious Diseases* 10, no. 2: 358–63, February. https://doi.org/10.3201/eid1002.030750

Powell, Martha. 2020. "What Role Can the Media Play in Managing the COVID-19 Outbreak?" *Infectious Disease Hub*. Accessed July 25, 2020. www.id-hub.com/2020/03/05/role-can-media-play-managing-covid-19-outbreak/.

Prati, Gabriele, and Luca Pietrantoni. 2016. "Knowledge, Risk Perceptions, and Xenophonic Attitudes: Evidence from Italy During the Ebola Outbreak." *Risk Analysis* 36 (10), 2000–2010. doi:10.1111/risa.12537.

"Q & A on Coronavirus COVID-19." World Health Organization. Accessed June 1, 2020. www.who.int/fr/emergencies/diseases/novel-coronavirus-2019/question-and-answers-hub/q-a-detail/q-a-coronaviruses.

Rajgor, Dimple, Meng Lee, Sophia Archuleta, Natasha Bagdasarian, and Swee Quek. 2020. "The Many Estimates of the COVID-19 Case Fatality Rate." *The Lancet Infectious Diseases*, March. doi:10.1016/S1473-3099(20)30244-9.

Ratzan, Scott, and Kenneth Moritsugu. 2014. "Ebola Crisis—Communication Chaos We Can Avoid." *Journal of Health Communication: International Perspectives* 19, no. 11: 1213–15, November. doi:10.1080/10810730.2014.977680.

Salek, Thomas A., and Andrew W. Cole. 2019. "Donald Trump Tweets the 2014 Ebola Outbreak: The Infectious Nature of Apocalyptic Counterpublic Rhetoric and Constitution of an Exaggerated Health Crisis. " *Communication Quarterly* 67, no. 1: 21–40. https://doi.org/10.1080/01463373.2018.

Scheufele, Dietram A., and David Tewksbury. 2006. "Framing, Agenda Setting, and Priming: The Evolution of Three Media Effects Models." *Journal of Communication*, no. 57: 9–20, November. doi:10.1111/j.0021-9916.2007.00326.x.

Schmidt, Carmen. 2020. "The COVID-19 Crisis and Risk Society in the Second Modernity." *Japan Today*. Accessed July 26, 2020. https://japantoday.com/category/features/opinions/the-covid-19-crisis-and-risk-society-in-the-second-modernity?comment-order=popular.

Seidu, Iddrisu. 2018. "And Ghana Was Scared: Media Representations of the Risk of an Ebola Outbreak in Ghana." *Online Journal of Public Health Informatics* 10, no. 2, September. doi:10.5210/ojphi.v10i2.9229.

Sell, Tara, Crystal Boddie, Emma McGinty, Keshia Pollack, Katherine Clegg Smith, Thomas A. Burke, and Lanie Rutkow. 2017. "Media Messages and Perception of Risk for Ebola Virus Infection, United States." *Emerging Infectious Diseases* 23, no. 1: 108–11, January. doi:10.3201/eid2301.160589.

Serbian Media During COVID-19 Pandemic. "Frederick Naumann Foundation." Accessed March 17, 2021. https://www.freiheit.org/es/node/21839.

Slovic, Paul. 1986. "Informing and Educating the Public about Risk." *Risk Analysis* 6, no. 4: 403–15, November.

Stojanovic, Millca. 2020. "Serbia Pins Coronavirus Blame on Returning Serbs 'Concealing Infection'." *Balkan Insight*. Accessed July 24, 2020. https://balkaninsight.com/2020/04/03/serbia-pins-coronavirus-blame-on-returning-serbs-concealing-infection/.

"Timeline of WHO's response to COVID-19." World Health Organization. Accessed July 21, 2020. www.who.int/news-room/detail/29-06-2020-covidtimeline.

Tran, Jueni. "Germany's Media During COVID-19." Accessed July 21, 2020. https://jia.sipa.columbia.edu/online-articles/germany%E2%80%99s-media-during-covid-19.

Villafranca, Paloma. 2012. "Los Encuadres Sanitarios en Prensa. Gripe A y Bacteria e. coli (The Sanitary Framing in Spanish Press: Swine Flu Virus and E. coli Bacterium)." *Revista Internacional de Relaciones Públicas (International Journal of Public Relations* 2, no. 4: 221–46, July.

Wieler, Lothar, Rexroth, Ute, and René Gottschalk. "Emerging COVID-19 Success Story: Germany's Strong Enabling Environment." *Exemplars in Global Health*. Accessed July 21, 2020. https://ourworldindata.org/covid-exemplar-germany.

Wimmer, Jeffrey, and Thorsten Quandt. 2006. "Living in the Risk Society." *Journalism Studies* 7, no. 2: 336–47. doi:10.1080/14616700600645461.

Young, Meredith, Geoffrey Norman, and Karin Humphreys. 2008. "Medicine in the Popular Press: The Influence of the Media on Perceptions of Disease." *PLoS One* 3, no. 10: e3552, October. doi:10.1371/journal.pone.0003552.

Yusuf, Ibrahim, Sani Yahaya, and Saleh Qabli. 2015. "Role of Media in Portraying Ebola in and Outside Africa." *Journal of Tropical Diseases* 3, no. 1: 1–2. doi:10.4172/2329-891X.1000152.

Zarocostas, John. 2020. "How to Fight an Infodemic." *The Lancet* 395, no. 10225: 676, February.

20 Abusing the COVID-19 pan(dem)ic

A perfect storm for online scams

Kristjan Kikerpill and Andra Siibak

Introduction

True to their opportunistic character, cybercriminals followed their unspoken motto of "never letting a good disaster go to waste" in fashioning a plethora of online schemes and scams during the COVID-19 pandemic. These online scams were and are largely based on social engineering, i.e., "any act that influences a person to take an action that may or may not be in his or her best interests" (Hadnagy 2018, 7). While all social engineering is not negative, the criminal applications of it are. For instance, the legal definition of fraud, i.e., "the causing of proprietary damage to another person by knowingly causing a misconception of the existing facts" (Riigi Teataja 2020, 209), emphasizes how malicious actors use deception and influence to get someone to do their bidding. Phishing attacks, i.e., computer attacks "that communicate socially engineered messages to humans via electronic communication channels in order to persuade them to perform certain actions for the attacker's benefit" (Khonji, Iraqi, and Jones 2013, 2092), including its subtypes, e.g., smishing (attacks via text message) and vishing (attacks using phone calls) increased by 600% during the COVID-19 pandemic (Jay 2020). Furthermore, recent reports which indicate that Google alone blocked 18 million COVID-19 related phishing attacks in one week in April and dealt daily with 240 million coronavirus themed spam messages (Kunert 2020) suggest that criminals enthusiastically grabbed the opportunity to profit from the pandemic.

Although online attacks are fairly common during times of social strife, e.g., forest fires and hurricanes (Grad 2020), literature focusing on the connection between social-engineering attacks and salient current events is scarce (Verma, Crane, and Gnawalli 2018). Even less is known about how salient current events can impact susceptibility to social-engineering attacks, including phishing (Williams and Polage 2018; Norris and Brookes 2020). Furthermore, despite the fact that various technical taxonomies of phishing attacks have been developed over the years (Pienta, Thatcher and, Johnston 2018; Das et al. 2020, 697), communication strategies and types in actual phishing attacks have received less attention (Kim and Kim 2013; Atkins and Huang 2013). To remedy this gap, our chapter contributes to the study of social-engineering attacks and their prevalence in current events, and further elaborates on the communication types present in such attacks. More specifically, we apply the RIFE scale of influence and impact (Kikerpill and Siibak 2019) to news stories regarding COVID-19 themed online scams that appeared in international media in January–April 2020. We propose using the RIFE scale as it consists of a matrix of four communication types, i.e., Robbery, Informational, Fraud, and Extortion, all of which are based on the intensity of communicated messages and the requirement for action from the side of the recipient. Since social-engineering attacks require some form of recipient action, the RIFE scale enables us to separate hoaxes and misinformation (Informational type) and purely technical cyber-attacks (Robbery type) from online scams that exploit human vulnerabilities, i.e., either through deception (Fraud type) or threats (Extortion type).

Methods and sample

Content analysis (Krippendorff 2004) was used for studying prevalent communication types in COVID-19 themed online scams. We relied both upon the RIFE scale as well as previous classifications of online scams when forming the categories for analysis, i.e., we made use of a priori coding. Both authors coded the news stories, which formed our sample, separately by following a common codebook we developed beforehand. As our aim was to also capture the variety in COVID-19 themed online scams and types of communication, single words, and phrases as well as sentences and paragraphs were employed as units for coding. We discussed the meanings of the codes and shared our interpretations throughout the process, but as we divided the news stories to be analyzed, intercoder reliability was not measured.

The news stories for the study were obtained through a Google keyword search, using the phrases "covid scam," "covid phishing," "coronavirus scam," and "coronavirus phishing." We conducted four separate queries, i.e., one for each month from January to April 2020, and further restricted the results by using the *allintitle* search operator, which set the requirement that every word in the search phrases must appear in the results' title. The words "coronavirus" and "covid" were both implemented in the searches because the name COVID-19 was given to the disease only during the period covered in the study (Nelson 2020).

The initial search results ($N = 1928$) were then evaluated for suitability and separated into categories of "mainstream media" (e.g., online versions of newspapers like the Guardian, the Washington Post; or websites of different radio- and TV stations, e.g., FoxNews) and "specialist media" (e.g., online news platforms dedicated to technology and cybercrime news e.g., BleepingComputer or Tech Xplore) or excluded. We excluded results that only contained video, were posts on social media, appeared on the websites of a private company (e.g., banks, law firms, insurance companies or healthcare providers, etc.), were published on the official websites of public authorities (WHO, FBI, etc.) or different NGOs.

We concurrently followed the RIFE scale to make further exclusions, i.e., to exclude news stories that pertained to Informational or Robbery type communications. Our search results did not include news items that solely covered a Robbery type communication, i.e., a purely technical attack in which the exploitation of human vulnerabilities would be a non-issue. However, due the various meanings attached to the word "scam," some Informational type stories, e.g., hoaxes about the curative power of boiled garlic with respect to the coronavirus (Best 2020), had to be excluded because these did not include an actual social-engineering attack that worked to the direct benefit of an attacker.

The findings and analysis presented in the next two sections are based on the final sample (N = 831) of news stories from mainstream (N = 618) and specialist media (N = 213) from January to April 2020 regarding COVID-19 themed online scams and phishing schemes, which fit either the Fraud type (section 2) or Extortion type (section 3) communication on the RIFE scale. In our analysis, we further elaborate upon the elements typical for the Fraud-type, referred to as "the Good Samaritan" communication, and the Extortion type, which we refer to as the "shock and awe" communication.

Fraud type, or "the Good Samaritan" communication

The parable of the Good Samaritan in the Gospel of Luke carries the moral of considering others as "your neighbor" and offering them support when needed. As the priest and the Levite had walked by a savagely beaten man, it was the Samaritan who took pity on the victim and cared for him (Biblegateway 2020). In transactional terms, it is possible to view the victim as in need of help (demand), the Good Samaritan recognizing the importance of the event (salience) and thus helping the person who was already ignored by many (supply). As described previously, the same three elements are also the building blocks of social-engineering attacks, and fraud. For example, the lack of preparedness prior to the COVID-19 pandemic meant that personal protective equipment was in high demand—con-artists were quick to recognize the importance of the situation and attempted to unload their "imaginary" supply (Kuner 2020). With coronavirus fears providing salience to the situation, various other demand and non-existent supply scheme connections were developed and employed by online scammers.

In January, i.e., in the introductory phase of the global pandemic, attackers and scammers played upon people's fears and the overall uncertainty regarding the novel coronavirus. The most prolific scam in January surfaced in Japan where people received emails that purportedly originated from a disability welfare agency and contained "important information" regarding local infection reports (Keach 2020). In fact, the files attached to the emails contained the Emotet malware capable of, among other things, stealing the users' personal information (Cohen 2020). January scams also exploited the growing concerns over the availability of protective equipment (Campbell 2020) and getting stuck due to travel restrictions (Fang and Wibawa 2020).

February scams and phishing attacks witnessed a heavy reliance on impersonating authorities, namely, the World Health Organization and the Center for Disease Control (CDC), to spread malware that was embedded in email attachments titled "safety measures" (Greig 2020). In February, con artists also began diversifying their use of electronic communication channels. In addition to emails, phone calls, text messages and bogus websites, even faxes were used to impersonate WHO in soliciting fake donations (Olenick 2020). However, the criminals often gave themselves away by asking that the donations be made in Bitcoin cryptocurrency (Greig 2020), which is still an unorthodox method for providing legitimate aid to global organizations. All such ruses were perpetrated under the guise of providing something that the people needed. In South Korea, for instance, people were warned of smishing attacks related to free face mask giveaways (Jun 2020) and a domain registered in Russia offered to sell willing online shoppers "the best and fastest test" for detecting the coronavirus (Venkat 2020).

In March, criminals continued soliciting donations and pushing the sale of non-existent treatments, vaccines, and personal protective equipment (Mitchell 2020). However, more advanced attacks were employed as well, e.g., embedding malware into a fake live-tracking map that mimicked the original Johns Hopkins University interactive dashboard (Pettit 2020) and thus taking advantage of people's desire to stay up to date on COVID-19 related information. Furthermore, robocalls, i.e., automated telephone calls that deliver a prerecorded message, were employed in offering unaware victims the chance at obtaining bogus COVID-19 home testing kits (Romm 2020). Additionally, with the glum reality of the spreading disease in full display during the month of March, scammers seized on the opportunity to impersonate governments and work various relief payment and tax refund offers into their phishing schemes in Canada and the UK (Alabi 2020; Carmichael 2020; Nilsen 2020).

Scams in the month of April were dominated in particular by including disease containment cues into phishing schemes. More specifically, smishing attacks in Ireland and the United States tried luring people into clicking on links in text messages, which notified recipients that someone they had come into contact with had tested positive for COVID-19 (Wall 2020; Hasco 2020). Additionally, with the rollout of stimulus checks in the United States, the Internal Revenue Service warned of the possibility of ensuing scams, e.g., con artists claiming that they are verifying people's personal information while actually stealing said information to perpetrate tax fraud (Lerten 2020). Financial relief was also offered in other formats, e.g., free Woolworths and Coles gift vouchers in Australia (Morton 2020) and bogus unemployment grants in South Africa (Lourie 2020). Moreover, surging unemployment entailed various scams that included bogus job offers, e.g., as a secret shopper (WMC 2020) or dog-sitter (Ahumada 2020). Evacuation scams also reemerged. For example, Vietnamese students were warned of con-artists taking advantage of the Vietnamese government's program of arranging flights back home for those struggling with COVID-19 (Nguyen 2020).

Cybercriminals adapted their lures and bogus offers to reflect important social developments over the course of four months. The initial state of uncertainty was met with fake information and the lack of personal protective equipment was countered with bogus online shops and non-delivery of face masks. Furthermore, the financial hardship experienced by many was included into scams in the form of relief payments, tax refunds and gift vouchers, i.e., anything that could be passed as providing economic relief to those hit hardest by the conditions and restrictions entailed by the spreading virus. Bogus donations for fake charities were solicited to help people that were doing even worse than the targets of the scams.

Extortion type, or "shock and awe" communication

Extortion type communications aim to startle the recipient and then immediately present it with a fallacious choice between bad and worse. In that sense, extortion type communications are the non-military equivalent of "shock and awe" tactics, which also often employ misinformation and deception to achieve a set goal (Rutherford 2004, 53–54).

In case of scams, criminals exploit the salient current event, and use urgency cues (Norris and Brookes 2020), to present the startled victims with a bifurcation fallacy (Van Vleet 2011, 15), i.e., making it seem as if there are only two choices available to the recipients and omitting the rest. For example, unaware victims in the UK received bogus text messages from con-artists pretending to be the government that contained a notification regarding a fine imposed on them for leaving their home too many times during lockdown (Salisbury 2020). In such cases, recipients who consider the smishing attack's contents to be legitimate, have a choice of either paying the fine or facing other, unknown consequences, which are left implicit in the message, but could be worse than accepting the fine. Yet, people receiving these fake fine notifications also had the options of ignoring the communication, notifying law enforcement, or attempting to verify the communication through methods external to the original message. Thus, the initial "shock" is necessary to try and get the recipient off balance, making them stop paying attention to what was omitted from the message.

Our sample did not include extortion type communications from January. In February, however, once the reality and severity of the situation had become clear enough, virus-related threats obtained sufficient potency. For instance, in South Korea, a scammer, who was pretending to be a confirmed coronavirus patient, contacted a restaurant owner and threatened to "tell everyone" that they had visited the restaurant, unless a sum was paid (Jun 2020).

The month of March saw the continued popularity of imposing fake fines on people who had supposedly left their household and thus broken established rules (Carmichael 2020). The most peculiar scam of all also emerged in March—a smishing attack in which criminals attempted to leverage a "mandatory online COVID-19 test" to get potential victims to click on a link included in the text message (WJIM 2020). News stories also reported an uptick in online blackmail attacks in March. For instance, in one such attack, the criminals claimed that they had gained access to an individual's personal information, knew their whereabouts, and threatened to infect the victim and their family with coronavirus unless a ransom was paid (Shein 2020).

In April, criminals kept bogus online COVID-19 test (Bisson 2020) and fake fine scams (Salisbury 2020) in circulation, and law enforcement took note of criminals threatening to infect others if a payment was not made (Cartwright 2020).

Furthermore, a form of blackmail, i.e., a "reputation attack," surfaced in April, when a real estate agent reported receiving a message in which he was notified that false negative reviews would be given to his company unless a specific sum is paid (Culot 2020). Bogus conditional transactions also emerged when scammers began leveraging the receipt of a stimulus check in return for a response in the 2020 US census (Leicht 2020), although the actual goal of the criminals was to obtain individuals' personal information by having them fill out fake census forms.

April also witnessed an important change in a classic extortion-type scam, i.e., threatening potential victims with disconnecting their utilities. Since local authorities had banned terminations during the crisis, scammers adapted their scheme and offered discounts on utilities instead, i.e., attempting to obtain personal information instead of direct payments (WHSV 2020). In this case, the criminals shifted their communication tactics from the extortion-type, which is conventionally employed in utility scams, to the fraud-type, i.e., switching from demands and threats to offering relief.

Discussion and conclusion

While con artists made use of an incredibly wide range of scams and circulated these scams through a variety of electronic communication channels, the attacks remained largely steady in their communication types, i.e., falling under the category of the fraud type ("the Good Samaritan") or the extortion type ("shock and awe"). Our sample showed that relief-offering fraud type communications emerged earlier than scams involving threats and demands. The earliest scams in January took advantage of the general uncertainty and need for information surrounding the emerging coronavirus crisis, providing a bogus supply of such information. As individuals scrambled to purchase necessary personal protective equipment, scammers seemed to conjure just what everyone needed. In February, the Good Samaritans were joined by "shock and awe" type communications, which relied heavily on the coronavirus' already established salience. Although not in the form of elaborated communication types, previous research (Atkins and Huang 2013; Williams and Polage 2018) has dealt with invoking a promise of reward or inflicting a potential sense of loss on the victims. Our analysis allowed us to detail the mechanics employed in achieving both of these goals, i.e., while the Good Samaritans embark on exploiting salient current events by recognizing various demands and offering a fake supply, scammers employing the "shock and awe" communication attempt to get the recipients off-guard first and then try to force the victims to make a poor choice to avoid loss.

Furthermore, our results clearly show that criminals adapt to ongoing social situations by changing the lures employed in various scams. The fact that certain schemes, e.g., notifications with respect to fake fines or bogus online tests for a disease, which cannot be tested for online, were retained by scammers through multiple months imply such schemes' success in exploiting unaware victims. More importantly, this notion also builds on how the salience of current events has been operationalized in previous studies (Williams and Polage 2018), i.e., relying on individuals' familiarity with certain events. Our study shows that while familiarity with an event is the so-called way-in scams' success relies on establishing personal relevance for the victim. This aspect could be explained by the difference between creating presumed relevance for an event under experimental circumstances and scams, which rely on a salient current event, being delivered to recipients who are actually living the circumstances exploited within the communication.

References

Ahumada, Rosalio. 2020. "Sacramento State Students Warned of Scam Offering Job After Coronavirus Order Lifts." *The Sacramento Bee*, April 23. Accessed June 7, 2020. www.sacbee.com/news/local/crime/article242252396.html.

Alabi, Leke Oso. 2020. "Taxpayers Targeted by HMRC Coronavirus Scam." *Financial Times*, March 11. Accessed June 6, 2020. www.ft.com/content/334ac60d-1f86-473f-a5dc-92b6f2d8bc56.

Atkins, Brandon, and Wilson Huang. 2013. "A Study of Social Engineering in Online Frauds." *Open Journal of Social Sciences* 1, no. 3: 23–32. doi:10.4236/jss.2013.13004.

Best, Shivali. 2020. "WhatsApp Coronavirus Scam Message Is Circulating—What to Do If You Receive It." *Mirror*, February 16. Accessed June 5, 2020. www.mirror.co.uk/tech/whatsapp-coronavirus-scam-message-circulating-21496450.

Biblegateway. 2020. "The Parable of the Good Samaritan." Accessed June 5, 2020. www.biblegateway.com/passage/?search=Luke+10%3A25-37&version=NIV.

Bisson, David. 2020. "COVID-19 Scam Roundup—April 6, 2020." *Tripwire*, April 6. Accessed June 7, 2020. www.tripwire.com/state-of-security/security-awareness/covid-19-scam-roundup-april-6-2020/.

Campbell, Chris. 2020. "Burnaby Residents Warned of Coronavirus Face Mask Scam." *Burnaby Now*, January 31. Accessed June 6, 2020. www.burnabynow.com/news/burnaby-residents-warned-of-coronavirus-face-mask-scam-1.24065902.

Carmichael, Hannah. 2020. "Warning as Scam Coronavirus Text Message Tricks Recipients." *The National*, March 30. Accessed June 6, 2020. www.thenational.scot/news/18344801.warning-scam-coronavirus-text-message-tricks-recipients/.

Cartwright, Lachlan. 2020. "Cyberscammers: Pay Up or We'll Infect Your Family with Coronavirus." *The Daily Beast*, April 29. Accessed June 7, 2020. www.thedailybeast.com/new-coronavirus-scam-threatenspay-up-or-well-infect-your-family-with-covid-19.

Cohen, Nancy. 2020. "Sophisticated Emotet Malware Loader Thriving on Unsophisticated Passwords." *Tech Xplore*, February 13. Accessed June 6, 2020. https://techxplore.com/news/2020-02-sophisticated-emotet-malware-loader-unsophisticated.html.

Culot, Caroline. 2020. "'I Have Been Paid to Carry Out a Reputation Attack': Boss Tells of Another Chilling Coronavirus Scam." *Eastern Daily Press*, April 4. Accessed June 7, 2020. www.edp24.co.uk/business/minors-brady-targeted-by-bribery-scam-amid-coronavirus-1-6593841.

Das, Avisha, Shahryar Baki, Ayman El Aassal, Rakesh Verma, and Arthur Dunbar. 2020. "SoK: A Comprehensive Reexamination of Phishing Research from the Security Perspective." *IEEE Communications Surveys & Tutorials* 22, no. 1: 671–708. doi:10.1109/COMST.2019.2957750.

Fang, Kai, and Tasha Wibawa. 2020. "Coronavirus Evacuation Scam Targets Chinese-Australians in Wuhan." *MSN*, January 28. Accessed June 6, 2020. www.msn.com/en-au/

news/australia/coronavirus-evacuation-scam-targets-chinese-australians-in-wuhan/ar-BBZoeJo.

Grad, Peter. 2020. "Router Phishing Scam Targets Global Fear Over Coronavirus." *TechXplore*, March 27. Accessed June 5, 2020. https://techxplore.com/news/2020-03-router-phishing-scam-global-coronavirus.html.

Greig, Jonathan. 2020. "Hackers Imitating CDC, WHO with Coronavirus Phishing Emails." *TechRepublic*, February 7. Accessed June 6, 2020. www.techrepublic.com/article/hackers-imitating-cdc-who-with-coronavirus-phishing-emails/.

Hadnagy, Christopher. 2018. *Social Engineering: The Science of Human Hacking*. Indianapolis: Wiley.

Hasco, Linda. 2020. "Do Not Click on This COVID-19 Text Message Scam, Authorities Warn." *PennLive*, April 17. Accessed June 6, 2020. www.pennlive.com/coronavirus/2020/04/do-not-click-on-this-covid-19-text-message-scam-authorities-warn.html.

Jay, Jay. 2020. "COVID-19 Related Phishing Attacks Grew by 600% Worldwide." *Teiss*, April 16. Accessed June 5, 2020. www.teiss.co.uk/covid-19-related-phishing-attacks-grew-by-600-worldwide/.

Jun, Ji-hye. 2020. "Voice, SMS Phishing Scams on Coronavirus Surging." *The Korea Times*, February 18. Accessed June 6, 2020. www.koreatimes.co.kr/www/nation/2020/02/119_283614.html.

Keach, Sean. 2020. "Beware the Sick 'Coronavirus Scam' Email That Lets Crooks Hijack Your Gadgets." *The Sun*, January 31. Accessed June 6, 2020. www.thesun.co.uk/tech/10861743/coronavirus-warning-email-scam-wuhan-hack/.

Khonji, Mahmoud, Youssef Iraqi, and Andrew Jones. 2013. "Phishing Detection: A Literature Survey." *IEEE Communications Surveys & Tutorials* 15, no. 4: 2091–121. doi:10.1109/SURV.2013.032213.00009.

Kikerpill, Kristjan, and Andra Siibak. 2019. "Living in a Spamster's Paradise: Deceit and Threats in Phishing Emails." *Masaryk University Journal of Law and Technology* 13, no. 1: 45–66. doi:10.5817/MUJLT2019-1-3.

Kim, Daejoong, and Jang Hyun Kim. 2013. "Understanding Persuasive Elements in Phishing E-Mails: A Categorical Content and Semantic Network Analysis." *Online Information Review* 37, no. 6: 835–50. doi:10.1108/OIR-03-2012-0037.

Krippendorff, Klaus. 2004. *Content Analysis: An Introduction to Its Methodology*. Thousand Oaks, CA: Sage.

Kuner, Dilip. 2020. "Explained: How Spanish Website Assisted Nigerian COVID-19 Face Mask Scam in Attempt to Fleece German Government of Millions of Euros." *The Olive Press*, April 15. Accessed June 6, 2020. www.theolivepress.es/spain-news/2020/04/15/explained-how-spanish-website-assisted-nigerian-covid-19-face-mask-scam-to-fleece-german-government-of-millions-of-euros/.

Kunert, Paul. 2020. "Google: We've Blocked 126 Million COVID-19 Phishing Scams in the Past Week." *The Register*, April 17. Accessed June 5, 2020. www.theregister.com/2020/04/17/google_coronavirus_spam/.

Leicht, Angelica. 2020. "Getting COVID-19 Emails from the Census Bureau? How to Tell Scams from the Real Thing." *KimKomando*, April 23. Accessed June 7, 2020. www.komando.com/coronavirus/covid-19-emails-census-bureau/736101/.

Lerten, Barney. 2020. "IRS: Don't Fall Victim to a COVID-19 Scam." *KTVZ*, April 2. Accessed June 6, 2020. https://ktvz.com/news/coronavirus/2020/04/02/irs-dont-fall-victim-to-a-covid-19-scam/.

Lourie, Gugu. 2020. "Coronavirus: Sassa Warns of COVID-19 Special Grant Scam." *Tech Financials*, April 26. Accessed June 6, 2020. https://techfinancials.co.za/2020/04/26/coronavirus-sassa-warns-of-covid-19-special-grant-scam/.

Mitchell, Jeff. 2020. "Scam Artists Capitalizing on Coronavirus Fears, Anti-fraud Centre Warns." *Durham Region*, March 19. Accessed June 6, 2020. www.durhamregion.com/ news-story/9910813-scam-artists-capitalizing-on-coronavirus-fears-anti-fraud-centre-warns/.

Morton, Nadine. 2020. "COVID-19 Scam Offering Grocery Vouchers with Coles, Woolworths." *The Leader*, April 2. Accessed June 6, 2020. www.theleader.com.au/ story/6708704/250-supermarket-voucher-too-good-to-be-true-scamwatch-warns/.

Nelson, Alex. 2020. "Covid-19: Why the Coronavirus Has Been Given Its New Name by the WHO—and What It Means." *iNews*, February 12. Accessed June 5, 2020. https://inews.co.uk/inews-lifestyle/travel/covid-19-coronavirus-name-who-china-virus-outbreak-why-explained-1555896.

Nguyen, Hannah. 2020. "COVID-19: Vietnamese Students Abroad Warned of Flight Scam." *Vietnam Times*, April 23. Accessed June 6, 2020. https://vietnamtimes.org.vn/ covid-19-vietnamese-students-abroad-warned-of-flight-scam-19680.html.

Nilsen, David S. 2020. "Multiple COVID-19 Coronavirus Scam Warnings Issued." *Paso Robles Daily News*, March 27. Accessed June 6, 2020. https://pasoroblesdailynews.com/ multiple-covid-19-coronavirus-scam-warnings-issued/106273/.

Norris, Gareth, and Alexandra Brookes. 2020. "Personality, Emotion and Individual Differences in Response to Online Fraud." *Personality and Individual Differences*. DOI: https://doi.org/10.1016/j.paid.2020.109847.

Olenick, Doug. 2020. "World Health Organization Warns About Coronavirus Phishing Scams." *SCMagazine*, February 19. Accessed June 6, 2020. www.scmagazine.com/home/ email-security/world-health-organization-warns-about-coronavirus-phishing-scams/.

Pettit, Harry. 2020. "Do NOT Click This 'Coronavirus Map'—It's a Dangerous Scam to Hijack Your Device." *The Sun*, March 18. Accessed June 6, 2020. www.thesun.co.uk/ tech/11201252/coronavirus-map-scam-hijack-device/.

Pienta, Daniel, Jason Bennett Thatcher, and Allen C. Johnston. 2018. "A Taxonomy of Phishing: Attack Types Spanning Economic, Temporal, Breadth, and Target Boundaries." In *Proceedings of the 13th Pre-ICIS Workshop on Information Security and Privacy, San Francisco, CA, USA, December* 1.

Riigi Teataja. 2020. "Penal Code of the Republic of Estonia." Accessed June 5. www.riigi teataja.ee/en/eli/506032020002/consolide.

Romm, Tony. 2020. " 'That Can Actually Kill Somebody': Scam Robocalls Are Pitching Fake Coronavirus Tests to Vulnerable Americans." *The Washington Post*, March 19. Accessed June 6, 2020. www.washingtonpost.com/technology/2020/03/19/ robocalls-coronavirus-test/.

Rutherford, Paul. 2004. *Weapons of Mass Persuasion: Marketing the War Against Iraq*. Toronto: University of Toronto Press.

Salisbury, Josh. 2020. "Warning Over Coronavirus Scam Texts Which Demand Money 'For Leaving the House'." *Southwark News*, April 3. Accessed June 7, 2020. www.south warknews.co.uk/news/warning-over-coronavirus-scam-texts-which-demand-money-for-leaving-the-house/.

Shein, Esther. 2020. "667% Spike in Email Phishing Attacks Due to Coronavirus Fears." *TechRepublic*, March 26. Accessed June 7, 2020. www.techrepublic.com/ article/667-spike-in-email-phishing-attacks-due-to-coronavirus-fears/.

Van Vleet, Jacob E. 2011. *Informal Fallacies: A Brief Guide*. Lanham: University Press of America.

Venkat, Apruva. 2020. "Phishing Campaigns Tied to Coronavirus Persist." *BankInfoSecurity*, February 20. Accessed June 6, 2020. www.bankinfosecurity.com/phishing-campaigns-tied-to-coronavirus-persist-a-13741.

Verma, Rakesh, Devin Crane and Omprakash Gnawalli. 2018. "Phishing During and After Disaster: Hurricane Harvey." *2018 Resilience Week 2018 (RWS), Denver, CO*: 88–94. doi:10.1109/RWEEK.2018.8473509.

Wall, Eva. 2020. "Irish People Issued Garda Warning About Sick COVID-19 Contact Tracing Text Scam." *Extra.ie*, April 9. Accessed June 6, 2020. https://extra.ie/2020/04/09/news/irish-news/irish-people-warned-covid-19-contact-tracing-text-scam.

WHSV. 2020. "Scammers Take New Approach to Classic Utility Scam Amid COVID-19." *WHSV*, April 27. Accessed June 4, 2020. www.whsv.com/content/news/Scammers-take-new-approach-to-classic-utility-scam-amid-COVID-19-569985421.html.

WJIM. 2020. "Another Coronavirus Scam to Look Out For." *WJIM*, March 27. Accessed June 7, 2020. https://wjimam.com/another-coronavirus-scam-to-watch-out-for/.

WMC. 2020. "BBB Warns of Coronavirus-Related Secret Shopper Scam." *WMC*, April 9. Accessed June 7, 2020. www.wmcactionnews5.com/2020/04/09/bbb-warns-coronavirus-related-secret-shopper-scam/.

Williams, Emma J., and Danielle Polage. 2018. "How Persuasive Is Phishing Email? The Role of Authentic Design, Influence and Current Events in Email Judgements." *Behaviour & Information Technology* 38, no. 2: 184–97.

Index